THE ZONDERVAN 2008

PASTOR'S ANNUAL

AN IDEA & RESOURCE BOOK

T. T. CRABTREE

ZONDERVAN®

ZONDERVAN.com/
AUTHORTRACKER
follow your favorite authors

We want to hear from you. Please send your comments about this
book to us in care of zreview@zondervan.com. Thank you.

ZONDERVAN®

The Zondervan 2008 Pastor's Annual
Copyright © 1987, 2007 by Zondervan

Requests for information should be addressed to:

Zondervan, *Grand Rapids, Michigan 49530*

Much of the contents of this book was previously published in *The Zondervan 1988 Pastor's Annual.*

ISBN-10: 0-310-27587-3
ISBN-13: 978-0-310-27587-9

Printed in the United States of America

07 08 09 10 11 12 • 10 9 8 7 6 5 4 3 2 1

CONTENTS

MISCELLANEOUS HELPS

PREFACE

Favorable comments from ministers who serve in many different types of churches suggest that the *Pastor's Annual* provides valuable assistance to many busy pastors as they seek to improve the quality, freshness, and variety of their pulpit ministry. To be of service to fellow pastors in their continuing quest to obey our Lord's command to Peter, "Feed my sheep," is a calling to which I respond with gratitude.

I pray that this issue of the *Pastor's Annual* will be blessed by our Lord in helping each pastor to plan and produce a preaching program that will better meet the spiritual needs of his or her congregation.

This issue contains some sermons by contributing authors who have been effective contemporary preachers and successful pastors. Each author is listed with his sermons by date in the section titled "Contributing Authors." I accept responsibility for those sermons not listed there.

This issue of the *Pastor's Annual* is dedicated to the Lord with a prayer that he will bless these efforts to let the Holy Spirit lead pastors in preparing a planned preaching program for the year.

ACKNOWLEDGMENTS

All Scripture quotations, unless otherwise noted, are taken from the *King James Version*. Additional translations used are the following:

The New English Bible, New Testament, copyright © 1961 by the Delegates of the Oxford University Press and the Syndics of the Cambridge University Press.

The Holy Bible, New International Version®. NIV®. Copyright © 1973, 1978, 1984 by International Bible Society. Used by permission of Zondervan. All rights reserved.

The New Testament in Modern English, by J. B. Phillips, copyright © 1964 by the Macmillan Company.

The New Testament: A Translation in the Language of the People, by Charles B. Williams, copyright © 1937, renewed 1965, assigned to the Moody Bible Institute.

CONTRIBUTING AUTHORS

Harold T. Bryson . . . . AM April 13
T. T. Crabtree. . . . . All messages other than those attributed
                                          to others
T. H. Epton . . . . PM May 4
William T. Flynt . . . . AM April 20, May 4
R. Furman Kenney . . . . PM December 31

JANUARY

■ Sunday Mornings

January is the month of new beginnings. The book of Genesis, which is the book of beginnings, is an excellent source for a series of messages focused on meeting personal needs.

Messages that center our attention on both the priority of God and the nature of God can strengthen our faith for the living of these days. "God Reveals Himself" is the suggested theme.

■ Sunday Evenings

A life of constant fellowship with God is essential for living the abundant life. The values of faith and obedience are emphasized. The theme is "Fellowship with God."

■ Wednesday Evenings

The genuineness of our worship experiences will determine the quality of the services we render both to God and for God. We worship the God of Abraham, Isaac, and Jacob. The theme is "Worship God in Spirit."

WEDNESDAY EVENING, JANUARY 2

Title: Calling upon the Name of the Lord

Text: "Then began men to call upon the name of the LORD" **(Gen. 4:26)**.

Introduction

It is impossible to know for sure all that is implied in the words of our text — "Then began men to call upon the name of the LORD" (Gen. 4:26) — but we can assume that a new beginning was made in consecration to God. It may be a reference to the beginning of the offering of prayers to God or to an act of dedication to God in which the descendants of Seth separated themselves unto God. This verse suggests that we could well begin each day by calling upon the name of our Lord.

I. A prayer of gratitude.

We could appropriately call upon the name of our Lord to express our gratitude. You can rejoice over the fact that the date 2007 will not appear on your tombstone. You still are among the living. You still have an opportunity to render loving service to your Lord, your family, and your fellow humans. You still have work to do. And you still have time to give praise to God and to be the means of imparting faith and encouragement to others.

II. A prayer for forgiveness and forgetfulness.

We should call upon the name of our Lord for forgiveness and forgetfulness. We need to have our sins forgiven so that we can have a clean conscience and unhindered fellowship with God. We need to be able to forgive ourselves and to forget the failures of the past as far as permitting them to hinder our witness and work for the Lord during the coming year. God will both forgive and forget our sins if we will but repent and confess (1 John 1:9).

We need to forget many things. Some let past successes cause them to coast during the present. Others let past failures serve as a stumbling block to their potential progress. Paul encouraged the Philippians to forget the past and press on toward the prize of the high calling of God in Christ Jesus (Phil. 3:13–14).

III. A prayer for wisdom.

We must call upon the name of our Lord for wisdom if we would walk through the year in the paths of righteousness. James, who challenged early Christians to practice pure religion, said, "If any of you lacks wisdom, he should ask God, who gives generously to all without finding fault, and it will be given to him" (James 1:5 NIV). If by faith we daily call upon our Lord for guidance, we can be assured that we will not go far astray nor fail to render a satisfying and acceptable service both to our Lord and to ourselves. The author of Proverbs encourages us to face the future with optimistic faith: "Trust in the LORD with all thine heart; and lean not unto thine own understanding. In all thy ways acknowledge him, and he shall direct thy paths" (Prov. 3:5–6).

IV. A prayer for help.

We need to call upon the name of our Lord for help as we cooperate with him in encouraging unbelievers to call upon his name for salvation. Myriad people around us do not know Christ as a personal Savior from sin. They have not discovered the joy of being the children of God through the gift of new life. They are still in their sins; they are away from God, lost. They need to hear the gospel from our lips and see its results in our lives so that they can be encouraged by the Spirit of God to come to our Savior during this new year. Paul wrote to the Christians in Rome, assuring them that our Lord is "rich unto all that call upon him. For whosoever shall call upon the name of the Lord shall be saved" (Rom. 10:12–13).

Conclusion

We will live this year one day at a time. We should rejoice over the opportunity to call upon the name of our Lord in each of these days. As the musical *Godspell* puts it (from a prayer of Richard of Chichester):

> *Day by day,*
> *Day by day,*

14

Oh, dear Lord,
Three things I pray:
To see Thee more clearly,
Love Thee more dearly,
Follow Thee more nearly,
Day by day.

SUNDAY MORNING, JANUARY 6

Title: "In the Beginning God"

Text: "In the beginning God created the heavens and the earth" (**Gen. 1:1 NIV**).

Hymns: "Come, Thou Almighty King," Anonymous

"God, Our Father, We Adore Thee," Frazer

"All Creatures of Our God and King," St. Francis of Assisi

Offertory Prayer: Our Father, we humble ourselves before your throne and offer ourselves as a gift to you. We bring our offerings for use in advancing your kingdom's work. Grant to us the privilege of knowing that through these gifts souls will be saved, lives will be transformed, suffering will be relieved, and your name will be glorified through Jesus Christ our Lord. Amen.

Introduction

January can be a month that begins more than the new calendar year. The child of God can use it to begin a new year of deeper worship and witness.

The book of Genesis deals with beginnings. It sets forth the beginning of creation, the beginning of humanity, the beginning of family life, the beginning of sin and disobedience to God, the beginning of suffering, and the beginning of God's effort to redeem and restore humans to a relationship of love and a fellowship of faith. Because of this, the book of Genesis is considered by some to be the most important book in the Bible.

Nearly everyone looks upon the book of Revelation as a book of insoluble mystery. It deals with the end of history and human existence as people normally understand it. The book of Genesis is just as wonderful and mysterious, for it deals with the beginning of human existence and provides us with a key that helps us understand many of the mysteries of life. A knowledge of the basic truths of the first three chapters of this wonderful book is absolutely essential if one is to begin to understand the Christian faith.

A lack of a proper understanding of the basic truths of these chapters causes many serious students to raise sincere questions concerning their faith. These three chapters provide a happy hunting ground for the foes of the Christian faith. It should be kept in mind that the writer of these words of Scripture was not concerned with giving a scientific explanation for the origin of humans or matter.

He did not conceive of himself as a historian who should be concerned with dates and events. He was a servant of God concerned with the activity and purpose of the eternal God as he sought to redeem humans from their sin.

This inspired writer was not interested in *when* or *how* the universe was created; he was concerned with the *who* of creation. He declares that Israel's God is responsible for the existence of all that is great and good and beautiful. He uses the word *bara,* translated "create," to refer to the exclusive work of God in bringing our world into existence. This word is never used of the work of humans. Only God can create something out of nothing. The inspired conveyer of this revelation of God's activity declares that the Creator worked in an orderly fashion, moving from the simple to the complex, with humans as the crowning climax of the creation. The devout Christian in a scientific age should rejoice to know that the source of all creation is our God and that the purpose of his creative activity was to provide for a human race who could walk and talk and serve him in love and faith.

These first three chapters in Genesis are said to serve three great purposes: they introduce God, they explain the world, and they interpret humankind.

I. God is introduced.

No attempt is made to prove the existence of God; he is simply introduced. His presence and power are taken for granted. The psalmist said, "The fool hath said in his heart, there is no God" (Ps. 14:1). God is introduced as a personal spiritual being. He acts! He speaks! He feels!

God is introduced as one who has existed from all eternity, antedating all things. He is back of all things, before all things, and above all things. He is the eternal and changeless God.

God is introduced as being supreme in power. He speaks the word and creates something out of nothing. He calls the universe into existence. He takes the dust that he has made and fashions man. Then he breathes into the man's nostrils the breath of life so that he becomes a living soul.

These chapters reveal God to be perfect in wisdom, for there is an orderly sequence in his creative activity that excels the finest assembly line in a modern industrial plant. One cannot help but see that God was revealing himself as benevolent and good, for careful preparation was being made in all of creation for the appearance of man.

II. The earth is explained.

Genesis declares that the earth and our universe were created by God. Matter is not eternal. It was not perfect at the beginning, but as the Spirit of God moved upon it, God was able to say that "it is good." The creative activity of God continued as he sought step by step to prepare the world for the coming of the Man who was to climax the divine creative work.

The first two chapters of Genesis celebrate the fact that the God of Israel is the creator and sustainer of all things. Because he is the creator, sustainer, and owner of all things, people should give the divine will reverent consideration.

III. Man is interpreted.

The psalmist raised the question: "What is man?" Many answers have been suggested for this question. The first three chapters of Genesis leave no doubt that man is a special creation. He is the crown and climax of God's creative activity.

The inspired writer declares that humans are creatures made in the image of God. "And God said, Let us make man in our image, after our likeness: and let them have dominion over the fish of the sea, and over the fowl of the air, and over the cattle, and over all the earth, and over every creeping thing that creepeth upon the earth" (Gen. 1:26). We are not to understand this as referring to a physical likeness to God but rather to the capabilities of knowing, responding to, and having immediate fellowship with God. In their rational, moral, and spiritual nature, people can walk and talk with God and come to resemble him in a manner impossible to other earthly creatures.

God planned for man's life to be one of joyful activity. God gave him beautiful surroundings, beloved companionship, and a pleasant occupation. Combined with these was the joy of communion with God.

Genesis 3 reveals Adam's unbelief, rebellion, selfish ambition, disobedience, and desire to find the abundant life outside the will of God. Tragic beyond description was the consequence of sin. The rest of the Bible is an inspired account of the consequences of human sin and of God's loving and merciful program of redeeming and restoring humans to the position of sonship and fellowship lost because of sin.

Conclusion

The text denies atheism, for the text assumes the being of God and introduces him as being behind, before, and above all things. The opening words of the Bible renounce materialism, for they declare that God created matter. As sovereign Lord, he must have first place in our lives. These challenging words should cause all of us to turn from fatalism, because our eternal God is free to work in his universe and in our hearts if we will cooperate with him.

Does it not seem wise and proper that since he is before, behind, and above everything that it is good that we should give him first place in our affections, our ambitions, and our actions? Since we are going to be journeying through a new year, we should travel trustingly in God's grace. Since life should be a mission, let's live it helpfully from day to day, following the example of our Savior who went about doing good. Since life during this new year will be a battle, we should depend on him for victory. And since God has loved us so freely, we should obey him eagerly and lovingly.

SUNDAY EVENING, JANUARY 6

Title: Walking with God

Text: "And Enoch walked with God: and he was not; for God took him" **(Gen. 5:24)**.

Introduction

People were made to walk and talk with God their Creator (Gen. 3:8). We find our highest possible happiness and most satisfying sense of achievement as we walk through life and beyond this life in fellowship with our Maker and Redeemer. Not only did Enoch live a happy life of walking with God, but even during Enoch's lifetime, God testified to his mind and heart that his life was well-pleasing to God (Heb. 11:5).

Throughout the Bible we are encouraged to walk and talk with our God. "Noah walked with God" (Gen. 6:9). Abraham was instructed by God, "Walk before me and be blameless" (17:1 NIV). God promised to walk among his people: "And I will walk among you, and will be your God, and ye shall be my people" (Lev. 26:12). The psalmist promised, "I will walk before the LORD in the land of the living" (Ps. 116:9). Paul challenged the Roman Christians to "walk in newness of life" (Rom. 6:4); and to the Colossians he said, "Walk worthy of the Lord unto all pleasing, being fruitful in every good work, and increasing in the knowledge of God" (Col. 1:10). One of the most inspiring thoughts to be found in all of God's Word is the truth that we were made to walk and talk with God. We are encouraged to believe that God wants to walk and talk with us: he wants us to walk before him and to follow after him. He who walks with God walks in a path of certainty and safety.

Those who walk with God walk in a happy road of life, for at the right hand of God, there are pleasures and joys forevermore (Ps. 16:11). Those who walk with God walk a highway of holiness and beauty that becomes more wonderful as the years go by. To walk with God is to walk in an honorable way. God will honor those who do so. And others will honor them as they behold their lives and are blessed by their character and are challenged by their influence. Jesus said that those who do the will of God will be honored by God (John 12:26). The apostle John declared that he who does the will of God abides forever (1 John 2:17).

Our Scripture reading speaks of the commencement, the continuation, and the consummation of Enoch's walk with God.

> *It is better to walk in the dark with God,*
> *Than walk alone in the light,*
> *It is better to walk with Him by faith,*
> *Than walk alone by sight.*
> *—Author Unknown*

I. The commencement of Enoch's walk with God.

The Scriptures say, "And Enoch lived sixty and five years, and begat Methuselah. And Enoch walked with God after he begat Methuselah three hundred years, and begat sons and daughters" (Gen. 5:21–22). It is a significant and happy hour when a home is blessed with a child. Parents should give serious thought to the course of their conduct as they face the responsibility of teaching and inspiring a child. Seemingly, the birthday of Enoch's first child was also the beginning of a wonderful relationship and fellowship with God for him. Parents should be careful not to lead little feet astray. The best insurance that they can have against doing so is to begin walking with God day by day if they have not already done so.

Some do not begin to walk with God until after they have fallen deep into sin and realize that they are wrecking their lives by walking in their own ways. The path away from God is always downward and leads to disappointment and destruction. If you are conscious of guilt and failure, and if life has lost its beauty and happiness, you should seriously consider returning to God in repentance and faith.

Others recognize their need to walk with God only when they see the emptiness and barrenness of life apart from him. The inner cry of the soul cannot be satisfied by the sawdust the world offers but only by the Bread of Life that heaven has to offer. The materialistic world with all of its honors and rewards cannot bring peace and joy to the human heart. Those come only from God.

Some resume their walk with God only when some tragedy comes to strike terror to their hearts and causes them to think on their ways. Every pastor could cite instances of believers who became busy with the cares of the world or preoccupied with its pleasures until an accident, an illness, or even a death brought them face-to-face with the fact that they have been following afar off. Or worse still, they may have actually forgotten their Maker and Redeemer. The neglect of the soul brings about a spiritual malnutrition that causes them to cave in when troubles come along.

Still others begin the delightful experience of walking with God when the road of their lives crosses the path of some genuine Christian whose life has a glow and glory about it. This creates a hunger and a thirst to such an extent that they seek the Savior as Lord and Master. Pray that your life might be such a witness.

Some hear the call of God to an exciting and satisfying walk as they read the pages of great books and especially the Bible. The Bible was written to reveal God to humans, the chief objects of his loving concern.

In one way or another the invitation comes. "He that hath ears to hear, let him hear." Everyone is invited to walk through life with God.

> *It is better to walk in the dark with God,*
> *Than walk alone in the light.*
> *It is better to walk with Him by faith,*
> *Than walk alone by sight.*

II. The continuation of Enoch's walk with God.

"And Enoch walked with God after he begat Methuselah three hundred years, and begat sons and daughters" (Gen. 5:22). Enoch's companionship with

God was not of a spasmodic nature. He not only made a wise and good beginning, he also followed through. On the good days and on the bad, he walked with God. On days of joy and on days of sadness, he walked with God. On days of prosperity and on days of depression, he walked with God. On days of ease and on days of hardship, he walked with God.

Enoch's life was not easy. He lived in an evil age. The wickedness of people was so great that it grieved the heart of God that he had even made them. Lust was the basis for marriage, and violence was prevalent. Compromise was the order of the day. Yet in this corrupt, wicked society, Enoch continued to walk with God.

Enoch was able to walk with God because he put his faith in God and found God to be trustworthy and faithful. He was acquainted with God. He was in agreement with God. He was the friend of God. God was his friend. He believed that God loved him, and he found out by experience that God did love him.

Nothing in the Scriptures would imply that Enoch did not walk the normal road of life even as he walked with God. He was no hermit who retired to a place of seclusion. The Scriptures do not say that Enoch sat with God. It says that he walked with God for three hundred years. Likewise, the followers of Jesus Christ can walk with him and talk with him in this age if we really want to and are willing to become better acquainted with him and willing to trust his purposes of love for us.

III. The consummation of Enoch's walk with God.

"And Enoch walked with God: and he was not; for God took him" (Gen. 5:24). The life of faith was thus crowned with glory by entrance into the life of perfect fellowship above. In the Revelation the living Christ says, "They shall walk with me in white; for they are worthy" (3:4). The culmination of the holy walk here on earth is to walk right into heaven itself with God. Heaven, someone has said, is where God is. If you walk with God in the here and now, then the joy and peace of heaven can be yours along the road of this life. We are citizens of the kingdom of heaven. As we walk with God, we walk in heavenly places now. Heaven is but the continuation, in a higher and richer form, of the heavenly walk here on earth.

Conclusion

If you are tired of walking in the way of sin, rebellion, loneliness, weakness, and failure, it is time for you to begin walking with God. Put your hand in the nail-scarred hand, give your heart to the Savior, and walk through life with God. Then one day you can walk through the curtain called death into the Father's heavenly home.

WEDNESDAY EVENING, JANUARY 9

Title: The Need for an Altar

Text: "So [Abram] built an altar there to the Lord.... There Abram called on the name of the Lord" **(Gen. 12:7; 13:4 NIV)**.

Introduction

Abraham, the man who became the friend of God as well as the father of the faithful, was an altar builder. When God would appear to him and bestow on him a blessing, a promise, or a commission, he would build an altar. All of us need to be altar builders.

The Bible does not tell us very much about these altars that Abraham built because it isn't important that we know everything about their construction. They do, however, symbolize a great truth and point out a basic need in our lives. Abraham built altars when he worshiped or when he moved from one place to another.

I. What is an altar?

For Christians an altar can be a place, an attitude, or a time when our thoughts and emotions are directed toward God. "God is a Spirit: and they that worship him must worship him in spirit and in truth" (John 4:24). We do not have to be in some specific place before we can worship, for God is a Spirit who cannot be restricted to a specific place. While man is limited to one place at one time, he also is a spirit and can worship God at any time or at any place.

We need to build altars that will call us to the holy privilege of prayer. As we do so, we will find that those altars become places and opportunities to offer to God the praise of our hearts and lips. As we spend time in deep heart searching and consideration of the blessings of God upon us, we will more meaningfully dedicate our time, talents, treasure, and testimony to the purposes of God.

Because Abraham was an altar builder, he found God's fellowship and friendship to be wonderful. His faith was strengthened by this so that he was able to believe when others would have disbelieved. Great strength came to him through worship. The inner man was kept strong.

II. Neglecting to build altars.

Fear captures the citadel of the soul when we neglect to worship. Abraham built no altar while he was in Egypt (Gen. 12:10–20). This most likely explains the reason for the fear that came over him at this time.

When fear captures the heart and the emotions, it is indicative of the fact that faith is either absent or that it has faltered. Faith must increase, and it can grow and be developed and strengthened. This growth occurs only as we give ourselves to worship. Worship is something infinitely more than just going to church and listening to the pastor's sermon. It is the response of the human soul to God as he reveals himself in any of many different manners.

21

Jesus spoke a parable to the end "that men ought always to pray, and not to faint" (Luke 18:1). The truth is that people will give up and at the same time cave in if they don't pray. By the building of altars along the way, Christians strengthen their faith, increase their joy, maintain their spiritual vitality, and guarantee a continuing Christian witness.

III. Building altars to God.

Many altars have already been built or are ordained as places and times for worship. The church where we are to come together as God's family for public worship is a divinely ordained altar. Stay close to your church. Love it sincerely and steadfastly. Remember that God's family is a human family, and don't let the sins of church members cause you to stumble or to neglect your altar of worship. Pray for the harmony of God's people. Pray for and participate in the work of your church as it carries on a crusade for our Lord.

Another altar where God would meet us is in the pages of the Bible. God will meet the deepest needs of our hearts as he did those of Abraham if we will but listen to his authoritative Word. The Bible is not just a history of what happened in the long ago. It is also a revelation of what God will do and what we can become today if we will but worship and work in cooperation with our Creator and Redeemer.

Conclusion

Every home should have an altar. If at all possible, the family should have a time each day for reading the Word of God and offering prayers of praise and confession and requests for guidance. If the entire family cannot be included, then the individual must build his own altar. This can be done at many different times during the day. For example, we can pray as we shave or dry our hair or as we make the bed or drive to work. Where there is a will there is always a way.

God will meet with you and bless you as you build your altars.

SUNDAY MORNING, JANUARY 13

Title: The Friend of God

Text: "I will make of thee a great nation, and I will bless thee, and make thy name great; and thou shalt be a blessing; And I will bless them that bless thee, and curse him that curseth thee: and in thee shall all families of the earth be blessed" (**Gen. 12:2–3**).

Hymns: "I've Found a Friend, Oh, Such a Friend," Small

"Jesus Is the Friend You Need," Reynolds

"What a Friend We Have in Jesus," Scriven

Offertory Prayer: Our heavenly Father, we come to you this morning with our offerings. We bring this portion of our time, talents, energies, and efforts and dedicate it to you. Bless this offering of our lives to your name's honor and glory and to the salvation of a lost world through Jesus Christ our Lord. Amen.

Introduction

One of the most highly revered men of the ancient world is Abraham. Modern Arabs, descendants of his son Ishmael, venerate him most highly. The multiplied millions of the Muslim world hold him in high honor as one of Allah's greatest prophets. The Jews look upon him with great reverence as the founder of their religion. Christians around the world recognize him as the father of the faithful. Abraham receives universal recognition and appreciation.

Three times in the Bible, Abraham is called the friend of God (2 Chron. 20:7; Isa. 41:8; James 2:23). In two of these passages, the speaker is God. Can any title surpass that which God gave to Abraham? Would you like to be a friend of God? Would you like to know that God is your dear Friend? It is a possibility for each of us.

One could define the mission of Christ in terms of making it possible for us to become the children of God. Indeed, it is a source of great joy to have the assurance that we are children of God. The apostle John marveled before this great truth. "Behold, what manner of love the Father hath bestowed on us, that we should be called the sons of God: therefore the world knoweth us not, because it knew him not. Beloved, now are we the sons of God, and it doth not yet appear what we shall be: but we know that, when he shall appear, we shall be like him; for we shall see him as he is" (1 John 3:1–2).

Paul took great pride and joy being a servant of the Lord Jesus. He reveals his gratitude and humility in using the word that means bond servant or slave when he describes himself as such. To be a servant of the Lord Jesus Christ is one of life's greatest privileges. He who spoke the word and called our world into being has given to each of his followers the privilege of being a worker with him in communicating the wonders of God's love to a lost and needy world.

Can you believe this? It seems too good to be true that we can have God as our Friend and that we can be numbered among his friends. On one occasion our

Lord said to his disciples, "Ye are my friends, if ye do whatsoever I command you. Henceforth, I call you not servants; for the servant knoweth not what his Lord doeth: but I have called you friends; for all things that I have heard of my Father I have made known unto you" (John 15:14–15). Jesus called his disciples by the title "friend." If he is the same yesterday, today, and tomorrow—and we believe that he is—then it is possible for us to be his friends also.

Human friendship has been thought of as a relationship between two or more people inspired by mutual respect, confidence, love, and a continuing desire to live and work for the other's welfare. Such was the relationship of Jesus and his disciples. Such was the relationship of Abraham with God. Such can be our joy and delight today.

I. God took the initiative in this friendship.

This is always the case. God comes to us first. We seek God because we are being sought by God. No reference is made to Abraham putting forth a great effort to find God. God found Abraham and revealed his purpose of grace and redemption to him. While he lived in Ur of the Chaldees, "The God of glory appeared.... And said unto him, Get thee out of thy country, and from thy kindred, and come into the land which I shall shew thee" (Acts 7:2–3). This was the first of many wonderful experiences in which God came to Abraham and communicated with him.

Nothing is said about the manner in which God appeared to or communicated with Abraham. It is possible that God communicated with him in the same manner in which he seeks to communicate with us today. Abraham had some limitations that we do not have. He had no Bible out of which he could read about God. He had no church whose fellowship inspired him to listen to the voice of God. In spite of these and other limitations, still he was able to experience God's presence. He was able to recognize the voice and respond to the will of his Creator.

The God who appeared to Abraham and communicated with him still speaks and seeks to establish an enriching friendship with those who are willing. He speaks to us through our conscience and by impressions in our spirit. He continually seeks to encourage us as his friends to introduce him to other potential friends. He seeks people through Sunday school teachers, pastors, and devoted friends or neighbors.

In Christ God came to our world to establish a personal and permanent friendship with those who are willing to walk by faith in and in cooperation with the Creator God who on the cross revealed himself as indescribable love.

II. This friendship was one of mutual faith.

James has this to say about God's friend: "Abraham believed God, and it was imputed unto him for righteousness: and he was called the friend of God" (James 2:23). Paul had paid Abraham this tribute of praise: "He staggered not at the promise of God through unbelief; but was strong in faith, giving glory to God;

and being fully persuaded that, what he had promised, he was able also to perform" (Rom. 4:20–21). Abraham's faith in God was the source of his spiritual greatness. Over and over references are made to the promises of God to Abraham, and his response is always one of faith. Abraham took God at his word. He put confidence in God's promises even when the fulfillment of those promises would have appeared hopeless from every standpoint. He believed that God was not only able and willing, but that he was actually going to do what he had promised. He never doubted the truthfulness or the faithfulness of his God who was also his Friend.

Not only did Abraham trust God, but God also trusted Abraham. A true friendship requires mutual trust and confidence. To Abraham the divine call came to be the leader and example of a long line of men and women who were to be God's servants and communicators of his redemptive purpose in the world.

Those who read with an understanding of redemptive history can clearly see the great commission of our Lord to his church enunciated in the call extended to Abraham to leave his home, his family, and his country, and to become the father of a nation that would make it possible for all nations to be blessed with salvation (Gen. 12:1–3). Here we have the beginning of the Jewish nation, which was to be God's spokesperson to the entire world. God entrusted to Abraham the responsibility of entering into a fellowship of redemptive effort that was to result in our salvation.

This same God, the God of Abraham, Isaac, and Jacob, continues this call to discipleship and friendship and redemptive activity through Christ and the church, his body. We can be the friends of God if we will but respond by faith as Abraham did, which leads to faithfulness.

III. This friendship was mutually satisfying.

The permanency of the relationship between God and Abraham proves that it was mutually satisfying. A genuine friendship is not formed in a moment. A friendship does not always grow fast. It usually is the result of years of experience in which there are high points and low points in which each party experiences the helpfulness of the other.

As the years went by, God saw progress being made in both the life and work of his servant and friend Abraham. Over and over God came to Abraham and restated his promises and interpreted his plan for his life. Again and again, Abraham built his altars for sacrifice, communion, and worship.

Life with this divine Friend was so satisfying and his confidence in both the divine love and purpose was so great that Abraham did not even hesitate when the command came to offer up his promised son Isaac as a sacrifice. As they neared the place of sacrifice, Abraham said to his servants, "Stay here with the donkey while I and the boy go over there. We will worship and then we will come back to you" (Gen. 22:5 NIV).

Here is demonstrated both his love for his heavenly Friend and his unfaltering faith in the divine purpose. He was determined to offer his son as a sacrifice, yet he was confident that both he and the lad would return to them after the experience of worship. The writer of the book of Hebrews says that even at the dawn of redemptive history, Abraham believed that "God could raise the dead, and figuratively speaking, he did receive Isaac back from death" (11:19 NIV).

This kind of faith will lead to a transforming spiritual experience today even as it did in Abraham's day. God is utterly trustworthy. He can be depended on. He cannot lie. He is the Friend all of us need. We are the friends he needs to carry forward his redemptive purpose in the world.

IV. Every friendship must be nurtured if it is to grow.

The wise man said, "A man of many companions may come to ruin, but there is a friend who sticks closer than a brother" (Prov. 18:24 NIV). This is just as true with the divine friendship as it is with human friendships. Christ Jesus has come that we might know God as Father and as Friend. Ours can be an increasingly wonderful fellowship and an ever-deepening friendship. God has taken the initiative in the Savior and in the gift of the Holy Spirit who came to dwell in the church as the divine administrator of God's continuing eternal purpose first revealed to Abraham.

There are several things that we can count on from Christ, who wants to be our Friend as well as our Lord and Savior. We need to move beyond becoming acquainted with him only in conversion and the new birth. We must also become his friends in the fellowship of service.

As we study the friendship that existed between Jesus and his disciples, it is possible to discover how our Friend will relate to us. First, we can count on him to give us advice. This is always expected between friends. In our human relationships, we expect advice and we receive it from our friends. Even if we do not take the advice of a friend, we are helped by it. It is wonderful to measure our thoughts against the opinion of our Savior as we study his written Word and hold communion with him in prayer as the living Word of God. He is full of counsel, and we would be wise to heed his advice at all times.

Again, we can depend on our divine Friend to defend us against all accusers. Paul rejoiced over the fact that no one could bring an accusation against the redeemed of God so as to imperil their relationship with God (cf. Rom. 8:33, 39). He is both able and determined that nothing in the past, present, or future will be able to separate us from the love of God. As a faithful person will defend the good name and reputation of his friend, even so the Savior ever lives to make intercession for us.

Another wonderful benefit of this friendship is that the Friend who sticks closer than a brother will both rebuke and correct us if we drift from the will of God for our lives. "Faithful are the wounds of a friend; but the kisses of an enemy are deceitful" (Prov. 27:6). Seldom do we have friendships that are close enough that we can both receive and welcome criticism that has all the appearances of being destructive or adverse. We usually hear compliments from our friends and criticisms from our enemies or at least from those who do not love us. We need to remember that Jesus considered Peter his good friend, yet he rebuked Peter more often than any of the other apostles. This is one of the most fearful duties of a genuine friendship because human nature does not welcome reproof.

All of us need at least a few friends whom we love and have faith in to the extent that we could receive even the most painful of personal rebukes from them without being offended. Our Savior can be such a friend if we will but permit him to be. By both the letter and the spirit of the Word of God, our Friend will rebuke us in our acts of omission and commission and in our attitudes or disposition if we will but read the Word reverently and prayerfully.

Last and by no means least, we can expect our Friend from heaven to show his appreciation for qualities of mind and spirit and actions of heart or hand that are commendable. It is most significant that in the letters to the seven churches of Asia Minor that the transcendent Lord who walked in the midst of the seven golden candlesticks saw things to commend as well as some things that deserved condemnation. He delights to commend us as we render acceptable service for God in ministry to others.

Conclusion

If you do not know Jesus Christ as your personal Savior, it is impossible to know him as your personal Friend. Become acquainted with him through repentance and faith. In your mind and heart, turn from the life of faithlessness and rebellion and begin to trust God for forgiveness and the gift of new life.

If you know him as Savior, you can know him also as Friend. Trust him implicitly. Believe even if you cannot see or figure it all out with your mind. The sin that does so easily beset all of us is the sin of desiring to walk by sight rather than by faith. Believe that all of God's purposes toward you are purposes of love. Obey his will for your life completely as it is revealed to you through Bible study, prayer, and worship. In his will, attempt that which is humanly impossible, trusting your infallible Friend for success in the end. You, like Abraham, can be the friend of God.

SUNDAY EVENING, JANUARY 13

Title: The Success That Failed

Text: "Abram dwelled in the land of Canaan, and Lot dwelled in the cities of the plain, and pitched his tent toward Sodom" **(Gen. 13:12).**

Introduction

The title of a sermon usually indicates something about the truth a pastor is seeking to communicate to his congregation. Considerable thought is usually given to the selection of an appropriate title. In studying the life of Lot, the nephew of Abraham, the pastor may choose from many appropriate titles. He could use "The Man Who Loved the World and Lost It." Lot did both of these. "The Way to Lose Your Influence" would make a good title, for Lot lost his influence completely.

Because all of us are tempted to live for the treasures of this world, Lot could speak powerfully concerning "The Tragedy of Living for One World Alone."

For those of us who are parents, Lot could serve as a warning signal concerning the peril of being "Betrayers of Our Children," for Lot did that when he moved into the suburbs of Sodom. Taking the line of least resistance is a natural human tendency, so this man's life could scream warnings of alarm to us concerning both "The Danger and Destiny of Drifters." Lot preaches a powerful sermon with his life and illustrates both "The Possibility and Price of Giving God Second Place."

We live in an age that has deified success. People are willing to pay almost any price for success. Many fail to realize that, like Lot, they can succeed and yet fail at the same time. Would you let Lot show you how you can succeed and fail at the same time?

I. Lot came to the time of decision.

Due to a combination of prosperity and crowded conditions, it was necessary that some adjustment be made concerning the flocks of Abraham and his nephew Lot. Abraham, wishing to be generous, gave Lot the privilege of making the first choice. "Abram said unto Lot, Let there be no strife, I pray thee, between me and thee, and between my herdmen and thy herdmen; for we be brethren. Is not the whole land before thee? Separate thyself, I pray thee, from me: if thou wilt take the left hand, then I will go to the right; or if thou depart to the right hand, then I will go to the left" (Gen. 13:8–10). The decision that Lot made on this occasion was decisive for his entire life. It determined his destiny during his lifetime, and it determined the message his life would have throughout redemptive history. His decision led to his destiny.

Behind every great success or great failure there is at least one significant decision and most likely many other decisions in harmony with the first one. The first big decision leads to many other little decisions that point in the same direction.

Lot faced the big decision of his life and made it without a proper appreciation of the values of what today we would call Christian influence and fellowship. He pitched his tent in the direction that would mean the moral and spiritual downfall of his own life and that of his family. It is most difficult to be a true follower of Christ if we deliberately expose ourselves to compromising influences.

Lot permitted covetousness to be the determining factor in his destiny-determining decision. Webster defines *covet* as "to desire; to long for, especially something belonging to another person." Our Savior went beyond this modern definition by considering covetousness as that attitude that judges success or real living in terms of the abundance of the things a man may possess. According to Jesus, a man could be completely innocent of wanting that which belongs to someone else and at the same time be filled with covetousness. To be covetous is to live life on a materialistic or secular level (cf. Luke 12:15–21). It is to be overly concerned with feeding the mouth and clothing the back. Success is measured in terms of the size and location of the house, the number and models of the cars in the driveway, the number and size of television sets, the balance in the bank, and how many people work either for you or under your supervision.

In this affluent society, it is most difficult for us to avoid being covetous. Some of the best minds in the country devote themselves to the art of cultivating our taste and creating a demand for their product, which can be secured only if we have the income from "vast herds of sheep" like those cared for by Lot's herdsmen. The Joneses are always a step ahead of us. The most winsome appeals are made to the pride of man as an inducement for him to provide certain luxuries, which are claimed to be necessities of life, for his family. Unless even the most devout Christian is on his guard constantly, he will drift into the way of thinking that caused Lot to judge success in terms of "stuff" instead of service to God and his fellow humans.

The biblical record does not indicate that Lot was a cheat or that he was dishonest. He was no crook. He simply made a decision concerning the direction that his life would take. He failed to count the cost of financial success when it involved moving toward a goal he had selected on a material basis alone.

Lot succeeded financially but failed miserably otherwise because he made this major decision without any consideration for the will of God for his life. Lot was not the last man to make that mistake. God has a mission and work for each of us. He can walk and talk with us along any road of legitimate endeavor if we are seeking to be his servants and if we are willing to be communicators of his message of love as we do so. God needs people in every bracket of life who will be his apostles, but they need to be his servants first and owners of sheep secondarily.

II. Lot pitched his tent toward Sodom.

I am not sure that Lot intended to become the first citizen of the city of Sodom. You can be sure that he never intended to become as much a part of that wicked city as he and his family finally became. He drifted in that direction by degrees, and finally, after a number of years, he found himself firmly established there.

Is it not true that one of the greatest perils we face is the peril of just drifting? We fail to ponder the path of our feet. We refuse to recognize, at least in some instances, that in choosing a certain way of life, we have automatically chosen the destination to which that road leads. This is true on our national highways, and it is also true on the road of life.

People continue to follow in the steps of this man who achieved success and yet failed at the same time. In our quest for financial success, a phantom that ever flees from our grasp, we neglect to be diligent students of God's Word. We give the church a minor place in our thoughts and affections. We neglect the inner cry of the soul for God, and we seek to satisfy our ambition for things by always trying harder. In the meantime, life is passing us by. Opportunities for Christlike service are fleeing. The spiritual welfare of the family receives only minor attention. All the while we are getting closer and closer to the city limits of the modern Sodom of our life's highway.

There are many mothers who put forth more effort to see that their daughters never miss a dance lesson than they do to see that those daughters come to know Jesus Christ as personal Savior. There are many fathers who will work like beavers to help their sons become star players on the Little League baseball team, yet they neglect to teach their sons how to play the real game of life according to the rules of the heavenly Umpire. It is possible to be on the way to success and failure at the same time.

III. Lot achieved success in time.

It is said that "Lot sat in the gate of Sodom" (Gen. 19:1). At the gates of ancient Middle Eastern cities, there were recesses that served as the offices of leading citizens. Here they made bargains, transacted business, and even administered justice. This would indicate that Lot had achieved a position of prominence in the city of Sodom. In modern terminology, we would say that he "had arrived."

Lot enjoyed the fruits of his labors, and no doubt everyone considered him to be a great success. We can imagine that he was a member of the chamber of commerce and a number of civic clubs and an officer in the local country club. He saw his daughters married to up-and-coming young men who had a great future in the business life of their city. Everything from a business standpoint seemed to be going his way. The tragedy of this success story is to be found in what Lot had lost in order to achieve this success.

IV. The day of reckoning came.

The day of reckoning always comes. We all face a time when all that we are and have is tested. Our individual lives are tested. Our family ties are tested. Our national character and strength are tested. Such was the case in Lot's day, and when Sodom was weighed on God's scales, it was found wanting. The city was past the point of hope and redemption.

God revealed that judgment was going to be poured out on the wicked city of Sodom (cf. Gen. 18:20–19:28). Abraham showed great faith in God and great compassion for Lot and others in Sodom by his intercessory prayer (Gen. 18:23–24). After much prayer on the part of Abraham, God promised to spare the city if ten righteous persons could be found in all of the city. The angelic messengers visited the city and failed to find that many.

The question has been asked as to why God would be willing to spare such a city for the sake of ten righteous people. Instead of thinking in terms of a reward for their righteousness, it would probably be closer to the truth to think that if ten could be found, this would provide a basis for hope that others would repent. Second Peter 2:7–8 speaks of Lot as being "distressed by the filthy lives of lawless men (for that righteous man, living among them day after day, was tormented in his righteous soul by the lawless deeds he saw and heard)" (NIV). Nothing is said of his bearing a testimony for God. He even failed to do so with his own wife and children. Perhaps he, like many moderns, just kept quiet about his religion.

The cities of Sodom and Gomorrah, because of the depths of wickedness and perversion to which they had descended, were sentenced to extinction and oblivion. Lot, the man who had pitched his tent toward Sodom until finally he found himself inside and a vital part of its business, was given a warning to flee. It is at this point that the extent of his failure can be observed.

When he was encouraged to flee from the city and take his loved ones with him, he discovered that he had no influence or power of persuasion. "Lot went out and spoke to his sons-in-law, who were pledged to marry his daughters. He said, 'Hurry and get out of this place, because the LORD is about to destroy the city!' But his sons-in-law thought he was joking" (Gen. 19:14 NIV). They did not believe him. They mocked him and ignored his warning.

This man who had succeeded financially began to realize that he had failed. He was destined to see his loved ones perish. He was to see his property go up in smoke and down in ashes. He was to come to the end of his journey of life in shame. The cost of achieving this kind of success was too high: Lot lost the privilege of having continuing fellowship with God. He missed the joy of an ever-increasing partnership with the God who was working to redeem the world. The joy of true success in life escaped him. He forfeited the chance to be listed among the great in God's hall of fame. He lost the possibility of having the approval of God upon his efforts. Perhaps his greatest disappointment was in his own home. And moreover, he would find himself without heavenly rewards.

Conclusion

There are some noble characters who serve as a green light and give us the "go" signal. They tell us that all is clear, the road is safe, and we may proceed along the way of life. There are others who serve as red lights that say "stop." Still other biographies would serve as amber lights that would encourage us to be very cautious.

Is the life of Lot a "stoplight" that God has placed on the road map of your life to warn you that defeat, disappointment, death, and destruction are ahead of you if you continue to pitch your tent in the direction of Sodom? Is Lot's life a "caution light" to encourage you to reexamine your aim or ambition, your attitude or affection to see if you are on a less direct route to Sodom? Are you letting God guide your decisions? Do you walk day by day so as to please him? Do you make your decisions on the basis of financial gain or loss?

It is much better to live in Canaan with God than to live among the cities of the plain and slowly drift toward Sodom. Let Lot give you some warnings for your life so that in succeeding you will not discover that actually you have failed.

WEDNESDAY EVENING, JANUARY 16

Title: The God of Abraham

Text: "Now the LORD had said unto Abram, Get thee out of thy country,... unto a land that I will shew thee: And I will make of thee a great nation" **(Gen. 12:1–2)**.

Introduction

Discovering the concept of God that possessed the hearts and minds of those who became spiritual giants is beneficial. By every manner of measuring, Abraham was a spiritual giant. Nevertheless, he was also a man of common clay. He was not perfect and without flaw. Thus, we should focus not on Abraham's spirituality, but rather on the God he worshiped—the same God we worship. We will grow spiritually and serve more effectively if we will relate to God as Abraham did.

I. Abraham's God was granted the right to command.

Scripture records that God appeared to Abraham and said, "Get thee out of thy country, and from thy kindred, and from thy father's house, unto a land that I will shew thee: ... So Abram departed" (Gen. 12:1–4). Abraham did not just play a game with God. He recognized God's sovereign right to command and responded with obedience. There is no substitute for obedience, and there can be no growth or progress in disobedience. Jesus said, "Why do you call me, 'Lord, Lord,' and do not do what I say?" (Luke 6:46 NIV).

II. Abraham's God had a purpose of grace.

Many Bible readers have missed the great commission as stated to Abraham. They have seen only the promise of God to bless Abraham and have missed the divine purpose for these blessings. The last phrase of Genesis 12:2 is actually a command: "You will be a blessing" (NIV). It is a statement of fact, but it is also a call for redemptive activity. The next verse speaks of a reflexive action in which all the nations of the earth will have the opportunity of blessing themselves through faith in that which God intended to accomplish through Abraham and his descendants.

Abraham perceived that behind all of God's purposes and commands there was a motive of love. What a difference it would make if we could but believe that all of God's movements toward us, all of his commands to us, and all that he would have us do is but the continuation of his love for us and for others.

The Evil One has been misrepresenting the character and nature of God from the very beginning. He never quits defaming the character of God. He will destroy what faith we do have if we do not prevent him from doing so.

The God of Abraham loves us, and he will bless us and make us a blessing to others if we will trust him and cooperate with him.

III. Abraham's God made many promises.

Abraham was lifted out of a pit of polytheism to become the father of the faithful and the head of a great nation because he believed that God was trustworthy and that he could be depended on to keep his promises. Paul said concerning Abraham's faith, "He staggered not at the promise of God through unbelief; but was strong in faith, giving glory to God; and being fully persuaded that, what he had promised, he was able also to perform" (Rom. 4:20–21). God trusted Abraham. Abraham trusted God. They walked through life together. God never did let Abraham down.

Have you found the great promises that God has made to us in the Bible? If you haven't, then your life has been greatly impoverished. To serve God acceptably, we must discover his great promises and cling to them. Otherwise we will depend on human effort and strength alone. Study the Word of God to discover these divine promises. Once you have found his promises, claim them and move forward in obedience, trusting him for the outcome.

Conclusion

We continue to worship the God of Abraham. He still has the right to command. He still has a purpose of grace. He still has promises for each of us. May God grant that we might relate to God as Abraham did.

SUNDAY MORNING, JANUARY 20

Title: The Test of Faith

Text: "Some time later God tested Abraham. He said to him, 'Abraham!' 'Here I am,' he replied." **(Gen. 22:1 NIV)**.

Hymns: "Have Faith in God," McKinney

"Faith Is the Victory," Yates

"Trust and Obey," Sammis

Offertory Prayer: Our Father, we come now to bring our tithes and offerings to you. Help us to realize the importance of giving our total selves to you. Help us to place ourselves on the altar as an act of worship. We offer to you our hands and our hearts. We give you our tongues, that they might tell the wondrous story of your love. Help us to be generous in our financial support of kingdom ministries. In Jesus' name. Amen.

Introduction

Few students look forward to the time of testing. Even a little pop quiz can be a cause for anxiety. Students experience much agony of soul as they cram for various examinations that sometimes occur with frightening rapidity.

Some people would discredit testing and say that the tension created by it is detrimental to students. However, all will have to admit that both the teacher and the student would be under some handicaps if there were no tests. Testing enables teachers to assess both their teaching methods and effectiveness. Frequently it is said that if 50 percent of the students in a particular class fail a test, it indicates that the teacher is failing to teach. By means of a test, students can determine the effectiveness of their own study methods as well as their intellectual effectiveness. While in some instances a test may create tension that leads to depression, in other cases it reveals progress that is both satisfying and exhilarating. Success can indicate that it is time to move on to a new plateau of investigation and achievement. Ours would be a confused world if there were no tests by which we could measure our progress or the quality of products available.

Did it ever occur to you that the heavenly Father might be interested in your spiritual progress? Does it not seem both right and natural to expect that our Lord, heaven's infallible Teacher, would test both the genuineness of our discipleship and our progress toward spiritual maturity? He did so during his earthly ministry (cf. Matt. 16:13–17). Some failed the test and flunked out before they came to an experience of conversion (cf. Matt. 19:16–17; John 6:66). Others made some very low grades. There were times, however, when students in the school of Christ passed with flying colors and received his congratulations.

In this morning's text, we read, "God tested Abraham." It is helpful to realize that when Satan tempts us, he always does it to bring out the evil in us so as to destroy us. His purpose is always determined by his wickedness and rebellion against God. When God puts us to the test, he always does so to bring out the good in us or to help someone else have the faith and courage to do that which is right. God never tempts us to do that which is evil. He never leads us astray (James 1:13–17). God's purposes toward us are always motivated by his love for us. This is true even when chastisement comes from him (Heb. 12:5–10).

From this experience that Abraham had with God, we can learn at least three valuable truths: (1) The divine purpose for tests to our faith can be discovered. (2) The response of Abraham to the test sets the pattern for us. (3) There are some thrilling principles that can encourage us as we face the tests of our faith.

I. The divine purpose for the test.

Abraham lived at the dawn of redemptive history. He was called out of a country and from association with a family that worshiped many gods. These heathen people were idolaters. They lacked a knowledge of the nature and character of the true God who had chosen Abraham to be the father of a nation through whom he would reveal himself to the world. In times of great need, these people resorted to human sacrifice. They came to the place where they thought that their gods demanded it. Human sacrifice was evidently a religious custom widely prevalent among the ancient Semites. This evil practice was condemned during the time of Moses, and the prophets repeatedly denounced this heathen act of worship (cf. Lev. 18:21; Jer. 7:31; Mic. 6:7).

If we would properly understand the nature of this test to which Abraham was put, we must assume that in his time the religious custom of human sacrifice prevailed among the peoples of the land. We must recognize him as a citizen of the age in which he lived. God put him to a test to prove the genuineness of his faith by a means that was common in that day, and it would not appear as outrageous or abominable to Abraham as it would to us.

34

The people of Abraham's day would have been greatly surprised and pleasantly pleased that his God would have restrained him from making the sacrifice. They were of the opinion that the gods demanded that they give up their most dearly beloved possessions as an act of appeasement. They would not be shocked by the command to make the sacrifice. Their amazement would arise from the wonderful experience of the firstborn being spared from the knife.

In testing Abraham's faith, God was seeking to bring out something good for Abraham, for Abraham's contemporaries, and for Abraham's posterity. This test revealed something about Abraham, but the greatest discovery to be made in this experience is what it reveals about God. God was seeking to reveal his character and his purpose for all people, and Abraham's faith was such that this revelation was successfully made.

By being put to this severe test by God, Abraham discovered something good about his own relationship to God. This test revealed that his love for his God was as genuine and as sacrificial as that of the heathen about him who gave up their most precious possessions in their foul and savage worship of the nature gods. Abraham discovered and revealed to others that his love and loyalty to his God were supreme over his love and loyalty to his family. His God had first place in his life. Now there could be no question about this. His was no easy, cheap, convenient faith. To know that your faith is the real article is of inestimable value.

This test of Abraham's faith was a means by which he proved his obedience and his love for God. He thus qualified himself to become a stimulating example to those who were to follow as they are called on to fulfill painful and difficult duties. God did not prove Abraham for his own satisfaction. He was seeking to provide an example that could serve as an encouragement to others. Nothing is more powerful than an example. Precepts are good, but an example puts our excuses to silence and tells us to press on toward success in the undertaking. He continues to encourage us to give our best to God.

II. Abraham's response is our pattern.

Abraham offered no excuses. He could have pleaded that such an act was contrary to nature. A father should not offer up his son as a sacrifice. He could have reasoned that the promise could not be fulfilled if the son of promise was slain. He remained silent as far as offering excuses was concerned. Evidently God had communicated with him in a manner in which he was accustomed. He knew what God wanted, and he was determined to do it.

Abraham did not delay doing what he knew he should do. He arose the next morning and made preparations to depart immediately for the place of sacrifice. He left the business of his flocks and herds and went immediately to the business of his God.

He did not confer with those who would oppose his action. No reference is made to a conference with his wife concerning whether it was advisable to do God's will. When the way is clear and plain as to what God would have us do, there is no need for us to have a multitude of counselors.

35

This burdened father did not call for a fanfare of trumpets as he rendered his service to God. He did not call in his neighbors to witness his heroic act of sacrifice. He knew that the Lord would be his witness, and that was enough for him. He had no desire for the applause of people. We need to be much on guard lest we serve and give out of a desire to win the acceptance and praise of others.

This man of faith and obedience did not waiver. He knew what God wanted him to do, and with dispatch he gave himself to the task. He did not dally with the Devil. He had a long time to think and consider during the three-day journey to the place of sacrifice, but he did not hesitate for a moment. He proceeded to the place of sacrifice. He did not even permit the servants to witness the act of sacrificial worship. "Stay here with the donkey while I and the boy go over there. We will worship and then we will come back to you" (Gen. 22:5 NIV). The trip up the mountain was made. The altar was erected. The wood was prepared. Isaac was bound and laid on the altar, and the hand of a loving father was stretched forth to slay his son as a sacrifice in obedience to the command of his God.

At this point, God interposed, and said, "Do not lay a hand on the boy. Do not do anything to him. Now I know that you fear God, because you have not withheld from me your son, your only son" (Gen. 22:12 NIV). Do we waver and complain bitterly when life brings hardships our way? Abraham's obedience was silent and immediate.

III. Thrilling truths for the present.

Abraham would encourage us to believe that the will of God for our life should be the law that we follow to the letter. Whatever God commands is not only good but also absolutely necessary if we would become what he would have us to be. Sometimes it is dangerous to try to figure out the way of everything before we attempt to do what God has commanded. In many instances, the why cannot be discovered until we are able to look back upon the entire experience, and then it becomes clear as crystal.

From this test in the school of difficulty, we should be able to learn that what God requires from us is not impossible. When God commands, he always provides strength to obey. God has all power, and he always bestows on us the power that is needful for the achievement of a task.

This command from God should inform us that God may permit or even send severe trials into our lives. We can be assured that our heavenly Father will be actively at work in each of these to bring out all possible goods to those who love him (Rom. 8:28). There are some great truths that equip one for unique service that cannot be learned by reading a book. These come to us only in the school of suffering. It is both wise and beneficial for us to be submissive to the will of God when the trials are painful or disagreeable. The awareness of his presence and the assurance that his purpose is motivated by love can bring peace and joy in the most frightful of circumstances.

From Abraham we can learn that at times God may require that we give up those dearest and most precious to us. We must not let our love for anyone or anything take first place in our life. Our loved ones will be safe, and we will not be deprived of them as long as our Lord has first place in our affections, ambitions, and actions.

Conclusion

From this test on the top of Mount Moriah, God revealed that he would provide the lamb for the sacrifice. This he did in the gift and death of his Son, Jesus Christ, on the cross of Calvary. God did not spare his own Son but delivered him up for us all. In this manner God proved his love for sinners (Rom. 5:8). John the Baptist proclaimed, "Behold the Lamb of God, which taketh away the sin of the world" (John 1:29). That is what the world needs. That is what each of us needs. Trust him today as your Lord that he might also be your Savior.

SUNDAY EVENING, JANUARY 20

Title: A Bowl of Stew

Text: "Then Jacob gave Esau bread and pottage of lentils; and he did eat and drink, and rose up, and went his way: thus Esau despised his birthright" **(Gen. 25:34; cf. Heb. 12:16–17)**.

Introduction

In the book of Hebrews, Esau is used as a warning to prevent us from making the fatal mistake of treating spiritual values, responsibilities, and opportunities as something cheap. The writer of Hebrews draws the attention of his readers to their high privileges and their sacred responsibilities; and at the same time he points out the fatal error of Esau, which can also cause our own downfall.

Esau sold his birthright for one mess of pottage. He sold out his future for a bowl of stew in the present. He had been out in the woods and fields on a hunting expedition. He came home famished. Jacob, his brother, was cooking a mess of red lentils. "And Esau said to Jacob, Feed me, I pray thee, with that same red pottage; for I am faint.... And Jacob said, Sell me this day thy birthright. And Esau said, Behold, I am at the point to die: and what profit shall this birthright do to me? And Jacob said, Swear to me this day; and he sware unto him: and he sold his birthright unto Jacob. Then Jacob gave Esau bread and pottage of lentils; and he did eat and drink, and rose up, and went his way: thus Esau despised his birthright" (Gen. 25:30–34).

Jacob's behavior of acting in an unbrotherly manner and driving a hard bargain in a time of great need cannot be condoned. It was a cruel act. On the other hand, Esau's foolishness is equally despicable. It indicates a weakness in his character and a base shallowness in his scale of values. It provides us with an index to the type of man he was.

Esau was Isaac's firstborn. One must understand and appreciate the position and privileges of the firstborn to know what Esau actually sold and what Jacob was so eager to possess.

I. The rights of the firstborn.

The firstborn in ancient Israel had unique privileges and responsibilities. They were dedicated and considered as belonging to God (Ex. 22:29). They occupied a position of honor next to their parents (Gen. 49:3). The firstborn received a double portion of the estate of the father (Deut. 21:17). He also succeeded as the authoritative figure in the family or kingdom (2 Chron. 21:3). Before the Aaronic priesthood was established, the firstborn was honored with the office of the priesthood and the administration of the worship of God.

The right of the firstborn thus carried with it both secular and sacred values. It was a position of prestige as far as business affairs were concerned. Perhaps the greatest significance was in the religious implications that this office possessed. In speaking of the church as the firstborn "whose names are written in heaven," the writer of the book of Hebrews speaks of present-day Christians as occupying a position similar to that which Esau sold for a bowl of stew in a moment of intense hunger.

It is our high privilege to be in the position of the firstborn of God in the world today. It is our high and holy privilege to render priestly services in the name of our Lord. We are to be the means by which the grace, mercy, and love of God are to be communicated to those who do not know Jesus Christ as a personal Savior from sin and as the giver of eternal life. Through each of us, the unbelievers about us are to come to a knowledge of the true God as he has revealed himself through the Christ who died and arose again from the dead. We are "a chosen people, a royal priesthood, a holy nation, a people belonging to God, that [we] may declare the praises of him who called [us] out of darkness into his wonderful light" (1 Peter 2:9 NIV).

This sacred position of privilege carries with it a great responsibility. God does not bestow on us the position and privileges of the firstborn merely for our selfish indulgence. God blesses us that we might be a blessing. Esau speaks with tears to warn us against the peril of despising our birthright and selling it for a mere "pot of stew."

II. Esau despised his birthright.

In a moment of temporary emergency, Esau bartered off his birthright for a pot of stew to satisfy the hunger of his stomach. Seemingly he did not properly appreciate the sacred privileges that went along with the birthright, and therefore he lightly and thoughtlessly transferred it to Jacob for the satisfaction of a momentary need.

In selling his birthright, Esau revealed himself as a careless, shallow fellow, living from hand to mouth, giving little or no thought to the higher values of the soul. He thus revealed himself to be a godless person (Heb. 12:16). He purchased the present satisfaction of an appetite at the price of something that would be of great value in the future. Later he was to regret this action, but it was too late to reverse his actions. This is always the case. We can never change a choice. We can only deal with the consequences of those choices.

III. Are you guilty of Esau's sin?

Probably all of us have followed in the footsteps of Esau more than we realize or would be willing to admit. Sin is deceptive, the Evil One is shrewd, and human nature is weak. Furthermore, the pressures of our competitive and materialistic society press in upon us constantly.

Esau lived for visible things and secured them by forfeiting spiritual and eternal values. It is easy to be captivated by the trinkets and gadgets that seem so necessary in our modern day. Many completely neglect worship and excuse their sleeping in late on the Lord's Day by saying that they just have to have their rest if they are going to successfully run the rat race during the week. Some have prospered to the extent that they have purchased a second home located in the country or by a lake; these homes then become the gods of the weekend.

Esau lived for sensual satisfaction rather than for spiritual achievement or service. His concern for the satisfaction of his hunger pains took priority over all other considerations. His stomach was more important than his mind, his soul, or the possible achievements of his hands and life. To consider yourself as a "stomach to feed and a back to clothe" is to rob yourself of your highest dignity as one who was made to walk and talk with God, and to lower yourself to the level of being a mere intestine that needs clothing. Without realizing what is happening, we can find ourselves treating ourselves in this manner before we know it. Our Lord said, "Man shall not live by bread alone, but by every word that proceedeth out of the mouth of God" (Matt. 4:4). Sad indeed is the fate of the man who comes to think of the chief end of living in terms of having only a bowl of stew.

Esau lived only for himself without being considerate of his family. He was willing to give up the position of opportunity for rendering a needed service for a bowl of stew that was already warm instead of taking a few minutes to prepare such for himself. He did not know the meaning of self-control or discipline. He did not have any built-in controls to provide guidance in a time of emergency.

There are many today who sell their future for the fleeting pleasures of the moment. Youth who do not study opportunities are automatically determining their destiny for the sake of some foolish pleasure of the present. Many young people, perhaps due to lack of parental training and example, sell their hopes for future happiness in marriage by insisting on participating in intimacies that should be reserved only for the married.

This man from the past, though he is dead, yet speaks to the present concerning the utter madness of flinging away greater future good for the temporary pleasures that are offered in the present. He who lives only for the present moment is acting as if he is on the same level with an animal.

Conclusion

Esau majored on his stomach and forgot about his soul. He lived for time and completely ignored eternity. He measured success in terms of the satisfactions of present appetites without regard to what was the highest and best for the future.

Esau made his fatal decision in a time of weakness and exhaustion. Temptation always comes at a time when we are most likely to yield. Our Lord was tempted when he had fasted and was "hungered." He did not sell his birthright. We do not have to. We were made for God, and our highest possible happiness is found in reflecting his glory and grace. We should give ourselves to him completely and constantly.

WEDNESDAY EVENING, JANUARY 23

Title: Redigging the Old Wells

Text: "And Isaac digged again the wells of water, which they had digged in the days of Abraham his father; for the Philistines had stopped them after the death of Abraham: and he called their names after the names by which his father had called them" (**Gen. 26:18**).

Introduction

Isaac had the misfortune of living in the shadow of a truly great father. Often it is exceedingly difficult for a son of such a father to achieve significance and recognition in his own right.

The Bible does not describe any great achievements of Isaac as it does of his father. However, Scripture records several times that he "digged again the wells of water, which they had digged in the days of Abraham his father; for the Philistines had stopped them." These wells were essential for the lives of both the families and the flock. Had it not been for these wells, they could not have survived. After Abraham's death, Philistines had destroyed these sources of refreshment and sustenance, and it fell to Isaac to rediscover and redig them.

I. Each generation must redig the old wells.

Every individual must find for himself or herself the source of spiritual vitality. Philistines who would deprive us and hinder us from finding the wells of salvation are still among us.

Each person is faced with the temptation to walk only by sight and not by faith. The pressures of a materialistic and competitive society take command of us and crowd out every thought concerning the spiritual.

If we permit the Evil One, who walks about as a roaring lion seeking whom he may devour, to engage our interests and activities to the extent that we forget where the wells of salvation are, for all practical purposes they have been stopped up as were the wells during the days of Isaac.

II. We must redig the wells of salvation.

Isaiah said, "With joy shall ye draw water out of the wells of salvation" (Isa. 12:3). And the psalmist said, "I will take the cup of salvation, and call upon the name of the LORD" (Ps. 116:13). Both the prophet and the psalmist refer to salvation as something more than just the initial experience with God. They are think-ing in terms of all that God has for his children. Desperately we need to realize that God's program for us is something more than a ticket to heaven. It is a total program for all of life.

    A. *We need to rediscover the well of the Word of God (Josh. 1:8; Pss. 1:2; 119:36, 92, 105, 140).*

    B. *We must redig the well of private prayer (Matt. 6:6).*

    C. *We must again come to the well of fellowship with the saints (Heb. 10:24–25).* Saints of the past and saints in the present can have a wholesome effect on our lives.

    D. *Another well that we need to redig with haste is the well of happy, joyful witnessing (Ps. 126:5–6).*

III. The result of redigging the old wells.

"The LORD shall guide thee continually, and satisfy thy soul in drought, and make fat thy bones: and thou shalt be like a watered garden, and like a spring of water, whose waters fail not. And they that shall be of thee shall build the old waste places: thou shalt raise up the foundations of many generations; and thou shalt be called, The repairer of the breach, The restorer of paths to dwell in" (Isa. 58:11–12).

Conclusion

Those who give themselves to the task of redigging these old wells of spiritual vitality will find for themselves divine guidance. Inward spiritual satisfaction will bless their lives. Spiritual refreshment and peace will be a reality.

SUNDAY MORNING, JANUARY 27

Title: "Behold, This Dreamer Cometh"

Text: "And they said one to another, Behold, this dreamer cometh" (**Gen. 37:19**).

Hymns: "Glorious Is Thy Name," McKinney

      "Arise, O Youth of God," Merrill

      "Lead On, O King Eternal," Shurtleff

Offertory Prayer: Our Father, you have given unto us the privilege of being your children. You have forgiven our sin. You have given us the gift of eternal life and the privilege of service to you and to others. Help us this day to give to you, with glad hearts, that with which you have seen fit to bless us. Accept it as an indica-tion of our love for you and as a token of our concern for the salvation of a lost world. In Jesus' name. Amen.

Introduction

Joseph, the son of Jacob, who later became the prime minister of Egypt, got into real difficulty as a young man because of his dreams. His childhood was not a particularly happy one. He was raised in a home where there was jealousy, envy, partiality, and even hate. His brothers held hatred in their hearts for him that led to murderous actions. Joseph was not entirely to blame for this. He was his father's favorite, and Joseph's older brothers felt that they were second-class members of their own household. This was one of the evil results of living in a society that practiced polygamy. They harbored no tender feelings toward Joseph, the elder son of Jacob's favorite wife.

Their smoldering hatred burst forth into action after Joseph, seemingly without elation and with innocent intention, reported on two different dreams that he had had. He told how "we were binding sheaves in the field, and, lo, my sheaf arose, and also stood upright; and, behold, your sheaves stood round about, and made obeisance to my sheaf" (Gen. 37:7). Hastily the brothers saw in this dream an omen that led them to believe that Jacob was going to exalt Joseph to the position of headship over the family at his death and that the dream was intended to secure their acceptance of this arrangement. Perhaps they had recognized something unique in Joseph's native endowment or character that led them to believe that he was superior. Or perhaps they recognized a divine significance in this dream that caused them to believe that he was appointed to leadership. They reacted with hatred and determination that such would not come to fulfillment.

Joseph had another dream that was interpreted by Jacob to have the same meaning as the first but with a wider range of significance. This dream concerned the heavenly bodies. The sun, moon, and eleven stars bowed to Joseph (Gen. 37:9), indicating that his father and mother and brothers looked to him in a position of prominence and sovereignty. Jacob, because he understood human nature, and perhaps because he detected the deep resentment of the other brothers, rebuked Joseph, but it is noticeable that he "observed the saying." Evidently he was deeply impressed with the remarkable similar implications of the twice-repeated dream, and it is even possible that he had cherished hopes for a fulfillment (cf. Gen. 42:6).

I. The study of dreams.

Dreams have been the subject of intense study from the beginning of time. They have been variously thought of as explaining the past, foretelling the future, serving as omens of good or bad fortune, and predicting the coming of great events.

Extensive studies have been made concerning the nature and significance of dreams. These studies reveal that every person dreams every night and that as one grows older, the amount of dreaming declines. They also reveal that dreams have meaning and give insight into the person doing the dreaming. A dream is a type of thinking that goes on while one is asleep. According to Freud, who was by no means infallible, dreaming is a primitive form of thinking that expresses the unconscious instinctual wishes and strivings of the individual doing the dreaming. Some psychologists believe that all dreams can be analyzed and shown to be wish fulfillments. The wish is a designation for a repressed unconscious, instinctual drive representation that is striving for discharge into consciousness. Dr. Vincent T. Lathbury has said that "the stimulus for a dream is often taken from some happening of the previous day. Then, by means of symbolism, pictorial representation, displacement, and condensation, this event is used as a backdrop or screen into which are woven the hopes, fears, and deepest strivings of the individual as conditioned by his past experiences in life" (*Encyclopedia Americana*, 9:32).

There are a great variety of opinions and theories concerning the nature and significance of dreams. Many believe that the unconscious mind is responsible for much that happens in life. Some scientists have reported that baffling problems have solved themselves during sleep. Some writers and philosophers say that many of their best passages and ideas come to them in dreams. Some dreams are foolish and even disgusting. Some are nightmares that frighten and disturb sleep. Some are indications of emotional sickness. Others are indications of potential achievement and greatness.

Joseph's dreams during his youth reveal something about his destiny in life. His dreams were prophetic. His brothers and his father interpreted them to be indications of the fact that he was the subject of a high destiny. The inspired writer of Genesis interprets these dreams as divine announcements of his future position of exaltation. His dreams were not considered as mere amusing stories but as indications of what he would do and be in the future.

Even in this modern day in which people seek to give a logical or psychological explanation of everything, we should not outlaw the thought that God can speak to us in or through a dream. The messianic age was described by the prophet as being a time when "your old men shall dream dreams, and your young men shall see visions" (Joel 2:28). He was not referring to a time when men would be visionary and unrealistic, but rather to the fact that by the help of the Holy Spirit the children of God would be able to see the divine program for their lives and the lives of others. The potential good that could come through responding to God with faith and faithfulness is so great that it seems too good to be true.

What are the dreams of your heart? Are they low and degrading? Are they shocking and embarrassing? Would you want them to come true? Would you be a better person if your dreams came true?

If you dream no high dreams, you will not achieve a high destiny in life. If you construct no air castles in your dreams, it is likely that you will build no cathedrals in your life. Someone has said, "If you will tell me what your dreams are, I can tell you what you will achieve in life."

II. The source of Joseph's dreams.

The thoughts behind these dreams were probably factors that Joseph's father had placed in his mind. He was the elder son of the wife whom Jacob loved. He would thus possess the right of the firstborn and hold the chief place in the household at the time of Jacob's death. As a badge of distinction, he had been given a "coat of many colors." He had been taught of the divine purpose for the family.

With these teachings from his father, it would not be unnatural for him to dream this type of dream.

The significant thing about these dreams for us is that Joseph later realized that they were visions of faith and were actually promises of God. These dreams, at least as far as we understand them from a human standpoint, were made possible by the teachings of a father. This thought should challenge every parent, pastor, teacher, or anyone else who is in a position to influence the thinking of those who need the stimulus of an inspiring and even prophetic dream. We should cherish our dreams—not those wild fantastic nightmares of the night, but the high ideals inspired by our Christian faith and the glorious promises of the Christian gospel.

III. The sufferings connected with Joseph's dreams.

Joseph was naïve and, seemingly with complete innocence, related the content of his dreams to his brothers and to his father. Possibly this was done within the family circle during a meal or some other time of relaxation. The brothers reacted immediately with resentment. This hatred was permitted to fester and finally resulted in murderous thoughts. Because of their hatred, they gave voice to the text and the chilling suggestion: "Come now therefore, and let us slay him, and cast him into some pit, and we will say, Some evil beast hath devoured him: and we shall see what will become of his dreams" (Gen. 37:20). Instead of actually slaying Joseph, they sold him to slave traders who carried him to Egypt and there sold him to Potiphar, an officer in the court of Pharaoh.

The point should be made that to dream dreams is not enough. This was not the case with Joseph. As he made progress toward his destiny, he not only suffered the resentment of his brothers but also the loss of companionship of his father while he was a prisoner in Egypt. While experiencing great success as a servant of Potiphar, he was severely tempted and slandered because he refused to yield to the wanton wishes of Potiphar's wife. He maintained his integrity, and again he suffered by losing his position and being imprisoned. It seemed that he could not win for losing. In all of this, it is possible to discern a sterling character, a genuine faith, and a steady progress in the school of suffering toward his destiny.

Joseph was no doubt strengthened and encouraged by the memory of his dreams. Evidently he maintained his communion with God in spite of discouragement and seeming defeat. He refused to do that which he considered to be a sin against his God and the man for whom he worked. He continued to press on in the university of hard knocks, and finally we see him graduating with honors as his God prepared him for his destiny of protecting and providing for his family who was to become a nation while living in Egypt.

IV. The substance of Joseph's dreams.

Many modern psychologists would say that our dreams are "wish fulfillments." It was because Joseph's dreams embodied his deepest ambitions that they were of real significance. Dreams are meaningful only when they represent the concentrated essence of our deepest waking thoughts and thus provide an index to our character. Evil thoughts that are permitted to dwell in the mind during our days come into expression in our dreams when there are no restraints or external conditions that would hinder. It is good to be able to awake and thank God that the dream was only a fantasy and not an actual deed. Joseph's dreams reveal his aspirations and purpose for being. The consciousness of a high and noble purpose provided a basis for hope and served as a constant challenge to him as he traveled toward his divinely ordained destiny.

What do you dream about? Are your dreams prophetic of your destiny? Do they reveal a character that is pure and unstained by dissipation or the desire to dissipate? Does the content of your dreams indicate a personal awareness of the purpose of God for your life? Does God's plan for your life ever appear in your dreams? Do your dreams serve to challenge you to put forth a more devoted effort to achieve God's high call for your life?

Conclusion

If you are not a follower of Jesus Christ, let me suggest that you dream of what it would be like to know him as your personal Savior. Do some serious thinking about what you are missing by shutting him out of your heart and your home. Perhaps your dream will come true. It can if you will but receive him even today.

If you have already trusted Christ as Lord and Master, why not dream of following him fully and cheerfully? Only God knows what can be achieved in and by your life if you would devote yourself to him to the extent that you dream about him.

Dream some about the home that he would have you to build. Construct some spiritual air castles, and then give yourself to making your dream come true.

"Behold, this dreamer cometh." Have you dreamed any dreams lately?

Life Sculpture

Chisel in hand stood a sculptor boy
  And his marble block before him,
And his eyes lit up with a smile of joy,
  As an angel-dream passed o'er him.
Carved the dream on that shapeless stone,
  With many a sharp incision;
With heaven's own light the sculpture shone,
  He'd caught that angel-vision.
Children of life are weak, as we stand
  With our lives uncarved before us,
Waiting the hour when, at God's command,
  Our life-dream shall pass o'er us.
If we carve it then on the yielding stone,
  With many a sharp incision,
Its heavenly beauty shall be our own,
  Our lives, that angel-vision.

45

SUNDAY EVENING, JANUARY 27

Title: Facing the Trials of Life Victoriously

Text: "God did send me before you to preserve life" (**Gen. 45:5**).

Introduction

Even the most faithful of God's children face trouble, sickness, suffering, disappointment, tragedy, and even catastrophe. This presents a real problem to those who have labored under the impression that if you trust God and try to do right that everything is bound to turn out fine. Sometimes it does and sometimes it doesn't as far as we are able to observe.

A pastor was visiting in a hospital room where there were four patients. He visited briefly with each, and as he came to the last one, he noticed that she was weeping. As he was preparing to leave, she said, "I don't see why I have to suffer like this. I have been so good." In this statement she revealed her concept of God and the motive for his righteousness. When suffering came she found herself in real trouble. Either something was wrong with her God or with her life. She had been laboring under the mistaken idea that if she sincerely tried to serve God, then she would escape suffering and trouble. Do you think in these terms? If so, you are in for some disturbing experiences, because in the pathway of each of us there will be storms and trials of one sort or another.

Joseph faced the trials of life victoriously. Did anyone ever experience tragedies more painful than those that threatened to overwhelm Joseph? He was the darling of his father's eye. He cherished fond dreams of the position of privilege and responsibility in his family. He enjoyed every opportunity life in his time could provide. Seemingly he had a safe and prosperous place prepared for him by his father.

Instead of giving him family love, Joseph's brothers envied him and hated him with murderous thoughts. Instead of killing him, they decided to do something that was less bloody and at the same time more profitable. They sold him into slavery to the Midianites who were passing by on their way to Egypt.

In Egypt the young man found himself well favored and successfully established in the home of Potiphar, an officer of Pharaoh. Everything was fine until the immoral wife of Potiphar began to tempt him. When he refused to become a party to her lust, she falsely accused him. This could have resulted in his death, but instead he was cast into prison. Had he been looking for an alibi for distrusting God, this would have been a good one.

Still later Joseph was forgotten by one who could have been his benefactor. He had every human right to be bitter, cynical, and utterly dejected. Somehow he remained in command of his spirit and faced this succession of severe trials victoriously. He survived and fulfilled the plan of God for his life. His exaltation to the position of prime minister in Egypt and to a place where later he was the means of saving his family from starvation is one of the true success stories of the Bible.

The absence of pessimism and hatred in Joseph's heart is remarkable. His conduct upon the arrival of his brothers is out of the ordinary. How was he able to forgive and to restore a warm relationship with those who had hated him so deeply and had mistreated him so cruelly? How was he able to meet all of these trials so victoriously? If we could learn his secret, perhaps life could be more beautiful and our Christian testimony could be more effective.

I. Facing life with true faith.

In "Faith's Hall of Fame," Hebrews 11, the inspired writer pays tribute to Joseph's faith. Joseph knew something about the purpose of his God. He also believed the divine promises. He believed that one day the children of Israel would return to the land God had promised them. He longed for the privilege of returning with them and being a continuing part of God's work on the earth. This faith took what might appear to be a strange expression. As Joseph faced death, he made a request of his people: " 'God will surely come to your aid, and then you must carry my bones up from this place.' So Joseph died at the age of a hundred and ten. And after they embalmed him, he was placed in a coffin in Egypt" (Gen. 50:25–26 NIV). In Exodus 13:19 we read of how Moses took the bones of Joseph with him as the children of Israel departed. Thus, throughout the entire period of the sojourn in Egypt, Joseph's mummy case served as a sermon to stimulate the faith of the Israelites.

Because of his faith in God, Joseph was able to achieve victory over the temptation to despondency and despair when he was sold as a slave by his own brothers. He who was in the process of being trained for a position of responsibility and honor found himself treated as a piece of property. He was demoted to the lowest rung of the social ladder, a position of shame and degradation. He could have yielded to an attitude of self-pity and despondency, but instead we observe him conducting himself so capably and faithfully that eventually he was exalted to the position of steward and placed in control of the complete estate of his master. He later lost this position because of foul slander. Still his faith did not dissolve nor did his courage disappear.

The second great trial that Joseph faced was that of temptation. The wanton wife of Potiphar was attracted to the youthful steward of her husband's business affairs and developed a consuming passion for him. Repeatedly she attempted to seduce him into committing adultery. To yield would have been the path of least resistance. Perhaps it could lead to advancement. The temptation was very real, and it did not cease. Not to yield was going to be dangerous. In spite of all of the pressure, Joseph maintained his personal purity and integrity. He was able to do so because he put forth an effort to remember his debt of gratitude toward his master who had trusted him so completely. He was also strengthened because his faith in God caused him to realize that impurity was an act of rebellion against his God. "How then can I do this great wickedness, and sin against God?" (Gen. 39:9).

Later Joseph faced an entirely different type of trial that was associated with prosperity. He became great. He occupied a position of prominence second only to Pharaoh. Great wealth was at his disposal. He was second in command throughout the country. It takes a steadier hand to carry a full bucket than one half full. In all of the record it is wonderful to see how practically and wisely Joseph conducted himself. Instead of letting his position "swell his head," he reacted with humility and diligence.

Joseph immediately established a program of thrift that would insure an adequate amount of food for the country. He went about his task in a diligent manner. He stayed with the job for seven long years and thus proved himself to be patient and persistent.

This man faced another great trial when he observed the coming of his brothers for food. The last time that he had seen them, their eyes had been filled with envy that expressed itself in murder for all practical purposes. The normal human reaction would have been to retaliate. What would you have done? It is most significant that Joseph reacted with forgiveness toward them and a recognition of the providential work of God in which even the crimes of his brothers had been a means used for the advancement of God's redemptive purpose. Only with the eye of faith could Joseph see through the maze and mystery of the deceptions, disappointments, hardships, and sufferings that had befallen him.

It can be safely assumed that this dawning of insight did not come to the mind of Joseph until the very moment when he revealed himself to his brothers. It was so wonderful and so unbelievable that Joseph repeated his interpretation of what had happened three times in just a few moments (Gen. 45:5, 7–8). He closes by saying, "So now it was not you that sent me hither, but God: and he hath made me a father to Pharaoh, and lord of all his house, and a ruler throughout all the land of Egypt" (v. 8). He does not excuse their envy, hatred, and murder but declares that God overruled and accomplished his good will in it all. Joseph sees his life as a plan of God from the divine perspective. His faith and faithfulness make this insight possible.

II. Faulty ways of facing the trials of life.

There are a number of natural reactions to trials, and all prove to be disappointing. Each of us to some degree has used these faulty ways of facing trouble. It is possible to react to trouble with resentment. When everything seems to go wrong, it is easy to develop a bitter attitude. A student can resent a teacher when he fails to make a high grade. A husband can resent his wife if married life is not perfect. A wife can resent her husband when there is not enough money to make necessary purchases. An employee can resent his employer when his job is not pleasant and profitable. Resentment can even be directed toward God, the church, or religious leaders.

Resentment is about the most expensive method that can be used for facing the trials of life. Hatred in the heart poisons the whole being. Resentment creates disturbances in all human relationships and deprives us of fellowship that could be enriching.

No comfort can come into the heart of the person who reacts to grief with resentment toward God for the death of a loved one. No peace can come to the mind of the person who in sickness or failure reacts toward God or family with resentment.

Another faulty method of responding to trials is resignation or fatalism. This viewpoint eliminates God and believes that a blind fate is responsible. Oftentimes those who react this way ascribe everything to the will of God and make no distinctions between his ideal will and his permissive will. They hold God responsible for everything. They simply say, "God willed it, and I must accept it." Many of the failures in our lives are our own fault, and many of our sufferings are due to the faults and mistakes of others. It is wrong to blame God for every unfortunate incident that happens and then to react with resentment and refusal to love and trust him.

Paul's word in Romans 8:28 is appropriate here. The New International Version presents a triumphant truth to those who are tempted to respond to troubles with blind resignation. "We know that in all things God works for the good of those who love him, who have been called according to his purpose." Even when trouble comes because of our own errors or because of mistreatment we experience at the hands of others, God will be at work in the circumstances to bring about something for our good. God is always on the job to teach us some new truth, to give us a new insight, or to provide us with the necessary strength and leadership for living a victorious life. God is no absentee God. His purposes toward us are always motivated by his love for us. We need faith to believe that our God is good and that he always wants that which is best for his children.

III. Growing a great faith.

Joseph faced trials in a manner that brought victory into his personal life and achievement that was of great benefit to others. He was able to rise above the trials and tragedies of life because of the genuineness of his faith in the presence and purpose of God in his life. It is basic to our Christian faith that we also can face the uncertainties of life with sufficiency if we do so with a genuine faith in God. "This is the victory that overcometh the world, even our faith" (1 John 5:4).

How do we come to possess a faith like that of Joseph and others who have faced the trials of life victoriously? Is there anything we can do to develop such a faith? We should recognize that such a faith is not only possible but also the will of God for each of us.

The writer of Hebrews points out the necessity for and also gives an excellent definition of the type of faith that we all need. "Without faith it is impossible to please him: for he that cometh to God must believe that he is, and that he is a rewarder of them that diligently seek him" (11:6). Faith is thus defined as the attitude and act of putting full confidence not only in the existence of God but also in the fact that he is a good God whose purposes toward us are always purposes of grace and mercy.

"Faith cometh by hearing and hearing by the word of God" (Rom. 10:17). There is no way by which we can have a faith adequate to give us victory over the trials and troubles of life if we are a stranger to the Bible. We should read the Bible not merely as a record of what happened in the past, but also as a record of what can happen in our lives if we will but trust and obey our Lord. God is the same

49

today as yesterday, and he will relate to us as he did to his children in the past if we will but walk with him in faith and faithfulness.

Triumphant faith comes as a gift from God and at the same time is something that we grow. It is appropriate for us to pray, "Lord, increase our faith," but at the same time we must trust his promises and give him a chance to prove that he is trustworthy. Faith develops by experiencing the faithfulness of the one in whom you put confidence. If one never puts faith in God in the laboratory of experience, it is unlikely that he or she will develop a great faith.

Faith that will provide us with access to the resources of God in times of great need will come as we look back and count our blessings and see what God has done in and for us in the past. Joseph's recognition of God's gracious purpose came when he looked back and saw how God had been at work.

If we will look back and see how good God has been in the past, our faith will be strengthened as we face the future. The poet said it this way:

> *I know who holds the future,*
> *And I know who holds my hand.*
> *With God things don't just happen,*
> *Everything by Him is planned:*
> *So as I face tomorrow*
> *With its problems large and small,*
> *I'll trust the God of miracles—*
> *Give to Him my all.*
>
> *—A. B. Smith*

Conclusion

Faith grows by degrees. First, you should put your faith in the good news of the gospel and receive Jesus Christ as your Savior and Lord. Trust him day by day for guidance and strength. Obey him completely as you understand his will for your life. Follow him closely and do not let anything cause you to drift away from the fellowship of your church or cause you to be so busy that you neglect to worship. Trust him to be with you and attempt to communicate with someone else about the goodness of God each day and you will discover that when the storms of life beat down upon you that your feet are on the solid Rock.

WEDNESDAY EVENING, JANUARY 30

Title: Seeing God Face-to-Face

Text: "And Jacob called the name of the place Peniel: for I have seen God face to face, and my life is preserved" (**Gen. 32:30**).

Introduction

There is nothing we need more than a vision of God. To come face-to-face with the living God can be a life-transforming experience. Such was the case for Jacob who was changed from Jacob the deceiver to Israel the prince of God.

I. Jacob was chosen by God.

    A. *The call to service revealed to Abraham (Gen. 12:1–3).*

    B. *God's purpose revealed to Jacob (Gen. 28:12–17).*

    C. *We are chosen (1 Peter 2:9–10).*

II. Jacob was complacent and neglectful.

    A. *We have no record concerning Jacob's prayer, praise, or piety while he was in Padan-aram.*

    B. *The record reveals his marriage, the increase of his family, and his great prosperity.* He was consumed with commercial activities.

    C. *How have you responded to God's plan for your life?*

III. Jacob was confronted by God.

    A. *The God of Bethel came to him (Gen. 31:13).*

    B. *The presence of God was with him (Gen. 32:1–2).*

    C. *A crisis developed (Gen. 32:3–8).*

        1. Jacob faced the wrath of an angry brother (32:6).

        2. Jacob recognized his utter helplessness (32:7).

    D. *Jacob prayed.*

        1. He appealed to God as a covenant God and Father (Gen. 32:9).

        2. He pleaded God's gracious promises (32:9).

        3. He confessed his own unworthiness and God's goodness and faithfulness (32:12).

    E. *Jacob's striving is related.*

        1. God took the first step. Jacob was made to see himself as he was and enabled to see himself as he could be.

        2. Jacob did not avoid this painful experience.

IV. Jacob was changed.

    A. *Jacob had a heart experience with God.*

    B. *God became real to Jacob.*

    C. *Jacob became Israel, the prince of God.*

Conclusion

The result of Jacob's face-to-face experience with God was a changed character. Such a change is possible for the man or woman who will spend time alone with God.

FEBRUARY

■ **Sunday Mornings**

This month's Sunday morning messages are based on the theme "Being a Genuine Christian in Today's World." Those who consider themselves to be Christians must behave the gospel if the world is to believe the gospel.

■ **Sunday Evenings**

Begin a series on the theme "The Promises of God" on Sunday evenings this month. If we are to walk by faith, we must trust in the promises of God.

■ **Wednesday Evenings**

Begin a series on the theme "The Child of God in Prayer." This theme is suggested for use beginning now and continuing through July. This lengthy series is suggested because of a deep conviction that all kingdom progress is made while on our knees in prayer. A preview of the titles and texts will indicate the great variety of needs that can be met by such a series.

SUNDAY MORNING, FEBRUARY 3

Title: What Does It Mean to Be a Christian?

Text: "And the disciples were called Christians first in Antioch" (**Acts 11:26**).

Hymns: "More Like the Master," Gabriel

"Take the Name of Jesus with You," Baxter

"Living for Jesus," Chisholm

Offertory Prayer: Our Father, we would sit at the feet of Jesus and hear him say that it is more blessed to give than to receive. Help us to believe this truth to the extent that we would determine to become a giver in every area of our lives. Today we give you our tithes and offerings. Bless us with a spirit of generosity as we do so. Grant to us the excitement of seeing good things happen through the wise and consecrated use of these funds for the advancement of your kingdom. In the name of our Savior. Amen.

Introduction

Christian is a fallen term cheapened by common usage. It now covers a multitude of religious ideas, error as well as truth, paganism as well as the revelation of God's divine truth. This term *Christian* has been stretched to the extent that it covers rationalistic modernism on one hand and a frothy sentimentalism on the other. It is ascribed to that which in some instances is gross worldliness and in other instances to that which is anything short of pharisaic self-righteousness. The term is used to describe that which is coldly ritualistic but also that which is nothing more than heated emotionalism. Is it possible that Christianity is failing to make a distinctive impact due to our failure to understand what it means to be a Christian?

Some apply the term *Christian* to all who have high moral standards and at the same time believe in the existence of God. Others claim this title simply because they are members of a church. Still others claim the privilege of wearing this title because they have had a conversion experience. Ideally, they have a right to do so. However, the great test comes in what others think of our witness. When they see our lives, are they able to call us Christian? Do they see the evidences of the presence of Christ in our lives? If so, only then should we claim this title for ourselves.

The disciples were first called Christians at Antioch. This was probably a term of derision because they were followers of the crucified Galilean. Evidently they thought and talked and acted in a manner that reminded their contemporaries of the Christ. What would your neighbors say about you? Is it possible for them to see features and characteristics in your life that resemble Jesus Christ? A government official in India once said to some Christian leaders, "If Christians would act like Jesus Christ, India would be at his feet." It is time for us to cease being satisfied with a low level of Christian living. We must demonstrate that genuine Christianity is something more than cushioned pews, enjoyable music, a comforting sermon on Sunday, and business as usual during the week.

I. To become a Christian one must first be saved.

It is absolutely impossible for one to be a Christian who does not have a personal redemptive relationship with the person of Jesus Christ.

Jesus said to Nicodemus, "Ye must be born again" (John 3:7). Individuals must repent—change their minds about the nature of God and the nature of sin and about self and others. Inseparable from genuine repentance, sincere faith must be placed in Jesus Christ as the Lord of life (Acts 20:20–21). As people respond to the gospel with repentance and faith, the Spirit of God brings about the miracle of the new birth within the soul. Believers become children of God (Gal. 3:26). They are now new creations (2 Cor. 5:17).

The new birth alone does not produce Christlikeness. The new birth makes possible a growth and development into Christlikeness. It is absolutely impossible for one to be genuinely Christian who has not first had an experience of commitment and conversion.

II. To be genuinely Christian one must be surrendered.

Jesus was surrendered completely to the will of God. "Jesus saith unto them, My meat is to do the will of him that sent me, and to finish his work" (John 4:34).

His surrender led to Gethsemane and Calvary. "Father, if thou be willing, remove this cup from me: nevertheless not my will, but thine, be done" (Luke 22:42).

Jesus spoke to the Galilean fishermen and said, "Follow me, and I will make you fishers of men. And they straightway left their nets, and followed him" (Matt. 4:19–20). As they forsook their nets, they began the journey that would lead them to the place where others would be able to bestow upon them the title Christian.

To be considered Christian, the convert must be identified with Christ through baptism. This is a visible symbol of an institutional relationship to Christ in which the individual accepts the demands and discipline of his lordship. To be genuinely Christian, the convert must be sincerely committed to the task of living the teachings of Jesus Christ. He or she must have a deep concern about keeping God's holy law. The Sermon on the Mount will be something more than just a beautiful passage of Scripture.

Commitment to the will of God will express itself in the home, throughout the community, within the business, and in every other area of life.

III. To be genuinely Christian the convert must be serving.

Jesus said, "My father worketh hitherto, and I work" (John 5:17). "I must work the works of him that sent me, while it is day: the night cometh, when no man can work" (9:4). Someone has said that the best biography of Jesus is that which describes him as one "who went about doing good" (Acts 10:38). There are many inactive church members, but an inactive Christian is a contradiction of terms, for when we cease to serve, we cease to be truly Christian.

The genuine Christian deliberately gives himself to the task of doing good and does so with humility and gratitude and without display. "As we have therefore opportunity, let us do good unto all men, especially unto them who are of the household of faith" (Gal. 6:10).

Conclusion

Who is sufficient for this ideal? It is impossible for the convert to be fully surrendered and graciously serving without the leadership and assistance of the Holy Spirit of God. A part of the wonder and the miracle of the new birth is the coming of the Holy Spirit to dwell within the heart of the believer (Gal. 4:4–6). The Holy Spirit dwells in the heart to produce the fruit of a Christlike spirit and a Christlike life (5:22–24). An old spiritual expresses the sincere desire of every believer:

> *Lord, I want to be a Christian*
> *in my heart, in my heart,*
> *Lord, I want to be a Christian*
> *in my heart.*

We must become Christlike within our hearts and minds before we can be called Christians.

A Definition of a Christian

A Christian is born of God, engrafted into Christ, and an habitation for the Holy Spirit. His nature is renewed, his mind illumined, his spirit changed.

He is not what he was, for grace hath made a difference; he is not what he desires to be, for grace is not yet perfected; he is not what he shall be, for grace shall be consummated in glory.

The knowledge of Christ is his treasure; the mind of Christ his evidence; the love of Christ his song; conformity to Christ his life; to be with Christ his preeminent desire.

By faith he rests on Christ, receives Christ, and looks to Christ. He heareth Christ's words, treadeth in Christ's steps, and seeketh Christ's approbation.

He speaks the language of the Savior's kingdom, reveres the Savior's statutes and laws, obeys His ordinances, wears His costume, and lives to His glory.

The life of Christ within him is the principle of his being, and because Christ ever lives, he shall live also. In the Christian, Christ lives, and speaks, and acts.

He is Christ's representative on earth, His witness before men, and His follower before God. The Christian hearkens to Christ's teachings, rests on Christ's sacrifice, avails himself of Christ's meditation, and cheerfully obeys Christ's royal laws. He inquires what would Christ have me know, what do, and what enjoy.

To know Christ, is Christianity intellectual; to obey Christ, Christianity practical; to enjoy Christ, Christianity perfected. As bread to the hungry, as water to the thirsty, as the rock in the sultry day, is Christ to the Christian.

The Christian is in the world, but not of it; among the world, but yet separate from it; passing through the world, without attachment to it.

The idolater boasts in his idols, the Mohammedan in the false prophet, and the Romanist in the virgin, but the Christian glories only in the cross of the Lord Jesus Christ.

The Christian is a man and may err, an imperfect man, and may sin; but a renewed man, and shall have his fruits unto holiness and the end everlasting life.

The Christian is a warrior, and must fight; but he is conqueror, and must prevail.

The Christian sojourns on earth, but dwells in heaven; a pilgrim in the desert, but an enrolled denizen of the skies.

The Christian is the impress of Christ, the reflection of the Father, and the temple of the Holy Ghost.

Contrast him with the infidel, in his faith; with the profligate, in his life; with the merely moral, in his heart; and with the Pharisee, in his spirit. His pedigree, from Jehovah; his nature, from heaven; and his name, from Antioch. Oh, Christian; great is thy dignity, refulgent thy glory, interminable thy blessed hope. All things are thine, thou art Christ's and Christ is God's.

—Author unknown

SUNDAY EVENING, FEBRUARY 3

Title: Standing on the Promises of God

Text: "He staggered not at the promise of God through unbelief; but was strong in faith, giving glory to God; and being fully persuaded that, what he had promised, he was able also to perform" **(Rom. 4:20–21)**.

Introduction

The Bible is a book filled with the promises of God to his people. Someone has calculated that there are at least thirty thousand promises in the Word of God. While this figure may appear to be extravagant, we must recognize that hundreds of promises have been made to us that we have failed to recognize and claim.

The book of Romans tells us that the secret of Abraham's spiritual achievement is to be found in his recognizing and clinging to the promises of God. He did not stagger back because of the mystery or miracle of the divine plan for his life. He was fully convinced that God was both able and willing to accomplish all that he had promised. May God grant us the insight to discover his promises and the faith to claim them.

Charles Haddon Spurgeon, the famous preacher of the last century, wrote a book still available today titled *Faith's Checkbook*. This book is a series of daily devotionals for use throughout the year. Each devotional is based on one of the great and precious promises of God. Concerning God's promises Spurgeon has said, "A promise from God may very instructively be compared to a check payable to order. It is given to the believer with the view of bestowing on him some good thing. It is not meant that he should read it over comfortably, and then have done with it. No, he is to treat the promise as a reality, as a man treats a check." How many of the promises of God have you discovered and claimed?

I. Promises for the present.

Many of the promises God made long ago are for those who live in the present if we will but recognize them and claim them by faith. There are very few promises made by God to his people in the past that have no relevant application for the present. God does not change with the passing of time. What he was yesterday he is today. What he did for his people yesterday he will do for us today. When we study the Word of God, we should place ourselves in the middle of the action and identify with biblical characters when such is appropriate. When God promised to forgive and to cleanse from sin in the past, we can be safe in assuming that we can claim his promise of such in the present upon condition that we sincerely repent. As God promised to guide in the past, so he promises to guide in the present if we are sensitive to listen and willing to respond.

II. Promises for the future.

The only thing certain about the future, as far as humans are concerned, is the fact of change. Nothing will be exactly the same tomorrow. In a world that moves so fast and in a time when humans have unlimited destructive power, it is easy to understand why many should be fearful as they face the future. On all sides there is a constant increase in anxiety and insecurity.

Children of God can be assured that in a changing world they worship an unchanging God. The promises that he has made will surely be kept. God is trustworthy and dependable. We need to discover the many precious promises concerning God's abiding presence and his providential care if we are to face each tomorrow with confidence and cheer.

III. Promises for his children.

By making promises to his children, God has revealed his desire to impart to them a blessing and to enrich their lives. The divine promises were not given to deceive or to encourage false expectations. The heart of the loving heavenly Father moves toward his children constantly with purposes of grace. His every intention toward us is good.

A study of the Bible and of Christian history will reveal that those who have endured the trials and difficulties of life and who have persisted and have gone forward to real achievement are those who studied the Word of God and discovered God's promises. These promises were claimed, and men and women moved forward depending on God to do as he had promised.

The margin of the Bible used by D. L. Moody contained the letters *T* and *P* on almost every page. When Mr. Moody was questioned about the appearance and the significance of these letters, he replied that the passage contained a promise from God to his children. The *T* indicated that he had tried the promise, and the *P* indicated that the promise had proven to be true in his own experience. How many times would these letters appear in the margin of your Bible? Without any fear of contradiction, it could be asserted that the number of *P*s would be determined by the number of times you trusted in God's promises. The writer of Hebrews affirms, "He is faithful that promised" (Heb. 10:23).

IV. Promises to the unsaved.

The Bible contains many promises from the redeeming Father to the unsaved. Forgiveness is promised on condition of repentance. Eternal life is promised to those who by faith make Jesus Christ the Lord of their lives. Acceptance by the Father is promised to all who will come to the Savior. Deliverance from the power of sin is promised to those who will break with the love of sin and come to him who conquered even death and the grave.

Conclusion

The conclusion of the whole matter is that we must accept the promises of God as being made personally to us, and we must claim them by faith. We must put our confidence in the truthfulness of God.

We must put the endorsement of our faith on the divine promise and present it at the throne of grace even as we would present a check to the cashier of a bank.

The promises of God are conditional. They are conditioned only by our faith and faithfulness. God is true. He is no liar. You can count on him. Put your faith in his promises and let the experience of the poet be your experience.

Standing on the promises of Christ my King,
Thro' eternal ages let His praises ring;
Glory in the highest, I will shout and sing,
Standing on the promises of God.
Standing on the promises that cannot fail,
When the howling storms of doubt and fear assail,
By the living word of God I shall prevail,
Standing on the promises of God.
Standing on the promises of Christ the Lord,
Bound to Him eternally by love's strong cord,
Overcoming daily with the Spirit's sword,
Standing on the promises of God.
Standing on the promises I cannot fall,
List'ning every moment to the Spirit's call,
Resting in my Saviour, as my all in all,
Standing on the promises of God.
                                    —*R. Kelso Carter*

WEDNESDAY EVENING, FEBRUARY 6

Title: The Model Prayer

Text: "After this manner therefore pray ye ..." **(Matt. 6:9)**.

Introduction

The prayer life of Jesus is most revealing. He lived in an atmosphere of daily prayer. His prayer life was never at the mercy of moods. Jesus did not permit prayer to be crowded out of his schedule. Persistence was a part of his prayer life.

"And it came to pass in those days, that he went out into a mountain to pray, and continued all night in prayer to God" (Luke 6:12).

Jesus was found praying during or before all of the great events of his career—at the time of his baptism, before the selection of the apostles, during his transfiguration, in Gethsemane, and even while on the cross. The prayers of Jesus contain the elements of communion, thanksgiving, petition, and intercession.

The disciples noticed the difference between Jesus' prayers and their own. His were short and small and real, while theirs were weak and stammering and unsatisfying. They felt an overwhelming need to know how to pray as the Savior prayed. They offered a prayer to him: "Lord, teach us to pray, as John also taught his disciples" (Luke 11:1). It is interesting to note that Jesus responded by teaching them how to pray.

We learn much about prayer by studying the prayers God answered. We can also profit by considering those requests that God refused to grant. The best place to learn about prayer is in the prayer that has been called the Lord's Prayer. It would be much more appropriate to give this prayer another title. Perhaps it should be called the "model prayer," for it presents a perfect pattern, a blueprint, a recipe, a model for our praying. It also could be appropriately called "The Disciples' Prayer," "The Children's Prayer," "A Kingdom Prayer," or "A Family Prayer."

Examine your prayer life. Have you followed the instructions of the Master Teacher at the point of praying with a proper motive and in a proper manner? Heaven's Teacher said, "After this manner, therefore, pray ye." The prayer that follows was never meant to be memorized and repeated, but to serve as a model.

A close study of this model prayer will reveal that it easily divides itself into three "looks." First there is the up-look to God. Then there is the in-look to personal needs. The third look is the out-look and permeates the prayer, because the plural possessive pronoun is used throughout rather than the first person singular.

The three vital elements of this prayer are communion, petition, and intercession.

I. First, communion must be established with God.

There must be a surrender of the heart to the will of God, and God must become the center of attention. His will and his work are of primary importance.

II. Petition is appropriate only after communion has been established and surrender to the will of God is real.

Usually we major on what we want. Our needs will be met adequately as we pray.

III. Intercession for others will then become one of the primary concerns of the person who is praying.

Our God, to whom we pray, is the Father of us all. Selfishness is unacceptable in prayer.

Conclusion

Prayer is everyone's gift and privilege. To pray is everyone's responsibility. The power of prayer is the power that is least exercised by the average believer. If we will but follow the teachings of our Savior, our prayers will help us see Christ more clearly, and we will rise up to be eager coworkers with God in the highest sense.

SUNDAY MORNING, FEBRUARY 10

Title: The Christian Approach to Economic Issues

Text: "He said unto them, Render therefore unto Caesar the things which be Caesar's and unto God the things which be God's" **(Luke 20:25)**.

Hymns: "This Is My Father's World," Babcock

         "He Leadeth Me," Gilmore

         "Serve the Lord with Gladness," McKinney

Offertory Prayer: Our Father, you have blessed us far beyond anything that we could ever merit. The gift of forgiveness and the blessing of eternal life have come freely to us from your loving heart. Not only do we thank you for blessings in the realm of the soul, but we also thank you for material blessings. We offer thanks for home comforts and for the satisfaction of bodily needs. Today, with tithes and offerings, we acknowledge your grace as the source of our blessings, and we make it possible for others to know of the gospel of your love through Jesus Christ our Lord. Amen.

Introduction

In today's world, there are two great economic systems engaged in a struggle that could win in our present civilization. Only time will reveal which, if either, survives. Christianity is not be identified with either capitalism or socialism. In the final analysis, both systems are built on a falsehood.

Socialism: People own property that is to be controlled by society instead of by the individual, as far as possible.

Capitalism: People own property that is to be controlled by the individual instead of by society, as far as possible.

Christianity speaks to both socialism and capitalism and says, "You are built upon a falsehood. God is the sole owner." This idea that God is the sole owner could save our civilization and bring about God's will on earth.

True Christians will seek to relate the teachings of Jesus Christ to their economic affairs as well as to their spiritual needs.

I. Economic principles according to the teachings of Christ.

    A. *Jesus believed in the right to hold property.*

        1. Thou shalt not steal.

        2. Thou shalt not covet.

B. *Jesus believed in the duty of honest toil (John 9:4).* We are obligated to partici-pate honestly and enthusiastically in needful work.

C. *Jesus believed in the law of mercy.*

　1. He illustrates this in the story of the rich man and Lazarus.

　2. The law of mercy is to be expressed in a generous ministry to the needs of human life.

II. Jesus recognized five ways in which money may be used legitimately.

A. *Money may be used to meet the basic needs of the family (Mark 7:10–13).*

B. *Money may be used to support religious institutions and the conduct of worship.* Jesus sanctioned the use of money to support the temple, as with the wid-ow's mite (Mark 12:41–44).

C. *Money may be used to minister to the poor.* There was little organized effort to relieve the poor during Jesus' time. He taught openhearted liberality toward the poor.

D. *Money may be used to enrich the emotional and intellectual life of men and women in acts of fellowship, friendship, and devotion.*

　1. Jesus attended a feast with publicans in the house of Matthew (Matt. 9:10–11). He often attended such occasions.

　2. Jesus commended Mary who lavishly anointed him with costly spike-nard ointment at a feast in Bethany (Mark 14:3–8).

E. *Money may be used to pay taxes to support the government (Matt. 17:24).* "Ren-der therefore unto Caesar that which is Caesar's and unto God the things which be God's" (Luke 20:25).

III. Jesus warned against the dangers in both the pursuit and possession of riches.

Jesus was not prejudiced against rich people, but he warned against the perils associated with the pursuit of riches.

A. *The danger of a false sense of security.*

B. *You cannot serve God and money (Luke 16:13).* God is to have no rival in the heart. To try to love both God and riches is to create a split personality.

C. *Riches tend to rupture fellowship.*

　1. This is not always true.

　2. Usually there is a gulf between the rich and the poor.

D. *People who give money first place in their hearts break both of the Great Command-ments.*

　1. They do not love God supremely.

　2. They do not love their neighbors as themselves (Matt. 7:14).

Conclusion

Christians must use money as servants of God rather than permitting them-selves to become the slaves of money. Christians must use their money to unite themselves with others in worthwhile interests rather than permitting their money to separate them from others. Christians must never let money keep them from higher things. Jesus left all to give himself in service to others. May God help us to hear him and to heed him as we face the economic issues of our day.

SUNDAY EVENING, FEBRUARY 10

Title: The Promise of Forgiveness

Text: "To him give all the prophets witness, that through his name whosoever believeth in him shall receive remission of sins" **(Acts 10:43)**.

Introduction

We all have problems. Some have health problems. Some face financial problems. Others are confronted with employment problems. More people than we realize have family problems. Each of us has specific personal problems. And we all have to deal with the problem of sin.

One theme that concerns all of us without exception runs throughout the Bible, and this is the forgiveness of sins. "All we like sheep have gone astray: we have turned every one to his own way" (Isa. 53:6). When the Word of God offers the forgiveness of sin, every one of us can say, "This means me."

One can choose from a great variety of attitudes and responses to sin. Some hold to the fancy that sin is an illusion, and they do not hesitate to deny the fact of sin. Others lull their consciences to sleep and ignore the presence of sin. Many attempt to hide their sin. All of us have sought to excuse, explain away, or cover our sins, only to discover that even if our sins are not found out by others, they find us out, for Scripture says, "Be sure your sin will find you out" (Num. 32:23).

The utter chaos in our world proclaims the undeniable fact of original sin. Humans have been and continue to be mistake makers. They sin against their God, they sin against themselves, and they sin against their fellow humans. They stand guilty before God, they stand guilty before the bars of their own consciences, and they stand guilty in the eyes of their fellow humans.

It is a part of the wonder of the gospel that forgiveness is offered to sinners. This is a truth that permeates the Old Testament. In the angelic announcement to Joseph concerning the babe that was to be born to Mary, it was said, "Thou shalt call his name Jesus: for he shall save his people from their sins" (Matt. 1:21). Following his resurrection, Jesus commissioned his disciples to evangelize the world. He said that "repentance and remission of sins should be preached in his name among all nations, beginning at Jerusalem" (Luke 24:27).

I. God's forgiveness is needed.

While a person may sin against himself or his sin may involve others, in the final analysis, all sin is against God. God can forgive in a manner that produces freedom and joy and a sense of healthy wholeness for which the heart hungers.

A. *A sense of guilt can be a blessing.* Guilt can lead to a creative experience. An attitude of self-judgment concerning failures toward God, toward self, and toward others, which leads to confession and correction, is always wholesome.

B. *A sense of guilt can be destructive.* Guilt can cripple and torment and produce a deep depression of heart and soul. It can lead to a sickness that in some instances results in suicide. Guilt that is unforgiven and unresolved can lead to a terrifying loneliness and sense of isolation. Hopelessness and despair capture the soul. Faith fails, and fear takes possession.

There are others who look upon guilt as being a most unhealthy state of mind. It must be recognized that some, because of failures of one sort or another, subject themselves to all of the torments of an unresolved guilt. While considering themselves as guilty defendants, they appoint themselves as a prosecuting attorney who issues one indictment after another. In this agonizing experience, they sit as a jury that finds the defendant guilty. Unless confession is made and forgiveness is experienced, they then appoint themselves as the judge who pronounces the sentence; and as the executioner they eliminate the defendant by what we call suicide. Perhaps this may appear as an extreme situation, but it happens more often than we realize.

The consciousness of unforgiven sin not only robs the child of God of valuable fellowship, but also makes Christian joy impossible.

II. God's forgiveness is adequate.

David speaks of the happiness of the man whose transgression is forgiven and whose sin is covered.

A. *David was guilty of the double crimes of adultery and murder.* Are there any more agonizing sins listed in the books of God or on the human conscience? Even though he was guilty of these terrible sins involving self, others, and God, he was able to experience forgiveness (Ps. 32:1–2). His sins are said to be covered. God holds them against him no more.

B. *The psalmist rejoiced in the assurance that God forgave all of our iniquities (Ps. 103:3).* He described this forgiveness in terms of removing our transgressions from us as far as the east is from the west (103:12).

C. *By the grace of God our sins are blotted out.* Through Isaiah the prophet God promised, "I, even I, am he that blotteth out thy transgressions for mine own sake, and will not remember thy sins" (Isa. 43:25). Not only does God blot them out, but he also promises with his forgiveness to forget. To completely forget is something only God can do.

D. *Our sins are cleansed by the blood of Jesus Christ (1 John 1:7).* The blood of Jesus Christ goes on and on cleansing us from the sin that would separate us from God.

63

III. God's forgiveness is available to all who will accept it.

A. *Forgiveness is offered to those whose sins are of the deepest dye.* "Come now, and let us reason together, saith the LORD: though your sins be as scarlet, they shall be as white as snow; though they be red like crimson, they shall be as wool" (Isa. 1:18).

B. *Wicked persons who are controlled by crooked thoughts are offered mercy and pardon if they will but change their attitudes, their way of thinking, and return to God (Isa. 55:7).*

C. *The preaching of the apostles contains the offer of forgiveness of sin and the gift of new life (Acts 2:38–39; 5:31; 10:43; 13:38–39).*

IV. God's forgiveness is offered to those who trust Christ as Lord and Savior.

A. *The act of God.* God was in Christ reconciling the world to himself. By his life, Jesus had met all the requirements of a perfect righteousness. By his death on the cross, Jesus was meeting the penalty of a broken law on behalf of all who would be willing to receive the remission of sins and the gift of new life through a faith that would make him the Lord of their lives. There is no remission of sin apart from his death on the cross for us.

  1. The forgiveness God offers is free. It cannot be bought with money or earned by effort.

  2. The forgiveness God offers is full. He forgives every sin. He doesn't do anything halfway. It is not a partial forgiveness, but a complete forgiveness that one receives from God.

  3. God's forgiveness is forever. When God forgives he forgets and remembers our transgressions against us no more.

B. *The attitude of man.* The human response to the act of God that affords this wonderful forgiveness is repentance toward God and faith toward the Lord Jesus Christ (Acts 20:21). Genuine repentance and saving faith are inseparable. One is negative while the other is positive. Repentance involves a turning from the life of sin and no faith, and faith involves a turning to the Christ in trust and surrender.

  Repentance is basically a change of mind with reference to God, self, sin, and others. Saving faith is the sincere acceptance of Jesus Christ as the Son of God and a trust in him to do what he promises to do.

Conclusion

As wonderful as forgiveness is, it does not remove the consequences of individual sins committed by the person who has received forgiveness. Forgiveness is an experience in which a broken relationship is restored and the offense is held against the offender no longer. The forgiven sinner is treated as if he or she had never sinned. This can be our experience with God through repentance and faith in Jesus Christ. To experience forgiveness provides one with a wonderful peace of mind and a consciousness of divine mercy. Forgiveness removes the fear of punishment and causes love to be warm and sincere.

How Far Is East from West?

How far is the East from the West?
It cannot be measured or proved;
But further than this, so the Bible tells me,
My sins have fore'er been removed.
How high are the heavens above?
An infinite measureless space;
But higher than this is the gift of God's love,
So great is His mercy and grace.
How deep are the depths of the sea?
A fathomless measure, you say;
But farther than this, so my Saviour tells me,
My sins are fore'er cast away.
They're gone and forgotten by God,
And God has removed every doubt;
For covered by blood are my many transgressions,
My sins are fore'er blotted out.
"Return unto Me," saith the Lord,
"For I have redeemed thee by blood,
Thy name is engraved on the palms of My hands,
And pardoned thou art, by thy God."
To Him we would joyfully sing,
Our praises to Him would ascend;
Our Saviour, our Shepherd, our Priest and our King,
Our true and unchangeable Friend.
—Anonymous

WEDNESDAY EVENING, FEBRUARY 13

Title: The God Who Hears and Answers Prayer

Text: "But when ye pray, use not vain repetitions, as the heathen do: for they think that they shall be heard for their much speaking. Be not ye therefore like unto them: for your Father knoweth what things ye have need of, before ye ask him" (**Matt. 6:7–8**).

Introduction

Our God definitely hears and answers prayer. He heard the prayers of Abraham and answered. Moses would testify that our God hears and answers prayer.

Elijah experienced remarkable answers to prayer. The apostles and the early church received repeated answers to their prayers.

Jesus, heaven's infallible Teacher, taught and believed that our God hears and answers prayer. Jesus used the relationship of a child to an earthly parent to illustrate not only God's desire to answer prayer, but also the manner in which he answers prayer. God's character does not change; his purpose continues even today.

When someone expresses a doubt concerning God's power to answer prayer, the words of Ethel Romig Fuller are appropriate:

> *If radio's slim fingers can pluck a melody*
> *From a night and toss it o'er a continent or sea;*
> *If the petal white notes of a violin*
> *Are blown across a mountain or a city's den;*
> *If songs like crimson roses*
> *Are culled from thin blue air,*
> *Why should mortals wonder*
> *If God answers prayer?*

In the words of the text that fell from the lips of Jesus, we are told that God is willing and ready and able to hear and to answer prayers.

"Evening, and morning, and all noon, will I pray, and cry aloud: and he shall hear my voice" (Ps. 55:17).

I. Like a wise earthly father, the heavenly Father provides many blessings for his children without them asking.

A. *He makes ample provision for our physical needs (Matt. 6:30).*
B. *Spiritual blessings are bestowed in abundance (James 1:17).*

II. Like a wise earthly father, the heavenly Father often awaits the request before bestowing the blessing.

"Ye have not because ye ask not" (James 4:2).
A. *Need must be recognized.*
B. *One must be able to utilize the gifts.*

III. Like a wise earthly father, the heavenly Father grants our petitions in a manner so as to develop the child.

A. *Parents are eager to provide books as they are needed and requested.*
B. *All good parents are eager to give guidance and instruction as it is requested.*
C. *An answered prayer is the bestowal of a responsibility.*

IV. Like a wise earthly father, the heavenly Father often denies the requests of his children.

A. *God denies our requests at times when we ask for stones instead of bread and for serpents instead of fish.*

66

B. *The heavenly Father will not bestow on us that which would be destructive.*
   1. Paul prayed for the removal of a thorn in the flesh (2 Cor. 12:7–10).
   2. The prayer of the mother of James and John received a negative reply (Matt. 20:20).

Conclusion

The heavenly Father always hears and answers our prayers. Sometimes his answer is yes and sometimes his answer is no, and on other occasions he answers, "Not yet." Nevertheless, "he spake a parable unto them to this end, that men ought always to pray, and not to faint" (Luke 18:1).

SUNDAY MORNING, FEBRUARY 17

Title: The Christian and the Racial Issue

Text: "Which now of these three, thinkest thou, was neighbour unto him that fell among the thieves? And he said, He that shewed mercy on him. Then said Jesus unto him, Go, and do thou likewise" **(Luke 10:36–37)**.

Hymns: "There's a Wideness in God's Mercy," Faber

" 'Whosoever' Meaneth Me," McConnell

"In Christ There Is No East or West," Oxenham

Offertory Prayer: Our Father, we recognize you as the source of all that is good and perfect. Because of your love for us, who are so unlovable, our lives have been enriched. We thank you for the gifts of life, health, and happiness and the privilege of work. We praise you for the abundance of material blessings that have come to us. We dedicate our ambitions, attitudes, and actions to you, and may your Holy Spirit lead each of us to live as givers. Deliver us from the peril of living only for the material. Teach us to give of ourselves and of our substance as generously as our Savior gave himself for us. In his name we pray. Amen.

Introduction

Jesus' choice of a Samaritan as the hero of his parable was not accidental or incidental. Racial difference was the occasion for problems that were acute, divisive, and controversial in that day. And in America today racial issues still have great emotional, social, religious, economical, and political significance.

I. The racial problem in our country.

A. *This problem is worldwide in significance.*
B. *It is a long-standing problem.*
C. *It is very complex, without a convenient solution.*
D. *Racial prejudice has continued to create pockets of hate.*
E. *We are part of the problem.*
   1. We are silent when we should speak.

2. We refuse to become involved.
3. We condone conditions our consciences condemn.
4. We make inaccurate generalizations.

II. What is the teaching of the Bible?

A. *The origin of the different races is not revealed in the Bible.* Genesis 9:24–27 is a passage used by segregationists to allege that God doomed Ham and his descendants (blacks) to perpetual servitude. A careful examination of this passage reveals the following.
 1. The curse was pronounced by Noah, not by God.
 2. The curse was pronounced upon Canaan and not Ham.
 3. The descendants of Canaan were the Canaanites, who were white tribes (Gen. 10:15–19). It is neither scriptural nor scientific to take isolated passages of Scripture and twist them so as to support the subjugation of blacks to whites as was done in slave days.
B. *God created humans in his own image (Gen. 1:27).*
C. *God "made of one blood all nations" (Acts 17:26).* We are all from the same source. We are one human family. Paul was speaking to a proud, intellectual, pagan people who felt that all except Greeks were barbarians.
D. *With God there is no preference of persons.* "God is no respecter of persons" (Acts 10:34).
 1. God's blessings are available to all.
 2. All are precious in his sight.
E. *Salvation is for all people of every race (Gal. 3:28).*

III. What can be done by the individual Christian?

A. *Face up to our responsibility to be Christlike as we face racial problems.*
B. *We can put ourselves in the place of those who are the victims of prejudice.*

> *If you discriminate against me because I am dirty,*
> *I can make myself clean.*
> *If you discriminate against me because I am bad,*
> *I can reform and be good.*
> *If you discriminate against me because I am ignorant,*
> *I can learn.*
> *If you discriminate against me because I am ill,*
> *I can improve my manners.*
> *But, if you discriminate against me because of my color,*
> *you discriminate against me because of something God Himself gave me and*
>   *over which I have no control.*
> —*T. B. Maston*

C. *We can obey the second greatest commandment (Matt. 22:39).*
D. *We cannot judge a brother (Rom. 14:7–12).*
E. *We can pray for guidance and grace.*

Conclusion

We can witness for Christ. Every soul is one for whom Christ died. Christ can solve the sin problem in every heart. Every person needs Christ.

SUNDAY EVENING, FEBRUARY 17

Title: The All-Sufficient Savior's Promise of Rest

Text: "Come unto me, all ye that labour and are heavy laden, and I will give you rest. Take my yoke upon you, and learn of me; for I am meek and lowly in heart: and ye shall find rest unto your souls. For my yoke is easy, and my burden is light" **(Matt. 11:28–30).**

Introduction

Of all the great promises in the Bible, the words of our text contain one of the most precious. Jesus came into a laboring and heavy-laden world. People were struggling under the burden of sin, fear, insecurity, and an empty, unsatisfying religion.

To the people of that day and to the people of this day Jesus extended an invitation that is universal in its appeal, all inclusive in its scope, positive in its promises, and eternal in its consequences. No one but a divine Savior would or could make a promise like this.

I. The invitation.

"Come unto me, all ye that labour and are heavy laden."

A. *This is the most extensive invitation ever extended.*
1. The weary worker is invited to come to Christ. Faith in him actually brings a renewal of the vital energies of life.
2. The weary worshiper is invited to come to Christ. Jesus was speaking to those who were burdened with empty religious observances. They were weary of the efforts to achieve their own salvation and to produce a satisfying self-reformation.
3. The weary worldling is also invited to come to Christ. The world with all of its promised pleasures cannot bring the peace and joy that are offered to those who forsake the life of faithlessness and begin looking to God for guidance and help.

B. *This is the most inclusive invitation ever extended.*
1. While innocent children are invited, the sinful reprobate is also included.
2. The rich as well as the poor are included.
3. The illiterate and the brilliant are both included.
4. Jesus does not only extend this invitation to those who are weary in active life but also to those who are weary in passive life. Whether your

69

burden is physical, mental, or spiritual, the living Lord, who is today what He was yesterday, invites you to come.

II. The promise.

"I will give you rest." The rest Jesus promises is more wonderful than that which comes as a result of a good night's sleep. He promises rest for the soul that can come only when a person is standing in a sure relationship with God.

A. *This promise of rest includes the privilege of sonship (John 1:12).* The people to whom Jesus was speaking were struggling by legalistic methods to achieve a position of acceptance with God. Jesus promised adoption as a gift to those who would receive him into their hearts as the Lord of life.

B. *This promise of rest includes forgiveness of sin (Luke 24:47).* People were laboring to atone for their own guilt. They were attempting to merit the favor of God. Jesus was proclaiming forgiveness as the gift of God to those who would repent and believe.

C. *This promise of rest includes the power of God.* Jesus was to make available to his disciples the inexhaustible resources of God for the living of fruitful lives. In the strength of this divine energy, they were to overcome the evil within and to resist the evil about them. With the power of God, they were to serve effectively doing God's will.

D. *This promise of rest includes provisions for the future.* For the Christian, death need not be a tragedy. In many instances, when life has been full and complete, death need not be sad. It is but a doorway through which a child of God walks out of one room in God's universe into the next room, where sin, suffering, and separation are no more.

III. The condition.

"Take my yoke upon you and learn of me." The invitation has been extended and the promise has been made, and now the condition for the fulfillment of the promise is revealed.

A. *This is an invitation to faith.* Jesus Christ invites people to consider his unique person, his marvelous words, and his miraculous works. Saving faith has been defined in terms of accepting Jesus Christ to be all that he claims to be and depending on him to do all that he has promised to do.

B. *This is an invitation to study.* By the term *yoke*, he invites us to accept his rule, his will, and his teachings as our basic philosophy and purpose in life. Receiving Christ as Savior is to become acquainted with him in a relationship that can be increasingly meaningful with the passing of time if we will fully accept him who is the Lord of love as our authoritative teacher and coach as we play the game of life.

C. *This is an invitation to practical obedience.* There is no benefit to be found in merely hearing the words of Christ. To accept this invitation requires that we agree wholeheartedly to live our life according to the divine plan.

Conclusion

The Savior assures us, "My yoke is easy and my burden is light." All of his purposes toward us are purposes of love. Consequently his yoke is easy. We are able to bear his yoke with the approval of our conscience. We follow him in the consciousness of his great love for us. We obey him with the help of the Holy Spirit. We are sustained by a great hope for the future. To come unto him and to follow him offers security and satisfaction. Only Christ can take care of the past, provide for the present, and take care of the future at the same time. Come to him now. Take his yoke upon you lovingly, cheerfully, and wholeheartedly.

WEDNESDAY EVENING, FEBRUARY 20

Title: Rewards Received in the Closet of Prayer

Text: "But thou, when thou prayest, enter into thy closet, and when thou hast shut thy door, pray to thy Father which is in secret; and thy Father which seeth in secret shall reward thee openly" (**Matt. 6:6**).

Introduction

Our Savior promises a reward to those who truly pray. In Hebrews 11:6 we find a similar truth affirmed. "But without faith it is impossible to please him: for he that cometh to God must believe that he is, and that he is a rewarder of them that diligently seek him." The Bible testifies from the beginning to the end that God is a prayer-hearing and prayer-answering God.

I. Misconceptions concerning prayer.

There are many misconceptions concerning the nature of this precious privilege of prayer. Prayer is not a blank check on which God's signature appears guaranteeing us anything on which we set our hearts. Neither is prayer a rabbit's foot or other charm warranted to preserve us from misfortune. Prayer must not be considered as a parachute project to be reserved for use in some extreme urgency. Certainly prayer is not a child's letter to Santa Claus. True prayer is never an attempt to change God's mind or bring him around to our way of thinking. Prayer is not a begging proposition in which we attempt to secure the sympathy of God. The Savior would assure us that the heavenly Father knows our needs even before we ask and is more eager to bestow his blessings upon us than we are to receive them.

II. The rewards of prayer.

Someone might raise the question, "Just what are the rewards of prayer?"

A. *One of the greatest blessings and one of the greatest rewards of prayer is a consciousness of the presence of God that comes to the person who is praying.* By its very nature, prayer is the bringing of oneself into God's presence, in the surrender of the mind and the surrender of the will to God. We come into

71

his presence to confess our sins. We come into his presence to express our gratitude. We come into his presence to make intercession for others. Thus, prayer is a bringing of oneself into a consciousness of the immediate presence of the living God.

B. *Another great reward that comes as a result of prayer is an awareness of the sin in one's life.* Isaiah went into the temple, and there he was blessed with a vision of God. His first reaction was an awareness of personal sin and guilt that led to confession. He said, "Woe is me! for I am undone; because I am a man of unclean lips, and I dwell in the midst of a people with unclean lips; for mine eyes have seen the King, the LORD of hosts" (Isa. 6:5). And close to this confession of sin, God gave to Isaiah a consciousness of cleansing as he was made clean and pure from sin. Thus, the young prophet was enabled to enjoy blessed fellowship with God and at the same time was equipped to serve God and others.

C. *Also, with this consciousness of sin and this awareness of cleansing from sin, there comes to the heart of the pray-er an inflow of spiritual power.* Jesus says that the heavenly Father gives the Holy Spirit to those that ask him. We need this divine power that will enable us to overcome the difficulties and the hardships, the troubles and trials of life. Isaiah writes, "But they that wait upon the LORD shall renew their strength; they shall mount up with wings as eagles; they shall run, and not be weary; and they shall walk, and not faint" (Isa. 40:31). Paul says, "I can do all things through Christ which strengtheneth me" (Phil. 4:13). And thus there comes as a reward to those who conscientiously pray, an inflow of divine power.

D. *The apostle Paul also speaks concerning another reward that comes as a result of prayer.* In Philippians he speaks of a peace that passes all human understanding. He says, "Be careful for nothing; but in every thing by prayer and supplication with thanksgiving let your requests be made known unto God. And the peace of God, which passeth all understanding, shall keep your hearts and minds through Christ Jesus" (Phil. 4:6–7). We discover a peace in the presence of God that is found in no other place. Isaiah writes, "Thou wilt keep him in perfect peace, whose mind is stayed on thee: because he trusteth in thee" (Isa. 26:3).

Conclusion

We have come apart during this midweek service for prayer. Let us each one now put forth an effort to enter a private cloister of prayer and talk to our heavenly Father concerning our individual needs and also concerning the needs of others. Let us approach him because we are his children and he is our Father. Let us approach him in the faith that he wants to give to us the blessings that we need.

SUNDAY MORNING, FEBRUARY 24

Title: The Christian and the Sexual Issue

Text: "Don't let the world around you squeeze you into its own mold, but let God remold your minds from within, so that you may prove in practice that the plan of God for you is good, meets all His demands and moves toward the goal of true maturity" **(Rom. 12:2 PHILLIPS)**.

Hymns: "Rejoice, Ye Pure in Heart," Plumptre

"Jesus, I My Cross Have Taken," Lyte

"I Would Be True," Walter

Offertory Prayer: Holy Father, help us this day to bring to you an offering in proper portion to the manner in which we have been blessed. Help us to know that we are not blessed so as to live a life of selfish indulgence. Help us to be good managers of all that we are and have as your servants. Accept our offerings and help us to give ourselves completely to you for your sake. Amen.

Introduction

What kind of God does the Christian worship? What kind of a Christ do we serve as our Lord? How would he have us relate to our world? How would he want us to be different from those who have no faith? In what way does the nature of our God influence the kind of life we live?

In addition to being a God of love and mercy, our God is a God of character. He is a moral God who places moral requirements on his people. Because of what he is, he cannot condone or encourage that which contradicts his character or that which is harmful and destructive to people. He forbids that we engage in that which is detrimental to self or to others. For him not to do so would be to show a lack of concern for us.

The moral laws of God are not the illogical requirements of a selfish despot who would deprive man of his freedom and of life in its finest form. The moral laws of God are as fixed and as unchanging as are the laws of nature. Apart from the moral law of God, life would become as chaotic and as uncertain as would nature if suddenly the law of gravity were to cease to function. When an individual or a nation ignores or transgresses either the moral law or the natural law of God, an act of self-destruction is committed.

The life of faith is a life related to the will of the God who has revealed himself as a moral God. Complete consecration to Christ is both positive and negative in its nature. It calls for a full dedication to God and a complete separation from a compromising and contaminating contact with pagan ways of life.

The children of God are constantly threatened (1 Peter 5:8). They face the continuing peril of a contaminating conformity to a way of life that is contrary to God's will. They are in the world but are not to be of this world. They worship a moral God who places moral demands on them. They live in constant contact with an immoral society that rejects God and the standards of righteousness.

The Christians at Rome were challenged to dedicate themselves fully to Christ and to guard against the perils of conforming to the pagan customs that prevailed in their city. They were to be dedicated fully to Jesus Christ and to live for him entirely. If they would achieve this goal, they must at the same time escape the degrading undertow of the society in which they lived. This was a real threat, because conversion had not created, and it does not create, an immunity to the pleasures of sin so easily available.

Even as it was necessary for the Christians in Rome to guard against the peril of letting the world of their day "squeeze them into its own mold," even so it is essential that modern-day disciples achieve and demonstrate a character and a way of life that are superior to that of a sinful world. To do this we must respond both positively and negatively. We must dedicate our all to God, and at the same time, we must escape from or rise above the degrading influences about us.

History is filled with stories of followers of Christ who have yielded to a low standard of moral responsibility and made shipwreck of their lives and brought great suffering into the lives of others. Homes have been destroyed. Children have been deprived of one or both parents. Churches have been weakened and made ineffectual. All have suffered emotional injuries that cannot be calculated.

I. The sexual crisis of our age.

If we would escape letting the world "squeeze us into its mold," we must recognize that there is a great disparity between the existing situation and what our Lord would have it to be. The Scriptures tell us that "the whole world lieth in wickedness" (1 John 5:19). It would appear that this is increasingly true as people flagrantly ignore and disobey the moral law of God that safeguards the home, protects womanhood, and provides for the security and training of children.

In 1956 a book by world-renowned Harvard sociologist Pitirim A. Sorokin was studied with great profit by young and old, believer and unbeliever alike. He introduced a term that became common across our country and even throughout the world in the title of his book, *The American Sex Revolution* (Boston: Porter Sargent). On the first page of this disturbing book, he says:

> Among the many changes of the last few decades a peculiar revolution has been taking place in the lives of millions of American men and women. Quite different from the better known political and economic revolutions, it goes almost unnoticed. Devoid of noisy public explosions, its stormy scenes are confined to the privacy of the bedroom and involve only individuals. Unmarked by dramatic events on a large scale, it is free from civil war, class struggle, and bloodshed. It has no revolutionary army to fight its enemies. It does not try to overthrow governments. It has no great leader; no hero plans it and no polit bureau directs it. Without plan or organization, it is carried on by millions of individuals, each acting on his own. As a revolution, it has not been featured on the front pages of our press, or on radio or television. Its name is the sex revolution.

In spite of its odd characteristics, this sex revolution is as important as the most political or economic upheaval. It is changing the lives of men and women more radically than any other revolution of our time.

These are not the words of a moralistic Bible preacher famous for a negative approach to moral issues but the studied opinion of a highly respected and well-known student of human affairs. This writer, after a careful study of history, continues, "During the last two centuries, and particularly the past few decades, every phase of our culture has been invaded by sex. Our civilization has become so preoccupied with sex that it now oozes from all pores of American life" (p. 19). How much more so today!

With historical perspective the author details the ever-increasing preoccupation with sex in literature, art, sculpture, music, the stage, the movies, television, radio, the popular press, advertising, the sciences, ethics, religion, and political life. He comes to a very disturbing conclusion:

> Thus, whatever aspect of our culture is considered, each is packed with sex obsession. Its vast totality bombards us continuously, from cradle to grave, from all points of our living space, at almost every step of our activity, feeling, and thinking. If we escape from being stirred by obscene literature, we may be aroused by the crooners, or by the new psychology and sociology, or by the teachings of the Freudianized pseudoreligions, or by radio-television entertainment. We are completely surrounded by the rising tide of sex which is flooding every compartment of our culture, every section of our social life. Unless we develop an inner immunity against these libidinal forces, we are bound to be conquered by the continuous pressure of a gigantic army of omnipresent sex stimuli. (p. 54)

There follows an analysis of the individual, social, cultural effects of an obsession with sex as it has affected the mental, emotional, and volitional integrity of people through the ages. In evidence that cannot be disputed, the author shows that a sex-obsessed society breaks both the divine and human law and eventually blows itself into smithereens because of the total absence of human values that make life worth living.

A half century after Professor Sorokin's book was published, one does not have to make a scientific survey to be convinced that conditions are even worse. The Internet is inundated with pornography in all forms. Magazines print feature articles on sex in terms that arouse curiosity and stimulate interest. Advertising is driven by sexual images and innuendos, and television shows and films promise more and more that panders to the lower nature. Adult bookstores can be found in nearly any large city in America. And newsstands are packed with books whose covers list titles that are shockingly vulgar.

One does not want to be a prophet of doom. No one should take delight in issuing threats or pronouncing forthcoming judgments on individuals or the nation. However, one cannot read the pages of sacred history in the Bible or secular history in our university libraries and escape the conclusion that we are in great peril as a nation. The peril on the inside may be more dangerous than the threat from without. The great civilizations that have marched across the pages of history have almost without exception collapsed from within before they were conquered from without. Such could happen to America. We are not immune from the law of cause and effect. We cannot claim a position of privilege with reference to the judgment of God on unrighteousness. Unless there are some radical changes, our nation is in great danger from moral collapse.

II. The Christian response.

What is the proper response for a Christian to make to the sex revolution? Dr. O. Hobart Mowrer has suggested that instead of calling it the sex *revolution*,

> more appropriate would be the term *devolution*, a turning or falling down, for there is little or nothing that is new in the so-called sexual revolution. It is in point of fact, very old stuff. Freedom for unfettered expression of the instincts characterized primitive man's earliest experience, and that is what we have been trying to get away from ever since. The notion that this is something we ought to try to move toward is pure illusion (quoted in John W. Drakeford, *The Great Sex Swindle* [Nashville: Broadman, 1966], 17).

Committed Christians will face this problem as they face other questions. What is the teaching of the Scriptures? What is the will of God for my life and for the lives of others? How can I live life according to the divine plan? As these questions are sincerely faced, the answers can be found. God has and will reveal the way that is best for all of us.

Dr. Wayne Oates, distinguished teacher of pastoral counseling, has warned ministers against the peril of offering simple answers to the complex problems of people who are much more familiar with the names of Kinsey, D. H. Lawrence, and Hugh Hefner than they are with Moses, Jesus, and Paul (*Pastoral Counseling in Social Problems* [Philadelphia: Westminster Press, 1982], 79–102). In spite of this warning concerning the problems confronting us in communicating with a secular world, the answer for the followers of Jesus Christ is simple: absolute chastity before marriage and absolute fidelity after marriage.

III. Practical suggestions for Christians.

A. *The gospel of divine forgiveness must be proclaimed to one and all who have broken the moral laws of God.* God is in the business of forgiving sexual sin even as he forgives other types of sin. David is a case in point. It should be understood that divine forgiveness of an illicit sex life does not remove the consequences of premarital or extramarital sexual transgressions. Forgiveness cannot remove the effects of a sexually transmitted disease or HIV/AIDS or erase the shattering emotional effects of giving birth to a baby outside of marriage. The unfaithful spouse finds it almost impossible to restore the faith he or she once enjoyed in the eyes of his or her companion.

B. *The individual Christian must guard against an attitude of self-righteous pride if it is possible for him or her to lay claim to a record of innocence as far as sexual sins is concerned.* It is very easy to become legalistic and proud at this point. Paul encouraged the Galatians to have a forgiving attitude toward those overtaken in a fault and at the same time to be very careful lest they likewise be tempted (Gal. 6:1–3).

C. *The Christian who follows the teachings of the Bible and the dictates of sober thinking will recognize that the only legitimate use of sex is confined to the marriage relationship.* Paul says, "The body is not intended for sexual immorality but for the service of the Lord, and the Lord is for the body to serve." He continues, "Keep on running from sexual immorality" (1 Cor. 6:13, 18 WILLIAMS).

D. *Jesus warned against the dangers of harboring lustful desires.* If disciples of Christ are to live lives of purity, they must keep their minds pure by refusing to permit evil thoughts to remain in their minds. Actions follow the thoughts, and Jesus warned against the possibility of committing adultery by means of the lingering lustful look. Evil desires must be dealt with radically and drastically (Matt. 5:27–30).

E. *The individual Christian should seek a Christian understanding of and appreciation for sex.* Sex is not basically sinful even though the subject has been taboo in the pulpit for entirely too long. In fact, most of us pastors have been derelict in our duty at this point. Most of us have given a negative interpretation or emphasis without declaring in positive terms what the Bible teaches at this point.

In Genesis 1–2 there are at least three guidelines to the purpose of sex: the completion of man's nature, the procreation of children, and the establishment of community in marriage. From a biblical standpoint and in actual experience, sex initiates marriage, consummates marriage, sustains marriage, enriches marriage, and fulfills marriage.

In the Old Testament sexual relations are considered proper only when associated with marriage. Marriage assumes unselfish and continuing love. Only in marriage can there be a mutual responsibility, not only of husband and wife for each other but also for any children that might be born. Only in marriage can there be a mutual and lasting respect based on appreciation of each other as persons rather than just things.

Conclusion

By the grace of God and with the help of the Holy Spirit, it is possible for the Christian to live a life of purity in the midst of a crooked and perverse generation. If we would be well-pleasing to our Lord, we must not let the world squeeze us into its mold. As parents we must be much more concerned about our children and give them every possible assistance to live a life of moral purity as they look forward to and prepare for Christian marriage.

SUNDAY EVENING, FEBRUARY 24

Title: The Promise of Light for the Road of Life

Text: "Then spake Jesus again unto them, saying, I am the light of the world: he that followeth me shall not walk in darkness, but shall have the light of life" **(John 8:12).**

Introduction

Light makes life, beauty, warmth, comfort, joy, and health possible. Without light the world would be a mass of coldness and death. What the sun does for the natural world Jesus Christ does for the world of humans—mind, soul, and spirit.

I. Jesus makes a sublime claim: "I am the light of the world."

Jesus declared, "I am come a light into the world, that whosoever believeth on me should not abide in darkness" (John 12:46). As the Light of the World:

    A. *Christ reveals the nature and will of the God of love.*

    B. *Christ serves as light by revealing and exhibiting the evil nature of sin.*

        1. Sin brings suffering and penalties into life.

        2. Sin creates a bad conscience.

        3. Sin enslaves the will.

        4. Sin hardens the heart.

        5. Sin causes one to lose the fellowship of God.

        6. Sin brings suffering into the life of others.

    C. *Christ, as the Light of the World, reveals the real meaning of life.*

    D. *Christ throws light on the mystery of death.*

    E. *Christ throws light on the issues of eternity.*

II. Christ issues a call to commitment: "He that followeth me."

Jesus extended this call not only to the disciples of John the Baptist, but he continues to extend this call even today.

    A. *Receive him as Lord and Savior (Rev. 3:20).*

        1. Everyone is mastered by something.

        2. Christ alone deserves first place.

    B. *Heed him as Teacher (Matt. 5:7).*

    C. *Imitate his example.*

III. To those who heed the call and follow him, Christ makes a twofold promise.

    A. *The negative side of the promise: "shall not walk in darkness."*

        1. The darkness of spiritual ignorance about God.

        2. The darkness of moral impurity.

        3. The darkness of unrelieved sorrow.

        4. The darkness of hopeless death.

B. *The positive side of the promise: "shall have the light of life."*
  1. He reveals to us the beauty and graciousness of the God of love. We need not be in darkness about the nature of God.
  2. He reveals the key to the life abundant—through worship, meaningful work, joyful witness, and unselfish giving.
  3. He takes away our fear of death by giving us the assurance that eternal life is a reality.

Conclusion

Come to him who is the Light of the World and discover the truth about God and life and eternity. As you walk in the Light, you will find yourself in possession of the truth and in the way of joy.

WEDNESDAY EVENING, FEBRUARY 27

Title: Watch the Manner of Your Praying

Text: "But when ye pray, use not vain repetitions, as the heathen do" (**Matt. 6:7**).

Introduction

Many professed followers of our Lord have become disenchanted with the privilege of prayer. They have decided not to pray because they have failed to receive any benefits from their previous efforts. Some have even been heard to say, "I don't believe God answers prayer. He has never answered any of my prayers."

If you find yourself in the group that has not received definite answers to your prayers, perhaps you should examine the manner of your praying. It is not enough just to be sincere. It is not enough just to be persistent. We must have a proper attitude and proper motive as we pray.

Matthew 6 begins with a warning: "Take heed." Stoplights are erected at street corners to prevent automobile accidents and the injury of pedestrians. When we ignore these warnings, disaster occurs. By his warning "Take heed," Jesus erects a stoplight to caution us against one of the most subtle foes of true spiritual achievement. He calls attention to the peril of performing religious duties so as to win the approval of people rather than the praise of God. Specifically he warns us against the peril of praying to be heard by people and consequently praised by them.

From earliest childhood, we have been taught to try to conduct ourselves so as to enjoy the approval of our parents. At a later stage in life, we were taught to study so as to have the approval of our school teachers. As we approached maturity, we were taught to so conduct ourselves as to win the approval of our employers. In the realm of our faith, we face the great temptation of seeking the praise and esteem of our fellow Christians. It is true that the vast majority of people are more influenced by what a person says than by what God Almighty thinks. Jesus teaches us that if the invisible and unspoken motive behind our prayer life is to receive the acclaim and to hear the applause of our fellow humans, then we have been paid in full and will have no reward from the heavenly Father.

79

In this portion of the Sermon on the Mount, our Lord is dealing with the motive behind our acts of righteousness. He uses three illustrations that show how the desire for the praise of people can corrupt the religious service that many of us seek to render. The giving of alms is an outward act of service in relationship to our fellow humans. We must beware lest we are benevolent solely to have the approval of others. Prayer is related to our relationship with God. Fasting is an inward experience calling for discipline of oneself.

By examining the manner of your praying, you may find the motive for your praying revealed. The motive is all important. Our Savior warns us against some perils.

I. Do not call for a fanfare of trumpets.

A. *The motive of the soloist is all important.*
B. *The choir should sing for the glory of God.*
C. *The preacher should hide himself behind the living Christ.*
D. *The giver should give so as to bring glory to God rather than to self.*
E. *Prayer is a personal, private, intimate conversation with God and should not be spoken so as to win approval of the human hearers.*

II. Do not stand on the corner to say your prayers.

A. *Prayer is not a speech to be made for human listeners.* Frequently you will hear someone say, "I cannot pray in public." If this statement were analyzed, you would actually hear the person saying, "I am not a public speaker." Admittedly, it is difficult to have your attention only on God with people all around you. Yet as you ask God to help you be more thankful to him, you become less needy of the praise of others.
B. *Compliments on the beauty of prayer offered in public should cause the one who voiced the prayer to examine his or her motives lest he or she fall into the temptation of praying for human approval.*

III. Do not pray like idol worshipers.

Worshipers of false gods think that somehow they will persuade their deity to yield to their requests. The child of God does not have to beg. We are to approach the throne of grace as children of the King. The Father knows us, loves us, and is more eager to please us than we are to be pleased.

Conclusion

The motive behind our prayers is all important. Our Lord said, "And whatsoever ye shall ask in my name, that will I do, that the Father may be glorified in the Son" (John 14:13). The purpose behind our praying should be that of bringing honor and glory to God rather than getting personal glory or gratification for our selfish desires. Examine the motive and the manner of your prayers if you want to receive the blessings God has for you.

MARCH

- ### Sunday Mornings

    With the theme "A Visit to Calvary," this month's messages point toward Easter. On the Sunday after Easter, begin the series "Following the Living Lord."

- ### Sunday Evenings

    Continue the series "The Promises of God."

- ### Wednesday Evenings

    Continue "The Child of God in Prayer" series.

SUNDAY MORNING, MARCH 2

Title: "Behold the Lamb of God"

Text: "The next day John seeth Jesus coming unto him, and saith, Behold the Lamb of God, which taketh away the sin of the world" (**John 1:29**).

Hymns: "Great Redeemer, We Adore Thee," Harris

           "My Saviour's Love," Gabriel

           "Come to the Saviour Now," Wigner

Offertory Prayer: Heavenly Father, we approach the throne of grace to thank you for the abundance of your blessings upon us. We offer you the love of our hearts and the labor of our hands. Bless our tithes and offerings so that the church can minister in your name and preach the message of your love to the whole world. For your name's sake. Amen.

Introduction

For many centuries the people of Israel had been longing and looking for the promised Messiah who was to redeem them from the curse of evil and from the inevitable consequences of sin.

There appeared on the scene a man, chosen and endowed by God, to prepare the way for the coming of the Messiah, and he was to do this by gathering about himself a group of people who by disposition would be prepared to become followers of and coworkers with the Messiah.

The piety of this man, John the Baptist, was so eminent that many people took him to be the Messiah. Again and again they came and asked him if he was the Promised One, the Anointed One, the one about whom the prophets had spoken. Again and again John the Baptist denied that he was the Promised One. He introduced himself simply as a voice crying in the wilderness, "Prepare the way for the coming of the Lord." He challenged people to turn away from the love of evil and turn to the way of personal faith and righteousness. Those who heeded his messages were thus prepared for the appearance of the Messiah.

Our Lord Jesus Christ, after living the first thirty years of his life in the city of Nazareth, went to John for baptism. Immediately following his baptism, he was led by the Spirit of God into the wilderness to be tested and to be tempted by the Evil One. After our Savior overcame these temptations and demonstrated his superiority to the power of Satan, we find him coming to John the Baptist again. When John the Baptist saw Jesus approaching, he said to his disciples who were gathered around him, "Behold the Lamb of God, which taketh away the sin of the world" (John 1:29).

This descriptive phrase by which our Lord was introduced came straight from the heart of the Old Testament prophets. From the book of Genesis through the Psalms and Prophets, the Messiah is frequently spoken of as the Lamb of God. The lamb was the animal of sacrifice by which atonement was made for sin. The ceremonial death of the lamb was a picture in which people's sins would be covered and removed and they would be forgiven through the blood of Christ. To the hearts of John's disciples, this phrase, "the Lamb of God," had a significance that it would not have for the modern-day man on the street if someone were to appear and say, "Behold the Lamb of God, which taketh away the sin of the world." The announcement of John contained eternal, timeless truth. In one sentence he stated the need of man and the provisions of God. Even for this modern day the imperative of John the Baptist rings down through the corridors of time, and there is nothing that we need more today than to "behold the Lamb of God, which taketh away the sin of the world."

I. The Lamb of God came because of sin.

We assemble from Sunday to Sunday in classroom and sanctuary in order that with the eye of our soul we might "behold the Lamb of God, which taketh away the sin of the world." This is a sight of which the eyes never grow tired. This is a sight that can always bless the heart, challenge the mind, sway the will, and deepen the faith. So, today it is my prayer that somehow during this service you might be able to "behold the Lamb of God, which taketh away the sin of the world." In this statement, "the sin of the world," John the Baptist was speaking about the world's greatest problem.

There are many superficial diagnoses of what ails the world. Some people believe that through education the ills of humanity can be eliminated. Certainly, the value of good education is not to be underestimated. Others believe that the solution to our problems here in America is to eliminate the slums and by means of an extensive urban renewal program eliminate the ghettos that are a constant breeding place for crime and delinquency. Definitely something needs to be done about this. Others would say that the greatest problem in the world today is the threat of terrorism. Somehow we need to recognize that these issues or problems are but the outcroppings of something that is deeper. The heart of our problem is *sin*.

When many of us think in terms of sin, we think of this little thing or that little thing or a particular act or attitude. We fail to recognize that these are but the fruit of a heart condition called sin. John the Baptist did not say, "Behold the Lamb of God, which taketh away the *sins* of the world." He went deeper than that. Jesus Christ came to deal with the core of the problem that plagues us all; he came "to take away the *sin* of the world." When John pointed to Jesus, he was pointing to the one who came to deal with our deepest need.

What is the greatest need of your heart and life today? Young people may say, "My greatest need is to finish my college education." Another person may say, "My greatest need is financial. I need money to pay off my debts." Couples experiencing marital discord may say that peace and harmony in the home is the greatest need they have. When we take all of these problems and analyze them, looking at ourselves as we really are, we come to realize that behind our uneasiness, behind our frustrations, behind our failures, behind our shortcomings, is this thing we call sin. It is not just a question of if the wife would do this or the husband would do that, everything would be all right. It is not merely if the son would quit doing this or the daughter would start doing something else, then everything would be perfect.

All of us need to recognize that our greatest need is for a solution to our sin problem. Only Jesus Christ can deal with this problem adequately. Only Jesus Christ can solve this problem for the world, for the nation, for your home, and for your individual life. If a man has skin cancer and considers it merely as a mild skin rash, he is in great danger. He is laboring under an illusion. Often we fail to diagnose what our problem really is, and consequently, we do not know how to treat it.

John the Baptist would point us to him who alone can deal with the deepest need of our lives. Jesus Christ came into this world not just to live a beautiful life or to give voice to pious platitudes. He did not come into the world merely to heal the sick, give sight to the blind, restore hearing to the deaf, and make the lame to walk. Jesus Christ came into this world primarily to deal with my sin problem and your sin problem. The angel said to Joseph concerning Mary, "She shall bring forth a son, and thou shalt call his name Jesus: for he shall save his people from their sins" (Matt. 1:21). Jesus himself said, "Even the Son of Man came not to be ministered unto, but to minister, and to give his life a ransom for many" (Mark 10:45). Paul wrote to the Romans, "God commendeth his love toward us, in that, while we were yet sinners, Christ died for us" (Rom. 5:8).

II. The Lamb of God takes away the punishment of sin.

Sin has never been a popular subject. It is a negative subject, and people do not like to hear about it. I do not even like to think about it. Yet it is the problem with which all of us must deal. Jesus Christ came into this world to take care of the sin problem and to help us with the biggest problems we have. He came into this world that he might bear the punishment for our sins. Sin must be punished. "The soul that sinneth, it shall die" (Ezek. 18:4). "The wages of sin is death" (Rom. 6:23). It is impossible to sin without suffering. Jesus Christ came into this world to suffer for our sins in the sense in which our sins separate us from God.

Jesus went to the cross and suffered condemnation, isolation, agony, and death as a substitute for us that he might bear the punishment of our sin (1 Peter 3:18). Our only hope of escaping a Christless, hopeless eternity is through the fact that Jesus Christ loved us to the extent that he died in our place on the cross. He took the "rap" for you and for me. He suffered in our place. You and I should "behold the Lamb of God" suffering the unutterable agony and anguish of the cross. The Scriptures tell us that Jesus Christ died for our sins. Paul wrote, "For I delivered unto you first of all that which I also received, that Christ died for our sins according to the scriptures" (1 Cor. 15:3). His death on the cross was not an accident in the plan of God. His death on the cross was not the death of an apostle of some lost cause. It was not an emergency venture. It was in the plan of God that Jesus Christ should demonstrate God's immeasurable love by dying in my place and your place.

Sometimes we forget that Jesus died for our sin. Behold, gaze upon, focus your attention upon him who came to take away the sin of the world. He took away the punishment of our sin — that punishment that would separate us from God — by dying on the cross in my place and your place.

III. The Lamb of God takes away the power of sin.

This Lamb of God comes into our hearts to take away the power of sin and to deliver us from the practice of sin and from the evil nature within us. "For sin shall not have dominion over you" (Rom. 6:14). We are not to be slaves of sin. God would not be a good God if he placed within our hearts a hunger and thirst for a holy life but did not also make available to us the resources and the strength to enable us to live a holy life. And so Jesus Christ came into the world that he might deliver us from the power, the practice, and the habit of sin.

A. *He does this by means of his church.* It is the plan and purpose of God that every one of his disciples be a part of the church, a community of the redeemed, a family of the forgiven, a fellowship of the twice-born, a group in whom the Holy Spirit dwells, a people who practice the law of love and live by the rule of mercy and mutual help and encouragement. The church is a part of God's plan to deliver us from the power of sin.

B. *Our Lord would deliver us from the power of sin through his Bible.* You cannot be victorious over the evil within you and you cannot escape the evil that is about you if you are a stranger to the pages of this blessed book, if you do not memorize its truths and hide them in your heart, if you do not feast your soul upon it as daily food, if you do not make it the rule of your life. "Wherewithal shall a young man cleanse his way?" the psalmist asked. "By taking heed thereto according to thy word" (Ps. 119:9). He bore this testimony: "Thy word have I hid in mine heart, that I might not sin against thee" (v. 11). As you take the precious, divine, living Word of God and make it a part of your way of life, you will find that this is God's way of helping you live a victorious life.

IV. The Lamb of God takes away the love of sin (2 Cor. 5:17).

Jesus Christ came into the world not only to take away the punishment of our sin and deliver us to a life of righteousness; he also came into our hearts and lives to destroy our love for sin. Many people have no interest in becoming a Christian because they are infatuated with the pleasures of sin. But these pleasures are counterfeit and destructive. Only with Jesus Christ in the heart can a person fall out of love with sin and fall in love with the righteousness, holiness, and purity that are good, kind, merciful, and gracious.

V. The Lamb of God will take us away from the presence of sin.

Ultimately, this Lamb of God who came to deliver us from the punishment, power, and love of sin will also deliver us from the very presence of sin.

Have you ever knelt to pray only to discover that the Evil One was in the closet of prayer with you and that in your most sacred moments, the most violent, sinful thoughts would enter your mind? Where did these thoughts come from? Well, they come from our sinful human nature and from the Evil One working to tempt and destroy each of us.

Have you ever been disturbed by the fact that even when you come to the house of God to worship you are out of tune with God? You can't seem to focus, and the message from God's Word doesn't seem to sink in. You eagerly wait for the pastor to pronounce the benediction so that you can go home. Have you wondered what is wrong? Paul writes in Ephesians 6 that we wrestle not against flesh and blood, but against the spiritual forces of darkness.

One of the wonderful things about heaven is that this Evil One that we have been talking about will be no more. Jesus Christ came into this world that ultimately he might deliver us from the presence of sin and take us into the home of his heavenly Father. There nothing shall enter in that can defile, pollute, or corrupt in any manner. There our praise to God will be perpetual. There we will be purified. And there by the grace of God we will worship and praise him without the limitations that we know in this life.

Conclusion

As followers of Jesus Christ, with the eye of our faith, let us behold the Lamb of God and adore him, love him, admire him, and obey him. Let us behold him and not only adore him, but also let us decide to serve him lovingly and obediently.

If you have not yet fastened your eyes on Jesus in faith to trust and receive him as your Savior, then do so today. He wants to be your Savior, teacher, friend, and guide. Your decision to receive him will permit him to take away the sin that has separated you from God.

SUNDAY EVENING, MARCH 2

Title: The Promise of an Eternal Love

Text: "God is love" **(1 John 4:8).**

Introduction

Abraham became a spiritual giant because he claimed the precious promises of God and moved forward in faith believing that God was trustworthy and would keep his promise. Abraham staggered not at the promise of God through unbelief but was strong in faith, giving glory to God, being fully persuaded that all that he had promised he was able to perform (Rom. 4:20–21). In this statement by the apostle Paul, we find an explanation of Abraham's greatness and a possible explanation for the spiritual weakness of many of God's children today. We lack a faith that will grasp the promises of God at their face value and march forward depending on God to do what he has promised. The apostle Peter speaks of the exceedingly great and precious promises of God by which we are to become partakers of the divine nature (2 Peter 1:4). A study of the Bible will reveal clearly that God is a promise-making and promise-keeping God. As we study the testimony of the saints, we observe that without exception they all testify that God is faithful to every promise he has ever made.

If we would be true to our faith and to our God, we must accept his promises and believe that he is able to perform that which he has promised. Without such a faith, spiritual success is impossible.

The Bible is a record of God's faithfulness in keeping his promises.

I. The promise of love.

Volumes have been written about the precious promises of God, but tonight I want to focus your attention on the divine promise of an eternal, undying love that we find in the Word of God.

A. *God spoke through Jeremiah the prophet, saying, "Yea, I have loved thee with an everlasting love" (Jer. 31:3).*

B. *God spoke through Isaiah to the children of Israel.* He said, "Can a woman forget her sucking child, that she should not have compassion on the son of her womb? Yea, they may forget, yet will I not forget thee" (Isa. 49:15). And thus the people of Israel were strengthened and sustained in days of adversity and hardship by an awareness of God's great loving care.

C. *The apostle Paul wrote to the Roman Christians, "Who shall separate us from the love of Christ? shall tribulation, or distress, or persecution, or famine, or nakedness, or peril, or sword?"* He replied, "Nay, in all these things we are more than conquerors through him that loved us. For I am persuaded, that neither death, nor life, nor angels, nor principalities, nor powers, nor things present, nor things to come, nor height, nor depth, nor any other creature, shall be able to separate us from the love of God, which is in Christ Jesus our Lord" (Rom. 8:35, 37–39). Paul rejoiced in a constant consciousness of this eternal love of God.

We urgently need this message of God's undying, eternal love today when there is so much hatred abroad and when there are so many things that would discourage us from living by the principle of love. If we were constantly aware of God's great love for us, surely it would strengthen our faith in him and cause us to rely on his promises and challenge us to do what he wants us to do.

II. The presence of love.

"Herein is love, not that we love God, but that he loved us, and sent his Son to be the propitiation for our sins" (1 John 4:10). God's promised love has been revealed most dramatically in the death of Christ on the cross for us. No limits are placed on the divine love (Eph. 3:18–19).

  A. *The love of God is as broad as the wide world.* It is wide without being shallow. It reaches out to include all people of all colors, countries, and cultures.

  B. *The love of God reaches to the farthest point in its quest to redeem and forgive.* It reaches back into the past and extends forward into the future. God always has loved us and always will continue to love us.

  C. *The love of God reaches down to find and bless us in our deepest need.* Sin cannot cover a person to the extent that the love of God is unable to reach down and lift him or her up.

  D. *The love of God has brought the Son of God down from on high to meet our deepest need.* We are all sinners without the power to save ourselves or to lift ourselves to a position where we would please God. What we were unable to do, God's love has done for us.

III. The purpose of love.

The promise of God's unending love for us is no sedative to lull our souls to sleep in spiritual indifference. Instead, it should be a constant motivating force to a life of trust and obedience (2 Cor. 5:14). The assurance of God's eternal, unchanging love can sustain us in times of difficulty or tragedy (Rom. 8:28). God, in love, will be at work in everything that happens to bring out every possible good for us. The constant awareness of God's love can make us rejoice even in the midst of chastisements that come upon us from God (Heb. 12:5–13). Even these events are motivated by his love for us (Luke 15:11–32).

Conclusion

The parable of the waiting father, often called the parable of the prodigal son, speaks of the promise of love. God loves you. He is looking at you. He is waiting for you. He will rejoice to welcome you and receive you. Come home tonight to the waiting Father whose love for you is eternal.

WEDNESDAY EVENING, MARCH 5

Title: The Prayers of the Pharisee and the Publican

Text: "He spake this parable unto certain which trusted in themselves that they were righteous, and despised others" **(Luke 18:9)**.

Introduction

The parable of the Pharisee and the publican is a simple parable with which we are too familiar. We disassociate ourselves from either the Pharisee or the publican. Consequently we miss the point.

I. Notice the parallels.

    A. *Both want to stand before God.*

    B. *Both go to the temple.*

    C. *Both seek to pray.*

    D. *Both approach God with a prayer of thanks.*

        1. The Pharisee's prayer of thanks is obvious.

        2. The publican's prayer of thanks is inferred from the fact that he recognizes that God is a God of mercy.

    E. *Both have examined their hearts seriously.*

        1. The Pharisee believes that he has a right to stand before God.

        2. The publican feels unworthy to stand before God.

II. Notice the path to self-knowledge.

Both of these men had a knowledge of themselves. By what system or measuring stick did they arrive at this concept of their relationship to God?

    A. *The Pharisee measured himself by looking downward.* Instead of looking upward, he looked about himself on a horizontal level and measured himself by his fellow man. He looked down at the publican and let the publican be his standard.

        1. This contributed to his pride.

        2. This encouraged complacency.

        3. This produced spiritual stagnation.

    B. *The publican looked up to God.* He let the divine standard be the rule by which he measured his life.

        1. He became aware of his sin.

        2. He confessed his guilt.

        3. He made a plea for mercy.

III. Notice the results.

    A. *The Pharisee went away from church unchanged.* He made no decisions that brought him closer to God. He experienced no broadening of vision. He became further detached and isolated in his spiritual self-satisfaction and complacency. Actually he had wasted his time and had fooled no one but himself. He had merely looked about himself and had not bothered to look up to God.

B. *The publican "went down to his house justified" (Luke 18:14).* This is a legal term that declares that his prayer was heard and that his plea was granted. His sin was forgiven. He was accepted by God. He entered into a relationship with God in which he would be treated as if he had never sinned.

Conclusion

What happens when you go to church? Do you look about yourself and congratulate yourself because you are not as other people are? Do you sit in your pew all swollen with pride because you are outwardly perfect and without flaw? If so, you have been looking down instead of up.

Thank God that we can bow our hearts, confessing our sins in the assurance that the God of mercy will hear and forgive our sins, and we can go home with the assurance that we belong to God.

SUNDAY MORNING, MARCH 9

Title: The Joy of the Cross

Text: "Jesus ... who for the joy that was set before him endured the cross, despising the shame" **(Heb. 12:2)**.

Hymns: "Hallelujah, What a Saviour," Bliss

"At Calvary," Newell

"Glory to His Name," Hoffman

"Must Jesus Bear the Cross Alone?" Shepherd

Offertory Prayer: Our heavenly Father, we offer you the gratitude of our hearts for your unspeakable gift to us in Jesus Christ, our Savior. We offer you the praise of our lives. We come in worship bringing the fruit of our labors, the results of the thoughts of our minds and the efforts of our hands, in the form of tithes and offerings. Help us to bring these gifts in an attitude of reverent worship. As you have given yourself for us, we give ourselves to you. Amen.

Introduction

We have heard many sermons on the sufferings of Christ on the cross. Words do not have the capacity to communicate the suffering Christ experienced as he died for our sins.

The loneliness of the cross was terrible. Jesus was forsaken by his friends. In the midst of his agony, he felt forsaken by God and cried out, "My God, my God, why hast thou forsaken me?"

The shame of the cross is frequently forgotten by modern-day Christians. Crucifixion was the ultimate in insult and public contempt for a criminal. It is impossible for us even to begin to understand the horror of the cross to the sinless soul of the innocent divine Son of God.

The writer of the book of Hebrews injects into our thinking an idea that appears to be contradictory. He makes much of the fact that a part of our Lord's motive for enduring the agony of the cross was for "the joy that was set before him" (Heb. 12:2). Is it possible that one could endure such agony, such loneliness, such shame, such horror, and yet experience joy in doing so? The writer of Hebrews says yes. There were at least three joys that led Jesus Christ to the cross.

I. The joy of glorifying God.

A. *In his great prayer, Jesus prayed, "Father, the hour is come; glorify thy Son, that thy Son also may glorify thee" (John 17:1).* To glorify means to "make known." Jesus came to the earth to make known the nature, character, and purpose of God. In this petition he prays that God might reveal the nature and the divine purpose of Jesus of Nazareth who was to be manifested as the Son of God in the miracle of resurrection. And Jesus, by this petition, is affirming his purpose to make known the nature and character of God by his death on the cross.

B. *What is God like?* He is the eternal Creator. He is the almighty Sovereign. He is the majestic and holy God. He is the God who is both righteous and just.

C. *The supreme revelation of the love, mercy, and grace of God is to be revealed in the display of his immeasurable love by the substitutionary death of Jesus Christ on the cross.* Jesus was eager to reveal once and for all that love and grace are at the very heart of God. He was seeking to repudiate in a manner that could not be disputed that God was totally different from that which he had been reported to be by the serpent in the garden and through all succeeding generations.

D. *The Devil has misrepresented the nature and character of God from the beginning of time.* People look upon God with resentment and try to evade and run from him because the Evil One has slandered his character with malicious falsehoods. By his death on the cross, Jesus refutes all of these and glorifies God, makes him known, and introduces him as the God of love and mercy and grace.

II. The joy of the highest possible personal achievement.

Could Jesus have escaped the cross? Perhaps this question is idle speculation, but it is evident that Satan thought that he could avoid the cross. Satan offered him the kingdoms of this world if he would but fall down and worship him. The heart of this temptation was a suggested escape from the cross and a convenient, inexpensive way to win the kingdoms of this world for God. Jesus rejected this suggestion and endured the cross because there was no other way to save people. In doing so, he was to achieve the highest possible destiny for his life.

A. *Apart from the sufferings of the cross, there could be no resurrection from the tomb and demonstration of the reality of eternal life.*

B. *Apart from the sufferings of the cross, there could be no crusade of love by gospel teams carrying the message of redemption to a lost world.*

C. *Apart from the sufferings of the cross, there could be for Jesus no divine approval and exaltation at the end of the way.*

D. *Jesus' first recorded words were "Wist ye not that I must be about my Father's business?"* From the cross, he cried, "It is finished." This was not the last gasp of a defeated idealist. It was the shout of triumph of one who had fully achieved his unique and divinely ordained destiny. It was, in a profoundly sober way, a shout of joy.

III. The joy of saving souls.

A. *Jesus endured the cross to experience the joy of saving you and me from sin.* We were slaves, and he came to set us free. We were guilty, and he came to cleanse us. We were helpless, and he came to rescue us. We were in a hopeless condition, and he came and gave us life.

B. *He died for our sins.* He makes forgiveness possible. He gives new life, eternal life, spiritual life, divine life.

C. *The joy of rendering the highest possible service to you and meeting the deepest need of your heart and life was a part of the joy that led Jesus to suffer the agony of the cross.*

Conclusion

Was the death of Christ on the cross a waste as far as you are concerned? If you have rejected him, then as far as you are concerned, he died in vain. Let his death on the cross be your death to sin. Let the life he revealed on the first Easter morn be your life.

Let his example challenge you to give your life completely to the divine plan. Determine to live so as to glorify God in your daily life that others might come to your Savior and be saved by his death on the cross and be transformed by his living presence.

SUNDAY EVENING, MARCH 9

Title: A Promise of Fifteen More Years to Live

Text: "I will add unto your days fifteen years" (**2 Kings 20:6**).

Introduction

Frequently we have heard it said, "We have no promise of tomorrow." Life is like a vapor that appears for a while and then fades away. We have only the promise of the present.

In the Old Testament, we read of how God used the prophet Isaiah to prophesy to King Hezekiah an extension of fifteen years of life. What would you do if you knew that you had fifteen more years to live?

Hezekiah was a godly statesman. The Scriptures say that he began his reign as king at the age of twenty-five and "did that which was right in the sight of the LORD, according to all that David his father did" (2 Kings 18:3).

Hezekiah came to the throne in a time when his nation was suffering from spiritual and moral decay. He immediately instituted religious reforms. He set out to obliterate idol worship.

Hezekiah was a man of great faith. "He trusted in the LORD God of Israel; so that after him was none like him among all the kings of Judah, nor any that were before him" (2 Kings 18:5). His rule enjoyed the blessings of God (v. 7). The borders of Judah were extended and Judah's defenses were strengthened (vv. 8–12).

Hezekiah lived a devout life of prayer (2 Kings 19:14–19). He knew how to talk with God. He lived on what men of old called "praying ground." In the midst of the prosperity and success of his reign as king, the prophet came with a sad message.

I. The prophet made a solemn announcement to the king.

"Set thine house in order; for thou shalt die, and not live" (2 Kings 20:1). The prophet of God announced to Hezekiah that he was approaching the end of his life and was to make preparation for his departure.

A. *People need to make preparation for death.*
1. Husbands seek to make economic preparation for death.
2. Every couple should make legal preparation for death by drawing up a will.
3. The most important preparation that can be made is spiritual preparation. Through repentance and faith, confession and trust, a man should commit himself to the grace and mercy of God as revealed in Jesus Christ.

B. *There are a thousand gates to death.*
1. Greatness in the eyes of the world will not prevent death from coming. Alexander the Great, Julius Caesar, Napoleon, George Washington, Roosevelt, and Churchill all died.
2. Great wisdom and extensive knowledge will not enable one to escape death. Scholars have died even as illiterates have died. College degrees do not enable us to avoid death.
3. Wealth cannot permanently postpone death. By means of wealth, a person can have the services of outstanding physicians and the facilities of vast medical centers, but eventually that person comes to the doorway of death.
4. Genuine piety and devout, unselfish service do not enable one to escape death. The noble, the strong, the famous, the good, the weak, and the wicked all eventually become feeble and die.

C. *Death gives us many warnings.*
   1. Empty chairs at home speak with a loud voice.
   2. Death claims victims daily.
   3. Some of us have already experienced a decline in physical vigor. Every gray hair in our head would speak to us as did Isaiah to Hezekiah, saying, "Set thine house in order, for thou shalt die, and not live."

II. Hezekiah's response to this sad news.

A. *The king desired privacy and prayer, so he turned his face to the wall and began to pray.* Most of us would need to talk with God if we were suddenly informed that death was only a few hours away.

B. *The content of his prayer.* "I beseech thee, O LORD, remember now how I have walked before thee in truth and with a perfect heart, and have done that which is good in thy sight" (2 Kings 20:3). Hezekiah was blessed with a clean conscience as he faced the record of his life, and this was a great source of comfort to him.

C. *The burden of his heart.* Scripture says, "And Hezekiah wept sore." We can well understand his grief and burden.
   1. He was at the prime of life, approximately only thirty-nine years of age.
   2. The religious reforms he had begun in the nation would perhaps fail if he were to die at this time.
   3. He had no son to succeed him on the throne.
   4. Hezekiah had no glimpse of the life beyond as we have it today. He lived on the other side of the empty tomb that has brought immortality to light.

D. *There was still much that needed to be done, and Hezekiah wanted to be a part of the work of God.* The Scripture tells us that God heard the prayer of the righteous king and spoke to Isaiah while he was still in the palace of the king. Isaiah was instructed to return and assure King Hezekiah that his prayer had been heard.

III. God's glorious promise of fifteen more years.

"And I will add unto thy days fifteen years" (2 Kings 20:6). Isaiah the prophet was given the privilege of announcing God's promise to Hezekiah. He had been informed that his lease on life was running out. He was now informed that his lease on life had been renewed and he had fifteen more years to live. How do you suppose Hezekiah responded to this good news? I can well imagine that his heart rejoiced with great gratitude and that even in the midst of his sickness he had a song of glad praise in his heart.

A. *Like Hezekiah, let us accept life as a gift from God.* It is difficult to define life. And it is possibly even more difficult to define death. Perhaps the most satisfying definition of life is to be found in terms of its being the gift of God.

B. *Like Hezekiah, let us recognize life as a trust from God.* God has entrusted us with the privilege of living. We are not to spend our lives in selfish pursuits.

93

God will hold us responsible for the manner in which we respond to the trust of life.

C. *Like Hezekiah, let us dedicate our lives to the glory of God.* To glorify God means to make God known. It is to let others know about our God.

D. *Like Hezekiah, let us see life as an opportunity to serve God.* By God's grace we have the privilege of being his sons. We also are granted the privilege of being his servants. We discover that life is really worth living when we begin to truly serve our God.

Conclusion

Someone has said that if we would make a quantitative impression on our generation, we must do it in a qualitative way. We have no promise that we will have fifteen years in which to worship and serve. We have no assurance that we will be able to love and live and give even one year from today. Perhaps our opportunity to be loyal and faithful and helpful will be no more than one year.

Note the words of the text, "I will add unto thy days fifteen years." Years are made up of days. We live life one day at a time. Yesterday has flown into the tomb of time. Tomorrow is but a dream. It is still in the womb of time. We have today in which to worship and work and witness for our Lord. Early in the twentieth century the *Baltimore Sun* conducted a contest, and a young lady named Mary Davis Reed received the prize after writing a poem in answer to the question, "What would you do if you had only one more year to live?"

One Year to Live

If I had but one year to live;
One year to help; one year to give;
One year to love; one year to bless;
One year of better things to stress;
One year to sing; one year to smile;
To brighten earth a little while;
One year to sing my Master's praise;
One year to fill with work my days;
One year to strive for a reward
When I should stand before my Lord,
I think that I would spend each day,
In just the very self-same way
That I do now. For from afar
The call may come to cross the bar
At any time, and I must be
Prepared to meet eternity.
So if I have a year to live,
Or just one day in which to give
A pleasant smile, a helping hand,

A mind that tried to understand
A fellow-creature when in need,
'Tis one with me, — I take no heed;
But try to live each day He sends
To serve my gracious Master's ends.

WEDNESDAY EVENING, MARCH 12

Title: "Our Father Which Art in Heaven"

Text: "Our Father which art in heaven" (**Matt. 6:9**).

Introduction

The Master Teacher encourages us to pray and also teaches us how to pray. The model prayer, often called the Lord's Prayer, is the perfect pattern that we should follow. It was not designed as a strait jacket to restrict our spontaneous petitions, but it is a "seed plot for new prayers."

The words of the text are actually the invocation, and they prepare the way for the seven petitions that follow. In this address or invocation the Savior gives us a unique revelation of the God to whom our prayers are to be offered.

I. Father.

Jesus came to reveal God to humans. People had thought of God and his people as the Potter and his clay, the Creator and his creatures, the King and his subjects, and the Judge and violators of the law. Jesus brought a unique revelation of God to the hearts of his disciples when he told them to think of God as their heavenly Father.

Jesus always addressed God as "Father" with the exception of the one time on the cross when he cried, "My God, my God, why hast thou forsaken me?"

Jesus did not consider all people to be the children of God (cf. John 8:44). He taught that in the miracle of the new birth a new relationship with God was created. This relationship is much closer than that which exists between the Creator and the creatures of his world. It is tender and affectionate and glorious.

The first recorded boyhood utterance of Jesus speaks of God as "my Father" (Luke 2:49). The dying cry of the Savior on the cross was "Father, into thy hands I commend my spirit" (23:46).

There is much difference between offering prayers to the omnipotent, eternal Creator God and bringing our needs to a warmhearted heavenly Father. Jesus would have us always remember that our prayers are to be directed to our heavenly Father.

A pastor was visiting one of the children's departments of the Sunday school. With appropriate comments, the teacher introduced him to the children. "This is our pastor." A bright-eyed lad of three interrupted and said, "This is my daddy."

There is much difference between being a boy's pastor and being his daddy. God is our Creator, but Jesus would lead us to trust him as our Father.

II. Our Father.

The first person singular possessive pronoun does not appear in the model prayer. Instead, the idea of family is implied by the use of the plural possessive pronoun "our."

We are not to pray as spoiled children full of selfish love and self-concern. Jesus teaches that as individuals we are to remember that we are members of a great family. The heavenly Father who is both wise and benevolent will not grant our petitions if we are seeking, from a selfish standpoint, that which would in any manner bring deprivation or destruction to one of his other children.

This petition recognizes the relationship that exists within the household of faith. If we are to pray effectively, we must do so as a child within the family. We cannot for one moment believe that God will give us special privileges that would be denied to other members of the family.

III. Our Father which art in heaven.

The heavenly Father to whom we pray is sovereign and supreme, majestic and holy, highly exalted on the throne of the universe. He has perfect knowledge of the past, present, and future. He knows where we have been, where we are, and where we will eventually be. He sees the end from the beginning. Because his purposes toward us are purposes of love, we can trust him, and we should come to him regularly for grace and mercy to help in time of need.

Conclusion

J. D. Jones of England tells of an incident that happened while crossing the ocean by boat that demonstrates the faith and love the truth that God is our Father can make possible. During a terrible storm, many of the people were overcome with fright. A little boy was aboard, and someone noted that he seemed perfectly poised and had complete control of himself. He was asked, "Why aren't you afraid like the rest of us?" The little boy replied, "My father is the captain of this ship, and I know that everything will be all right." With the attitude of the little boy, let us approach the heavenly Father in prayer.

> *I'm a child of the King,*
> *A child of the King,*
> *With Jesus my Savior*
> *I'm a child of the King.*

SUNDAY MORNING, MARCH 16   PREACED 08

Title: "Behold Your King"

Text: "And Pilate wrote a title, and put it on the cross. And the writing was, JESUS OF NAZARETH THE KING OF THE JEWS" (**John 19:19**).

Hymns: "Rejoice, the Lord Is King," Wesley

"Crown Him with Many Crowns," Bridges

"Praise Him! Praise Him!" Crosby

Offertory Prayer: Our heavenly Father, you have given your very best to us. Help us to bring our best to you. Help us to offer to you the best of our time, the best of our thoughts, and the best of our talents. Today we bring the fruits of our labors. Bless them to meet the needs of a lost and perishing world, through Jesus Christ our Lord. Amen.

Introduction

Jesus Christ was first introduced to the people by John the Baptist as "The Lamb of God, which taketh away the sin of the world."

The last introduction of Jesus was performed by Pilate, the Roman governor. In presenting Jesus to the mob who clamored for his crucifixion, with these words, "Behold your king," Pilate said far more than he realized. This cowardly Roman governor failed to perceive that Jesus was indeed the King of Kings and Lord of Lords. He most likely spoke these words of truth concerning Christ out of scorn for the Jewish people whom he hated.

It was the common custom in those days when a criminal was executed that a brief description of the charge for which he had been condemned be written on a placard and placed on the instrument of execution, that passersby might know what had brought him to that end. Pilate had an inscription made, which was printed in three languages and placed on the cross of the dying Redeemer. The inscription read, "JESUS OF NAZARETH THE KING OF THE JEWS."

Why was the charge written in three languages—Greek, Latin, and Hebrew? Perhaps the reason was to make sure everyone in the crowd could read it. Jerusalem was packed with visitors at this time from all parts of the world. But another hand than Pilate's was in it. It was the hand of Providence, for Greek, Latin, and Hebrew were the three great languages of the world. Each of them represented an era of history. Each symbolized a great world movement.

Greek was the language of culture and science—it was the language of the men of letters. Providence was proclaiming that Jesus was King over the realm of culture.

Latin was the official language, the language of civil law and politics, of government, of the Roman Empire. Providence was proclaiming Jesus to be King over the realm of government.

Hebrew was the national language of Palestine. It was the language of revealed religion. It was the language of the Law and the Prophets. Providence was claiming Jesus to be King in the realm of religion, in the realm of the spirit.

97

Today culture and education, law and government, religion and ethics should behold and reverence and worship the King of Kings and Lord of Lords. With a spirit diametrically opposed to that which Pilate had—that is, a spirit of utmost respect for him who was crucified—I urge you to consider seriously Christ's title. We need to behold our King in his full glory.

I. Behold your King in the councils of eternity (John 1:1, 14).

The apostle John, in philosophical terms, tells us that the eternal God, who before time began spoke and called light to shine, in time clothed himself in human flesh and walked the face of the earth as a man. Neither his life nor his death on the cross was an accident. From before the foundation of the world in the councils of eternity it was ordained that Jesus Christ should be our King.

II. Behold your King in the manger cradle.

A. *The babe in Bethlehem's manger was the fulfillment of Old Testament prophecy (Isa. 7:14; 9:6).*

B. *The wise men came seeking, saying, "Where is he that is born King of the Jews? for we have seen his star in the east, and are come to worship him" (Matt. 2:2).*

C. *An angelic host announced his birth by means of a heavenly anthem.*

> *I know not how that Bethlehem's babe*
> *Could in the Godhead be;*
> *I only know the manger child*
> *Has brought God's life to me.*
> *—Harry Webb Farrington*

III. Behold your King among the crowds.

A. *When Jesus "saw the multitudes, he was moved with compassion on them, because they fainted, and were scattered abroad, as sheep having no shepherd" (Matt. 9:36).* When the King stood in the presence of human need and sorrow, his heart quivered with sympathy and his eyes were a fountain of tears. He did not turn his ears or his eyes away from the needs and troubles of the world.

B. *The Christ was deeply moved by the spiritual depression of the people.* "They fainted."

C. *The kingly Christ was deeply disturbed by the spiritual destitution of people.* "They were scattered abroad as sheep having no shepherd."

D. *The kingly Christ sees, seeks, and sympathizes with shepherdless souls today.* "The same yesterday, today, and for ever" (Heb. 13:8).

IV. Behold your King in the classroom.

A. *"Never man spake like this man" (John 7:46).*

B. *"He taught them as one having authority, and not as the scribes" (Matt. 7:29).*

C. *The Christ who was a kingly teacher came to lead men to a true and complete knowledge of the character and purpose of God.*

1. "Philip saith unto him, Lord, show us the Father, and it sufficeth us ... he that hath seen me hath seen the Father" (John 14:8–9).
2. "No man hath seen God at any time; the only begotten Son, which is in the bosom of the Father, he hath declared him" (John 1:18).
   D. *He reveals man's duty toward God.* "And he answering said, Thou shalt love the Lord thy God with all thy heart, and with all thy soul, and with all thy strength, and with all thy mind; and thy neighbor as thyself" (Luke 10:27).
   E. *Jesus taught us the science of successful human relations.* "Therefore all things whatsoever ye would that men should do to you, do ye even so to them: for this is the law and the prophets" (Matt. 7:12).
   1. Man to man.
   2. Husband and wife.
   3. Parent and child.
   4. Employer and employee.

V. Behold your King upon the cross of Calvary.

A. *Here we come to the central purpose of his coming into the world (Mark 10:45).*
B. *At the cross the seriousness of sin is disclosed.*
C. *At the cross the justice of God is revealed.*
D. *At the cross the love of God is demonstrated.*
E. *At Calvary ... our sins were suffered for (1 Cor. 15:3; 2 Cor. 5:21; 1 Peter 1:18–19).*
F. *At Calvary we see the basis for God's hope for a redeemed race.* He has no other plan. Here man makes the decision that determines his eternal destiny.

VI. We shall all behold the King coming in the clouds.

A. *John 14:1–3.*
B. *Acts 1:11.*
C. *"Behold, he cometh with clouds; and every eye shall see him, and they also which pierced him: and all kindreds of the earth shall wail because of him" (Rev. 1:7).*
D. *A day is coming when the same words that Pilate had written above the cross of Calvary are going to be sung around the throne, not in Greek, Latin, or Hebrew, but by people from all nations in the perfected language of heaven.*

Conclusion

I beseech you, I encourage you, I beg you to make Jesus your King. Let the Lord of indescribable love become the master of your heart.

"And being found in fashion as a man, he humbled himself, and became obedient unto death, even the death of the cross. Wherefore God also hath highly exalted him, and given him a name which is above every name: That at the name of Jesus every knee should bow, of things in heaven, and things in earth and things under the earth; and that every tongue should confess that Jesus Christ is Lord, to the glory of God the Father" (Phil. 2:8–11).

SUNDAY EVENING, MARCH 16

Title: The Promise of Fruit to the Sower

Text: "They that sow in tears shall reap in joy. He that goeth forth and weepeth, bearing precious seed, shall doubtless come again with rejoicing, bringing his sheaves with him" **(Ps. 126:5–6)**.

Introduction

It is possible that the words of our text provided inspiration to the life and ministry of our Lord. He understood his own mission in terms of sowing the good seed of the Word of God in the hearts of people. He also considered those who received his Word and became his followers as the good seed of the kingdom (Matt. 13:1–9, 37–41).

The words of our text serve as an Old Testament commission to personal witnessing on the part of the people of God. They contain a precious promise of fruitfulness to those who give themselves to the task of sowing the seed of divine truth in the hearts of others (John 15:8).

Personal witnessing is the most neglected form of Christian service. This could be due to normal timidity, a feeling of spiritual unworthiness, the fear of making a mistake, or a lack of training or experience, or it could be due to spiritual laziness, unconcern, and a preoccupation with other things. We can be certain that the Devil will do all in his power to keep us from the task of sowing the seed of the gospel in the world.

Perhaps more of us would be at work in the task of bearing a personal witness if we visualized ourselves as seed sowers rather than soul winners. In reality soul winning is the work of God rather than man. Soul winning emphasizes the techniques and the methods used by the seed sower. Emphasis should be placed rather on the dynamic and creative power of the gospel as the Holy Spirit blesses the personal witness of the one sowing the seed.

The text contains a clear promise of fruitfulness to the spiritual seed sower. This is a promise that should excite and challenge not only the pastor and those who teach in the church, but every believer.

I. The seed sower places himself in proper position to receive the fulfillment of God's promises.

    A. *The Bible is a book of God's promises.*

    B. *To claim the richest of God's promises, one must be seeking to save the lost from sin.*

    C. *The unlimited resources of heaven are for the use and benefit of those who serve as servants of the Christ (Matt. 28:18–20).*

II. The seed sower can be assured of the presence of the living Christ.

    A. *"For where two or three are gathered together in my name, there am I in the midst of them" (Matt. 18:20).*

    B. *"Lo, I am with you alway" (Matt. 28:20).*

C. *"I will never leave thee, nor forsake thee" (Heb. 13:5).*
   1. He is present to commend.
   2. He is present to convict.
   3. He is present to counsel and to challenge.
   4. He is present to give courage.
   5. He is present to convert the unbelieving.

III. The seed sower can enjoy the peace of being in harmony with God's will.

   A. *A Jewish rabbi wrote a wonderful book titled* Peace of Mind. Billy Graham is the author of a book titled *Peace with God*. Tension comes when a man's life is not in harmony with the will of his Maker.
   B. *Peace of mind and heart comes when there is a coordination of our will with the will of our Maker and Redeemer.*
   C. *Never are we so close to the center of God's will as we are when we are busy at the task of sowing the seed of divine truth in the hearts of those who have not yet discovered the joy of knowing Jesus.*

IV. The seed sower experiences the thrill of rendering life's greatest possible service.

   A. *Of inestimable value is the service rendered by the excellent school teacher.*
   B. *Who could estimate the value of the service of a good physician in a time of illness?*
   C. *Above and beyond the mental or physical service is that rendered by the individual who sows the divine truth in the mind and heart, which makes possible a transforming experience with God.*
   1. This is the greatest possible service that you can render to the individual involved.
   2. Families are blessed. A man is changed into a Christian husband and father. A woman becomes a Christian wife and mother. The conversion of a child makes possible a great blessing to a future family.
   3. Community service is important. What could contribute more to a community than to help an individual become a Christian citizen?
   4. The greatest honor and glory that we can bring to God is to lead someone to trust him and to yield his life to the claims of his love.

V. The seed sower can be assured of eternal rewards.

   A. *The rewards hereafter (Dan. 12:3).* The only possible way by which people can lay up treasures in heaven is to invest their time, talents, treasures, and testimony in that which is going to heaven. Only as the currency of this world is changed into the souls of humans will we have rewards in heaven.
   B. *Rewards in the here and now.* The text declares that the seed sower "shall doubtless come again with rejoicing, bringing his sheaves with him." Paul speaks of those who had come to know Christ through his ministry as being his children in the spirit and as being his joy and his crown (Phil. 4:1).

An unusually close and warm relationship is created between individuals when one gives and the other receives the word of truth about God's love.

Conclusion

Paul said, "I have planted, Apollos watered; but God gave the increase" (1 Cor. 3:6). If we wait until we possess the power to cause the seed to germinate, we will never experience the joy of reaping a harvest. Only God can cause the gospel seed to germinate in the heart and bring about the gift of forgiveness and the implanting of new life. Our task is to sow the seed joyfully, constantly, expectantly, and as winsomely as we possibly can. God has promised us the joys of reaping a spiritual harvest if we will busy ourselves at the task of sowing the seed.

WEDNESDAY EVENING, MARCH 19

Title: "Hallowed Be Thy Name"

Text: "Hallowed be thy name" (**Matt. 6:9**).

Introduction

The model prayer contains an invocation or address and seven petitions. The first three petitions are centered on God. They concern God's name, God's kingdom, and God's will. These petitions are intended to permit God to work within the heart of the one praying. The second section of the model prayer focuses attention on human needs: our need for bread, for forgiveness, for guidance, and for deliverance from evil. The model prayer closes with an anthem of praise.

In the first section of this blueprint for prayer, the Master Teacher encourages us to take a larger interest in God's cause. We are to place ourselves by the side of God. We are to agree with and accept the divine purpose for our personal lives and the rest of the world.

The first petition is perhaps the most misunderstood, overlooked, and ignored of the seven petitions. To "hallow" means to "regard as holy" or to "hold in reverence." Subsequent petitions flow from this one.

It would be beneficial for us to learn to think biblically about the sacred name of God. We would worship and pray more properly. In ancient thought it was assumed that the personality of a man was bound up with his name. The name of God to the Hebrews was his signature, his monogram, his seal or stamp. In his name God was revealing his unique, divine person. The name of God reveals who he is, what he is, and what he is going to do. Jesus considered the Father's name beautiful and holy.

In this model prayer Christ encourages us first to be concerned with the unique and holy character and purposes of our Father.

Today we do not have as much reverence as we should have. This is probably due to the fact that we have lost a sense of the holiness of God. We have lowered him to the level of a "chum" instead of paying tribute to him as our Creator. Somehow we need to regain a sense of reverence for the God of holiness.

I. The attitude of reverence illustrated.

The proper attitude toward the holiness of God is easier to illustrate than to define. Isaiah's experience in the temple (Isa. 6:1–8) provides us with a proper human response to the God who is thrice holy. Isaiah's experience was one of deep humility and a sincere confession of guilt and unworthiness. He fell on his face in awe before the holy God.

The apostle Peter recognized both the deity of the Christ and his own humanity and unworthiness when he beheld the miraculous catch of fish. "When Simon Peter saw it, he fell down at Jesus' knees, saying, Depart from me; for I am a sinful man, O Lord" (Luke 5:8).

John's experience with the living Lord on the isle of Patmos (Rev. 1:17) illustrates the attitude our Lord is encouraging when he teaches us to pray, "Hallowed be thy name."

If we are to pray properly, we need to understand the divine nature of holiness. The disciples did not take liberties with Jesus. By what and who he was, he inspired holy awe. The Father to whom we pray is the God before whom the angels veil their faces and the redeemed fall down on their knees.

II. Ours is a profane world.

The word *holy* originally meant "separate and apart." Then it referred to that which was separate and dedicated to the service of God. In its later development, it took on a moral significance of being pure and without sin or imperfection. The Holy One of Israel is a moral God who places moral demands on his people.

The opposite of "hallowed" is profane. People treat themselves and God's world as if neither belonged to God. We have secularized life and the world. People ignore God, and consequently life is incomplete and disappointing. To offer this petition is to pray that the individual and society and the world might recognize God's holiness and dedicate themselves to him.

III. A plea for divine intervention.

To pray "hallowed be thy name" is a request for God to reveal and declare his character of holiness. This would actually mean that the one praying would be asking God to burn out the dross and eliminate all that is profane from the mind and heart. It requests that God will rule and overrule in the heart and life so that the holy name of God will not be treated lightly or be blasphemed.

IV. A promise to cooperate.

Jesus here encourages us to have an attitude of reverence toward God and God's will in every area of our lives. By this petition we express the sincere adoration of our hearts for the holiness and purity of our God. We acknowledge our love and affection for him because of who he is. And we dedicate ourselves to him for the same reason.

Conclusion

It is said that the great architect Sir Christopher Wren gave instructions during the construction of St. Paul's Cathedral in London that if any of the workmen were heard using profanity on the job, they were to be dismissed without exception. Profanity is a verbal expression of an attitude that is the opposite of the opening declaration of the model prayer. Profanity, if analyzed, is a request that God will act in a manner contradictory to his holy character. By the words "Hallowed be thy name," our Lord teaches us to enter the presence of God on our faces rather than tromping in with muddy boots.

SUNDAY MORNING, MARCH 23

PREACHED 3-23-08

Title: Good News from a Graveyard

Text: "He is not here: for he is risen, as he said, Come, see the place where the Lord lay" (**Matt. 28:6**).

Hymns: "Christ, the Lord Is Risen Today," Wesley

"Christ Arose," Lowry

"He Lives," Ackley

Offertory Prayer: Our Father, on this day we are dramatically reminded of your rich blessings toward us and of the debt of gratitude we owe you. You have revealed the extent of your love for us in the sufferings and death of your divine Son, Jesus Christ. In his resurrection from the tomb, you have revealed your purpose to give us victory over death and the grave and to provide for us an eternity of fellowship with the redeemed in the home of the Father. Our gifts of tithes and offerings are inadequate to express our gratitude, so help us to give ourselves totally to you through our Lord Jesus Christ. Amen.

Introduction

The message of Christianity is good news from a cemetery. Graveyards are always melancholy places because they are associated with grief, sadness, and separation from our loved ones. The cemetery is the last place from which one would expect to receive good news.

From the beginning of time, man has raised the question that was articulated by Job. "If a man die, shall he live again?" (Job 14:14). Century after century the small and the great, the wise and the foolish, the rich and the poor, the young and the old marched into the silent, clammy chambers of death. People stood in fear of death and the tomb. It remained for Jesus Christ, the God-man, to come with an authentic answer to Job's painful, perplexing question.

I. The basic truth of Christianity.

The basic truth of Christianity is found in this angelic announcement: "He is not here: for he is risen, as he said, Come, see the place where the Lord lay. And go quickly, and tell his disciples that he is risen from the dead" (Matt. 28:6–7). The Easter message is not an argument. It is a divine proclamation. The angels declared that Jesus Christ had conquered death and had risen to life. The apostles experienced his living presence to the extent that they died martyrs' deaths rather than surrender their faith and deny their relationship to him. The Scriptures record at least eleven appearances of the living Christ to the disciples. The empty tomb spoke with a shout to declare that he was no longer dead. The present strength of Christianity is a dramatic testimony to the presence of the living Christ who has walked the corridors of time.

II. The message of the empty tomb.

During the last six months of our Lord's earthly ministry, he sought repeatedly to instruct his disciples concerning the necessity and nature of his forthcoming death on the cross. They found these teachings impossible to understand and they sought by every means at their command to prevent Christ from going to the cross.

His shameful and horrible death on the cross was, for them, a great personal tragedy. He was their dearest friend. They had placed their complete confidence in him. They had pinned their hopes for the future of their nation on him. His death, for them, was a great political tragedy because they expected him to be a nationalistic messiah who would deliver Israel from the domineering power of Rome. His death on the cross, for them, was a public disgrace. There was no more shameful manner in which a man could die. Jesus was condemned as a common criminal and sentenced to death by crucifixion. This was a fate so horrible that Roman law forbade the crucifixion of a Roman citizen even for the most heinous crime.

It was not until the mysterious miracle of the first Easter morn that they began to understand what the Savior had been trying to communicate to their minds and hearts.

A. *The empty tomb declared to their minds and hearts that Jesus Christ was really the divine Son of God (Rom. 1:4).* Jesus Christ of Nazareth had worked in a carpenter shop. He had walked about Galilee. He had become hungry like other men. He had experienced weariness and exhaustion. He knew loneliness and sorrow.

He was a man, but he was also God. He gave sight to the blind; he made the deaf hear; he made the lame walk; he brought the dead back to life. He commanded the winds to cease their blowing, and they obeyed. He ordered the waves of the sea to be calm, and without hesitation they carried out his orders. On several occasions he claimed to be the Son of God. He had the audacity to forgive sin. He claimed to have the power to lay down his life and also to take it up again. This was the boldest of his

105

claims. It was the fulfillment of this claim that authenticated the truth of all of his teachings and declared him once and for all to be the God-man. He was the eternal God with a human body.

B. *The empty tomb declares that his death on the cross made atonement for our sins (Rom. 4:25).* The hymn writer said, "Jesus paid it all. All to Him I owe. Sin had left a crimson stain. He washed it white as snow" (Hall). With reverence let us ask, "How can we know that the death of Jesus Christ took care of the sin that separates the souls of humans from God?" The resurrection is the answer.

When Jesus was baptized, a voice came out of heaven, saying, "This is my beloved Son, in whom I am well pleased" (Matt. 3:17). On the Mount of Transfiguration, God again expressed his approval (Matt. 17:5). And he did it once again shortly before our Lord's passion. Jesus endured the agony of false accusations and judicial condemnation, which were followed by his indescribably horrible death for the sins of humans.

Have you wondered what the reaction of the heavenly Father was to this awful event? The resurrection is the answer. The substitutionary death of Christ on the cross perfectly met the requirement of a just and holy God who will bring every sin into judgment. God was pleased with what had been accomplished by Christ on Calvary that people's souls might be saved from the penalty of their sin, death.

C. *The empty tomb was for the apostles, and for us, a promise of victory over death and over the grave.* Jesus had said to Martha before his death on the cross, "I am the resurrection, and the life: he that believeth in me, though he were dead, yet shall he live: And whosoever liveth and believeth in me shall never die" (John 11:25–26). He also said, "Because I live, ye shall live also" (John 14:19). This is good news for all of his disciples now living who will one day find themselves in a graveyard if our Lord delays his return.

By his resurrection from the dead, Jesus was giving a dramatic demonstration of the reality of immortality. Eternal life is real.

III. Ours is a living Savior.

"I am he that liveth, and was dead; and, behold, I am alive for evermore" (Rev. 1:18).

A. *Christianity must be defined in terms of a relationship to a living Lord.* His living presence is a fact more solid than the mountains, more firmly established than the stars. This truth should revitalize our worship, for we come together, not in memory of a dead Christ, but in fellowship with a living Lord who said, "Where two or three are gathered together in my name, there am I in the midst of them" (Matt. 18:20).

B. *That he is alive makes prayer more meaningful, for when we pray in his name, we requisition the needed resources from the bank of heaven for the carrying on of his kingdom's work.*

C. *Sacrificial service is more meaningful and worthwhile because the resurrection proves that God will bring every good work to fruition (1 Cor. 15:58).*

D. *By his living presence, he would unify our efforts and command our very best.* Because he is alive and with us, we should be encouraged to abstain from evil. We should be bolder in attempting what is difficult. We can receive comfort from him in time of sorrow.

Conclusion

The living Savior offers the gift of eternal life now. "I am come that they might have life, and that they might have it more abundantly" (John 10:10). He is able to save completely all who come to him by faith, because he lives forever to make intercession for them. He can deliver you from the sentence of spiritual death, and he will one day deliver you from physical death. He offers you the gift of eternal life now if you will but receive him as your Savior and Lord.

SUNDAY EVENING, MARCH 23

Title: The Promise of His Abiding Presence

Text: "For where two or three are gathered together in my name, there am I in the midst of them" (**Matt. 18:20**).

Introduction

Dr. A. J. Gordon, a famous preacher of the nineteenth century, titled his auto-biography *How Christ Came to Church*. In the introduction, Dr. Gordon relates how that on a Saturday night, wearied from the work of preparing the next day's sermon, he fell asleep and had a dream. He was in the pulpit before a large congregation, ready to begin his sermon, when a stranger entered and passed slowly up the left aisle of the church, looking first to one side and then to the other as though silently asking with his eyes for a seat. He made a mental note of the presence of the visitor and determined that at the conclusion of the service he wanted to meet him. After the benediction had been given, the departing congregation filled the aisles, and soon they were gone. The stranger had disappeared with them.

Dr. Gordon approached the man by whom the stranger had sat and with genuine interest asked, "Can you tell me who that stranger was who sat in your pew this morning?" In the most matter-of-course way, he replied, "Why, do you not know that man? It was Jesus of Nazareth." With a sense of keenest disappoint-ment, he said: "My dear sir, why did you let him go without introducing me to him? I was so desirous to speak with him." And with the same nonchalant air, the gentlemen replied, "Oh, do not be troubled. He has been here today, and no doubt he will come again."

The rest of the book explains and applies the tremendous truth that dawned upon the mind and heart of the dreaming pastor. He realized for the first time in his life that if the promise of the Son of God, "Where two or three are gathered together in my name, there am I in the midst of them," means what it says, then Jesus of Nazareth is present every Sunday morning when his followers assemble for worship.

Dr. Gordon's ministry experienced a spiritual revolution. He was made vividly aware that Christ would be present to assist and that he should preach with one supreme motive: that of pleasing his living Lord.

Do you come to the house of God with the expectation of having an experience with the Christ who has promised to be present with his disciples always?

As the Savior gave his missionary mandate, he promised those who were obedient, "I am with you always." The apostles experienced his living presence. John described his experience with the living Lord on the isle of Patmos, saying, "I saw seven golden candlesticks; and in the midst of the seven candlesticks one like unto the Son of man" (Rev. 1:12–13).

I. Christ is always present to commend.

A study of the seven epistles to the seven churches of Asia Minor contains words of commendation. Christ will commend those things that are worthy in our life and work if we will but make ourselves sensitive to his presence when we come to worship.

What could he commend in your life? Could he commend your attitudes and actions in the home? Would he be able to commend your ambitions in the business world?

II. Christ is always present to convict.

We shy away from this. Many people think of God only in terms of his being a killjoy. They see him as some kind of a policeman who is wanting to apprehend them and punish them for wrongdoing.

God hates sin but loves the sinner. God hates sin because by its very nature sin is destructive. God is against sin because of what it does to people. Peace-loving people are against war because war is evil. Doctors are the sworn foes of disease. God would not be God if he were not against evil.

When God forbids something, he does so with our best interest at heart. When God requires us to do something, it is always for our good and for the good of others. Thus, Christ convicts about all attitudes and actions that are destructive to either ourselves or to others.

Only a hopeless egotist would be so conceited as to say that he had already eliminated all evil from his life and had arrived at the highest possible moral excellence.

III. Christ is always present to counsel.

There is a recurring refrain throughout these epistles to the church: "He that hath an ear, let him hear what the spirit saith unto the churches." Throughout these epistles, specific instructions are given to individual churches concerning changes that should be made. As we come together for worship and witness, for prayer and praise, the living Lord who is always present would not only speak to us collectively, but also individually.

    A. *He will counsel us concerning character.*

    B. *He will give us counsel concerning our companions and family opportunities and responsibilities.*

    C. *He will give us counsel concerning the choice and conduct of our professional career.*

IV. Christ is present to comfort and to cheer.

    A. *Over and over our Lord counseled his disciples to have faith rather than to surrender to their fears.* He convinced them that the life of faith was the life of victory.

    B. *Not only did our Savior bring courage, confidence, and cheer into the hearts of the disciples as they faced life, but he also gave to them comfort and hope as they faced the experience of death.* By his resurrection from the dead, he assured them that death was not the end. He gave to them a demonstration of the reality of life eternal.

Conclusion

With the promise of a marvelous companion, the Lord is present to command. He has promised to be with us in all of our ways throughout all of our days, always as we obey him. He will be with us in days of sunshine and in days of shadow. He will be with us in days of strength and days of weakness. He will be with us in the day of battle and in the day of victory.

The precious promise of his abiding presence was not designed as a sedative to create a complacent conscience. It was given to provide us with an incentive to give ourselves without reservation in worship and service to God.

WEDNESDAY EVENING, MARCH 26

Title: "Thy Kingdom Come"

Text: "Thy kingdom come" (**Matt. 6:10**).

Introduction

In teaching his disciples to pray, "Thy kingdom come," Jesus instructed them to pray for the most magnificent blessing the world can receive. This is a prayer for the rule of Christ to be active, effective, and triumphant in every area of our lives. The answering of this prayer would have an effect upon our attitudes, our actions, and our ambitions.

By this petition the Master Teacher instructs us to pray for the extinction of all tyranny whether in individuals or in multitudes. If we truly offer this petition, we are praying for the exposure and destruction of all corruption—both inward and outward. Our Lord would have us to pray for truth and righteousness to be supreme in all parts of government, art, science, and social life. By offering this petition, we send a cry up to God for help in our personal efforts to do his will on earth even as it is done in heaven.

Today millions of Christians can *say* this disciples' prayer, of which "Thy kingdom come" is one of the seven petitions. Nevertheless, only a very few have learned how to *pray* it. This petition implies not a blind fatalism, but rather a vibrant, victorious faith in the ultimate victory of God.

I. Jesus and the kingdom.

At the age of twelve, Jesus visited Jerusalem with Joseph and Mary. While he was there, he entered into the temple and sat in the midst of the teachers of the Law, both hearing them and asking them questions, and all who heard him were astonished at his understanding and answers. When Mary and Joseph found him there, Mary asked him to explain his actions, and he replied, "Wist ye not that I must be about my Father's business?" Having so answered, he rejoined them and returned to Nazareth where he remained until he was thirty years of age.

One night Jesus locked the door of the carpenter shop for the last time. He must be about his "Father's business." That business was to bring God's kingdom on earth. The text of his first sermon was, "The kingdom of heaven is at hand" (Matt. 4:17). The kingdom of God was the one theme of his preaching throughout his earthly ministry. On every occasion he spoke to his disciples about the kingdom of God, and even on the resurrection side of the grave he continued to discuss it with them.

II. God on a throne.

By this petition, "Thy kingdom come," Jesus calls our attention to the fact that God occupies the throne of the universe. When we think of a kingdom, it is natural for us to think also of the king. Before instructing his disciples to pray for the coming of the kingdom, Jesus revealed the nature of the king in the statement "Our Father which art in heaven." While the God to whom we pray is high and holy, sovereign and supreme, Jesus taught his disciples to think of the King of the universe as their heavenly Father.

There are in the minds of men many erroneous notions concerning God. Some see only one side of his nature, and consequently, their opinions are warped. Many think of him only in terms of his being a sovereign Lord, the Creator, the Ruler of the earth. They think of service to him in terms of slavish labor. They think of reluctant submission to one mightier than themselves. They fear that surrendering to him will call for a sullen resignation to a blind fate and to the painful execution of unwelcome duties. They fail to realize that when a person first prays this prayer in faith, the miracle of the new birth takes place and they become children of God; they acquire a new nature that brings them into a relationship with God in which they delight in the law of the Lord.

Service is motivated by love and gratitude. The Lord Jesus Christ urges us to pray for the coming of the kingdom of a loving and good God whose will is perfect.

III. Make it personal.

The Bible speaks of the kingdom of God as a thing of the past, a reality in the present, and a prospect in the future. God has been working to bring about his rule of love among people in the past. God is seeking to lead people to accept his will for their lives in the present. The Bible points forward to a day when God's will will be done perfectly by all the redeemed after the consummation of this age.

This is an evangelistic petition, for by praying it we are asking for the salvation of those about us.

This is a missionary petition, for by praying it we are asking for the salvation of a lost world.

This is a dedicatory petition, for the one who truly offers this prayer pledges to cooperate with the will of God as he or she comes to understand it. We must not be content to pray, "Thy kingdom go," which is a rather inexpensive petition, but if we would see God's kingdom come and his will be done on earth as it is by the angels in heaven, we must let his work be done in our hearts.

When God's grace and mercy are considered, it should be easy for us to pray, "Thy kingdom come." His way is always the best way. His way, ultimately at least, is always the happiest way.

Conclusion

This is a prayer that we should pray constantly. It is a petition that we should offer before the throne of grace daily. Cheerfully, we should offer this petition because of the blessings it will bring to our own lives and to the lives of others. Perhaps the most important thought that should come to us is that this is a prayer that we need to pray immediately.

SUNDAY MORNING, MARCH 30

Title: "He Goeth before You"

Text: "But go your way, tell his disciples and Peter that he goeth before you into Galilee: there shall ye see him, as he said unto you" (**Mark 16:7**).

Hymns: "The Day of Resurrection," Neale

"I Know That My Redeemer Liveth," Pounds

"Lead On, O King Eternal," Shurtleff

Offertory Prayer: Holy Father, help us during this service to receive every blessing that you have provided for us. Help us to give ourselves and all that we are to you. Accept our tithes and offerings as tangible expressions of our gratitude and stewardship. Bless these offerings to the coming of your kingdom into the hearts and lives of other men and women, boys and girls. In the name of Jesus we pray. Amen.

Introduction

Great spiritual benefit can come to those who by faith will visit the empty tomb and discover the reality that ours is a living Savior. The resurrection of Jesus Christ from the dead transformed an indescribable tragedy into a wonderful triumph.

The death of Christ on the cross afflicted his disciples with a great personal sorrow. They were crushed with grief. To the disciples the crucifixion of the Savior was a great political disappointment. They had focused their patriotic hopes on him for political freedom and for national deliverance from the tyranny of Rome.

Christ's shameful death on the cross was nothing short of the greatest public tragedy that they had ever experienced. Jesus had been condemned by the religious courts; then Pilate, the Roman governor, had authorized Christ's death by crucifixion. Their leader had been thus exposed to official public ridicule and condemnation to death.

Only as these facts are recognized can one even begin to understand the trembling amazement and excitement that captured their intellect and emotions when they discovered that the Savior had conquered death and the grave. They responded with both fear and faith to the angelic announcement that "he goeth before you into Galilee: there shall ye see him, as he said unto you" (Mark 16:7).

I. The triumphant Savior.

Christ's resurrection was more than just the raising of one to life again. It was a creative act of God in which the deity of Jesus Christ was declared and his victory over the forces of evil was affirmed.

A. *The resurrection declared Jesus to be triumphant over wickedness in high places:*
1. In Jerusalem.
2. In Rome.

B. *Triumphant over sin.*
C. *Triumphant over Satan.*
D. *Triumphant over death and the grave.*

II. Spiritual power available.

The resurrection of Jesus Christ was wrought by the power of God. The power utilized in raising him back to life is made available to his followers for the advancement of his kingdom.

A. *The exceeding greatness of his power toward us.* "And what is the exceeding greatness of his power to usward who believe, according to the working of his mighty power, which he wrought in Christ, when he raised him from the dead, and set him at his own right hand in the heavenly places" (Eph. 1:19–20).

B. *"Now the God of peace, that brought again from the dead our Lord Jesus, that great shepherd of the sheep, through the blood of the everlasting covenant, make you perfect in every good work to do his will, working in you that which is well-pleasing in his sight, through Jesus Christ; to whom be glory for ever and ever" (Heb. 13:20–21).*

C. *"Jesus came and spake unto them, saying, All power is given unto me in heaven and in earth" (Matt. 28:18).*

We make a fatal mistake if we assume that we must carry on God's work in human strength alone. Through the power revealed in the resurrection, which became available in the church on a permanent basis on the day of Pentecost, the Christian is to follow the living Lord.

III. The angelic announcement is still relevant: "He goeth before you."

The transcendent but ever-present Lord continues to draw near to us. He continues to go before us if we obey his commands of love. He promised, "For where two or three are gathered together in my name, there am I in the midst of them" (Matt. 18:20).

In the Great Commission he declared, "I am with you alway, even unto the end of the world" (Matt. 28:20).

A. *He will lead us to the mountaintop of prayer (Luke 9:28).*
B. *He will lead us into the valley to serve (Luke 9:37–42).*
C. *He will be with us to provide warning and strength for the time of temptation (1 Cor. 10:13).*
D. *He will come and provide comfort in our time of sorrow (John 11:23–26).*
E. *Finally, he will receive his people into the mansions of God (John 14:1–6).*

Conclusion

By his presence, the Savior would challenge us both to a greater faith and to a greater faithfulness. If we can but respond to his living presence, Bible study will be more delightful, worship will be more vital, prayer will be more exciting, service will be more challenging, and sacrifice will be more significant.

This living Savior offers to one and to all the double offer of forgiveness and new life if you will but turn from the life of no faith to repentance and then receive him by faith as the Lord of your life.

SUNDAY EVENING, MARCH 30

Title: The Promise of His Personal Return

Text: "And, behold, I come quickly; and my reward is with me, to give every man according as his work shall be" **(Rev. 22:12)**.

Introduction

The last chapter of the New Testament is a most significant one, for in the twenty-one verses that constitute this chapter, there are three clear promises of the Savior to return to the earth for his own. They are found in Revelation 22:7, 12, and 20. It appears that our Lord wanted to impress upon his disciples that he would return.

There are differences of opinion concerning the events surrounding the second coming of Christ. It would seem wise for us to forget some of our theories and concentrate on the central fact that our Lord has promised to return and that his coming is imminent.

Following our Lord's ascension, his disciples anticipated and eagerly longed for the return of the Lord. With great zeal for his kingdom, they labored in the daily hope that he would appear and fully establish the kingdom of God on earth. I am persuaded that if twentieth-first-century Christians properly understood the love of God and his redemptive purpose, they would have the same eagerness as the apostle John did for the Lord's return (Rev. 22:20).

I. The promise of his coming.

    A. *The central theme of Old Testament prophecy is the first advent of the Savior.*

    B. *The most often mentioned event in the New Testament is the second coming of Christ.* It is referred to over three hundred times. One of each twenty-five verses deals with it.

    C. *Christ promised to return (John 14:1–3).*

    D. *The apostles repeatedly made reference to the Lord's return (1 Thess. 4:13–18).*

    E. *The angels said that Christ would return (Acts 1:11).*

II. The program of his coming.

    A. *It will be personal (1 Thess. 4:16).*

    B. *It will be visible to all (Acts 1:11; Rev. 1:7).*

    C. *It will be sudden (Matt. 24:44).*

    D. *It will be mysterious (2 Peter 3:10).*

    E. *It will be triumphant (Matt. 24:30).*

He came at first in lowliness,
  but he will return in great dignity.
He came at first in poverty,
  but he will return in wealth.
He came the first time alone;
  he will return with all his holy angels.
He came the first time in weakness;
  he will return in great power.
He came the first time in humiliation;
  he will return in great exaltation.
When he was here before, he was "despised and rejected of men,"
  but when he returns, every knee will bow before him
  and every tongue shall confess his lordship.
                              —*Author unknown*

III. The purpose of his coming.

A. *Christ will raise the dead and transform the living (1 Cor. 15:51–54).*
B. *Christ will exercise final judgment upon the deeds of men and their response to his offer of mercy through his redemptive work on the cross (Acts 17:31).*
   1. It will be a time of reward (Rev. 22:12).
   2. It will be a time of reunion (1 Thess. 4:14).
   3. It will be a time of separation (Matt. 25:31–46).

IV. Preparation for his coming.

A. *The saved.* Jesus encouraged his disciples to be alert and responsive to the will of God if we would be completely ready (Matt. 24:42–51). Careful attention should be given to the matter of our personal habits and to the service we should be rendering to others.
B. *The unsaved.* The unsaved are not ready for the Lord's return. Their greatest need is to recognize Jesus as their one hope and as the one whom God appointed Savior and Lord. If they would be ready, they must first respond in repentance and faith (Acts 17:30–31).

Conclusion

People are able to live the abundant life only when they have made the necessary preparation to meet the issues of eternity. While the Lord may delay his coming for decades, the fact remains that each of us could meet him at any moment through the doorway of death. While preparation pays off in every area of life, there is no place where preparation pays off so richly as in the matter of a person being ready to meet his or her Maker. Today is the day of salvation.

APRIL

- **Sunday Mornings**

    Continue the series "Following the Living Lord."

- **Sunday Evenings**

    Begin a series titled "The Person and Work of the Holy Spirit in the Early Church."

- **Wednesday Evenings**

    Continue the series on prayer.

WEDNESDAY EVENING, APRIL 2

Title: "Thy Will Be Done"

Text: "Thy will be done in earth, as it is in heaven" (**Matt. 6:10**).

Introduction

A seminary student was at least honest when he filled out a questionnaire to provide information concerning his experience and preferences for a profile to be used in helping him locate his first pastorate. One question asked, "Where would you like to locate?" In reply the seminary student said, "Anywhere the Lord leads—in Georgia."

We must understand the nature of God's will. Jesus thought of the will of God as the sovereign wisdom and justice and goodness by which all things are governed. This is an utter contrast to the attitude that considers the will of God to be that which a cold, cruel fate imposes. Some associate the will of God only with tragedy, when in reality the will of God is something to be embraced rather than endured.

We put too much confidence in our own wisdom. The heavenly Father does not wish to crush our will and make us into slaves. Instead, he wants to eliminate the discord and the destructive tensions of life and to enable us to live a life of harmony and beauty. To surrender to his will is to purify, exalt, and enrich our will.

We fear God's will because we fail to take the long look and recognize that life does not cease when death comes. God sees on both sides of the curtain that we call death.

Wise parents insist that children be studious. These parents know the value of preparation by experience. The principles and guide rules these parents establish for their children are not indications of a desire to restrict the development and suppress the happiness of their children, but rather to bring out the best that the children are capable of doing. Even so it is with the will of the heavenly Father.

I. A confession that we have departed from God's will.

If we would properly understand the petition "Thy will be done in earth as it is in heaven," we must confess that we have departed from God's will. "All we like sheep have gone astray; we have turned every one to his own way; and the LORD hath laid on him the iniquity of us all" (Isa. 53:6). We have departed from God's will in our conversation, our conduct, our choices, and our careers.

This confession acknowledges that our failures and frustrations are the result of our ignoring God's will. Here is the real cause for our inward unrest, our frustrations, our recurring unhappiness.

By praying this prayer, we acknowledge humankind's responsibility for the mess in which the world finds itself.

II. God has a will for this earth.

God is no absentee God who created the world and then forsook it to its own fate. While he is sovereign and supreme above the universe, he is very present in our world.

The universe itself is constantly obedient to the will of the Creator. The clouds float through the sky in peaceful obedience to his will. The stars burn and glisten against the night according to his will. The planets roll in their mighty orbits and revolutions according to his will.

The angelic hosts perfectly obey the will of God in heaven. There is no interruption in their obedience because of sin. No resistance to his will because of temptation. No flaw in the doing of his will because of weariness. No pain or guilt in their actions because of a rebellious will. The obedience of the angelic host is free, constant, spontaneous, and happy.

The heavenly pattern of submission to the will of God is to be our pattern here on this earth. To the degree that we follow the heavenly pattern of submission to the will of God, to that same degree we cooperate with God in the bringing of his kingdom here on earth. He would have us to experience the holy happiness and harmony of a heavenly life here. This is the abundant life that Jesus Christ is eager to make a reality for each of us.

It is with this purpose in mind that Jesus sets before us the proper pattern for our prayer habits. Our first concern is to be with God's will, God's way, and God's work. When God's will, and God's way, and God's work have their proper place in our attitudes, ambitions, and actions, the deepest needs of our lives will have already been supplied.

When Jesus taught his disciples to pray, "Thy will be done in earth, as it is in heaven," he was giving them the divine blueprint by which they were to build a significant life of achievement that would bring complete satisfaction to their hearts and lives.

III. The plea behind the petition.

This petition is a plea for help in making the divine will a regulator of our attitudes. The disciples were encouraged to pray for divine help in bringing the crookedness of their thinking into harmony with the straightness of the mind and heart of God. Behind this plea is a cry for help in letting the divine will become the standard and rule for all of our ambitions. The disciples were encouraged to pray for divine assistance until they sought to make the divine will the road map for all of their future activities.

Conclusion

The will of God is done constantly in heaven without failure. Joyfully and without weariness, the angels carry out God's wishes, desiring only the glory of God. The angels serve with humility. Without hesitation the will of God is done instantly in heaven. If we would experience the delights of the heavenly life in the here and now, we need to pray sincerely and regularly, "Thy will be done in earth, as it is in heaven," and at the same time promise to do God's good will as we understand it.

SUNDAY MORNING, APRIL 6

Title: The Living Lord Draws Near

Text: "It came to pass, that, while they communed together, and reasoned, Jesus himself drew near, and went with them" **(Luke 24:15)**.

Hymns: "Our Lord Christ Hath Risen," Plunket

"I Know That My Redeemer Liveth," Pounds

"Close to Thee," Crosby

Offertory Prayer: Our Father, this is the day you have made. We will rejoice and be glad in it. We come to bring an offering of our substance to you. Accept these tithes and offerings and bless them in the ministries and growth of your kingdom. In Jesus' name we pray. Amen.

Introduction

Our Scripture lesson reveals the sad fact of human blindness to divine nearness. Although the risen Christ is everywhere present, we may not be able to see him or recognize his presence at all times.

This record of two disciples' journeying to Emmaus carries with it many important teachings. It brings before us how the risen Christ in a special sense draws near to each one of us; how he adds himself to the two or three gathered together in his name; how he journeys with us; how he enlightens our reason and fires our affections; how he abides under the shelter of our dwellings; how at some supreme moment, it may be, he allows us to see, with the eyes of the spirit, a brief vision of his majesty.

The disciples learned that first Easter that they were not left with just the memory of a dear Lord. They were to walk in intimate fellowship with the living Lord who had conquered death and the grave. He was and continues to be all that he had been and even more. They discovered in his presence a warmth, a graciousness, and a power superior even to that which they had felt before his crucifixion.

I. The living Christ draws near to us now, as to those unknown wayfarers, with purposes of love.

A. *These two disciples on the way to Emmaus were disappointed and despondent.* The future indeed looked dark. An uncharted and unpromising road loomed up in front of them. They had placed their faith in Jesus Christ for pardon, peace, power, and a purpose for the future. His death on the cross and burial in a tomb had plunged them into despair.

B. *He who was infinite, indescribable love was near to them as they walked toward their home to press into their hearts the peace, and power, and purpose for living that they thought was gone forever.* With love, he drew near to them to quiet their fears, to instruct their minds, to increase their faith, and to restore their hope and confidence. Even so, he would come and walk the road of life with us today.

II. The living Christ draws near to us when we assemble together in his name.

"Where two or three are gathered together in my name, there am I in the midst of them" (Matt. 18:20).

A. *Those who neglect to assemble themselves together with the church deprive themselves of an enriching and transfiguring experience with the living Lord (Heb. 10:25).*

B. *God comes to meet with his people.* Such has always been the case. God wants to dwell in the midst of his people and walk and talk with them. The living Christ who walked "in the midst" of the seven golden lampstands wants to speak to our minds, warm our hearts, and mold our wills to harmonize with the truth that sets us free from sin and failure.

C. *The living Christ comes into the midst of his people to commend deeds well done.* He comes to complain concerning our shortcomings and our ways of self-destruction. He also comes to counsel, to challenge, to command, and to cheer according to the riches of God's grace and according to the deepest needs of his people.

III. The living Christ draws near to us when we give ourselves to the study of God's Word.

"And beginning at Moses and all the prophets, he expounded unto them in all the scriptures the things concerning himself.... Then opened he their understanding, that they might understand the scriptures" (Luke 24:27, 45).

Only Jesus Christ gives meaning to the Scriptures. Only as we let the Holy Spirit lead and guide our thinking will we be able to understand the great truths of God. Many attempt to read and to understand the Scriptures without any thought for divine guidance and assistance. But if faith comes by hearing and hearing by the Word of God, then it follows that God will speak to our hearts as we read his Word. Christ will speak authoritatively to our lives as we give ourselves to the study of his written words in the New Testament. To neglect God's Word is to impoverish our own spiritual life. The living Christ would speak to us and give us words of guidance and hope and cheer if we will reverently and prayerfully study the divine truth.

IV. The living Christ draws near to us in our homes.

"But they constrained him, saying, Abide with us; for it is toward evening, and the day is far spent. And he went in to tarry with them" (Luke 24:29).

    A. *These were average, ordinary believers to whom the Christ appeared and with whom he walked.* When they invited him to come into their home, he responded, and they had as their guest the very Lord of heaven and earth.

    B. *The living Christ will come into our homes and bless us as we face the common duties, responsibilities, and opportunities of life.* He would assist parents who seek to provide a spiritual atmosphere conducive to the moral and religious development of their children. He would guide children and young people as they make the choices that will determine their destinies.

V. The risen Christ draws near to us as we seek to serve a needy world.

    A. *In meeting the physical and spiritual needs of those about us, we are actually rendering service to the Christ.* "Inasmuch as ye have done it unto the least of these my brethren, ye have done it unto me" (Matt. 25:40). Very few of us realize that a service in the name of Christ is actually a service to Christ. Many opportunities come to us for fellowship with him as he uses our time and resources to render ministries of mercy to those about us.

    B. *This living Christ has promised to be near to us and even with us as we bear a Christian witness to the unbelievers about us (Matt. 28:20).* The promise of his presence is made to those who in their going about from place to place seek to persuade others to become his disciples. This promise and command are inseparably linked together.

VI. The risen Christ draws near to us in the time of trial and in the hour of death.

The journey from Jerusalem to Emmaus is an allegory of many a life, both in its apparent sadness and in its final joy.

    A. *While the road ahead may seem bright and sunny with much promise of success, sooner or later there will be sickness and sorrow, troubles, and eventually death itself.*

B. *The living Lord, who is the same yesterday, today, and forever, will come to us and will walk the road of life with us to provide us with counsel, comfort, and cheer.*
C. *By the resurrection from the dead, Christ assures us that death itself is a defeated foe and the grave will have no final victory over us.*

Conclusion

If you would have this living Christ to draw near to you, to meet the deepest needs of your heart and life, and to bless you with the gifts of heaven, then you should draw near to him now. Trust him for the forgiveness of all sin. Receive him that you might receive the gift of new life. As the days go by, develop a warm friendship with him, and you will discover that he has given you the abundant life in the here and now that will be more perfectly realized in the life beyond this life.

SUNDAY EVENING, APRIL 6

Title: The Promise of the Holy Spirit

Text: "And it shall come to pass afterward, that I will pour out my spirit upon all flesh; and your sons and your daughters shall prophesy, your old men shall dream dreams, your young men shall see visions" (**Joel 2:28**).

Introduction

The Bible contains many rich promises from God to his people. Our lives will be greatly impoverished if we do not discover these promises and claim them for our own lives.

The Old Testament focuses primarily on promises concerning the coming of the Messiah who is to be the Savior. There are also a number of promises concerning the coming of the Holy Spirit that were to find their fulfillment in that which took place on the day of Pentecost. With great profit we need to look to these promises that we might enter into our full inheritance as the children of God.

I. The promise of the Father through the prophet Joel.

We read a promise concerning the outpouring of the Holy Spirit upon the church: "And it shall come to pass afterward, that I will pour out my spirit upon all flesh; and your sons and your daughters shall prophesy, your old men shall dream dreams, your young men shall see visions: And also upon the servants and upon the handmaids in those days will I pour out my Spirit" (Joel 2:28–29). The word "afterward" in this passage is very significant. It refers to an experience in the future concerning all of the children of God that was not true at the time when Joel was writing.

In Old Testament times the Holy Spirit came upon individuals to endow them with ability and strength for a special task. He came as a unique gift from God to enable them to render a needed service.

A. *The Spirit of God came upon Gideon, and he was led to blow the trumpet and call the people to arms against the Midianites (Josh. 6:3–4).* The Spirit enabled him to be a judge, a deliverer, a military leader for Israel.

B. *The Spirit of God came upon Samson and blessed him with mighty muscular power by which he broke the bands that imprisoned him (Judg. 15:14).* He fought against the Philistines and achieved a great victory because of the gift of the Spirit.

C. *The Spirit of God came upon Saul and filled him with righteous indignation because of the cruel purpose of the Ammonites against the people of Jabesh-Gilead (1 Sam. 11:6).* Saul issued a call to arms and led them to victory and became Israel's deliverer. Later in his life, we read that following his disobedience, "the Spirit of the LORD departed from Saul, and an evil spirit from the LORD troubled him" (16:14).

D. *From the day when Samuel anointed David to be the future king of Israel, the Spirit of God came upon him (1 Sam. 16:13).* Later, after David had committed great sin, we hear him in his prayer of confession making a plea for forgiveness, adding, "take not thy holy spirit from me" (Ps. 51:11). David was standing in holy horror of the possibility that he was going to experience the same fate as did Saul. David knew from observation the agony that Saul had experienced because he had been forsaken by the Spirit. As a shepherd lad with great musical ability, he had been invited to the palace of Saul to try to soothe his distressed nerves with beautiful music. He prayed that he might be spared that awful fate.

Through Joel, God promised that in a later era he would pour out his Spirit upon all flesh. This is to be a new departure in the activity of God.

II. The promise of the Savior.

As the Savior approached the end of his public ministry, he began to inform the apostles of the necessity of his substitutionary death on the cross. They were greatly disturbed and cast down by this sad news. They could not understand, and so they rebelled against the idea.

Not only did he promise them a heavenly home at the end of the way (John 14:1–3), but he also promised them the gift of the Holy Spirit.

Our Savior sought to instruct them, to comfort them, and to assure them that the future was not going to be as they feared. Consider Jesus' promises in John 4:16–18:

A. *"I will pray to the Father."* The Holy Spirit is to come as an answer to the prayer of the Son to the Father. Actually, the Holy Spirit is the gift of the Father to the Son following his crucifixion, resurrection, and ascension to the Father (Acts 2:33).

B. *"Another Comforter."* Both of these words are very significant. When Jesus speaks of a Comforter, he is not talking about a person who would come to you in a time of sorrow to wipe away tears of grief. The word translated

"Comforter" literally means "one called to walk by the side of." Jesus had walked by their side for more than three years. Their lives had been inseparably united with each other.

The word "another" is also a significant word. The language of the New Testament contains two words, both of which are correctly translated "another." The word *allos* means "another of the same kind." Jesus, when talking about the Comforter, "one called to work by the side of," uses the word *allos*—another of the same kind as himself.

C. *"That he may abide with you forever."* In contrast to the brief three-and-a-half-year ministry of the Savior, the Holy Spirit is to abide with the disciples forever, as long as the ages roll.

D. *"Whom the world cannot receive."* The word "receive" can also be translated "seize" or "arrest." It is so translated concerning the action of the soldiers when they came and arrested Jesus in the Garden of Gethsemane. The Savior is actually promising to his disciples a Comforter of the same kind as he is, which the wicked, ungodly world will not be able to seize or arrest or crucify on the cross. This will be the case because the Holy Spirit will dwell within the heart and life of each child of God.

This precious promise from the Savior tells us that the Spirit of the eternal God is to dwell within each of us. God is as close to us as our breath. "Know ye not that ye are the temple of God, and that the Spirit of God dwelleth in you?" (1 Cor. 3:16).

Conclusion

Have you responded to this great truth with reverent faith? Today it is more wonderful to have the Holy Spirit within each individual heart than it would be to have the physical presence of Jesus Christ as he was during his earthly ministry. Respond to the fulfillment of this promise of the Savior with reverent humility and faith. Cooperate with the divine Spirit, for he seeks to reproduce the character and disposition of Christ in your life. Follow his leadership as he guides you in both witnessing and working for our Lord.

WEDNESDAY EVENING, APRIL 9

Title: "Our Daily Bread"

Text: "Give us this day our daily bread" (**Matt. 6:11**).

Introduction

Jesus taught his disciples that God the Father is interested in the bodies as well as the souls of humans. Neither is to be neglected or ignored. Between the prayer of surrender and the prayer of confession, the heavenly Teacher placed the prayer for physical necessities.

Our prayer is to be directed to the heavenly Father whose love wants the best for his children. His wisdom knows what is best for them; his power does that which is best for them.

By this petition Christ encourages us to bring all our needs to the Father, things small and large, things secular and sacred, things material and moral. The particular emphasis in this petition is on physical needs.

I. This petition recognizes God as the giver of daily bread.

We often boast of our high standard of living. We give constant praise to our American system of free enterprise. We often forget that the Giver of all good gifts is our heavenly Father. We are all debtors to the generosity of God.

It is easy to deprive God of the glory that belongs to him at this point. We are not very thankful because we are not very thoughtful. If we sincerely offer this petition, we pledge thankful recognition to God for our blessings.

> *Back of the loaf is the snowy flour,*
> *And back of the flour the mill,*
> *And back of the mill, the wheat, the shower,*
> *The sun and the Father's will.*
> —*Maltbie D. Babcock*

II. This petition requests God's presence in our daily work.

The prayer for daily bread is not an encouragement to idleness, for it does not rule out human effort. Jesus did not encourage anyone to be a parasite.

God is vitally interested in our economic life. Daily bread, and all that this signifies, is necessary if we would have the strength for kingdom service. All prayer would die on our lips if it were not for bread.

The pursuit of bread can cause people to lose sight of the true ends of life. We are to live for the advancement of the kingdom of God rather than for piling up a huge supply of bread. As a Greek proverb says, "We do not live in order to eat, but we eat in order to live."

III. This petition recognizes our brother's need for bread.

Eight times in the prayer we find the words "our," "we," or "us." We are to remember God's children everywhere when we pray. This petition requires that we volunteer to refrain from greedily grasping after that which belongs to another.

Conclusion

By this petition the Savior encourages us to trust our tomorrows into the hands of our heavenly Father. He is capable of providing for us adequately. This wonderful truth could relieve many of our fears and anxieties. The psalmist has said, "I have been young, and now am old; yet have I not seen the righteous forsaken, nor his seed begging bread" (Ps. 37:25). The heavenly Father will surely be in our tomorrows even as he was in our yesterdays.

SUNDAY MORNING, APRIL 13

Title: The Risen Christ Makes Us Happy

Text: "And when he had so said, he shewed unto them his hands and his side. Then were the disciples glad, when they saw the Lord" (**John 20:20**).

Scripture Reading: John 20:19–29

Hymns: "Great Redeemer, We Adore Thee," Harris

"Jesus Lives and Jesus Leads," Hood

"Crown Him with Many Crowns," Bridges

Offertory Prayer: Our heavenly Father, help us to worship you in spirit and in truth this day. Keep our minds concentrated on the many bountiful blessings of life that we might not complain about our circumstances. Help us to remember how you endured hardships and discomforts, perils and dangers, ultimately giving your life that every person who believes in you may have abundant life.

We ask today that you will lead us as we give our money. We acknowledge that you have given us health and strength to earn these material goods. With our tithes we acknowledge that everything we have belongs to you. We adore your name and earnestly desire that through the use of this offering people all over the world will learn of you. We pray this in the name of him who is Lord of all, Jesus Christ. Amen.

Introduction

In the third year of Jesus' ministry, there came a fateful Friday. For three years Jesus had ministered to humankind, and during this time the Jewish leaders sought to put him to death. They finally accomplished their intentions by using unjust accusations. The Jews conspired with the Roman authorities to have Jesus crucified.

After Jesus' death, few people were happy. Pilate, the Roman governor, suffered miserable flashbacks. He knew that he had allowed an innocent man to be crucified. Roman soldiers knew before breath had left Jesus' body that someone more than a man died that Friday. Perhaps Herod tried to erase the memory of Jesus through a night of carousing, but Jesus lingered on his conscience to make him miserable. Each member of the Sanhedrin undoubtedly suffered from guilt. Tired and irritable travelers returned to their homes after the close of the Passover festival. But probably the saddest people in Jerusalem were Jesus' disciples. Their Messiah had died on a cross.

On Sunday evening following that Friday, the risen Christ came to these dejected, disillusioned, and miserable followers. The Bible says, "Then were the disciples glad, when they saw the Lord" (John 20:20). They were glad because the same Jesus who died now visited with them in a live presence. Their dearest friend had returned from the grave.

125

The sad disciples' experience with the risen Lord could mean much to contemporary followers of Jesus. Often the circumstances of life make us unhappy, but when we come into Christ's presence, we can rejoice, for in his presence there is fullness of joy. What really made the difference with the first-century disciples was not an announcement of the resurrection, but the appearance of Jesus. Let us learn some ways that Jesus can make modern disciples happy.

I. The risen Lord deals with our fears.

The circumstances of life bring fear. The disciples assembled in an upper room after Jesus' crucifixion. They feared for their future. Various happenings in life cause Christians to be afraid. Fear takes many forms. We fear losing our job, getting sick, being criticized, growing old, facing death, as well as numerous other things.

Fear brings negative consequences. The disciples could not do what Christ wanted them to do with their raging fear, for fear filled them with negative thoughts and robbed them of maximum efficiency. Fear leads to greater fear. It weakens us and puts us in a position that makes us susceptible to the very thing we fear. But the risen Christ can deal with our fears. To a panic-stricken group, Jesus said, "Peace be unto you" (John 20:19). Jesus provides courage to face fear.

II. The risen Lord develops our faith.

Even though these men had lived intimately with Jesus for three years, their faith was not yet perfect. Jesus had taught them on numerous occasions about his resurrection, but they did not believe. Likewise, our faith is immature. We need to be continuously developing the character of the Master. Modern disciples often fail to claim Jesus' promises. Such neglect robs us of growth experiences in the Lord. Our faith grows as we read the Word and hide God's promises in our hearts. To develop our faith, we must encounter the risen Lord daily.

III. The risen Lord discloses the future.

Many people live in despair over the future. Perhaps the disciples in the upper room talked despairingly of what the future would bring and surrendered to the finality of physical death. Several years ago when archaeologists excavated Roman cemeteries, they noticed that almost all grave markers had seven letters carved on them—NFF NS NC. These are the first letters of the words in four brief sentences familiar to the Roman world—*Non fui. Fui. Non sum. Non curo*—which means, "I was not. I was. I am not. I do not care." Something akin to their feeling may have filled the disciples.

The risen Lord disclosed a glorious future by showing himself alive. He had been crushed to death, but now he stood before the disciples with nail-pierced hands and feet. He arose the Victor from the "dark domain" of death. Because he lives, every one of his followers will live also.

Conclusion

Have you found joy amid the troubled conditions of today's world? You cannot find happiness apart from the risen Lord. Seek Jesus' presence today and let him bring happiness to your life. Christ is here! He waits for your openness. As he did for the disciples on that Sunday evening, he can dispel your fears, develop your faith, and disclose a glorious, victorious future after death.

SUNDAY EVENING, APRIL 13

Title: The Presence and Purpose of the Holy Spirit

Text: "And it shall come to pass in the last days, saith God, I will pour out of my Spirit upon all flesh: and your sons and your daughters shall prophesy, and your young men shall see visions, and your old men shall dream dreams" (**Acts 2:17**).

Introduction

An aged Oklahoma farm couple found it difficult to rent a farm on which they could earn a living. When their difficulty was discovered by their son, now a machinist living in the city, he requested that his father look for a farm that was for sale. After several weeks of searching, a quarter section was found. The son purchased it, and by monthly payments over a period of years, the debt was finally eliminated. The parents died, but the son continued to own the farm. In the late 1950s oil was discovered on the property, and the royalties exceeded a thousand dollars per month. The oil had been beneath the surface all along and no one knew about it. The machinist had been a rich man and did not know it.

We who have trusted Jesus Christ are rich beyond our wildest imaginations. The overwhelming majority of us have never even begun to understand or to experience our special legacy or inheritance. The Scripture tells us that all of the resources of God are available to us.

It has been said, "It takes money to make money." This is a truth that is accepted as fact. It is also true that spiritual resources are essential for spiritual achievement and for kingdom advance.

Many of us have entered into the riches of salvation from sin by the way of the cross. Some of us have visited the empty tomb to discover that ours is a living Savior who wants to be our companion along the road of life. Only a few of us have visited the upper room to experience and to understand the full impact of the gift of God at Pentecost.

Some of us have been afraid to investigate this spiritual experience. The Devil has determined to encourage us to bypass this event. Consequently, our spiritual experience has been shallow and superficial. Our understanding of God's plan and purpose has been incomplete. Our service has been unsatisfying, and our efforts at witnessing have been unsuccessful.

I. "What meaneth this?" (Acts 2:12).

    A. *"There came a sound from heaven" (Acts 2:2).* Three times during Jesus' ministry a voice came from heaven expressing divine approval and attestation that Jesus was the Son of God. On the day of Pentecost a sound like a rushing, mighty wind came from heaven. But it was not a wind; it was a sound *like* a rushing, mighty wind.

    B. *"And there appeared unto them cloven tongues like as of fire, and it sat upon each of them" (Acts 2:3).* This appears strange to us, but to the devout Hebrew, it would have been recognized immediately as the appearance of the glory of God. Numerous times in the Old Testament God's presence is manifested with fire. The Angel of the Lord appeared to Moses in a flame of fire out of the midst of a bush that was burned and not consumed (Ex. 3:2). The fire of God fell upon Elijah's offering in the contest with the prophets of Baal (1 Kings 18:36–39). The fire of God fell and consumed David's sacrifice on the altar he built in the threshing floor of Ornan (1 Chron. 21:26–28). Fire came down from heaven and consumed the offerings and sacrifices when Solomon dedicated the temple (2 Chron. 7:1–3). By this means God revealed himself. He endorsed and authenticated Elijah as being a true prophet. At the same time Baal worship was rejected.

        The cloven tongues of fire on the day of Pentecost formed an appearance of the glory of God upon the members of the church which the Lord had commissioned and commanded to tarry until they received the promise of the Father.

    C. *They were all filled with the Holy Spirit, and they began to speak with other tongues declaring the wonderful works of God.* People from fifteen countries heard them speak in terms that were intelligible. They understood them as they proclaimed the wonderful works of God.

II. "Be this known unto you" (Acts 2:14).

Peter repudiated the explanation that the members of the church were drunk. He declared that they were witnessing a unique fulfillment of Old Testament prophecy before their eyes. As the angels had announced to the shepherds that a Savior had been born, even so Peter announces that the Holy Spirit, promised through Joel the prophet and Jesus the Christ, had come to dwell in the church to begin a ministry that would continue until the end of the ages.

III. "This is that" (Acts 2:16).

Peter announces to all who are concerned that the divine successor whom Joel and Jesus had promised had actually made his appearance.

    A. *The Comforter had come.* Repeatedly Jesus had spoken concerning the coming of the Comforter (John 14:16, 26; 15:26; 16:7, 13).

    B. *The Teacher had come.* Jesus had promised his disciples that when the Comforter did come, "He shall teach you all things, and bring all things to your remembrance, whatsoever I have said unto you" (John 14:26). The Holy

Spirit teaches only the things of Christ, yet he teaches more than Christ taught. He reveals the universal scope of the gospel.

C. *The Reprover had come (John 16:7–8).* Only the divine Spirit of God can bring about conviction of sin in the heart of an unbeliever and reveal his deep personal need for the forgiveness of sin and for the gift of new life.

D. *The Energizer had come.* Jesus had commanded his disciples to tarry in Jerusalem until they received the Holy Spirit (Luke 24:49). From the day of Pentecost the servants of Christ labored with supernatural energy.

Conclusion

The Holy Spirit who began his ministry in the church on the day of Pentecost is as close to the heart of the redeemed as the air we breathe. It is unnecessary for us to pray that he come to us. He has already arrived. We need to recognize his presence and fully surrender ourselves in cooperative activity with him as he leads day by day. Let us not be guilty of grieving him by ignoring him. Let us trust him to do what only God can do as we seek faithfully to do what we can do as we sow the gospel seeds of divine truth in the soil of the hearts of those about us. As the farmers trust the sun to germinate the seed planted in the soil, let us sow the gospel message and trust the Holy Spirit to bring about the birth of new life as people respond to Jesus Christ in faith.

WEDNESDAY EVENING, APRIL 16

Title: "Forgive Us Our Debts"

Text: "Forgive us our debts, as we forgive our debtors" **(Matt. 6:12)**.

Introduction

Christ the Lord gave his disciples a perfect pattern for the prayers we are to offer to the heavenly Father. This pattern should be studied closely and followed correctly.

There is a very significant conjunction in this perfect pattern for prayer. The word "and" links the petition for daily bread to the confession of sin and the plea for pardon. "Give us this day our daily bread. *And* forgive us our debts, as we forgive our debtors." The suggestion is that just as we need to go to him for daily bread for daily needs, even so we should go to him for daily forgiveness for daily sin. As the physical body is nourished by food and needs to be renewed in vitality day by day, even so the spiritual nature needs to be made clean and white by confession and cleansing every day.

I. This plea for pardon acknowledges sinfulness.

This is one petition that our Savior never needed to offer for himself. He alone has lived a life without sin. Not only have all of us sinned in the past but we are also sinners in the present. In spite of the fact that some deny, ignore, excuse, or seek to conceal sin, its reality continues to be painfully present. Sin sears the conscience and brings about a breach of fellowship between the child and the Father. Only when sin is confessed and forsaken can the fellowship be restored and enjoyed.

II. This plea would encourage us to deal drastically with our debts.

Each of us needs to recognize the nature of our sin and reflect on the consequences of our rebellion and our disobedience. We need to face up to our unmet obligations toward God, toward others, and toward self. We need to pray, "Father, let me know the measure of my debt and guilt," because sin in the heart is a malignant force that affects the lives of those about us.

The spirit of this petition calls for an attitude of grief over past failures that will lead to positive and constructive action in both the present and the future.

III. This plea for pardon includes others.

We need not only to confess our individual sins but also to lift the debts of others before God for forgiveness. Moses, Nehemiah, Isaiah, and our Lord prayed that the sins of others might be forgiven.

We are sinners collectively as well as individually. Our nation today is in great social turmoil because of the collective greed and selfishness of our forefathers. We are part of a society that permits and tolerates that for which we would not want to assume individual responsibility.

IV. This plea reveals the divine strategy for heavenly happiness on earth.

If we would experience the forgiveness of God, we must forgive those who have sinned against us. God wants to deal with each of us on the basis of forgiveness. To forgive is more than to ignore or to forget an offense. To forgive means to "hold it against him no longer" and to restore a broken relationship with warm feelings. To forgive is to remember and yet at the same time not to carry a grudge.

Divine forgiveness is possible for all who will repent, confess, and forsake their evil ways.

Human forgiveness is essential if we would purge our hearts of the malice, hatred, and desire for revenge that poison our joy. To have an unforgiving spirit blocks the channel by which we experience the peace and happiness of divine forgiveness.

When Jesus counseled the disciples that they must be willing to forgive until seven times seven (Matt. 18:21–22), he was pointing out the absolute necessity of the offended party eliminating from his or her own heart the poison and hatred that corrode and destroy the human spirit.

Conclusion

Our Lord knew that each day his disciples had need of forgiveness. He also knew that every day they would need to forgive others. Consequently, he linked together in an inseparable way the plea for pardon with the promise to forgive. God has forgiven us. It is possible by his help for us to forgive both ourselves and those who sin against us. After we forgive, we will begin to experience some of the joys of heaven on earth.

SUNDAY MORNING, APRIL 20

Title: Appearance by the Sea

Text: "Jesus showed himself again to the disciples at the sea of Tiberias" (**John 21:1**).

Scripture Reading: John 21:1–19

Hymns: "Praise to God, Immortal Praise," Barbauld

"Rejoice, the Lord Is King," Wesley

"Is Your All on the Altar?" Hoffman

Offertory Prayer: By your providence, O Lord, we are placed on a kindly earth. We confess that our actions sometimes spoil the heritage you have given us. Make our hearts tender to care for the needy, and make our minds strong to solve the problems that frustrate us. Consecrate these offerings that your name and your ways may be known and loved, through Jesus Christ our Lord. Amen.

Introduction

It is difficult for us to feel what Jesus' disciples felt in their sense of utter defeat at Calvary and the joy of triumph in his resurrection appearances. We know the end of the story by the time we know the beginning. But for those who experienced it initially, it was a time of great suspense and surprise, sorrow and joy. Never have human beings felt such a wide range of emotions in so short a space of time as they passed from the depth of despair to a victory that defied comprehension.

Jesus had risen from the dead. The disciples had seen him and heard him speak. Yet as the postresurrection days stacked themselves upon each other, they seemed to have found themselves with time on their hands. Peter made the simple announcement, "I'm going fishing," and six other disciples said in essence, "Me too."

The disciples' night of hard work on the open sea of Galilee was fruitless. In the early dawn, they saw someone standing on the shore whom they took to be a stranger. He called out a greeting and, either from his vantage point or from supernatural knowledge, he gave instructions for the next net casting. Following his advice, they made a great catch of fish. Bringing their catch to the shore, they recognized the risen Christ.

Jesus' postresurrection appearance by the sea and the circumstances of the disciples' great catch are beautiful suggestions that life is not all tragedy, that we can engage in purposeful activity that makes sense. But there is more than symbolism and analogy here. Three accomplishments may have been intended through this appearance by the sea.

I. Reality of the resurrection.

Many people said that the appearances of the risen Christ were nothing more than visions the disciples had. Jesus' sudden appearance behind locked doors and his disappearance in the same manner added to the mystery. The Gospels go far out of their way to establish the fact of an empty tomb and a risen Christ who had a body that still bore the marks of the nails and the sword thrust in his side.

Jesus' appearance by the sea adds to the firmness of the resurrection foundation. Jesus pointed out a place to cast their nets. He had kindled a charcoal fire and already had begun to cook fish before the disciples reached shore. Such things as these certainly could not have been the figment of someone's imagination; they were not seeing a spirit or a ghost.

The appearance by the sea may well have been a reminder of their calling.

II. Reminder of the disciples' calling.

These seven disciples needed to be reminded of the work to which they had been called. We can imagine the ridicule they faced on the village streets and the puzzlement they had within their own minds. They had seen the risen Lord, he had made them promises, they had been called to high service for him and the world. Yet nothing happened that could give them a "handle to catch on to." Still they waited, and there were more days when they did not see him than days when he appeared. These delays put strain on tired minds.

Quite suddenly, we may guess, Peter announced, "I'm going fishing," and as the others joined him, they got that accustomed feeling of having something to do. What were they thinking as they moved away from the shore? Were they getting a feel for the fisherman's life again? Were they going to turn their backs on the real adventure, to settle down, disillusioned if not outright cynical, contemptuous of their idealism? Was Christ's call to them fading out? Notice what the Scripture has to say.

A. *"That night they caught nothing" (v. 3).* This is more than a note of mere human failure. The Bible makes a good case for the sanctity and dignity of common work, but that is not the point here. For men who are called to serve God vocationally, an occupation of their own choosing different from this, however useful in human estimation, is destined for disappointment.

B. The Scripture goes on to say, *"Just as day was breaking, Jesus stood on the beach; yet the disciples did not know that it was Jesus" (v. 4 RSV).* Note the contrast between night and day. They went their own way during the night, and their efforts were fruitless. Daylight brought revelation and identity. Note also the contrast between the lake and the shore. On the lake they toiled without success. On the solid ground of the shore, Jesus gave rewarding directions and prepared breakfast. Could their failure to recognize Jesus be traced to their failure to follow him?

C. *Jesus asked them while they were out on the lake, "Children, have you any fish?"* They answered him, "No" (v. 5 RSV). The affectionate form of address used here by Jesus suggests his special sympathy for them, his tender, almost fatherly, care for men who had so quickly forgotten their true calling and had come up against the brick wall of failure.

D. *Jesus was preparing breakfast and soon invited them to gather around and eat.* After breakfast Jesus asked Peter three times, "Do you love me?" After the apostle's affirmative reply each time, Jesus said successively, "Tend my lambs," "Shepherd my sheep," and "Tend [or feed] my sheep" (vv. 15–17). The lesson Jesus was teaching them seems to be this: the ministry to which they were called, the apostolic life, required that they learn to trust him to provide for their daily bread.

The renewal and deepening of their call dates from this appearance by the sea. With this experience to look back upon, there will be no more turning aside from the duties of apostleship. Christ's commands here are set in the complex context of fishing and a meal: fishing because the apostles must draw people to Christ, a meal because they must provide for the new converts as he has provided for them.

Joseph Addison Richards has described these experiences of Peter and the disciples in a way that appeals to many of us.

The Master of My Boat

I owned a little boat a while ago,
And sailed the morning sea without a fear,
And whither any breeze might fairly blow
I steered my little craft far or near.
Mine was the boat,
And mine the air,
And mine the sea,
Nor mine a care.
My boat became my place of mighty toil,
I sailed at evening to the fishing ground,
At morn my boat was freighted with the spoil
Which my all-conquering work had found.
Mine was the boat,
And mine the net,
And mine the skill
And power to get.
One day there came along that silent shore,
While I my net was casting in the sea,
A Man who spoke as never man before.
I followed Him; new life began in me,
Mine was the boat,

But His the voice,
And His the call
Yet mine the choice.
Ah! 'twas a fearful night out on the lake,
And all my skill availed not, at the helm,
Till Him asleep I waked, crying,
"Take Thou the helm—lest water overwhelm!"
And His the boat,
And His the sea,
And His the peace
O'er all and me.
Once from the boat He taught the curious throng
Then bade me cast my net into the sea;
I murmured but obeyed, not was it long
Before the catch amazed and humbled me.
His was the boat,
And His the skill,
And His the catch,
And His my will.

Jesus' appearance by the sea made his resurrection more real to the disciples, and it reminded them of their calling.

III. Restatement of the church's function.

A third thing Jesus' appearance accomplished was the restatement of the church's function. Jesus' threefold question to Peter about love cannot be confined to the individual disciple. From it, all of us must learn that the essence of discipleship is love and that the response of that love is service. Love does not ask permission to do good things; it has done them already. The church, to the extent that it is truly Christ's people, loses its life in a ministry to the world. The church should have no time to fuss about itself, its image, or its prestige. The church denies its Lord when it becomes self-centered and pampered, fondling its own achievements, admiring its own righteousness or orthodoxy, caressing its own virtues. The church's function in the world is to be light and salt.

Conclusion

The church is not a reservoir where the Water of Life is stored; it is the spring where the Water of Life arises in the lives of Christ-centered Christians and flows out to others. If you love Christ, you will serve him through a love that reaches out to gather in the sheep and tend the flock of God.

SUNDAY EVENING, APRIL 20

Title: The Power of the Holy Spirit

Text: "But ye shall receive power, after that the Holy Ghost is come upon you: and ye shall be witnesses unto me both in Jerusalem, and in all Judaea, and in Samaria, and unto the uttermost part of the earth" **(Acts 1:8)**.

Introduction

The disciples of our Lord were most inadequate for the task he commanded them to carry out. They were ordinary people, much like those of our congregation today.

Their inadequacy and the limitation of their understanding are dramatically demonstrated by a question they put to the Lord just before his ascension: "Lord, wilt thou at this time restore again the kingdom of Israel?" This was an expression of a desire for political and earthly authority. Jesus replied by revealing that God had something in store for them that was far more wonderful than a restoration of the Jewish kingdom. He said, "It is not for you to know the times or the seasons, which the Father hath put in his own power. But ye shall receive power, after that the Holy Ghost is come upon you" (Acts 1:7–8). When Jesus spoke of that "which the Father had put in his own power," he was referring to the power of the authority of God. When talking about the power of the Holy Spirit in verse 8, he used an entirely different word — *dynamin* — referring to a divine energy that would come upon and take possession of the disciples and enable them to do all of the things God was commanding them to do.

Jesus was talking about a power other than that with which the world is familiar. Men know much about muscle power, mechanical power, electrical power, financial power, political power, and military power, but there is a dearth of knowledge about spiritual power.

The Savior was referring to enabling power, redeeming power, delivering power, creative power that would make it possible for his disciples to advance God's kingdom in a pagan world.

As one studies the experience of the disciples on the day of Pentecost and during the years that followed, it is easy to observe that they possessed spiritual power. This power manifested itself primarily in the ministry of witnessing. The Holy Spirit came to empower them for witnessing.

I. The power of a new insight into the purpose of God.

Jesus had said that when the Comforter would put in his appearance that he would guide them into all truth (John 16:13). For the first time, many of the teachings of Jesus Christ began to have meaning to the apostles. They remembered the things he had said, and for the first time they understood. Paul refers to this new insight and understanding in a passage that has frequently been quoted as a reference to heaven (1 Cor. 2:9), when in reality he is talking about

135

the spiritual realities or insights the Holy Spirit has revealed to the eyes of those who are responsive to the Spirit (1 Cor. 2:10).

Peter's sermon on the day of Pentecost is what we would call a biblical or theological sermon. He was explaining the truth of God. He was equipped to do so by the power of a new insight.

II. The power of a new liberty of utterance.

One of the immediate effects of the coming of the Holy Spirit was a miracle of ecstatic language as the disciples began to speak concerning the wonderful works of God. There were people present representing at least sixteen different nationalities and languages. Many of these would be departing shortly for their home. By this miraculous hearing of the mighty works of God in their native tongues, the advancement of the gospel was greatly expedited.

It was a common belief among pagans throughout the ancient world that their gods communicated to humans by means of an ecstatic language. Pentecost and the miracles associated with it were a divine attestation to both believers and pagans that the God of Israel had a message for the world through the church.

A remarkable thing about the members of the early church was the fact that they went everywhere preaching the gospel. C. E. Autrey has said that they went everywhere "gossiping the gospel." Their timidity disappeared, and with exuberant joy they shared the good news of what God had done, not only in Jesus Christ, but in their own hearts. This is the great need of the church today. Only as each disciple becomes a witness can we hope to win our world to faith in Christ.

III. A new power of persuasion.

"Now when they heard this, they were pricked in their heart, and said unto Peter and to the rest of the apostles, Men and brethren, what shall we do?" (Acts 2:37). These early disciples discovered that as they bore a personal testimony concerning their experience with Jesus Christ and declared that through faith in him the deepest need of their lives had been met, other men and women listened to them with hungry hearts. They discovered that even in controversy they were able to put to silence the arguments of unbelievers, and people were persuaded to believe in Jesus Christ (4:33).

This power of persuasion was particularly evident in the ministry of Stephen who was confronted by those who rejected the Christ, and the record says "they were not able to resist the wisdom and spirit by which he spake" (6:10). Today the church needs a power of persuasion that can come only from the Spirit of God to convince people to forsake the ways of sin and to follow Jesus Christ in the paths of righteousness.

IV. The power of a new boldness in witnessing.

On the day of Pentecost, Peter, who had shrunk back in cowardice before the question of a maid, stood forth as bold as a lion to interpret what God had done and to proclaim Jesus of Nazareth as indeed the Messiah (Acts 2:22–36). There was within him an inner compulsion to testify and to persuade others to yield the throne of their hearts to Jesus Christ whom God had made "both Lord and Christ."

It is interesting to note how these early disciples reacted to persecution. It is a bit surprising to the modern Christian that they prayed that God would "grant unto thy servants, that with all boldness they may speak thy word" (Acts 4:29). In spite of the fact that they were beaten, the record says, "and daily in the temple, and in every house, they ceased not to teach and to preach Jesus Christ" (5:42).

Conclusion

This unusual boldness in witnessing was due to the fullness of Holy Spirit power. The tragedy of the modern-day Christian is that our negative response to the presence and power of the Holy Spirit has deprived us of spiritual insight, intimidated our testimony, destroyed our power to persuade, and caused us to be cowardly silent about the wonders of the gospel. May God help us to recognize and to respond to the Holy Spirit in a manner that will vitalize the church, energize the individual witness, and evangelize an unsaved world.

WEDNESDAY EVENING, APRIL 23

Title: "Lead Us Not into Temptation"

Text: "And lead us not into temptation" (**Matt. 6:13**).

Introduction

To even begin to understand this particular petition the Lord included in the model prayer, we must recognize that there is a difference between the temptation that is initiated by Satan and the test to which God puts us.

God is not the author of evil. God does not induce anyone to participate in that which is sinful and destructive. When God places some burden upon us, he does so to bring out the good rather than the bad. When Satan places some burden on us or some obstacle before us, he is seeking to bring out the bad and lead us into something harmful.

The text has presented a problem to many. C. C. Torrey translates it, "And let us not yield to temptation." A. T. Robertson renders it, "Do not allow us to be led into temptation." Phillips translates it, "Keep us clear of temptation." The ancient theologians interpreted it to mean, "Do not suffer us to be led into temptation."

By this petition our Lord, recognizing a problem that will be with us continually, encourages us to trust in God implicitly.

I. The Christian has to struggle daily to be victorious over temptation.

It is not easy to be genuinely Christian. It is no easy accomplishment to live a life that is blameless and without spot in a corrupt world.

A. *Forgiveness does not assure the conquest of evil.* One cannot relax in the confidence that he is immune to evil. The gift of eternal life does not eliminate our lower nature. The miracle of new life that comes in conversion imparts a hunger after righteousness.

B. *Temptation will be a part of our experience as long as life lasts.* It is one of the conditions of our existence. Even Christ was tempted in the wilderness to do wrong. He was tempted to shrink back from his duty.

  1. Temptation can come from the circumstances about us.
  2. Temptation can come to us through those who love us.
  3. Temptation can come from evil desires within us.
  4. Temptation to do evil also comes from the Devil.
  5. Tests, trials, even troubles may come in the providence of God, but they come to develop and perfect us and not to degrade and destroy us (James 1:12–14).

II. Jesus encourages us to love righteousness and to hate sin.

A. *To sincerely offer this petition is to experience a fear of sin.* Only a fool will treat sin mildly or lightly. It is never wise to be courageous against a temptation to do wrong. It is never smart to be overly confident in the face of temptation, "Let him that thinketh he standeth take heed lest he fall" (1 Cor. 10:12).

B. *A genuine desire for inward righteousness will lead one to offer this petition continuously.* A mortal hatred of sin and an intensive hunger after righteousness are basic essentials for becoming a genuine Christian.

III. A consciousness of personal weakness will cause us to offer this petition.

A. *Peter was overconfident concerning his love for and his loyalty to the Lord (Matt. 26:33–35).* Consequently, he neglected to respond to the invitation to prayer and fell asleep. It was only normal that he should follow afar off, and at the moment of testing, he denied any knowledge of or relation to the Lord Jesus. There might have been a different story to tell if he had not been so overconfident.

B. *The apostle Paul had a great fear of failure that produced a spirit of humble trust and rigid discipline.* "But I keep under my body, and bring it into subjection, lest that by any means, when I have preached to others, I myself should be a castaway" (1 Cor. 9:27).

IV. We are taught to pray for divine help when temptation comes.

A. *God is our greatest defense in the time of temptation.* We must rely on him for power to overcome.

B. Personal defenses can be utilized for victory.

  1. Self-respect should challenge us to overcome temptation.
  2. Christian training and tradition can strengthen us.

3. Concern for those whom we love and those who love us can challenge us not to yield to temptation.
4. Scripture verses that have been memorized can provide us with inward strength.
5. The desire for divine approval can help us.

Conclusion

The presence of Jesus Christ assures us of victory if we will cooperate with him. "Ye are of God, little children, and have overcome them: because greater is he that is in you, than he that is in the world" (1 John 4:4).

SUNDAY MORNING, APRIL 27

Title: The Commission of the Living Lord

Text: "Go ye therefore, and teach all nations, baptizing them in the name of the Father, and of the Son, and of the Holy Ghost: Teaching them to observe all things whatsoever I have commanded you: and, lo, I am with you alway, even unto the end of the world. Amen" **(Matt. 28:19 – 20)**.

Hymns: "The Light of the World Is Jesus," Bliss

"We've a Story to Tell," Sterne

"Rescue the Perishing," Crosby

Offertory Prayer: Our heavenly Father, through the testimony of others we have learned of your great love for us. We thank you for the gift of salvation. Gratitude compels us to desire to share the good news of your love with a lost world. Today we bring our tithes and offerings that the ministry of preaching and teaching and healing through Jesus Christ might be carried to all parts of the earth. Bless these tithes and offerings. To that purpose we pray in Jesus' name. Amen.

Introduction

After twenty centuries of Christian history, the church finds itself in the embarrassing position of having been disobedient to the Lord's command to the extent that the majority of the inhabitants of our world are still not Christians. We have treated the Great Commission as if it were a "great omission."

We need to face up to the urgency of our unfinished task. We need a burning sense of our spiritual obligation. We need to be overwhelmed with our spiritual opportunities.

Our Lord's commission contains the divine strategy for world redemption. The overwhelming majority of us have failed to catch the imperative note in this mandate of the Master to his church. Consequently, our failure to fulfill God's purpose for us is pathetic enough to make the angels weep.

That we have neglected to heed the imperative and to accept the claims of the Great Commission upon us is dramatically revealed by our spiritual complacency. We rejoice over the fact that salvation has been provided and that God is a great and good and loving heavenly Father. Evidently we have construed it to be the supreme objective simply to dwell in the secret place of the Most High, to cultivate the inner devotional life and aim at personal holiness. Consequently, many individuals and churches have isolated themselves in sanctified seclusion. They have disowned their redemptive mission. Our reference is not primarily to those who have placed themselves within the confines of a convent or monastery, but to those who walk the streets and rub shoulders with John Doe every day yet are as silent as a tomb concerning the wonderful works of God. The church that does not vibrate with a fervent missionary spirit has ceased to be a moving, conquering force and has become a dead ecclesiastical machine.

We need to face up to the fact that Jesus' precious promise "I am with you alway, even unto the end of the world" is not an unconditional promise. It has an evangelistic and missionary setting. It is associated with fidelity to the task of soul winning.

We need to sit at the feet of the risen Master and hear his imperative challenge. We need to recognize that evangelism and missions are not left to the whim or preference of the individual church member. The Great Commission places some legitimate claims on the life of each follower of Jesus Christ.

I. The commission is based on the claim of divine ownership.

A. *"The earth is the Lord's, and the fullness thereof; the world, and they that dwell therein" (Ps. 24:1).*

B. *"What? know ye not that your body is the temple of the Holy Ghost which is in you, which ye have of God, and ye are not your own?* For ye are bought with a price: therefore glorify God in your body, and in your spirit, which are God's" (1 Cor. 6:19–20).

C. *"Whether therefore ye eat, or drink, or whatsoever ye do, do all to the glory of God" (1 Cor. 10:31).*

II. The commission is based on the claim of our Savior's lordship.

"All power is given unto me" (Matt. 28:18).

A. *Jesus is the risen and glorified Lord.*

B. *Christ is Lord over all and of all.*

C. *Our lives are to be lives of obedience to incarnate love.*

D. *We represent, and are to proclaim, Christ's lordship.*

III. The commission is based on the claim of spiritual debtorship.

"I am debtor both to the Greeks, and to the Barbarians; both to the wise, and to the unwise" (Rom. 1:14).

A. *Each of us is personally indebted to Jesus Christ.*

1. Ours should be the love of the forgiven.

2. Ours should be the gratitude of the redeemed.
B. *It is a debt we can never fully pay.*
C. *We make payments on this debt by witnessing to the unsaved.*
D. *This is a debt that is inescapable.* There is no way to evade, avoid, or delay it. No substitute is acceptable. This passionate debtorship has taken the pain out of martyrs' fires, the shame out of crucifixions, and the fear out of persecutions for twenty centuries.

IV. The commission places us under a destiny determining trusteeship.

Our response to this trust determines the spiritual welfare of those about us as well as our significance to the kingdom of God.

A. *The gospel has been committed to our trust.* Christ has placed his redemptive work in our hearts and hands. Evangelism is not something tacked on to a person's Christianity that he or she may choose to take or leave. It is at the very heart of our new experience of God in Christ. It can never be the province of a few enthusiasts—a sideline specialty for those who happen to have a bent in that direction. It is the distinctive mark of being a Christian.
B. *This trusteeship is personal.*
C. *This trusteeship is perpetual.*
D. *This trusteeship is urgent because so much is involved.* Our lives, our time, our talents, our testimonies, and our treasures should all be invested in a manner that will help us to be faithful to our trust.

V. This commission is issued out of the compassionate heart of heaven's only Savior.

A. *Christ came that the world might be saved from sin.*
B. *Christ died that the world might be saved.*
C. *Christ lives eternally to offer, through us, salvation to a needy world.*

Conclusion

Each Christian should relate personally to the Great Commission. In this commission there is one dominant and controlling imperative while all of the other verb forms are participles. In the original Greek the central verb is formed on the noun for "disciples" and should be translated "make disciples." The word translated "go" is a participle and could be translated "going" or "as you go." Our Lord is saying to all of his disciples, "As you go about from place to place, involve yourself in the privilege and responsibility of making disciples."

If you have not yet discovered the joy of being a Christian, then the good news of the gospel is for you and you should and can receive Christ as your Savior today.

SUNDAY EVENING, APRIL 27

Title: The Path to Holy Spirit Power

Text: "But ye shall receive power, after that the Holy Ghost is come upon you: and ye shall be witnesses unto me both in Jerusalem, and in all Judaea, and in Samaria, and unto the uttermost part of the earth" **(Acts 1:8)**.

Introduction

The newspapers carried the account of the death by starvation of a very wealthy woman. She had isolated herself from friends and relatives to the confines of her mansion. At a time when she could have had the best of medical care and the most appropriate of foods, she suffered illness that led to her death. This is comparable to the condition in which many children of God find themselves. With the inexhaustible resources of God available, they live impoverished lives of spiritual weakness instead of enjoying the abundant life that is available through the presence and work of the Holy Spirit.

The only explanation for the marvels of the period of history we call the apostolic age is to be found in the early Christians' relationship to the Holy Spirit. These disciples — a baffled, disappointed group of Jewish peasants, untrained and inexperienced in the arts of communication — launched a movement that established their leader as the King of Kings, superior even to Caesar. Without political endorsement, without social or intellectual prestige, without financial resources, they marched through a pagan, materialistic empire proclaiming Christ with a power that was more than that which is merely human. The explanation for their unusual achievements is to be found in the text "and they were all filled with the Holy Ghost" (Acts 2:4).

What has been your response to the Holy Spirit who came to dwell in the church on the day of Pentecost as the divine administrator of God's redemptive activity in the world?

I. The peril of a negative response.

   A. *Like some during the apostolic period, we can make a negative response by simply ignoring the presence of the Holy Spirit within our heart.* "What? know ye not that your body is the temple of the Holy Ghost which is in you, which ye have of God, and ye are not your own?" (1 Cor. 6:19).
   B. *Many followers of our Lord live lives of spiritual loneliness and weakness because they are uninformed of the glorious presence of the Holy Spirit who came to dwell in their hearts in the miracle of the new birth (Gal. 4:6).* The Holy Spirit is not able to render his greatest service when his presence is ignored.
   C. *Paul warned the Thessalonian Christians against quenching the Spirit (1 Thess. 5:19).* Did you ever see someone hastily pinch the fire out of a candle with his fingers? Paul is saying, "When God builds a fire in your heart, don't choke the life out of it. Don't pour water on the divine spark."

D. *Have you ever had an inward hunger for prayer?* Would you quench this leading of the Holy Spirit? Every impulse to pray is the invitation of God to receive a blessing. Not to respond is to quench the Spirit.

E. *Have you ever had a hunger to read the Word of God?* Because of the press of circumstances, did you postpone eating the Bread of Life and drinking the milk of divine truth? If so, you quenched the Spirit.

F. *Has compassionate concern for an unsaved person caused you to feel that you should tell him or her about Jesus?* Have you also been guilty of making excuses? God was at work seeking to use you to communicate the gospel, and you were guilty of quenching the Spirit.

II. Three steps to Holy Spirit power.

As one studies the New Testament, there are at least three positive responses to the Holy Spirit that make possible the release of divine energy in the lives of the individuals involved.

A. *The first step toward experiencing this power is associated with faith (Gal. 3:2, 14).* We must have information concerning the presence, the purpose, and the power of the Holy Spirit. We must move beyond this information to a personal faith in the activity and the availability of the Holy Spirit to do the work of God in and through us.

It is said that Stephen was "a man full of faith and of the Holy Ghost" (Acts 6:5).

Barnabas was a man "full of the Holy Spirit and of faith." We cannot hope to experience the fullness of the power of God until we believe sincerely that God's power is both able and available.

The disciples patiently and trustingly waited for the promised power that became available on the day of Pentecost. They lived and labored and served effectively because of the divine energy of the Holy Spirit.

B. *The second response is that of prayer.* The Holy Spirit power came to the church and into the lives of individual members because of persistent and united prayer. Genuine prayer creates a spiritual atmosphere in the heart that makes it possible for the Holy Spirit to take charge of the mind, the emotions, and the will.

Real prayer is more than just saying, "Gimme, gimme," to God. Fundamentally, it is a worship experience in which we position ourselves in faith, humility, gratitude, and surrender before the throne of grace. In prayer, we both receive what God has for us and we give what we are and what we have to God. If the experience of prayer is neglected, one cannot hope to be filled adequately with the divine energy that is necessary for effective Christian service.

C. *The third step to experiencing the Holy Spirit's power is obedience (Acts 5:32).* It is not a question of our being able to secure the power of the Holy Spirit as much as it is a question of the Holy Spirit taking charge of us and using us in kingdom activities. The individual believer is to be the instrumental

143

agent, and the Holy Spirit is the directing and enabling agent. To be filled with the Holy Spirit implies the absence of a selfish, disobedient spirit. When the will is surrendered and the body is yielded, the Holy Spirit is able to use us in a mighty manner to bring the blessings of God into the lives of those about us.

Conclusion

God the Father has been described as Deity invisible. Christ is Deity manifested. The Holy Spirit is Deity communicated. May God help each of us to enter into the experience of faith, prayer, and surrender that we might labor for him in the fullness of the power of the Holy Spirit.

WEDNESDAY EVENING, APRIL 30

Title: "Deliver Us from Evil"

Text: "Deliver us from evil" (**Matt. 6:13**).

Introduction

Real prayer calls for real cooperation with God. The perfect pattern of prayer, which closes with this petition, contains seven petitions, each of which is designed to meet specific needs in various areas of life.

This petition is the climax of the prayer as it is the object of Christ's coming into the world. The great evil of the world is sin — the source and fountain of all the other evils in the world. The Greek text may be translated "the evil" or "the evil one."

When we pray "deliver us from evil," we pray against everything that ruins and makes us wretched; against the slavery of sin; against all of the wickedness, cunning, and malignity of the Devil or of man. We should uplift our souls in prayer against all of the trouble and pain and confusion, worse than death, that evil has brought into the world.

This is a prayer for self, for family, and for others.

I. By this petition Jesus registers divine opposition to all evil.

A. *Sin is that which is contrary to God's will.*

B. *Sin, by its very nature, is destructive to the being and happiness of God's creatures.*

C. *God, by his very nature, will never condone, approve, or tolerate sin. He is eternally opposed to sin, just as doctors are opposed to cancer.*

D. *God loves us very much and wants to save us to the extent that he gave his Son for us (John 3:17).*

E. *Christ died to save us from evil (Gal. 1:4).*

F. *The heavenly Father will help us destroy the roots of evil in our hearts.*

G. *The heavenly Father can deliver us from reaping the fruits of evil in later life.*

II. By this petition we are encouraged to trust God for spiritual strength.

A. *Divine power is available for human weakness.*

B. *Divine deliverance is possible for those who are enslaved.* "O wretched man that I am! who shall deliver me from the body of this death? I thank God through Jesus Christ our Lord" (Rom. 7:24–25).

C. *Divine power and deliverance come through surrender to God.*

III. This petition contains a pledge to cooperate with the divine Deliverer.

A. *Only God can deliver us from evil (Eph. 6:10–13).*

B. *God delivers us from the guilt and penalty of evil through Christ (Rom. 6:23).*

C. *God delivers us from the power of evil through the Holy Spirit (Gal. 5:16–18).*

D. *God delivers us from the practice of evil through the truth of his Holy Word (Ps. 119:9, 11, 105).*

E. *God delivers us from the work of evil by putting us to work in his kingdom (Phil. 2:12–13).*

Conclusion

The complete answer to this petition comes after the end to this life. Heaven is a place of perfect holiness where we shall be delivered from both the presence and the practice of evil. Meanwhile, day by day, we should pray "Deliver us from evil" and do God's will.

MAY

■ Sunday Mornings

Conclude the series on "Following the Living Lord" on the first Sunday of the month, and begin a new series titled "Serving Christ in Marriage and Building a Christian Home" on Mother's Day. The primary objective is to enrich the quality of marriage and family life. This series will conclude on Father's Day.

■ Sunday Evenings

Conclude the series on "The Holy Spirit in the Early Church" on the first Sunday and begin a series titled "Preparing to Serve Christ in Marriage and Building a Christian Home," primarily for the young and unmarried. This series is also directed toward parents who are helping their children prepare for Christian marriage.

■ Wednesday Evenings

Continue the series on "The Child of God in Prayer," giving special attention to the hindrances to prayer.

SUNDAY MORNING, MAY 4

Title: Departure without Tears

Text: "Then he led them out as far as Bethany, and lifting up his hands he blessed them. While he blessed them, he parted from them. And they returned to Jerusalem with great joy, and were continually in the temple blessing God" **(Luke 24:50–53 RSV).**

Scripture Reading: Acts 1:1–11

Hymns: "Rejoice, the Lord Is King," Wesley

"Jesus Shall Reign," Watts

"Crown Him with Many Crowns," Bridges

Offertory Prayer: O God, we acknowledge your goodness to us beyond measure. We acknowledge, too, our debt to the forefathers of our Christian faith. As a result of what you have put in their hearts and minds, the influence of our offering today will be felt in many parts of the world. May our material resources be made increasingly available to your work so that the Good News can be proclaimed more universally. Through our Savior's name. Amen.

Introduction

No one enjoys saying good-bye to a loved one. Some people will go to much trouble to avoid this unpleasant experience. Joseph Parker, one of the great English preachers of former days, preferred that visitors in his home not say good-bye upon departure. He and his wife, early in marriage, agreed not to say good-bye to each other upon parting, and they lived up to the promise.

We are not likely to go to such extremes in dealing with life's inevitable separations. Yet our unpleasantness is pronounced in varying degrees, depending on how close the departing person is to us and the degree of finality we fear is in the good-bye.

One would expect, therefore, that the disciples would be heavyhearted when Jesus left them. His ascension had all the marks of finality about it, yet they shed no tears over his departure. There can be no question about their love for him. They were heartbroken and puzzled when he told them, prior to his crucifixion, of his departure. We might have expected an account of the ascension to read as follows: "And it came to pass that he parted from them and was carried up into heaven, and they worshiped him and returned to Jerusalem with hot tears that blinded their eyes and with hearts breaking in the sorrow of farewell. And they said one to another, 'It was beautiful while it lasted, and now we must get on without him in a world, which, in his absence, has turned cold and bleak and gray.'"

As strange as it may seem, there is nothing of this gloom and sadness surrounding the ascension of Jesus. Instead, those early Christians "returned to Jerusalem with great joy, and were continually in the temple blessing God."

I. Consider, first, the scriptural basis for this observation—departure without tears.

Jesus met his disciples in the vicinity of Jerusalem for private instructions. Then "he led them out as far as Bethany, and he lifted up his hands and blessed them." This is an exact reversal of the triumphal entry and symbolized their following him to the ends of the earth. "And it came to pass, while he blessed them, he was parted from them, and carried up into heaven." How appropriate that the last recollection the disciples have of their Lord is of his blessing them as they stood together on the high ground overlooking Jerusalem!

"And they worshipped him, and returned to Jerusalem with great joy." This verse follows logically from the thought of the previous one. Worship is properly given to the ascended Christ because he is ascended. The disciples returned to Jerusalem, obedient to the Lord's previous command and in expectation of the fulfillment of the promise.

The account in the book of Acts has much to add. It tells of a cloud receiving Jesus out of the disciples' sight. The "cloud" is to be understood both literally and symbolically. It seems that an actual physical cloud hid Jesus from the disciples' view, and that when the cloud lifted, he was no longer visible. But there is more involved than the literal. God's relation to his people and the world was often through the use of a cloud. At the time of the exodus, the Lord led and protected his people by a cloud. The cloud covered the mount at the giving of the Law. When the tabernacle was completed, the cloud came upon it to signify God's abiding presence. On the Mount of Transfiguration, the cloud signified God's presence. In the ascension, the cloud was without doubt, for the disciples, a powerful symbol of the return of Jesus to the Father.

The Acts account talks about "two men standing by the disciples in white apparel." The appearance of angels in the narrative suggests that, for the disciples, there was the dawning realization of spiritual truth, which the author, and probably the apostles, could express in no other way. "Ye men of Galilee, why stand ye gazing up into heaven?" (Acts 1:11). This is a contrast between the insignificant and earthly as over against the divine and eternal. It is the realization that the Lord who is tabernacled *here* really belongs *there*. The disciples sensed that this was the last appearance of its kind. But there is to be a future coming, in some sense, for so he promised. How? When? Where? Who can know? In some way his coming will be similar to his departure — mysterious but certain. Greater precision than this is hardly to be expected in speaking of the mystery of the consummation of all things.

II. There was departure without tears because the disciples had no sense of loss.

The ascension was not in any sense a good-bye. The ascension of Jesus expresses a certain finality as far as its place at the end of a group of narratives is concerned. It marks the end in time of the whole series of events that the Gospels proclaim. The events of the thirty-plus years of Jesus' earthly life can be narrated somewhat, but not exactly, as ordinary earthly events can be narrated. The event that started the series of earthly events on its way and the event that brought the series to its close cannot be confined to the language of narration. The incarnation and the ascension are the "brackets" that enclose the earthly life of the Lord. Or, to change the metaphor from mathematics to music, they are the "bridge passages" that link the earthly events to the eternal world.

What happened at the ascension does not, however, exactly reverse what happened at the incarnation. The world is not the same place after the Lord's ascension as it was before he became man. It is permanently different from what it was because of what he accomplished. Jesus remains eternally man — "the same yesterday, and to-day, and for ever" (Heb. 13:8). In him man has been raised to the throne of God. The Godward aspect of this truth is expressed in the epistle to the Hebrews as the eternal intercession of Christ as High Priest on behalf of humankind. The manward aspect is expressed in the Pauline phrase, "Our citizenship is in heaven" (Phil. 3:20 NIV). The unity of heaven and earth for the Christian is guaranteed by the indwelling of the Spirit through whom Christ is eternally present on earth.

The ascension marks the completion of a ministry, beginning with the resurrection, in which Jesus successfully aimed at carrying the sense of his presence beyond the need of the sense. Without seeing, hearing, or touching him, they knew him to be near. Read the New Testament carefully, remembering that the Epistles were written before the earliest Gospels, and you will recognize that the apostles preached his risen power and abiding presence more than they preached the glory and splendor of his life.

Jesus went out of the sight of his disciples, and after Pentecostal power had come upon them, they went out to be witnesses of what they had seen and heard. They heralded the Good News, the news commanded attention and produced conviction, and salvation by faith in Jesus followed. Witnessing to that truth by word of mouth and by their daring, holy living, they captured for the living Christ the Old Roman Empire, which was falling to pieces.

Conclusion

The New Testament leaves no doubt about the believer's reunion with the ascended Christ. It will be in the Father's house, in the completeness of our human nature, and it will never end. So we must not try to stay on the mount of vision. Returning to our Jerusalems, let us continue on our way rejoicing.

SUNDAY EVENING, MAY 4

Title: The Holy Spirit as a Fire

Text: "There appeared unto them cloven tongues like as of fire, and it sat upon each of them. And they were all filled with the Holy Ghost, and began to speak in other tongues, as the Spirit gave them utterance" (**Acts 2:3–4**).

Scripture Reading: Isaiah 4:2–4; Acts 2:1–4

Introduction

Many of us love an open fireplace. The flickering light, crackle of fire, smell of burning wood, and direct heat of a cheerful flame serve as therapy. Most of us do not have such fireplaces. But God has always had his fireplaces. The burning bush, the brazen altar of the tabernacle, Mount Carmel, and his Pentecost people — these are just a few of God's fireplaces. The only fireplaces he has today in all the world are the hearts of his people. The Holy Spirit appeared "like as of fire." Hebrews 12:29 declares, "Our God is a consuming fire." Isaiah spoke of "the spirit of burning" (Isa. 4:4). We are to be filled with the Spirit. The fire of the Holy Spirit is to burn in the fireplaces of our own hearts. He is all that fire is, and he does all that fire does.

I. Fire consumes.

The bonfire of Ephesus consumed the bad books (Acts 19:19). Fire consumed Sodom. Moses said to Israel, "Understand therefore this day that the LORD thy God is he which goeth before thee; as a consuming fire he shall destroy them, and he shall bring them down before thy face" (Deut. 9:3). When the sin of Achan was discovered, the people stoned him and burned him with fire (Josh 7:25). A spiritual ecology also cries for action. If we would but let the fire of the Holy Spirit fill us, all that is undesirable in us would be consumed. You see, one does not have to worry much about what to do with what has already been burned up.

II. Fire purifies.

Do you recall the testimony of Isaiah? The house was filled with smoke, and where there was smoke, there was fire (Isa. 6:4). After his confession, one of the seraphim came to him, "having a live coal in his hand, which he had taken with the tongs from off the altar; and he laid it upon [his] mouth, and said, Lo, this hath touched thy lips; and thy iniquity is taken away, and thy sin is purged" (vv. 6–7).

The presence of so much that is impure about us is surely the result of the fact that the fire does not burn within us. The way to get cleaned up is to get burned out. And the Holy Spirit is the divine conflagration without which we shall remain cluttered and polluted.

III. Fire prepares.

Following the resurrection, our Lord appeared to his disciples by the Sea of Galilee. One of the sweet verses from the story states that "as soon as they were come to land, they saw a fire of coals there, and fish laid thereon, and bread" (John 21:9). The food was made ready with fire. We push back a good many spiritual groceries and label them as inedible simply because we do not allow the Holy Spirit's fire to make them savory. The intolerable becomes delightful following the fire.

Could it be that we ourselves are raw and repulsive because we have not been made ready with the fire?

IV. Fire cheers.

Seeing a burning lamp in the window brings cheer. Seeing a campfire in the night brings cheer. Coming in from the winter cold to an open fire brings cheer. Without the Spirit we are caught in the cold grip of despair. With the Spirit we are cheered on to victory.

One of unique word pictures of Jesus declares, "His eyes were as a flame of fire" (Rev. 1:14). The flame brought terror to the enemies, but it brought cheer to the friends. The Holy Flame cheers us!

V. Fire softens.

The psalmist declared that "as the wax melteth before the fire, so let the wicked perish at the presence of God" (Ps. 68:2). Isaiah prophesied, "As when the melting fire burneth . . . , the nations may tremble at thy presence" (Isa. 64:2).

The Holy Spirit softens the heart of the sinner. He makes people responsive. He prepares them to be remolded, remade, regenerated. The people of God could spare themselves a lot of fatigue and failure by depending on and responding to the softening of the Spirit.

VI. Fire unites.

The unity of metals comes only through applied fire. Much of the unity of ingredients in our food comes because of fire. Likewise, God's people are united by the power of God's fire. The two disciples on the way to Emmaus were united as their hearts burned within them (Luke 24:32). Fellowship is dependent on the Flame.

VII. Fire empowers.

We fail to get up much steam in many of our endeavors because we do not have enough fire under the boilers. In our do-it-yourself determinism, we insist on our spiritual programs of flameless cooking. We are powerless because we are flameless. Our half-baked ideas come from our half-heated ovens.

Let us be reminded often of our Lord's clear words, "Ye shall receive power after that the Holy Ghost is come upon you" (Acts 1:8).

Conclusion

A. *The fire for God's fireplaces is the Holy Spirit.*
B. *The consuming, purifying, preparing, cheering, softening, uniting, and empowering of God's holy fire can be ours.*
C. *Let us prayerfully yield and say, "Set my soul afire, Lord, set my soul afire."*

WEDNESDAY EVENING, MAY 7

Title: "Lord, Teach Us to Pray"
Text: "Pray without ceasing" **(1 Thess. 5:17).**

Introduction

Jesus lived in constant communion with God. There was never a time when he was away from God. He never felt at a distance from God except when he was dying on the cross as sin-bearer.

Jesus often prayed, and evidently during these times his disciples were aware of unusual blessings coming to him as a result of prayer. For at the end of one of his prayers, one of the disciples voiced the request of all, saying, "Lord, teach us to pray" (Luke 11:1).

Jesus assumed that his disciples would want to pray (Matt. 6:6). In several instances, Jesus encouraged them to pray. In our text, Paul encourages the disciples at Thessalonica to "pray without ceasing." He was not suggesting that they remain on their knees in a physical posture of prayer constantly; rather, he was insisting that they have a habit of prayer and not break it. He was challenging them to be constantly aware of and open to God. This is needed today.

I. If we would overcome temptation (Mark 14:38).

There is no way by which children of God can be victorious over the temptations that beset them from without and from within if they neglect to correct their scale of values and restore the vital energies of life through communion with God in prayer.

Temptation is an experience of life. No one is immune, and there is no way to escape being tempted. It is yielding to temptation that is sinful.

II. If we would overcome the Devil (Eph. 6:10–12).

Some people do not believe there is a Devil. Those who have accepted this idea have already been devoured by the Devil without realizing it (1 Peter 5:8).

Jesus experienced opposition by the Devil, and Paul had firsthand experiences with the Devil (2 Cor. 2:11). The late Ellis A. Fuller used to say, "I have no difficulty believing in the existence of a living personal devil. He offers me advice as to how I should conduct my life every morning before I eat breakfast."

If we would be victorious, we must not only resist the Devil, but we must also draw near to God in prayer (James 4:7–8).

III. If we would receive the blessings of God (James 4:2).

Prayer is the divinely appointed channel through which we are to receive the promised blessings of God. Through prayer we rise up to be coworkers with God in the highest sense. Prayer brings us into contact and true harmony with the will of God. While we pray, God shares his concern for a lost world with us. As we pray, God bestows upon us the blessing of a burdened heart for individuals with whom we are acquainted. He bestows upon us the wisdom and the divine energy necessary for carrying out his purposes on earth.

Not to pray is to be irreligious. Prayerlessness is an injustice to our own spiritual welfare. The neglect of prayer explains the spiritual poverty and weakness of today's church.

The biblical records reveal that the men and women whom God was able to use were men and women who had the habit of prayer. A study of Christian history will reveal that those who became spiritual giants were those who prayed more than their contemporaries.

IV. If we would be effective witnesses (Acts 4:31).

Prayer creates an atmosphere in which it is possible for the Spirit of God to do his work in the heart of the pray-ers. Changes can take place in their hearts that enable them to bear a winning witness of Christ to the unsaved.

A study of both sacred and secular history will reveal that every great spiritual revival was preceded by and permeated with serious heart-searching prayer. If you as an individual would be an effective witness, you must give yourself to prayer. Your church must become a praying church if you would be a soul-winning church. Genuine prayer is inseparably connected with effective Christian witnessing.

Conclusion

Do we need any further encouragement to pray? Let us develop the habit of private prayer and not break it. Let us develop a prayer partnership with someone and share our spiritual burdens. Let us make our church "a house of prayer."

SUNDAY MORNING, MAY 11

Title: The Marks of a Great Mother

Text: "And the woman conceived, and bare a son: and when she saw him that he was a goodly child, she hid him three months" **(Ex. 2:2)**.

Hymns: "Have Faith in God," McKinney

"O Blessed Day of Motherhood," McGregor

"Faith of Our Mothers," Patten

Offertory Prayer: Our Father, on this special day we would pause to thank you for your wonderful gifts to us through our mothers. Help us to be mindful that every good and perfect gift is from you. You have been most generous toward us. As we give our tithes and offerings, help us to be grateful for your great love toward us in the giving of your Son in our place on the cross for our sins. In Jesus' name. Amen.

Introduction

Today I will be speaking to mothers and not about them. A man's best friend is not his dog. A man's best friend is his mother. Every child needs a good mother. Would that all of us could be grateful to God for a good mother.

In this age of selfishness and materialism, we need to look at the virtues that present mothers and future mothers would do well to seek.

Jochebed, the mother of Moses, possessed many of the marks of goodness and greatness that are needed by mothers of today.

I. Jochebed ("The Lord Is Glorious") had a good husband.

He was of the tribe of Levi (Ex. 6:20). We can assume that he shared the same faith, ideals, and hopes as did his wife. Every woman needs a Christian husband.

    A. *Many women find their greatest opponent to the proper rearing of children in the father of their children.*

    B. *The husband can and should help his wife to be a great mother.*

II. Seemingly Jochebed recognized parenthood as a glorious responsibility.

    A. *She was willing to disobey a king to preserve the life of her child.*

    B. *She risked her own life.*

    C. *Hers was the joy of creation and preservation.*

    D. *Motherhood for her was a service to God and to her nation in a time when both needed what only good mothers could do.*

III. Jochebed was a woman of vision.

"He [Moses] was a goodly child" (Ex. 2:2). Acts 7:20 tells us that he was exceedingly fair. Hebrews 11:23 tells us that "he was a proper child."

    A. *She had prophetic insight.*

    B. *She saw the possibilities of a life.*

1. For her nation.
2. For her God.
3. For future generations.
C. *She recognized that the baby was designated for spiritual purposes. She determined to cooperate with the purpose of God for her child.*

IV. She was a mother of faith (Heb. 11:23).
A. *Faith in God.*
B. *Faith in herself under God.*
C. *Faith in her child.*

V. She was a mother of courage and sacrifice.
A. *She would not accept defeat.*
B. *She wanted to do all in her power to meet the need of the hour.*

VI. She was more than just a parent; she was a teacher for God.
A. *Children need more than the material things of life.*
B. *Children need to have the inspiration and guidance of things spiritual.*
    1. She taught Moses the truth about God.
    2. She pictured for Moses the heroes of the faith.
    3. She taught Moses to be sympathetic toward the unfortunate.
    4. She taught Moses to be intolerant toward injustice.
    5. She taught Moses about the God of Israel.

Conclusion
Every child needs a genuine Christian mother, one who knows, loves, worships, and serves God. No one can give your child a Christian mother except you. Determine to let God help you and cooperate fully with him as he works in your mind and heart that your children might have the best possible mother.

Husbands, your wife must have a Christian husband who is sympathetic and cooperative if she is to be the kind of mother God wants her to be. With God's power you can help your wife provide your children with the kind of mother they need.

If you have not already received Jesus Christ into your heart, do so today so that he might dwell in your home and bless your children through you. There are many things you are unable to provide for your children, but with God's help you can give them a Christian mother.

SUNDAY EVENING, MAY 11

Title: The Serious Business of Marriage

Text: "And I will make thee swear by the LORD, the God of heaven, and the God of the earth, that thou shalt not take a wife unto my son of the daughters of the Canaanites, among whom I dwell" (**Gen. 24:3**).

Introduction

In our Scripture text for today, it is plain to see that Abraham considered that the proper marriage of his son Isaac was of great importance. He put forth every possible effort to secure a wife for his son. Intelligent consideration and earnest faith in God were combined in searching for a companion.

Failure to realize that marriage is serious business is one of the tragedies of our day and the chief cause of countless broken homes.

There is no step pertaining to our earthly life more solemn or fraught with deeper meaning than choosing a marriage partner, yet often that step is taken with little consideration of what is involved. A real marriage does not just happen; it is the most difficult achievement in the field of human relations, exacting every ounce of ability and effort that one man and one woman can put into it.

If there is one career above all others that demands prayerful consideration and careful preparation, it is marriage. Circuit Judge L. D. Miller of Chattanooga, Tennessee, who handled more than twenty-five thousand marriage failures in his long career, unreservedly asserts that over 40 percent of those marital tragedies resulted from hasty marriages of the physically and mentally immature.

I. Marriage is serious business because so many people are involved.

Marriage is no lark; it is no adventure for the carefree days of youth. It is a decision that will affect one for life and perhaps for eternity, and not only oneself but also one's partner and any children God may send.

    A. *The parents of the couple are involved.*

    B. *The community has a stake in every marriage.*

    C. *The schools are involved.*

    D. *The church is affected by the success or failure of marriage.*

II. Marriage is serious business because of the heavy obligations involved in this relationship.

Since marriage is such a serious business, it follows that the same rules govern its success as govern other careers. Every successful career demands adequate preparation, intelligent earnestness, persistent industry, and the will to succeed.

A married man may give proof of power to rule an empire, master abstruse sciences, and write immortal volumes, yet if he fails in his marriage career, he is a failure. A married woman may win the plaudits of the world for her contributions to medical or scientific research, art, poetry, or music, yet if she fails in her marriage, she is a failure.

III. Marriage is serious business because of the suffering involved in its failure.

A happy and successful marriage is one of life's greatest blessings. On the other hand, an unhappy marriage is among the cruelest afflictions that can befall anyone.

A. *The parents of the couple who fail suffer.*

B. *The children who are deprived by divorce of the love of both parents suffer.*

C. *There is no way by which a marriage can fail without both husband and wife suffering a shattering experience.*

Elizabeth Barrett Browning said, "A woman finds heaven or hell on her wedding day."

IV. Marriage is serious business because God has given specific guiding principles to insure its success.

A. *Monogamy.* It is the divine plan that one man and one woman be united as husband and wife (Gen. 2:18, 22–23).

B. *Fidelity.* God would have the husband and wife to live together in steadfast faithfulness to each other (Matt. 19:4–5).

C. *Permanency.* In God's plan marriage is a permanent and responsible relationship that is to continue as long as life lasts (Matt. 19:6–9).

D. *Mutual love.* The husband and the wife are to maintain a steadfast, unbreakable spirit of goodwill toward each other (Eph. 5:22–23).

V. Marriage is serious business because success is so wonderful.

A. *Successful marriage creates a home where security and affection are provided.*

B. *Successful marriage makes possible a creative relationship in which husband and wife and children experience growth toward their greatest possible potential.*

C. *Successful marriage can be a little bit of heaven on earth because it is a place of holiness and happiness.*

Conclusion

It is expedient to desire and to determine that since marriage is so serious, you will put forth the necessary effort to make your individual contribution toward mutual fulfillment in marriage. Your best efforts are impossible without first seeking God's face.

WEDNESDAY EVENING, MAY 14

Title: Hindrances to Answered Prayer

Text: "Ye ask, and receive not, because ye ask amiss, that ye may consume it upon your lusts" **(James 4:3)**.

Introduction

There are those who bear testimony to the sad truth that thus far they have never received a definite answer to a prayer they have offered. Due to their failure to receive a specific answer, they are inclined to be skeptical about prayer. They have assumed that God does not answer prayer.

The failure to receive answers from God can be due to many things. Some think of prayer as a means by which they present their selfish requests to the Giver of all good and perfect gifts. They think of prayer only in terms of saying, "Gimme, gimme." They failed to recognize that prayer is the divinely ordained channel through which the child of God requisitions from the throne of grace those things that are essential in the work of the kingdom.

The Scriptures teach that there are a number of different attitudes that can obstruct the answer to prayers that we might offer.

I. The text reveals that selfishness voids our prayer requests.

The Scriptures teach that God is under no obligation and has made no promise to hear the selfish requests of his children (Mark 10:35–40).

II. Unconfessed and unforsaken sin in the heart hinders prayer.

A. *Psalm 66:18.*
B. *Isaiah 59:1–2.*
C. *Jeremiah 5:25.*

III. Giving God second place hinders prayer (Ezek. 14:3).

When we permit anything or anyone to usurp the place that belongs to God in our heart, we are automatically depriving ourselves of the privilege of receiving the needed blessings that can come from God through prayer.

IV. The mistreatment of a brother or sister can hinder prayer (Matt. 5:23–24).

One can be guilty of mistreating a brother or sister by not making restitution. He cannot then offer acceptable worship and prayers before God. When Zacchaeus was converted, a part of his decision was to make restitution for any mistreatment that others had received at his hands (Luke 19:8).

V. The harboring of a grudge will deprive us of forgiveness (Mark 11:25–26).

Hate in the heart makes it impossible for one to receive and experience the forgiveness of God as long as there is no intention to forgive and to remove the grudge that is held against another. This is one of the chief reasons why many prayers go unanswered.

Conclusion

Perhaps the greatest hindrances to prayer are not those that are present while we are praying, but rather those that keep us from even attempting to pray. The author of our text also said, "Ye have not because ye ask not" (James 4:2). Our sinful lower nature does not encourage us to pray. The Devil will do all that he can to prevent us from praying. The pressures of a competitive world will crowd out prayer and prevent us from praying as we permit them to do so. God eagerly invites us to pray.

> ### Take Time to Pray
> ### James 4:2
>
> *I got up early one morning,*
> *   And rushed right into the day;*
> *I had so much to accomplish*
> *   That I didn't have time to pray.*
> *Problems came tumbling about me,*
> *   And heavier came each task.*
> *"Why doesn't God help?" I wondered.*
> *   He answered, "You didn't ask."*
> *I wanted to see joy and beauty,*
> *   But the day toiled on, gray and bleak.*
> *I wondered why God didn't show me.*
> *   He said, "But you didn't seek."*
> *I tried to come into God's presence,*
> *   I used all my keys at the lock.*
> *God gently and lovingly chided,*
> *   "My child, you didn't knock."*
> *I woke up early this morning,*
> *   And paused before entering the day;*
> *I had so much to accomplish,*
> *   That I had to take time to pray.*
>
> *   —Author unknown*

SUNDAY MORNING, MAY 18

Title: Building a Christian Home

Text: "Except the LORD build the house, they labor in vain that build it: except the LORD keep the city, the watchman waketh but in vain" (**Ps. 127:1**).

Hymns: "Tell Me the Story of Jesus," Crosby

"The Christian Home," Spitta

"Lead Me Gently Home, Father," Thompson

Offertory Prayer: Our heavenly Father, we thank you for your blessings upon us through the home. May our tithes and offerings be used to bring about the conversion of boys and girls and men and women who will be able to serve you better in their homes. Bless this act of worship as each of us brings of our material substance to express our gratitude and to indicate our concern for the advancement of your kingdom through Jesus Christ our Lord. Amen.

Introduction

In our society there are four basic institutions: the state, the school, the church, and the home. Of these four, the home is of supreme importance.

The home has a profound influence on the state, school, and church whether it is Christian or unchristian. When the home is genuinely Christian, the church can wield a spiritual impact on society and culture, the school can do the best possible job of stimulating the intellect, and the state is most secure from foreign invasion as well as from inward deterioration.

Because of the profound influence of the Christian home for good and because of the alarmingly high percentage of marriage failures, we need to discover the sources of strength and do all that we can to insure the success of marriage and family life.

One does not accidentally build a Christian home. R. E. Luccock has said:

In the experience of millions, the inheritance received from a Christian home is the richest endowment of our lives. Many young men and women now in high school and college will go out to lives of distinguished public and professional service. But none will render any greater service than the young person who goes out to make a home that will be a strong fortress and a shining glory for other lives, some of them yet unborn." (in John Charles Wynn, ed., *Sermons on Marriage and Family Life* [Nashville: Abingdon, 1956], 23)

What kind of a home are you building?

I. In building a Christian home, a proper location should be chosen.

A. *Near to the church.*

B. *Close to the school.*

C. *As safe as possible.* Moral dangers are often far greater than physical dangers.

II. A solid foundation must be laid if one is to build a home that will last.

A number of different items go into a building's foundation: brick and steel, mortar and stone. A number of ingredients go into the foundation of a Christian home.

 A. *Active faith in God.* It is a terrible thing to shut God out of the lives of little children. "And thou shalt teach [God's words] diligently unto thy children, and shalt talk of them when thou sittest in thine house, and when thou walkest by the way, and when thou liest down, and when thou risest up" (Deut. 6:7).

 B. *Delight in the Bible as the Word of God (Ps. 1).*

 C. *Active participation in the worship and work of the church (Heb. 10:24–25).*

 D. *Family worship as a part of the normal routine of living.*

III. A Christian home needs a number of different rooms.

The houses in which we live have many different rooms. You will find bedrooms, bathrooms, dining rooms, dens, living rooms, family rooms, closets, utility rooms, storage rooms, attics, storm cellars, and garages. Each of these rooms serves a function.

In the Christian home, there are a number of rooms you should have if you would achieve success.

 A. *A Christian home has a room called "gratitude."* This room should be used by the entire family.
  1. Gratitude releases joy.
  2. Gratitude inspires.
  3. Gratitude creates a sense of personal satisfaction.
  4. Gratitude makes hardships easier.

 B. *A Christian home has a room called "forgiveness."* "Let not the sun go down upon your wrath" (Eph. 4:26).

 C. *The Christian home has a room called "sharing."*
  1. "Bear ye one another's burdens, and so fulfil the law of Christ" (Gal. 6:2).
  2. Share responsibilities.
  3. Share joy.

 D. *The Christian home has a room called "courtship."*
  1. Romantic love should continue.
  2. Courtship encompasses all of the kind actions that take place between a couple preceding to marriage. An attitude of persistent goodwill must continue if husband and wife are to be happy and if they are to provide an atmosphere of affection for children.

 E. *The Christian home has a room called "helpfulness."*
  1. Parents help each other.
  2. Parents help children.
  3. Children help parents.

IV. The construction of the Christian home begins in the moment of spiritual dedication.

    A. *Jesus will come into your home as he came into the home of Zacchaeus, bringing salvation if you will permit him to do so (Luke 19:5).*

    B. *Jesus will come into your home as a friend, as he did in the case of Mary, Martha, and Lazarus, if he is welcome (John 11).*

Conclusion

Like Joshua, make a decision and declare from the heart, "As for me and my house, we will serve the LORD" (Josh. 24:15).

SUNDAY EVENING, MAY 18

Title: A Marriage Ceremony Seriously Considered

Text: "Nevertheless let every one of you in particular so love his wife even as himself; and the wife see that she reverence her husband" **(Eph. 5:33).**

Introduction

Often husbands and wives have been heard to say, "I was so scared I didn't hear a word that the preacher said during our wedding ceremony." Due to both the excitement and the seriousness of the occasion, such a statement is altogether possible. Perhaps it would be wise and profitable for both the unmarried and the married to give some serious consideration to a marriage ceremony under circumstances more conducive to a proper understanding of what is really involved. (Photocopying the following ceremony and outline, or a ceremony of your own construction, for distribution to the congregation would be helpful.)

I. Marriage is a divine institution.

Marriage Ceremony

Holy and happy is the sacred hour when two devoted hearts are bound by the enchanting ties of matrimony. Marriage is an institution of divine appointment and is commended as honorable among all men. Marriage is God's first institution for the welfare of the race. In the quiet bowers of Eden, before the forbidden tree had yielded its fateful fruit or the tempter had touched the world, God saw that it was not good for the man to be alone. He made a helpmate suitable for him and established the rite of marriage while heavenly hosts witnessed the wonderful scene in reverence.

The contract of marriage was sanctioned and honored by the presence and power of Jesus at the marriage in Cana of Galilee and marked the beginning of his wondrous works. It is declared by the apostle Paul to be honorable among all men. So it is ordained that a man shall leave his father and mother and cleave unto his wife, and they two shall become one flesh, united in hopes and aims and sentiments until death alone shall part them.

II. Marriage is a covenant relationship.

If you, then _____ (Groom), and _____ (Bride), after careful consideration, and in the fear of God, have deliberately chosen each other as partners in this holy estate, and know of no just cause why you should not be so united, in token thereof you will please join your right hands.

III. Christian marriage is based on and requires genuine love.

Groom's Vow

_____ , will you have this woman to be your wedded wife, to live together after God's ordinance in the holy estate of matrimony? Will you love her, comfort her, honor and keep her in sickness and in health, and forsaking all others, keep only unto her so long as you both shall live?

Answer: I will.

Bride's Vow

_____ , will you have this man to be your wedded husband, to live together after God's ordinance in the holy estate of matrimony? Will you love him, honor him, and keep him in sickness and in health, and forsaking all others, keep only unto him so long as you both shall live?

Answer: I will.

IV. Christian marriage assumes the acceptance of a mutual responsibility for each other's happiness.

I, _____ (Groom), take you, _____ (Bride), to be my wedded wife, to have and to hold from this day forward, in prosperity or adversity, in sickness or in health, in advances or reverses, to love and to cherish till death do us part, according to God's holy ordinance, and thereto I pledge you my faith.

I, _____ (Bride), take you, _____ (Groom), to be my wedded husband, to have and to hold from this day forward, in prosperity or adversity, in sickness or in health, in advances or reverses, to love and to cherish till death do us part, according to God's holy ordinance, and thereto I pledge you my faith.

V. Christian marriage requires mutual fidelity.

Then are you each given to the other for richer or poorer, for better or worse, in sickness and in health, till death alone shall part you.

From time immemorial the ring has been used to seal important covenants. The golden circlet, most prized of jewels, has come to its loftiest prestige in the symbolic significance which vouches at the marriage altar. Its untarnishable material is of the purest gold. Even so may your love for each other be pure and may it grow brighter and brighter as time goes by. The ring is a circle, thus having no end. Even so may there be no end to the happiness and success that come to you as you unite your lives together.

Do you, _____ (Groom), give this ring to your wedded wife as a token of your love for her?

Will you, _____ (Bride), take this ring as a token of your wedded husband's love for you, and will you wear it as a token of your love for him?

Do you, _____ (Bride), give this ring to your wedded husband as a token of your love for him?

Will you, _____ (Groom), take this ring as a token of your wedded wife's love for you, and will you wear it as a token of your love for her?

You have pledged your faith in and love to each other in the sight of God and these assembled witnesses and have sealed your solemn marital vows by giving and receiving the rings. Therefore, acting in the authority vested in me as a minister of the gospel by this state, and looking to heaven for divine sanction, I now pronounce you husband and wife.

VI. Christian marriage involves permanency.

Therefore, what God hath joined together, let not man put asunder.

Conclusion

An appropriate conclusion for a serious consideration of a marriage ceremony might involve all of the husbands and wives present in a repetition of their marriage vows. Let each of us join simultaneously in a renewing of our wedding vows and promises to the glory of God and to the enrichment of our marriage.

WEDNESDAY EVENING, MAY 21

Title: "For What Should We Pray?"

Text: "Likewise the Spirit also helpeth our infirmities: for we know not what we should pray for as we ought" **(Rom. 8:26)**.

Introduction

B. H. Carroll said, "Our most lamentable ignorance is in regard to prayer." If we knew the proper manner of effective praying and the proper things for which we should pray, and then if we would pray, life's greatest difficulties would be solved. Our text is a statement of our need for knowledge and guidance in prayer. Assurance is given that the Holy Spirit will aid us if we are responsive to his leadership in prayer.

James, whose epistle encourages us in the practice of true religion, warns us against the peril of being selfish when we pray. All of us have been guilty of offering selfish prayers. Even the apostle Paul gives expression to his difficulty at this point in the text.

Assuming that our motives are not completely selfish, we are given definite guidance concerning the things for which we can pray and expect an affirmative answer.

I. We are to pray for grace to help in time of need (Heb. 4:14–16).

Sooner than we think, all of us will come to a time of desperate need. We will be in a position where only God can help us with our real need. Because we have a faithful High Priest who is compassionate and approachable, we are to pray for grace and mercy to help in time of need.

II. We are to pray for that which will glorify God (John 14:12–14).

Many people have been guilty of spiritual embezzlement because of an incomplete knowledge of the teachings of this passage of Scripture. We have been guilty of drawing up a list of wants and uttering them in a prayer that we closed with the phrase, "This we ask in Jesus' name." This can be a form of spiritual forgery that will be detected when presented to the "divine cashier." To pray "in Jesus' name" means something more than just attaching that phrase to the end of our prayer. Literally, to pray in Jesus' name means "to offer the prayer that the Christ would pray if he stood in your place" and to do so in order "that the Father may be glorified in the Son." To glorify means "to reveal, to publish, to make known." Jesus is here authorizing us to requisition those things that are needed in order that people might come to a knowledge of the nature and character of God.

Prayer has been described as a "company credit card" for use in the business of advancing the kingdom of God. It is illegal to use a company credit card for purely selfish purposes (cf. Col. 4:2–4).

III. We are encouraged to pray for the sick (James 5:16–17).

Our Savior is concerned about the physical well-being of people as well as their spiritual welfare. While on earth, he ministered to the suffering people about him. By what he did, we should be encouraged to pray his blessings upon the efforts of doctors, nurses, medical research scientists, and all who give themselves to a ministry of healing.

While recognizing that death, a penalty which all must pay, is inevitable, we should have no hesitation to believe that our Savior still heals the sick and restores health much as he did during his earthly ministry. There should be no conflict between our recognition that a terminal illness usually precedes the experience of death and our faith to believe that in many instances it is the will of God for the sick to recover completely.

IV. We are encouraged to pray for wisdom (James 1:5–7).

While we are in the midst of an "information explosion," there is a dearth of wisdom. A person can possess all of the information contained in a library and yet not possess wisdom. True wisdom is the gift of God. It has been defined as "sanctified horse sense" or "divine know-how" (Prov. 4:7; 9:10).

V. We are to pray for forgiveness (1 John 1:9).

A day never goes by during which we do not sin. We have sins of omission, sins of commission, and sins of disposition that need to be confessed and forsaken. God has promised to forgive and to cleanse us upon the condition that we confess and forsake known sin. We need to ask him to forgive us of known sins and to expose to us those unknown.

Conclusion

By the language of our lives and with the words of our lips, we are to encourage those about us to pray for salvation (Rom. 10:13). We are to encourage them to heed the efforts of the Savior to come into their heart (Rev. 3:20). They alone can pray the prayer that can bring the salvation of God into their lives.

SUNDAY MORNING, MAY 25

Title: Dealing with Difficulties in the Home

Text: "Finally, be ye all of one mind, having compassion one of another" (**1 Peter 3:8**).

Hymns: "This Is the Day the Lord Hath Made," Watts

"Guide Me, O Thou Great Jehovah," Williams

"Just When I Need Him Most," Poole

Offertory Prayer: Holy Father, you who are the creator and the sustainer of life, to you we come with gratitude for the inner disposition that causes us to want to worship you. We thank you for the inward prompting of your Holy Spirit that would ever draw us closer to you. As an act of worship, we bring our tithes and offerings for the advancement of your ministry of mercy in the world. Bless both the gifts and the givers for Jesus' sake. Amen.

Introduction

Theodore Adams tells of a couple who had been happily married for sixty years. When interviewed and asked for the key to their success they suggested, "Do unto one another as you would a month before marriage."

Someone has said that the ABCs of success in marriage are: Always Be Christian.

I. A great variety of problems plague the home.

A. *Some problems grow out of the inevitable crises of life.*
   1. Financial difficulties.
   2. Relocation to a new community.
   3. Separation from loved ones.
   4. Illness.
   5. Death.

B. *Marriages suffer because of character failure.*
   1. Dishonesty.
   2. Cheating.
   3. Infidelity.
   4. Gambling.
   5. Drinking.
C. *Marriages often collapse because there has been no growth of love and the relationship deteriorates into nothingness.*
D. *Another problem that often leads to unhappiness and suffering is incompatibility.*
   1. This could be discovered before marriage by those who have ears to hear and eyes to see.
   2. If partners are unwilling to adjust, compromise, and work, they will experience much unhappiness.

II. Some scriptural suggestions that involve work.

A. *Conduct yourself so as to win the unsaved companion to the Christian way of life (1 Peter 3:1–6).*
B. *"Be ye all of one mind."* Seek to unite in one great common way of thinking (1 Peter 3:8).
C. *"Having compassion one of another."* Have compassion toward each other (1 Peter 3:8).
D. *"Love as brethren."* Practice a persistent spirit of good will toward each other (1 Peter 3:8).
E. *"Be pitiful."* Be tenderhearted toward each other (1 Peter 3:8).
F. *"Be courteous."* Give attention to the little courtesies of life (1 Peter 3:8).
G. *Return good for evil (1 Peter 3:9).*
H. *Watch your tongue (1 Peter 3:10).*
I. *Hate the evil and love good (1 Peter 3:11).*
J. *Pursue peace (1 Peter 3:11).*
K. *Always pray (1 Peter 3:12).*

Conclusion

All marriages face difficulties. Some marriages fail. Other marriages succeed. The difference between success and failure is not to be found in the absence of difficulties, but rather in the dedication of both husband and wife to work together continuously to achieve success and to fulfill God's plan for their lives. May God help you to deal with the difficulties in your home in a Christian manner. Christ the Lord will guide you and assist you if you will permit him to do so.

SUNDAY EVENING, MAY 25

Title: Preparing for Marriage

Text: "Be ye not unequally yoked together with unbelievers: for what fellowship hath righteousness with unrighteousness? and what communion hath light with darkness?" **(2 Cor. 6:14)**.

Introduction

A Russian proverb goes like this: "Before embarking on a journey, pray once. Before leaving for war, pray twice. Before you marry, pray three times."

An Arabian proverb says, "Choose your horse from a hundred, your friend from a thousand, and your wife from ten thousand."

Marriage is serious business, for it involves a lifelong journey with one partner. Preparation for this journey is vital, and very sane and sage judgment should be used in this preparation. Broken hearts and wrecked homes would be the rare exception if serious and prayerful thought was given to the matter of making proper preparation for marriage.

Success that results from mere chance is extremely rare in any area of life. Happiness in marriage is never an accident. It is always an achievement. How a marriage turns out is the exact working out of the law of cause and effect.

What you and your mate bring into marriage is as important, if not more so, than what you do after you are married, as far as success or failure is concerned.

There are at least two kinds of preparation for marriage—immediate preparation and long-distance preparation. This message concerns itself primarily with long-distance preparation for marriage.

I. Choose the best possible home for your birth and growth toward maturity.

O. T. Binkley said, "The best possible preparation that a young person can have for marriage is to be born and raised in a happy home." One must admit that you cannot choose this kind of home before birth.

A. *If your parents make a success of their marriage, the chances are good that you will make a success of yours.* The basis for your marriage has been laid in your own home. The examples you observed and absorbed will be the basis for your own happiness or failure in the career of marriage.

B. *There is a close relationship between childhood impressions of family life and the achievement of married happiness as an adult.*

C. *Your personality is affected for good or for evil by the family relationship with which you are familiar.*

D. *What you, or your companion, are or will be depends in no small way on how you were trained and what you were taught.*

It is in our childhood homes that we learn the primary virtues and character traits that determine what we will be as adults.

167

While it is true that a young man marries a young woman and a young woman marries a young man, in reality they also marry the background, training, family traditions, relatives, and so forth of each other.

II. Keep yourself worthy of the best.

A. *Determine to resist all outside pressures that would lead you to conform to the lowest common denominator of morality.*
B. *Resist all inward inclinations that would be degrading and that would lead to harmful aftereffects.* Much pressure is brought upon young people to consider moral standards as obsolete and to live a life without regard to Christian standards of absolute chastity before marriage and absolute fidelity after marriage. Both the church and the home must put forth a better effort in the future than has been put forth in the past to help young people know not only what the Christian standard is, but the reason behind the Christian standard.

III. Make yourself worthy of the best.

A. *Ask yourself, "What do I have to offer in a marriage partnership?"*
B. *Determine to increase your ability to bring out the best in yourself so as to bring out the best in others generally and in your companion particularly.*
  1. Physical.
  2. Intellectual.
  3. Social.
  4. Economic.
  5. Moral and spiritual.

IV. Find or select someone who can bring out the best in you.

There are at least three tests which your prospective life companion should pass with flying colors if you would achieve success in marriage.

A. *The test of the heart.* This test is placed first, not because it is of primary importance, but because it is usually first chronologically. There should be romance in marriage.
B. *The test of the head.* Take a good hard look at your prospective companion. Are you willing to dedicate your life completely to making this person happy? Does he or she have the capacity to help you experience lasting happiness? This test is often the one applied by your parents to your choice of a companion.
C. *The test of the soul.* Will this person encourage and stimulate your faith in God and your commitment to the Christian way of life? Does he or she share a common faith with you?

Conclusion

If a prospective companion fails on any of these tests, your chance of success is not very great. If your companion passes these three tests, and if both of you will dedicate yourselves without reservation, then, by the grace of God, you can have a successful marriage.

WEDNESDAY EVENING, MAY 28

Title: The Prayers of Jesus

Text: "And it came to pass, that as he was praying in a certain place, when he ceased, one of his disciples said unto him, Lord, teach us to pray, as John also taught his disciples" **(Luke 11:1).**

Introduction

There was something about the prayers of Jesus that created within the hearts of his disciples a hunger to pray. They requested that he teach them to pray, and he complied. A study of some of the prayers our Lord offered can provide us with guidance concerning some of the things for which we can pray and expect an answer from God.

I. Jesus prayed for the Holy Spirit before he began his ministry (Luke 3:21–22).

We can be genuinely Christian in our inner life, and we can render Christian ministries only when we are blessed with the presence and power of the Holy Spirit. Prayer in this respect is in reality a surrender of ourselves to the leadership and guidance of the Holy Spirit.

II. Jesus prayed when people misunderstood the spiritual nature of his kingdom (Matt. 14:15, 22–23).

It is easy for us to be so concerned about "loaves and fishes" that we fail to perceive spiritual realities. Frequently we substitute common sense for the venture of faith. We insist on walking by sight. We are guilty of being very materialistic. We prefer to work things out by ourselves rather than to walk by faith.

As Jesus prayed that his disciples might understand the spiritual nature of his kingdom, even so we should pray for spiritual insight.

III. Jesus prayed before selecting his apostles (Luke 6:12–13).

As Jesus faced one of the major decisions of his life, that of choosing his disciples, he felt a need for prayer.

We should face every decision not only with our best intelligence, but also with complete openness to God for direction. Life would be much more meaningful and we would make fewer mistakes if we moved forward, as it were, on our knees. The heavenly Father would prevent us from making some tragic mistakes if we would but counsel with him.

IV. Jesus prayed a prayer of thanksgiving for the success of his disciples (Luke 10:17–21).

All of us find it easy to pray in times of great need when it seems that the situation is hopeless. The heart cries out to God for help. It is not wrong for us to do so, but we should be just as eager to thank God for his blessings upon us as we are to plead for his help. Paul specifically instructed the Philippian Christians to offer thanksgiving with their petitions (Phil. 4:6).

V. Jesus prayed that his crucifiers would be forgiven (Luke 23:34).

This is the ultimate expression of the forgiving spirit. If our Lord could pray this prayer while hanging on a cross, with his help we can pray for the forgiveness of those who have sinned against us, and we can pray for the grace that will make it possible for us to have an attitude of forgiveness toward all who have mistreated us.

VI. Jesus prayed a prayer of committal for his soul (Luke 23:46).

This was not the dying gasp of a helpless Savior; rather, it was the deliberate act in which the Savior dismissed his spirit and committed it into the care of the heavenly Father (John 10:18).

Conclusion

Each of us can commit our soul into the hands of the Savior now. We can trust him for guidance throughout life. We can ask for counsel as we commit to him our ways. We can face even death with calmness and courage because we have committed ourselves to the love and mercy of God, who saves all who call on him (Rom. 10:13).

JUNE

■ **Sunday Mornings**

Conclude the series "Serving Christ in Marriage and Building a Christian Home" on Father's Day, and begin a series with the theme "Inspiration from the Psalms" the next week.

■ **Sunday Evenings**

Begin a series of expository sermons based on Hebrews 12. The theme could be "Challenges to Consecrated Christian Living."

■ **Wednesday Evenings**

Continue the series on "The Child of God in Prayer" by using specific prayers of individuals as they approached our heavenly Father in their time of need.

SUNDAY MORNING, JUNE 1

Title: Love — The Law of the Home

Text: "But now abideth faith, hope, love, these three; and the greatest of these is love" (**1 Cor. 13:13 ASV**).

Hymns: "Wonderful Story of Love," Driver

"Something for Thee," Phelps

"Somebody Needs Your Love," McKinney

Offertory Prayer: Holy Father, you have given us your Holy Spirit to dwell within us collectively as your holy temple. We come now bringing the results of our work, the fruit of our efforts, to you. Accept these tithes and offerings and through them render a spiritual ministry to lives that are in need. Through Jesus Christ, our Lord. Amen.

Introduction

Some years ago 750 married couples were asked, "What, in your judgment, is the most important factor making for happiness in home life?" The answer given by the largest number was "religion lived daily in the home."

Love is at the heart of our Christian faith. Throughout both the Old and New Testaments we are told that love for God and love for others are the genuine expressions of spiritual religion. To be genuinely Christian is to live by the principle of love day by day within the home. In an atmosphere created by love, each member of the family can find the stimulation and creative encouragement that makes for true fulfillment.

When Jesus spoke of love as being the badge of Christian discipleship (John 13:34–35), he was referring to Christian love rather than romantic love. He was referring to the Calvary kind of love (3:16) rather than erotic love. While romantic love is one of the essential ingredients for happiness in marriage, the home that is built on this kind of love alone has its foundation resting on sand rather than on solid rock.

The first and greatest of the commandments requires of each of us that we love God with the totality of our being (Matt. 22:37). Love for our neighbors is to be our primary manner of relating to them (v. 39). The principle of love is said to be the royal law by which we are to regulate our lives as the children of God (James 2:8). In writing to the Ephesians, Paul encouraged husbands: "Husbands, love your wives, even as Christ also loved the church, and gave himself for it; ... So ought men to love their wives as their own bodies. He that loveth his wife loveth himself. For no man ever yet hated his own flesh; but nourisheth and cherisheth it, even as the Lord the church" (Eph. 5:25, 28–29).

It would appear that if one law were to be selected as a guideline for constant use in the home, love — genuine Christian love — would be the best.

I. The preeminence of love in the home (1 Cor. 13:1–3).

In talking about the various expressions of spiritual religion, Paul points out that love is the essential motive. It takes love to make both religion and life complete.

A. *Love is more important than eloquence (v. 1).*
B. *Love is more important than knowledge and intellectual achievement (v. 2).*
C. *Love makes faith meaningful (v. 2).*
D. *Love must motivate benevolence (v. 3).*

II. The properties of love in the home (1 Cor. 13:4–8).

While romantic love is said to be impossible to define, Paul has done an excellent job of setting forth some of the qualities of Christian love both in its negative and in its positive expression.

A. *Love is patient (v. 4).* Patience is one of the most urgently needed qualities in the home. The husband and the wife must be patient with each other's imperfections. Children never attain perfection, and parents must be patient, for only time and growth can take care of some things.

Without patience with each other, real happiness is impossible.

B. *Love is kind (v. 4).* Kindness is a virtue. Patience endures difficulty, while kindness reaches out aggressively to do good.

The members of the family must go out of their way to accommodate each other with continuous acts of kindness. Children need to be taught to be kind not only to one another, but also to pets. The attitude and practice of kindness are acquired. The home is the place where it is most important that we practice kindness in our relationships to others.

C. *Love demonstrates confidence (vv. 4, 7).* Christian love is not jealous. Instead of suspecting or surmising, love believes the best rather than the worst about others. Jealousy and envy indicate self-love and are a confession of a feeling of inferiority.

Both husbands and wives should conduct themselves so as never to shake the confidence of their companions in their truthfulness and integrity. At the same time, Christian love will always believe the best.

D. *Love practices good manners (v. 5).* Real love inspires one to an attitude of kindness and courtesy that eliminates rudeness. Courtesy in the home is as essential as the conduct that insures good public relations at the place of business. Husbands and wives should continue to practice the courtesy that caused them to be able to win their spouse's heart during the days of courtship.

E. *Love is not self-centered (v. 5).* Christian love does not insist on its own way. Christian love concerns itself with the happiness and well-being of the person who is loved.

Selfishness and Christian love are opposites. Children are born with a self-centered nature. As they grow toward maturity in Christ, this tendency toward being self-centered should be discarded. Some people, however, never grow out of the self-centeredness of early childhood.

Selfishness, in the final analysis, has probably caused more homes to break up than any other factor. To genuinely love another person is to be concerned primarily with that person's happiness or well-being. Christian love does not seek its own way, but instead seeks that which is best for others.

F. *Love is gentle (v. 5).* It is not easily irritated and does not harbor resentment. It does not maintain a list of gripes and does not carry a sackful of grudges. Instead, it meets problems with an attitude of gentleness and kindness.

There are difficult days in life that necessitate gentle treatment. The husband and wife must guard against the tendency to be irritable or resentful when everything does not go properly.

G. *Love rejoices in and practices righteousness (v. 6).* Instead of rejoicing in things that are wrong, love rejoices in doing that which is right. Within the happy home, the husband and wife will always seek to do what is right toward each other.

H. *Love is optimistic (v. 7).* It always sees the good in others. It majors on opportunities rather than obstacles. It cheerfully faces duties rather than majoring on difficulties.

I. *Love is characterized by determination (v. 8).* Christian love is not shallow or superficial. It is not defined by moods or impulses. The mind and the will are only partially involved. There is a firm determination to demonstrate a persistent, unbreakable spirit of goodwill.

173

III. The permanence of love (I Cor. 13:8–13).

Christian love is permanent and imperishable. It refuses to fail. This kind of love begins with God and will continue with him throughout eternity. Christian love is eternal.

Conclusion

A time will come when faith will give way to sight and hope will be realized by achievement, but even in heaven, as long as the ages roll, love will prevail. Because God has loved so abundantly, let us determine to live more completely by this prevailing law of the kingdom of heaven.

SUNDAY EVENING, JUNE 1

Title: Finding a Wife

Text: "Whoso findeth a wife findeth a good thing, and obtaineth favour of the LORD" **(Prov. 18:22)**. "Houses and riches are the inheritance of fathers: and a prudent wife is from the LORD" **(Prov. 19:14)**.

Introduction

Our texts for this evening's message tell us that a good wife is indeed a wonderful blessing from God. In our society it is up to the individual young man to find, to woo, and to win as his bride a woman who is potentially one of God's greatest blessings.

Proverbs 31 presents a directory of qualities for wives and mothers. It is a beautiful picture of how noble a wife and mother's life may be. It is an exhibit to young men of what they should seek in a companion. It is an ideal to which young women should aspire.

Every young man needs to face up to the fact that he cannot build a good home without the right kind of a wife.

I. What are you seeking in marriage?

A. *Are you seeking something that is merely fanciful?*
B. *Are you mature enough to consider facts realistically?*
C. *The proper kind of marriage meets three basic human needs:*
   1. The need for security.
   2. The need for significance.
   3. The need for affection.

II. The instructions of a queen mother.

The last chapter of the book of Proverbs contains words of wisdom from a mother to her son that can be studied with great profit.

A. *Most parents are vitally interested in the happiness of their children.* This is particularly true with reference to marriage.

B. *Parents can and should teach their children some of the basic fundamental truths concerning this most important of human relationships.* This is an obligation and not merely an option.

C. *The queen mother speaks primarily concerning character traits of a good wife and mother.* As a young man selects a wife, he needs to recognize that he is also choosing the mother of his children.

III. Characteristics of a good wife and mother.

A. *Virtuous (v. 10).*

B. *Trustworthy (v. 11).*

C. *Benevolent (v. 12).*

D. *Industrious (vv. 13–19).*

E. *Sympathetic with the needy (v. 20).*

F. *Domestic in her interests (vv. 21–22).*

G. *Strong and honorable (v. 25).*

H. *Wise and kind in her speech (v. 26).*

I. *Able to lead her children and challenge her husband in the things of God (vv. 28–30).*

J. *Beautiful on the inside (v. 30).*

Conclusion

Fortunate indeed is the young man who can find, woo, and win as his wife one who has at least the potential and the intention to achieve the ideals suggested by King Lemuel.

Such a wife and mother as described above would need as her husband a man who was saved and who was definitely committed to the task of living a genuine Christian life. Determine to let God give you guidance as you make the choice of your life's companion, and then determine to do all you can to help her to become the kind of wife and mother described in this last chapter of the book of Proverbs.

WEDNESDAY EVENING, JUNE 4

Title: The Prayer for Sight

Text: "And Jesus stood still, and called them, and said, What will ye that I shall do unto you?" (**Matt. 20:32**).

Introduction

The Scriptures tell us that as Jesus passed by, two blind men were sitting by the wayside begging. In ancient Israel it was the custom for the blind or crippled to sit in the dust by the roadside and beg. These two blind men had heard about the miracles of Jesus. At his touch disease fled away. Death gave up its victims. He did many wondrous things, and his fame spread throughout the whole country.

The blind men sat and wished that some day Jesus would come down the road where they sat in the dust.

One day someone said to them, "Jesus of Nazareth is coming." These blind men realized this was the time for them to make a personal plea to Jesus, and they began to shout for his attention. Although the people tried to hinder them, Jesus heard their cry of distress and stopped and asked these men a personal question. He did not say, "What will ye that I shall do *for* you?" but "What will ye that I shall do *unto* you?" Those who have made a successful contribution to our lives are those who have been permitted to do something to us rather than for us. Because of his grace and power and because of the faith of these two blind men, they were blessed with the restoration of their sight.

I. "Have mercy on us, O Lord, thou son of David" (Matt. 20:30).

A. *These blind beggars recognized the unique person of Christ.* They addressed him as "O Lord, thou son of David."

B. *They were persistent in their prayers.* They refused to let the multitude hinder them from making their plea (Matt. 20:31). We could well follow their example to the point of being persistent in the habit of prayer and then refusing to break the habit.

C. *Jesus heard their prayer.* In spite of the efforts of the multitude to silence the beggars and in spite of the noise of the crowd, he heard their cries of distress.

D. *Once sight had been returned, the beggars rejoiced exceedingly and followed Jesus (Matt. 20:34).*

II. "What will ye that I shall do unto you?" (Matt. 20:32).

A. *Jesus has promised to be in the midst of those who come together in his name (Matt. 18:20).*

B. *Christ is present tonight confronting us with the question, "What will ye that I shall do unto you?"* A service that he can render to us is always more wonderful than something that can be done for us.

Is it possible that we need to make the same request that the blind men made? Are we suffering from the inability to see or to hear him? On one occasion Jesus asked his disciples, "Having eyes, see ye not? and having ears, hear ye not?" (Mark 8:18).

On another occasion the Master said, "Blessed are your eyes, for they see: and your ears, for they hear" (Matt. 13:16).

III. "Lord, that our eyes may be opened" (Matt. 20:33).

To possess the blessing of perfect eyesight is to be rich indeed. To have the capacity to arrive at a clear mental perception is a blessing of immeasurable worth. To be blessed with spiritual eyesight, the ability to see spiritual reality, is a blessing that comes only from God. Let us pray that the Lord will open our eyes in this respect.

A. *Lord, help me to see the spiritual poverty of my soul (Matt. 5:3).* Spiritual satisfaction is a serious hindrance to both personal growth and kingdom progress. This was the sin of the Laodiceans (Rev. 3:17).

B. *Lord, help me to see the sin in my life that is displeasing to you.* When the eye of Isaiah saw the Lord, he also saw the sin in his own life (Isa. 6:5). He was convicted of sin, he confronted his sin, and he experienced cleansing.

C. *Lord, help me to see the spiritual resources that are available for kingdom effort (Matt. 28:18; Acts 1:8; Eph. 1:19–20; Phil. 4:13).*

D. *Lord, help me to see the value of a lost soul (Prov. 29:18; John 3:16).*

E. *Lord, help me to see where I fit into the divine plan (John 20:21–23).* Protestant Christians interpret this passage to mean that every disciple is to be a part of God's program by which forgiveness is communicated to those who will believe. For believers to avoid their responsibility as witnesses is to retain unbelievers in their sins.

Conclusion

Eyesight is a wonderful privilege and a priceless blessing. Let us ever pray that God will help us to see not only physical realities but also spiritual realities. If we give ourselves in undivided loyalty to him, it will be our delight and joy to see God as real in the present as well as in the future when we, by his grace, enter heaven (Matt. 5:8).

SUNDAY MORNING, JUNE 8

Title: "Today I Must Abide at Thy House"

Text: "And when Jesus came to the place he looked up, and saw him, and said unto him, Zacchaeus, make haste, and come down; for today I must abide at thy house" **(Luke 19:5).**

Hymns: "Come, Thou Almighty King," Anonymous

"Jesus Is All the World to Me," Thompson

"Let Jesus Come into Your Heart," Morris

Offertory Prayer: Our Father, we thank you for your gift of life to us. We thank you for your blessings to us throughout this past week. We praise you for the blessings you have in store for us in this service. Help us to recognize our need to be a giver. Help us to believe that the highest possible happiness is to be found as we give ourselves to some good cause bigger than ourselves. In this faith we bring our tithes and offerings to you this day through Jesus Christ our Lord. Amen.

Introduction

Our nation is constantly in peril. We face the danger of an international war that could make a cinder heap out of our world. We are in political peril if ungodly people gain control of our government. We confront the peril of a secular and materialistic spirit. Possibly, the greatest peril that we face is that of the dissolution of our home life.

Marriage and the family have been affected far more than we realize by the false information that is communicated to us through the media, movies, and television programming. Repeatedly viewing images of fornication, adultery, and homosexuality have caused Christians to become numb to the fact that what they are viewing is sin and an abomination to God. Thus, immorality has become commonplace in today's society and our homes are threatened.

A common phrase in marriage ceremonies is, "The home is God's first institution for the welfare of the race." Dr. George W. Truett said concerning the Christian home that it is "God's citadel of an enduring social order, above church and state."

The local church is vitally involved in the quality of the home life of its membership. It takes good homes that produce good families to make a church both good and great in its community.

I. The nature of the Christian home.

Dr. O. T. Binkley has said some appropriate things about the nature of the Christian home.

 A. *A Christian home is a home that is dedicated to God.* As the sun is at the center of our solar system, even so God is at the center of a Christian home.

 B. *A Christian home is a home where Christ is known, trusted, and obeyed.* The husband loves (Eph. 5:25–29). The wife respects (v. 33). The children obey (6:1–3).

 C. *The wedding vow is considered as an unconditional commitment to each other, before God, before the state, before family, and before friends.*

 D. *The Christian home is a home in which there is a creative relationship between parents and children.* It is not just a place where we eat and sleep. Rather, it is a place where we seek to make a spiritual contribution to each other. It is a place where persons growing toward spiritual maturity are found. It is a place where the church and the Bible are at the center. It is a place where people love God with their hearts as well as with their minds.

II. The need for Christian homes.

 A. *Everyone needs a Christian home that:*
    1. Provides a sense of security.
    2. Supplies the need for love.
    3. Provides character training.
 B. *Children need a Christian home.*
 C. *The church needs Christian homes.*
 D. *The schools need Christian homes.*
 E. *The nation needs Christian homes.*

III. Christ wants to come into your home now.

A. *"Today I must abide at thy house" (Luke 19:5).*

B. *"This day is salvation come to this house" (Luke 19:9).*

C. *Trust Christ as your Lord and Savior.*

D. *Let him come in as the abiding Guest and Adviser.*

E. *Let him occupy completely.*

Conclusion

A marriage begins when two people freely and fully decide to enter into a lifelong intimate relationship with each other. If you are among the young and unmarried, you should determine even now that your future home will be Christian. This will affect your choice of a companion and guide you in preparing for Christian marriage.

If you are already married, Christ wants to meet your deepest needs in the home. Trust him today. Cooperate with him, beginning today, that your home might be truly Christian.

SUNDAY EVENING, JUNE 8

Title: Choosing a Husband

Text: "The wife is bound by the law as long as her husband liveth; but if her husband be dead, she is at liberty to be married to whom she will; only in the Lord" **(1 Cor. 7:39)**.

Introduction

Our text speaks of marriage as being a permanent relationship for as long as life lasts. It also speaks concerning the possibility of a second marriage for the wife if her husband should die. A regulation concerning the choice is mentioned: "only in the Lord." The apostle is declaring that if a Christian widow chooses to remarry, she must restrict her considerations to those who profess faith in the Lord Jesus. If this be the case concerning the second marriage, surely the same regulation would hold true with the first marriage.

The Bible does not provide us with many specific instructions concerning the selection of a husband or wife, but it does provide us with some guiding principles that are applicable to us all. It might be enlightening to look at the first home to delineate some of these principles.

I. The first wedding (Gen. 1:27–28).

A. *God made both man and woman.*

B. *God made them different from each other.* They are to complement and supplement each other.

C. *God made them for each other.*

1. For companionship.

2. To glorify God.

3. For propagation of the race.

D. *God made this marriage as a model for all humanity.*

II. Choosing a life companion.

What kind of a husband do you want? Will just any kind be acceptable? What do you have to offer? Use your heart, your head, and your soul in making the choice.

A. *Your happiness depends on a right choice.*

B. *Your success depends on a right choice.*

C. *Others will be affected by your choice.*

1. Your parents.

2. Your church.

3. Your community.

4. Unborn children.

III. Factors to be considered in making your choice.

A. *A Christian's marriage is to be "only in the Lord" (1 Cor. 7:39).*

1. To marry a non-Christian is to disobey the revealed will of God (2 Cor. 6:14–16).

2. To do otherwise is to imperil your own happiness. Someone has facetiously said, "If you marry a child of the Devil, you can expect to have trouble with your father-in-law."

B. *A young woman is to choose one whom she can reverence (Eph. 5:33).* In this very significant passage, Paul uses the ideal relationship between a husband and wife to illustrate the mystical relationship between Christ and his church. It also provides some suggestions concerning qualities a young woman should seek in a husband.

Nothing is said directly about a wife loving her husband, though it is implied. Specifically the passage says she is to submit herself unto her husband as unto the Lord (Eph. 5:22), and she is to reverence her husband. The apostle is clearly implying that marriage should not be entered into unless there is a basis for genuine respect and reverence.

In a day when a tremendous importance is placed on love being the basis for marriage, there needs to be a recognition that true, lasting love between husband and wife is based on reverence.

IV. Practical questions to be considered.

A. *Are you really well acquainted with him?*

B. *Does he possess a vital faith in Jesus Christ?*

C. *Does he possess genuine character?* It is better to marry a man who is worth a million dollars but doesn't have a cent than to marry a man who has a million dollars but isn't worth a cent.

D. *Is he kind and generous?*

E. *Is he thoughtful and unselfish?*

F. *Is he absolutely honest and truthful?*

G. *Would he be a good father to your children?*

Conclusion

A pastor had finished a sermon to young people concerning the choice of a companion. Following the service, a very wise and experienced judge came by and said, "Pastor, everything that you said was true, but there was one other thing that you could have said to them. Marriage is still the biggest gamble they will ever make."

There is an element of risk in every marriage. In choosing your husband, you need to use the highest part of your intellect as well as the deepest emotions of your heart. Make your choice before the throne of grace, and then ask God to help you determine with all of your heart that you are going to achieve success. God will then work with you.

WEDNESDAY EVENING, JUNE 11

Title: A Prayer for Cleansing

Text: "And, behold, there came a leper and worshipped him, saying, Lord, if thou wilt, thou canst make me clean" (**Matt. 8:2**).

Introduction

If we would read the Word of God in a manner so as to feed our soul, we must let it speak to our condition. There is some message for us in every book and chapter if we have eyes to see and ears to hear what God would say to us.

We can learn much about prayer by taking notice of both the prayers Jesus answered and those he declined to answer affirmatively. The prayer of the leper is no exception.

I. The leper's condition.

The leper was acutely conscious of his leprosy and was overwhelmed by his uncleanness. During the days in which our Savior walked the earth, there was a stigma attached to those who had leprosy. They were considered ceremonially unclean and were not permitted to enter the temple area. They were quarantined from normal association with the healthy. In the ancient world, leprosy was the most terrible of all the diseases. The physical effects of leprosy and the spiritual effects of sin have some remarkable parallels.

A. *Sin on the moral plane, like leprosy on the physical plane, is the most awful thing that ever afflicted humanity.* No pen or picture can portray its horror or its devastation.

B. *Sin, like leprosy, is the most loathsome, polluting, deforming, unclean thing in the universe.*

C. *Sin, like leprosy, is deceitful in its workings.* Only time will reveal the terrible effects of sin as it is permitted to have its way in life.

D. *Sin, like leprosy, is in a sense contagious.* By continuous contact with those of evil and degrading habits, one exposes himself to the peril of yielding to temptation.

E. *While leprosy was practically incurable by human skill, only God can deal adequately with the problem of sin.*

F. *Sin, like leprosy, separates one from that which is clean.* The sinner is utterly unfit for heaven and the society of pure and holy beings until he or she is purified and made clean. As leprosy separated people from their fellow humans, so sin separates people from their friends, family, and worst of all, God.

II. The leper's prayer.

A. *He came to Jesus with reverence.* He worshiped Jesus as Lord.

B. *He came to Jesus with confidence.* It was a dangerous thing for a leper to approach a rabbi. Often stones were thrown at lepers as they came too close. The compassion of the Savior had been manifested in a manner that encouraged the leper to have confidence in his tenderness.

C. *The leper came in humility.* He made no demands upon Jesus. He issued no orders. He gave no instructions. He did not question the power of Jesus. His only concern was the willingness of Jesus: "Lord, if thou wilt, thou canst make me clean." He placed himself at the mercy of the Savior. He desired to be clean.

III. The Savior's reaction.

A. *Compassion.* Mark's gospel tells us that Jesus was moved with compassion (Mark 1:41). The Savior's heart suffered with the leper.

B. *Tenderness.* The compassion of the Savior caused him to do something that probably overwhelmed the soul of the leper. In tenderness Jesus stretched forth his hand and touched him. Never before or since has a touch of the hand spoken so tenderly and at the same time so strongly. It had been a long time since the leper had felt the touch of another's hand.

C. *Cleansing.* With a word, the sovereign Lord cleansed the leper of his terrible disease.

IV. The leper cleansed.

A. *The cure was instantaneous and complete.* It was the result not of human but of divine power.

B. *A marvelous change was accomplished; instead of being diseased, he was healthy.* In the place of foul repulsiveness, the leper's flesh became as clean as a baby's. Instead of being an outcast from society, he was restored to his community, his friends, and his family.

V. The leper's reaction.

A. *Jesus forbade a public proclamation of the leper's cleansing until after he had been declared cured through the proper channels prescribed for such (Lev. 13:1–17, 29–46; Matt. 8:4).*

B. *The cleansed leper was unable to contain himself (Mark 1:45).* To be clean after being unclean was a privilege so indescribably wonderful that he could not keep it secret. From the depths of his being, there was a volcanic eruption of joy that could not be repressed.

Conclusion

The joy of forgiveness, the consciousness of being clean through the blood of Christ (1 John 1:7), should motivate all of us to be joyful communicators of what Jesus has done and what he can do.

SUNDAY MORNING, JUNE 15

Title: "Our Father Which Art in Heaven"

Text: "Our Father which art in heaven, hallowed be thy name" (**Matt. 6:9**).

Hymns: "God, Our Father, We Adore Thee," Frazer

"Great Is Thy Faithfulness," Chisholm

"Faith of Our Fathers," Faber

Offertory Prayer: Eternal Father, you who are the giver of every good and perfect gift, we come to you today and give you offerings from our material substance. We thank you for life. We are grateful for health. We rejoice in the privilege of work, and we thank you for prosperity. Take these tithes and offerings as symbols of our desire to give ourselves completely to you through Jesus Christ our Lord. Amen.

Introduction

It is difficult for some people to love God because they have been deprived of an earthly father whom they could love sincerely and steadfastly.

The right kind of father can be a child's best teacher about God. A good father is a happy combination of strength and tenderness, righteousness and mercy. The wrong kind of father can cripple a child's emotional and spiritual well-being. Today I want to lead you to a better understanding and a deeper appreciation of the heavenly Father.

Jesus came to reveal God to man. "Philip said unto him, Lord, shew us the Father, and it sufficeth us. Jesus saith unto him, Have I been so long time with you, and yet hast thou not known me, Philip? He that hath seen me hath seen the

183

Father; and how sayest thou then, Shew us the Father? Believest thou not that I am in the Father, and the Father in me? The words that I speak unto you I speak not of myself: but the Father that dwelleth in me, he doeth the works" (John 14:8–11).

In the Gospels God is spoken of as "Father" more than 150 times (e.g., Jesus said, "I and my Father are one" [John 10:30]). This name was in the first recorded boyhood utterance of Jesus: "Wist ye not that I must be about my Father's business?" (Luke 2:49). This name was in his last dying cry: "Father, into thy hands I commend my spirit" (Luke 23:46).

People had thought of God and his followers in a number of different ways: a Shepherd and his sheep, a Potter and his clay, a Creator and his creatures, a King and his subjects, a Judge and violators of the law.

Jesus came to give us new truth about God so that we might walk lovingly in his way and so that we might have abundant life here and now.

Jesus taught his disciples—and all believers—to think of God as a heavenly Father.

Jesus did not consider all people to be the children of God (cf. John 8:44). He taught that in the miracle of the new birth, the spiritual birth, the birth from above, a new relationship was established with God that was much closer than that which exists between a Creator and the creatures of his world. This new relationship is tender, affectionate, and glorious.

I. God is a perfectly wise and consistent heavenly Father.

    A. *In contrast to even the best of earthly fathers, the heavenly Father perfectly knows our deepest needs even before we could request his blessings in prayer (Matt. 6:8).*

        1. He looks upon our needs with purposes of love and compassion.

        2. He is more eager to meet these deep needs than we are to have them met. "If ye [earthly fathers] then, being evil, know how to give good gifts unto your children, how much more shall your Father which is in heaven give good things to them that ask him?" (Matt. 7:11).

    B. *In contrast to even the best of natural fathers, the heavenly Father always acts toward us in a manner consistent with our highest good.* In the very beginning, the Evil One put doubt in the mind of Eve, the mother of us all, concerning the goodness of God. "Ye shall not surely die: For God doth know that in the day ye eat thereof, then your eyes shall be opened, and ye shall be as gods, knowing good and evil" (Gen. 3:4–5).

        1. The heavenly Father prohibits only that which is destructive.

        2. The heavenly Father challenges us to do that which is truly constructive and beneficial.

        3. The heavenly Father disciplines us for our good (Heb. 12:5–12).

        4. The heavenly Father punishes only when he is forced to do so. He dare not condone that which is destructive. When we continue toward moral perversity or disobedience, he will manifest his displeasure in a manner that may cause us to think that he is angry with us.

II. God is a gracious and providing Father.

  A. *God is gracious and loving.*

    1. He does not need to be bribed.

    2. We cannot merit his grace and love.

  B. *The heavenly Father provides the necessities for moral and spiritual health and happiness.* He is more interested in the fruits of life than he is with mere leaves and roots.

  C. *We need to trust implicitly in the providing Father who feeds the sparrows and clothes the lilies.*

    1. He has given us the Bible for nourishment.

    2. He has given us prayer for communion and fellowship.

    3. He has given us the Holy Spirit for guidance.

    4. He has given us a needy world in which to work.

  D. *At the end of the road, he has provided a house with many rooms (John 14:1 – 3).*

III. God is a restrained and suffering heavenly Father.

  A. *God has placed some restraints on his own power by giving people the privilege of choice.* He did not desire the worship of robots.

  B. *The heavenly Father suffers as only infinite love can suffer when his children persist in ways that will bring tragedy.*

IV. God is a merciful and forgiving heavenly Father.

  A. *The parable of the prodigal son presents an indescribably beautiful picture of the waiting Father.*

  B. *The psalmist grasped this truth.* "Like as a father pitieth his children, so the LORD pitieth them that fear him. For he knoweth our frame; he remembereth that we are dust" (Ps. 103:13 – 14).

    1. Without money and without price.

    2. Without pomp, ceremony, or ritual, the wayward son returned to the merciful and forgiving father.

V. God is a saving and keeping heavenly Father.

  A. *John 3:16.*

  B. *John 10:27 – 30.*

  C. *Romans 5:8.*

  D. *1 John 3:1.*

Conclusion

On this Father's Day, it would be wise for every father to have a genuine faith in and a loving relationship to the heavenly Father. If you are still outside the family of God, then receive Jesus Christ into your heart that you might become a child of God by faith.

Perhaps the greatest gift you can give your child is to be a father who will help your child understand and relate to the heavenly Father. The earthly father should be a replica of the heavenly Father.

You can be one of God's dear children. You can be a member of his loving family. You can have access to the heavenly home at the end of the way if you will let Christ be at home in your heart and life in the here and now.

SUNDAY EVENING, JUNE 15

Title: "As for Me and My House, We Will Serve the Lord"

Text: "As for me and my house, we will serve the Lord" (**Josh. 24:15**).

Introduction

Life is made up of a continuous series of decisions. Some choices that we make are seemingly inconsequential. However, when one looks back and considers the road that he or she has traveled, it is sometimes shocking to discover how significant some relatively small decisions have turned out to be.

Tonight we consider the decision of a man who lived long ago. Let this man's example, though he has been dead for many centuries, speak to you and encourage you to make a similar decision.

I. This was a man's decision.

It was no feminine voice that spoke these words: "As for me and my house, we will serve the Lord."

A. *We usually think of the mother as being the one mainly responsible for making the home Christian.*

B. *Joshua was not a weakling.* He was a mighty military leader.

C. *Joshua recognized the importance of the home being a spiritual sanctuary.*

D. *The wife alone cannot produce a Christian home.*

II. Joshua made a decision to put first things first.

A. *He saw the importance of being successful in his family life.*

B. *The family today has many foes.*

1. The competitive materialistic spirit of the age in which we live can be detrimental. We overemphasize the importance of things.

2. Liberal ideas about marriage and divorce permeate our society.

3. Alcohol abuse presents a threat to many homes.

4. Partners struggle to persevere in problems.

5. Resentment builds when forgiveness is not given.

III. Joshua's decision was an act of dedication.

A. *He recognized that he was a steward of his home life.*

B. *We need to determine that the will of God as revealed in Christ is to be the standard of conduct in our homes.*

IV. Joshua's decision invited God to come into his home.

A. *A Christian home is a spiritual fellowship with Christ at the center.*

B. *A Christian home is the producer of Christlike character.*

C. *A Christian home provides the sense of security that only love can produce.*

D. *A Christian home is a home where differences are settled using the Bible and prayer.*

E. *A Christian home is a home where unconditional love is the rule.*

F. *A Christian home makes a positive spiritual contribution to each member of the family.*

Conclusion

The head of the house must make a decision such as Joshua made. When Jesus taught his disciples to think of God, he did not present them with a mother image but rather a father image. By being the right kind of father, you can enable your children to have faith in the fatherhood of God.

May God help you to arrive at the same destiny-determining decision that Joshua made.

WEDNESDAY EVENING, JUNE 18

Title: Nehemiah's Prayer

Text: "And it came to pass, when I heard these words, that I sat down and wept, and mourned certain days, and fasted, and prayed before the God of heaven" **(Neh. 1:4).**

Introduction

Nehemiah rendered a great service to his nation. He was generous and faithful and was possessed by a splendid patriotism. He had a great love for his country. He was a businessman with a great love for God in his heart. A part of the explanation for the greatness of Nehemiah is to be found in his prayer life. Like spiritual giants in every generation, Nehemiah prayed more than his contemporaries.

I. The burden of a great need.

A. *Nehemiah was the trusted servant of Artaxerxes, king of Persia (1:1; 2:1–8).*

B. *News came of the desperate circumstances of those who had returned to Jerusalem from the captivity (1:2).*

C. *The returnees were suffering great deprivation (1:3).*

D. *The wall of Jerusalem was broken down, and the gates had been burned (1:3).* This meant that the people had no protection and were at the mercy of the powerful.

E. *Nehemiah presented the burden of his concern before the throne of God.*

187

II. An exalted concept of God (1:5).

A. *He prayed to the Lord God of heaven.*
B. *He prayed to the great God.*
C. *He prayed to the covenant-keeping God.*

III. A confession of sin.

A. *There was a personal confession of sin (1:6).*
B. *There was a confession of corporate or collective sin (1:7).*

IV. Claiming the promises.

A. *Nehemiah pleaded the promises of God (1:9).*
B. *Nehemiah trusted God to hear his prayer (1:10).*

V. Personal dedication to redemptive processes (1:10).

A. *Nehemiah trusted God to do what only God could do.*
B. *Nehemiah pledged himself to do what he and others were capable of doing.*

Conclusion

Great needs in our life or in the lives of those about us should encourage us to pray as did Nehemiah. Sincere prayer on our part is a pledge to cooperate with God in his work.

SUNDAY MORNING, JUNE 22

Title: A Guest in the House of God

Text: "Lord, who shall abide in thy tabernacle? who shall dwell in thy holy hill?" **(Ps. 15:1).**

Hymns: "O Worship the King," Grant

"Purer in Heart, O God," Davison

"Nothing Between," Tindley

Offertory Prayer: Our Father, this is the day you have made. We accept it as a gift and as a trust from your loving hand. You are the giver of every good and perfect gift. We thank you for life, for health, for ability, and for the opportunity to work and earn material benefits. We rejoice in the opportunity to offer upon your altar the fruits of our labors as an expression of our grateful worship to the end that the needs of the kingdom might be met. Bless these gifts to the relief of human suffering and to the salvation of souls. In Jesus' name. Amen.

Introduction

The Bible opens with a picture of man walking and talking with God. God had made man and placed him in a garden. Here he enjoyed beloved companionship in the midst of beautiful surroundings. And he was given a pleasant and satisfying occupation.

The Bible closes with a picture of God dwelling with the redeemed of all ages in an eternal home where ignorance, poverty, pain, disappointment, failure, death, and separation are unknown (Rev. 21:1–4).

Humans began with God. Their final destiny is intended to be with God if they will but respond to the divine efforts to forgive and redeem. It was sin that wrecked man's Garden of Eden. The Bible is a record of the activity of a gracious God who through the ages has sought to win people away from the way of rebellion and self-destruction. God would persuade us to walk by faith and obedience the way to fullness of joy and satisfying achievement.

I. The psalmist hungered for fellowship with God.

Psalm 15 was written by a man who assumed that many others would like to find again the position of privilege and security with God that had been lost because of sin. This hunger and delight in the presence of God is repeated many times in the hymnal of the ancient Hebrews. "How amiable are thy tabernacles, O LORD of hosts! My soul longeth, yea, even fainteth for the courts of the LORD: my heart and my flesh crieth out for the living God" (Ps. 84:1–2). The psalmist continues: "For a day in thy courts is better than a thousand. I had rather be a doorkeeper in the house of my God, than to dwell in the tents of wickedness" (v. 10).

A. *To dwell in the presence of God was to enjoy safety.* "I was glad when they said unto me, Let us go into the house of the LORD" (Ps. 122:1). "He that dwelleth in the secret place of the most High shall abide under the shadow of the Almighty" (91:1).

   People need the security of a sense of the presence of God in this modern age when the only thing that is certain is change. People's hearts are easily captured by fear when they have no awareness of the presence of God in the events that are taking place about them.

B. *The psalmist believed that the highest possible human satisfaction was to be found in God's presence.* Life apart from God was barren and incomplete, but with him life could be joyful. "Thou wilt shew me the path of life: in thy presence is fullness of joy; at thy right hand there are pleasures for evermore" (Ps. 16:11).

C. *David pictured this experience in terms of a feast prepared by the divine Host.* "Thou preparest a table before me in the presence of mine enemies: thou anointest my head with oil; my cup runneth over" (Ps. 23:5).

D. *The psalmist had observed that those whose character and purpose of life permitted them to enjoy the friendship and fellowship of God enjoyed a wonderful stability that was to be desired by everyone.* He declares this conclusion in the last sentence of the psalm. "He that doeth these things shall never be moved" (15:5). The writer of Psalm 1 had made the same observation. He described the fruit of the life of the man who lived in the house of God in beautiful terms: "He shall be like a tree planted by the rivers of water, that bringeth forth his fruit in his season; his leaf also shall not wither; and whatsoever he doeth shall prosper" (1:3).

II. A pointed question is put to God.

The psalmist pictures God as dwelling in a tent pitched perhaps out in the wilderness. The Hebrews loved to think of God's earthly dwelling as a tent or house of curtains. The low, spreading tent with its curtain represented the clouds that veiled God in heaven.

A question is put to God. Inquiry is made as to what kind of traveler is worthy to halt and crave hospitality from Jehovah. Who shall be found worthy to be a citizen of Zion? Who can be a guest and dwell as a permanent resident?

The tent on the holy hill is the tabernacle David built on Mount Moriah when he removed the ark from the house of Obed-edom to Jerusalem. It is thought of here as the place of the divine presence and of the community of God gathered around this holy place. The idea is not that of frequenting Zion as a place of worship, but of dwelling there. It is a picture of communion and participation in God's favor.

The question is asked for a twofold purpose. In the first place, the question was raised in order to exclude men, whose lives were wicked and hypocritical, from coming to the sanctuary and altar with a false and superstitious idea that these appointments of worship possessed some mystical virtue that could secure exemption from punishment or a toleration of falsehood, impurity, and wrong. The question is a repetition in another form of the positive declaration in Psalm 5:4: "For thou art not a God that hath pleasure in wickedness: neither shall evil dwell with thee." It is declared that God's holy court with all of its sacred privileges is a place of blessing and honor only for those whose character is true and pure.

III. A detailed answer is given.

Verse 2 gives a positive answer to the pointed question that had been directed to God. The answer is not to be taken as a direct answer from God. The psalmist presents himself as a suppliant before God: he reads, as it were, what is passing through God's heart, and he himself answers in accordance with the mind of God the question that he had just asked.

A. *Those who would dwell with God must walk uprightly.* Walking is used to represent the habitual course of life. Their way of life must be blameless, innocent, sincere, and complete. There must not be any known unconfessed and unforsaken sin in their lives. In all of the essential features of the character, there must be a sincere practice of genuine religion.

B. *The guest in the house of God is one who works righteousness.* His life is one of positive goodness. As our Lord went about doing good, so must his followers do something more than just make a good profession with the mouth. Their words must be accompanied by good deeds. They must be workers for God and for their fellow humans.

C. *To have the privilege of dwelling in the holy hill of God, guests must practice a rigid control over the use of their tongues.* Perfect truthfulness should characterize the speech of the children of God. Those with whom God will be pleased are the ones who do not permit their tongues to communicate that which is untrue, hurtful, and destructive to others. They are those who can be counted on to be honest and truthful in all of their conversation.

D. *The negative side of this truth is also spotlighted.* Those who would be God's guests will have some great refusals in their lives. They will refuse to use their tongues destructively. They will not be guilty of slander. They will not be talebearers. Others will not be able to accuse them truthfully of being gossips. They will not spread false reports.

    The church, the home, and the community would be greatly benefited if each of us would try to let our tongues be genuinely converted. Several questions could be asked with great profit before repeating many of the things that come to our ears. Is it truthful? Is it kind? Would I be willing to face the people with the criticism or story which I have heard and which I am tempted to repeat? Will Christ be pleased with the repetition of this story? We must let Christ censor our thoughts if we would regulate our words, because the tongue reveals the thoughts that we harbor in the mind.

E. *God's guests are doers of good to their neighbors rather than doers of evil.* This is possible because of the love of God within those who dwell with God.

F. *The inspired writer further discloses that those who are granted to dwell with God are those who have integrity and who honor those who are genuine and worthy and utterly abhor those who are reprobate.* A reprobate is one who is insincere, counterfeit. The guest of God refuses to whitewash iniquity even when iniquity is personified in one who claims or appears to be great.

G. *Such persons are further described as those who are dependable to the extent that they refuse to back out on a contract even if they discover that they are going to suffer loss.*

H. *Furthermore, those who dwell with God must refuse to profit from the pain of the unfortunate.* In the days of the psalmist, people did not borrow money except in times of great necessity. Those who loaned money were dealing with souls in pitiful distress. Only drought, famine, war, sickness, or some other tragedy caused people to borrow. Those who enjoyed God's favor were never to take advantage of the sufferings of the helpless. Money was to be loaned as an act of mercy rather than a means of making a high profit. Usury and bribery were two of the most common and flagrant offenses against justice. The psalmist declares that those who are guilty of taking advantage of the unfortunate, the widow, or the orphan should not expect to enjoy the presence and the favor of the God of Israel.

Conclusion

    They who would dwell with God and enjoy his presence, his protection, and his provisions must be men and women of high ethical and moral character with genuine faith and a faithfulness that expresses itself in kindness and mercy. Who is sufficient and adequate? Only through Jesus Christ can our sins be forgiven and can we find the inward strength and guidance that can make possible for us a life of fruitful fellowship with God and his people.

SUNDAY EVENING, JUNE 22

Title: Listen to the Witnesses

Text: "Wherefore seeing we also are compassed about with so great a cloud of witnesses ..." **(Heb. 12:1).**

Introduction

The text is a fertile plot containing many seeds of divine truth. These seeds have germinated and brought forth roots that have blessed the hearts and challenged the minds of God's servants through the ages.

The cloud of witnesses that surrounds us includes all of the saints who have preceded us. Some have surmised that they are eyewitnesses, spectators, beholders of that which transpires on the earth today. The inspired writer uses a figure of speech from the world of sports. He writes from the perspective of the center of a great arena. The saints are engaged in what appears to be a gladiator conflict in which death appears to be certain. The seats of the amphitheater are filled, not with idle spectators who have a thirst for blood, but rather with the heroes of the faith who have trusted God and have persevered even to the point of martyrdom. They are in the bleachers not merely to watch, but to share and to challenge and to inspire their successors now living to continue to hold to their faith and to do their best in the struggle of life.

If we would grasp the full import of this challenge, we need to recognize that the word *witness* is a word with legal connotation. In the New Testament this word is used of the testimony of the early disciples as if they were standing in a court of law with truth pertinent to the case under consideration. A witness is required and permitted to bear testimony concerning facts that he has seen or experienced. His testimony must follow out of a firsthand personal knowledge. The writer of the text visualizes this cloud of witnesses as testators rather than spectators.

The unsaved world was the jury who listened to the testimony of the early Christian witnesses and decided on the basis of that testimony whether Jesus of Nazareth was indeed the Christ of God. In the words of the text, those who have a testimony are bearing a witness to believers to encourage them to remain faithful and steadfast and to persevere.

I. An illustrious list of honorable witnesses.

Hebrews 11 has been called faith's "Hall of Fame." Actually, it contains a list of the witnesses with an abbreviated biographical sketch and with a hint concerning the testimony that they would give to those who now find themselves in the midst of the battle of life.

    A. *Abel would encourage us by faith to give God our best (11:4).*

    B. *Enoch would challenge us to walk with God in the midst of a crooked and perverse generation (11:5).*

    C. *Noah would challenge us to escape the consequences of sin (11:7).*

D. *Abraham would challenge us to obey God whatever the cost (11:8–19).*

E. *Isaac, Jacob, and Joseph would challenge us to trust God implicitly to accomplish his purpose in the future (11:20–22).*

F. *Moses would challenge us to trust God through the difficulties of the present with a view of the ultimate achievement and reward in the future (11:23–30).*

II. Continuous, recurring truths.

As witness after witness speaks from his place in the bleachers of heaven's amphitheater, certain great truths are emphasized over and over for the benefit of those who struggle under the burden of responsibility and strive to rise up and grasp spiritual opportunities.

A. *Believe in faith as a way of life.* Without exception the saints of Old Testament history speak from the witness stand to declare that God is faithful and trustworthy. They would encourage us to believe that we can count on God to keep his promises. They would declare that God is honest and honorable and does not play cruel jokes on those who trust him either in life or in death.

B. *The way of obedience is the pathway to achievement.* By faith they obeyed God as they understood his will for their lives. There is no substitute for obedience. Kingdom progress waits upon obedient disciples. Disobedience always produces disappointment. Obedience may bring hardship and difficulty, but it produces spiritual success.

C. *The way of sacrifice leads to significant achievement.* Without exception the real heroes of our faith have been men and women who have denied themselves their selfish desires and have given themselves unreservedly into the services of their God and their fellow humans.

III. You are the jury.

A. *Do you have faith in the witnesses who have borne a testimony concerning the faithfulness of God and the way to the life abundant?*

B. *Will you trust your life, your time, and your energy unto the services of God with whom these men walked and talked?*

C. *The decision is yours.* Without faith in God, it is impossible to please him. To distrust him is to insult him. To distrust him leaves a man to his own resources.

Conclusion

Let your mind and your heart be convinced that God is a good God and that his way of life, though difficult and dangerous at times, is in the long run the wisest and most satisfying life that one can live. Because of the accumulated testimony of many witnesses, be encouraged to trust God completely and obey him cheerfully.

WEDNESDAY EVENING, JUNE 25

Title: The Prayer of a Thief

Text: "And he said unto Jesus, Lord, remember me when thou comest into thy kingdom" **(Luke 23:42)**.

Introduction

The dying thief on the cross was unable to enter a temple to pray. It was impossible for him to fold his hands or to lift his hands in prayer. He could not go off to some quiet place alone and offer up his prayer to God. His only chance now was to pray while hanging on the cross.

Our God is Spirit, and they who worship him must worship him in Spirit and in truth. For this we can be grateful. While it would be unwise for us to wait until we are in sad circumstances similar to those of the thief, his prayer experience can be very helpful to each of us.

I. The thief was in a pitiful plight.

    A. *He was nailed to a cross.* Death was approaching with great certainty.

    B. *He believed in a God to whom he was responsible (Luke 23:40).*

    C. *He acknowledged that his death on the cross was the result of crimes he had committed.*

    D. *He had a belief in a future life and was aware of his unpreparedness for such (Luke 23:42).*

    E. *He was totally helpless.* There were no works that he could perform, and there were no ceremonies that he could observe. In the eyes of observers, there could be no doubt but that he was doomed for both time and eternity.

II. The thief offered a plea for pardon.

"Lord, remember me when thou comest into thy kingdom" (Luke 23:42).

    A. *The dying thief had somehow perceived the innocent perfection of Jesus.* "This man hath done nothing amiss" (Luke 23:41).

    B. *The thief acknowledged his guilt and confessed his sin.* "And we indeed justly; for we receive the due reward of our deeds" (v. 41).

    C. *The thief made no attempt to explain or to excuse his sin.*

    D. *The thief made a public confession of his faith in the kingship of the Christ who was officially being crucified.* "Lord, remember me when thou comest into thy kingdom" (Luke 23:42). Thus he spoke to Jesus as to a king and prayed to him as if he were God.

        1. His prayer was a single, short sentence.

        2. His plea was humble in that he only requested to be remembered.

        3. His prayer was utterly sincere, for he was an accused sinner on the brink of eternity.

194

4. His prayer was courageous, for by so praying he identified himself with Christ and expressed his condemnation of those who had brought about the execution of Christ.

III. The thief received a precious promise.

"Today shalt thou be with me in paradise" (Luke 23:43). By this precious promise Jesus assured the thief that he was willing, ready, and able to meet his deepest needs.

A. *Jesus assured him that life does not end in physical death.*
B. *Jesus promised him the privilege of continuing fellowship.*
C. *Jesus revealed that entrance into the heavenly home is immediate when death occurs.* Note that Jesus said the forgiven thief would be with him in paradise "today." To be absent from the body is to be present with the Lord (2 Cor. 5:8).
D. *Jesus' promise reveals that salvation comes in the moment of trust and surrender.*

> *Not the labors of my hands*
> *Can fulfill Thy law's demands; ...*
> *Nothing in my hand I bring;*
> *Simply to Thy cross I cling.*
> —A. M. Toplady

Conclusion

The thief had a chance to be saved, and he seized it. He would encourage us to believe that all of God's dealings with sinners are based on God's unmerited grace as people respond to him by faith.

The thief sets a good example for every sinner. The Lord can and will hear our prayers if we are sincere in seeking him.

SUNDAY MORNING, JUNE 29

Title: Show Forth His Salvation

Text: "Sing unto the Lord, bless his name; show forth his salvation from day to day" **(Ps. 96:2)**.

Hymns: "Praise Him, Praise Him," Crosby

"When I Survey the Wondrous Cross," Watts

"Since I Have Been Redeemed," Excell

Offertory Prayer: Our Father, as Jesus sat by the treasury and saw the widow give her last coin, help us to be aware that he knows perfectly both the amount that we give and the amount that we retain for our own use. Help us to give in a manner that would bring us his divine approval. Help us to give because of love for you and because of love for others. Help us to give, not grudgingly, but out of hearts filled with gratitude for all of your good gifts to us. Help each of us to know that it is impossible for us to outgive the God who gave his Son for us. In Jesus' name. Amen.

Introduction

Many Christians believe that the missionary imperative of our faith is based on the Great Commission alone. A sincere study of the Old Testament will reveal that God always intended that his people should be an evangelistic and missionary force through whom he could reveal his grace and mercy, his power and purpose, his holiness and righteousness, his love and salvation to a needy race.

The trumpet-toned commission of our Lord can be heard faintly in this Old Testament hymn, for the psalmist calls attention to Israel's missionary charter. This grand coronation anthem falls into four stanzas: The first stanza invites Israel to assume its high vocation as the Lord's evangelist. The second stanza sets God high above the idols, the nothings, which were worshiped by the pagan nations of the earth. The third stanza invites the people of all nations to enter the temple gates to worship and to honor and bless the name of the Lord on an equal basis with the Jewish people. The fourth and final stanza calls upon nature in all of its heights and depths and lengths and breadths to praise the Lord for his greatness and goodness.

The text describes our mission. We are to "show forth his salvation." The method for doing this is disclosed. A demonstration is called for in the words "show forth his salvation from day to day." The message of ancient Israel and of the modern church is disclosed in the words "show forth his salvation."

I. Our mission is defined: "Show forth his salvation."

We do well if our life is an anthem of praise to the Lord. By this anthem of praise we are to communicate to the unsaved about us the wonders of God's grace toward all people.

From the very beginning, our faith has been a missionary faith and God has been seeking to reach more and more people with the message of his redeeming love. God's great missionary purpose began with Abraham. And his all-inclusive redemptive purpose was disclosed in his command to Jonah to go to the wicked city of Nineveh.

Today those who are in the church occupy the position of privilege and responsibility that was once enjoyed by Israel. "But ye are a chosen generation, a royal priesthood, an holy nation, a peculiar people; that ye should show forth the praises of him who hath called you out of darkness into his marvelous light: Which in time past were not a people, but are now the people of God: which had not obtained mercy, but now have obtained mercy" (1 Peter 2:9–10).

II. Our method is described: "Show forth his salvation from day to day."

A. *We are to show forth his salvation by what we are.* One picture is worth a thousand words. We are to be living demonstrations of the difference Christ can make. We are to be exhibits of his gracious love. We can be samples of his transforming power.

A pastor and a visiting evangelist visited an unsaved husband in the home where the claims of Christ were brought to bear upon his heart. The man was open, appreciative, and responsive. After some discussion, the three knelt in prayer and the unsaved man trusted Jesus Christ as his Lord and Savior. After a time of rejoicing, the guests departed, and as they were leaving, the pastor, Dr. A. D. Foreman, said, "You could tell by the way that man talked that he had faith in his wife's religion. I can always tell after talking to a man for ten minutes if he has faith in his wife's religion."

Actually, the pastor and the evangelist did not convince the man that he should trust Jesus Christ as his Savior. The wife's daily life had already accomplished this task. They were able to lead him to be decisive and to definitely yield his life to his wife's Savior.

B. *We are to show forth his salvation by what we believe.* What a person believes affects his or her behavior. We need a great faith in the love of God, but we also need to believe in the wrath of God. It is good to believe that there is a heaven, but we must also believe that there is a hell. Only as we believe in our divine origin and our divine destiny by God's grace will we live the life of faith and service.

C. *We must show forth his salvation by what we do.* Our task is that of being Christ's hands and feet on earth.

> *Christ has no hands but our hands*
>   *To do His work today,*
> *He has no feet but our feet*
>   *To lead men in His way,*
> *He has no tongue but our tongues*
>   *To tell men how He died,*
> *He has no help but our help*
>   *To bring them to His side.*
> *We are the only Bible*
>   *The careless world will read,*
> *We are the sinner's gospel,*
>   *We are the scoffer's creed,*
> *We are the Lord's last message,*
>   *Given in deed and word.*
> *What if the line is crooked?*
>   *What if the type is blurred?*
> *What if our hands are busy*
>   *With other work than His?*
> *What if our feet are walking*
>   *Where sin's allurement is?*
> *What if our tongues are speaking*

> *Of things His lips would spurn?*
> *How can we hope to help Him*
> *And hasten His return?*
> —*Annie Johnson Flint*

III. Our message is disclosed: "Show forth his salvation."

    A. *We must introduce God to a lost, needy world.* He is the living, personal, holy, saving, redeeming God. The world needs to know the wonders of his grace and wisdom, peace and power, joy and victory.

    B. *We must interpret man to our world.* He is the crowning climax of God's creative activity. While man was made in the image and likeness of God, by his sin he has created a Frankenstein that threatens him with self-destruction. The wonder of it all is that in spite of his rebellion and wickedness, he is the object of God's redeeming love.

Conclusion

With the language of both our life and our lips, we are to bear a personal testimony to the world about us concerning the gracious God who has revealed himself as indescribable love in Jesus Christ.

Our mission is glorious. The method is simple. The message is for all. May God help you today to respond according to the deepest longings of your heart, the highest thoughts of your mind, and the leading of God's Holy Spirit.

SUNDAY EVENING, JUNE 29

Title: "Render Therefore unto Caesar"

Text: "And he said unto them, Render therefore unto Caesar the things which be Caesar's and unto God the things which be God's" **(Luke 20:25)**.

Introduction

As we approach the day on which we celebrate the signing of the Declaration of Independence, it is appropriate that we pay tribute to our country and offer praise to God for his blessings and his guidance upon the founding fathers of our country. Our nation is often the envy of the world. We are fortunate to be the citizens of a great nation like America.

We have both a Christian and a patriotic duty to help our nation to be a better place in which to live, work, and worship.

In our text the Savior enunciated the principle that, while first place always belongs to God, the state (or Caesar) occupies a place in God's plan for our lives.

No one passage of Scripture deals with the whole duty of a Christian to either his national or local government. But Paul's epistle to the Romans (13:1–7) does give some specific instructions concerning the proper Christian attitude and responsibility to the duties of citizenship.

I. We are to be subject to the state because government is a divine institution (Rom. 13:1).

II. Resistance to constituted authority is disobedience to God and will be punished (Rom. 13:2).

III. Governmental officials, viewed ideally, are God's ministers appointed to encourage what is good and to punish what is evil (Rom. 13:3–4).

IV. Only evildoers have anything to fear from properly constituted authority (Rom. 13:4).

V. The laws of the country should be obeyed because it is the right thing to do rather than because of the fear of the consequences of disobedience (Rom. 13:5).

VI. The power of taxation is legitimate, and the payment of taxes is a Christian duty (Rom. 13:6).

VII. The Christian should fulfill his many obligations to the state (Rom. 13:7).

Conclusion

In his epistle to Timothy, Paul encouraged that "supplications, prayers, intercessions, and giving of thanks, be made for all men; for kings, and for all that are in authority; that we may lead a quiet and peaceable life in all godliness and honesty" (1 Tim. 2:1–2). We have a responsibility to God to remember our governmental officials in prayer. Our desire for peace and harmony and our concern for the welfare of others should cause us to pray for our leaders.

On the Fourth of July some will explode fireworks. Many will display the flag. Others will go to picnics. Perhaps the greatest service that we could render to our nation would be to spend some time in earnest prayer that it might be worthy of God's continued blessings.

JULY

- ■ **Sunday Mornings**

    Continue the series "Inspiration from the Psalms."

- ■ **Sunday Evenings**

    Continue the series of expository sermons based on Hebrews 12, following the theme "Challenges to Consecrated Christian Living."

- ■ **Wednesday Evenings**

    Conclude the series "The Child of God in Prayer."

WEDNESDAY EVENING, JULY 2

Title: The Prayer of a Great Sinner

Text: "Have mercy upon me, O God, according to thy lovingkindness: according unto the multitude of thy tender mercies blot out my transgressions" (**Ps. 51:1**).

Introduction

May God spare each of us from sinning in the same manner and to the same degree in which David sinned. Adultery and murder are two heinous sins. One does not have to have a Christian's conscience to be shocked and horrified at the sins of a man whom the Bible describes as a man after God's own heart. Perhaps one of the reasons why David was so described was due to the manner in which he confessed his sin. While some deny the fact of sin and others ignore the presence of sin and still others attempt to hide or to excuse sin, David dealt with his sin — upon his knees.

I. David made a plea for pardon.

A. *David acknowledged his sin as his own responsibility (Ps. 51:3).*

1. He claimed every bit of the guilt.
2. He did not blame a generation that had lowered its standards.
3. He did not blame circumstances that had "thrown the two of them together."
4. He did not blame Bathsheba.

B. *David confessed the nature of his sin.*

1. Transgressions (*pesha*). This word pictures a rebellious soul guilty of willfully transgressing the law of God.

200

2. Iniquity (*awon*). This word means crookedness or twistedness. He recognized that his life was out of tune and out of touch with God.

3. Sin (*hatah*). The word means to miss the mark, to fall short of the aim. David had deliberately transgressed the holy law. Consequently, his life had become twisted, warped, and made an ugly thing. The result was that he fell below God's aim and purpose for his life.

C. *The king cast himself upon God's mercy.* His only hope was in God's mercy. He used three words that reveal the longing of his heart before God.

1. Blot out my transgressions (Ps. 51:1).
2. Wash me. Wash out my defiled and unclean heart (Ps. 51:2).
3. Cleanse me from my sin; make me clean enough for the eyes of God.

II. David made a plea for purity (Ps. 51:7).

A. *David did not want pardon alone.* He wanted to be made clean so that he could be admitted to his old place in God's plan for his life (Ps. 51:7).

B. *He prayed for an inward condition of being right with God.*
1. Create in me a clean heart.
2. Renew a right spirit within me.

C. *Restore unto me.* David wanted to regain the music in his soul that had been lost because of sin (Ps. 51:8). He wanted to hear the joy bells of heaven again.

D. *"Restore unto me the joy of thy salvation" (Ps. 51:12).*

III. David made a promise to serve (Ps. 51:13 – 15).

A. *"Then will I teach transgressors thy ways."*
B. *"Sinners shall be converted unto thee."*
C. *"My tongue shall sing aloud of thy righteousness."*
D. *"My mouth shall show forth thy praise."*

Conclusion

Psalm 32 is the testimony of a forgiven sinner who tries to describe the joys of knowing that his sins have been forgiven. Even God could not eliminate the consequences of David's sin, but God could and did forgive the guilt of his sin.

As a confessor of sin, David provides a good example for all of us. Instead of ignoring or concealing or attempting to explain our sin, let's be wise enough to acknowledge sin, confess sin, and forsake sin.

SUNDAY MORNING, JULY 6

Title: "Serve the LORD with Gladness"

Text: "Serve the LORD with gladness: come before his presence with singing" **(Ps. 100:2).**

Hymns: "Rejoice, Ye Pure in Heart," Plumptre

          "Serve the Lord with Gladness," McKinney

          "He Keeps Me Singing," Bridgers

Offertory Prayer: Holy Father, we thank you for this church family. We thank you for what it means to this community and to your work around the world. We rejoice now in the opportunity to bring our offerings to you that the work and ministry of this church might be prosperous and successful. May your blessings be on these offerings to that end. In Jesus' name we pray. Amen.

Introduction

Psalm 100 issues seven challenges to the heart of the redeemed. An invitation is extended for us to participate in joyful praise and service. The psalmist calls for positive service, regular service, continuous service, and wholehearted service. Service motivated by glad, joyful hearts is what the world needs, what the church needs, and what God needs; and it is something you can render.

I. Serve the Lord with gladness, for this is the natural and proper response of the redeemed.

    A. *Gratitude will produce joyous service.*

    B. *Reason affirms that our service should be joyous.*

        1. God is our Creator.

        2. God is our Redeemer.

        3. God protects us.

        4. God's purposes for us are purposes of love.

        5. God has provided a home at the end of the way.

II. Serve the Lord with gladness to be saved from inward collapse and the pursuit of unworthy objectives.

    A. *It is easy to forget God.*

    B. *People neglect God and misunderstand him.*

    C. *Worship and service are as essential for happy living as food and rest are necessary for healthy living.*

    D. *We all are busy, but what are we busy doing?* One of the great tragedies of our age is that people are giving first-rate loyalty to third-rate causes. Serious thought should be given to that which should have top priority in both our interests and our investments. Where do God's will and God's work figure into your plans? If you are not working for God in some way, you are giving yourself to something that is unworthy of your best.

III. Serve the Lord with gladness to achieve and experience moral and spiritual fulfillment.

    A. *Deep within the human breast there is a hunger for fulfillment and achievement.*

    B. *There are many ways in which we seek for this happiness.*

       1. Some ways are deceptive and destructive.

         a. Some search for the highest good in the realm of material things.

         b. Some seek happiness in sensual pleasure.

         c. Some try numerous other pathways.

       2. We should always seek constructive opportunities.

         a. Education.

         b. Community service.

         c. A deep commitment to the Lord and a life of unselfish service motivated by his love are the most satisfying achievements one can experience.

IV. Our service must be joyous if we are to be true representatives of Christ.

    A. *Jesus' beautiful personality served as a magnetic power, drawing multitudes to hear his message.*

    B. *Only as our life is characterized by gladness and joy can we hope to attract others to the Christian way of life.* "These things have I spoken unto you, that my joy might remain in you, and that your joy might be full" (John 15:11).

V. Serve the Lord with gladness.

    A. *God loves you.*

    B. *God is able to give you victory in life.*

    C. *God can use you to bless others if you are willing and available.*

    D. *Your life can take on new beauty and new meaning if you respond to God's purpose for your life with gladness and joy.*

Conclusion

If you are still among the unsaved, God will be glad to forgive you and to bestow on you the gift of new life. He will not force his grace and salvation upon you, but he offers it to you freely through Jesus Christ. Today, turn from the life of unbelief and from the waste of sin and gladly entrust yourself into his hands.

SUNDAY EVENING, JULY 6

Title: "Lay Aside Every Weight"

Text: "Wherefore seeing we also are compassed about with so great a cloud of witnesses, let us lay aside every weight, and the sin which doth so easily beset us, and let us run with patience the race that is set before us" **(Heb. 12:1)**.

Introduction

Followers of Christ who would be truly Christian and accept God's will for their lives must expend as much moral and spiritual effort as a champion athlete expends in winning a race.

Spiritual trophies are not won by those who warm the bench. The crown of victory, which the Heavenly Umpire wishes to bestow, will not be granted to those who fall by the wayside and drop out of the race (Gal. 6:9).

Athletes lay aside all of the weights and hindrances that would prevent them from achieving their objective. Often, football players will wear heavy coats as they sit on the sidelines, but they lay these aside when it comes time to play.

There are some things that the disciples of our Lord must lay aside if we are to achieve our destiny. The weights that must be laid aside are either sinful or, in some instances, legitimate activities. Some things are not harmful within themselves but must be given up if we are to give ourselves unreservedly to the work of God.

I. Lay aside the weight of spiritual immaturity and inexperience.

Newborn Christians are but babes in Christ. They can only understand on a child's level the things of God. They can only do what children can do. God does not expect newborn Christians to be able to render the same service that is expected from experienced and mature disciples.

A tragedy of tragedies is that many disciples remain spiritual babes and never give themselves to a discipline of growth and training that makes it possible for them to render significant service for the Lord.

The gospel tells us that even "Jesus increased in wisdom and stature, and in favour with God and man" (Luke 2:52). There is nothing sinful or wrong about being a newborn babe in Christ, but to remain such indefinitely is a sin against God, self, and a needy world.

II. Lay aside the weight of self-righteous self-satisfaction.

One of the greatest foes to spiritual growth is an attitude of self-satisfaction. All of us have been guilty of looking about us with a critical spirit and patting ourselves on the back for our achievements when we beheld the failures and deficiencies of others.

A. *By parable and precept, the Savior pointed out the tragedy of self-righteousness.* The first beatitude, which is the foundational characteristic of an ideal citizen of the kingdom of God (Matt. 5:3), demonstrates how out of place the attitude of self-righteousness is.

B. *The parable of the Pharisee and the publican contains a pointed message for the saved and unsaved alike at this point (Luke 18:9–14).*

C. *The sin of the Laodicean church was primarily an attitude of spiritual self-satisfaction with the status quo (Rev. 3:17).*

As church members, we must not permit ourselves to become a pious self-centered circle of people who come together only for emotional "self-edification."

III. Lay aside the weight of an unforgiving spirit.

Injuries because of either the actions or talk of others are inevitable. There is no way by which we can please everyone. There is no way by which we can escape criticism. At times others will deliberately seek to harm us in one way or another.

Jesus counseled his disciples that they must forgive until seventy times seven (Matt. 18:21–22). As long as attention is directed toward the offending party who needs forgiveness, it is impossible to understand and appreciate what Jesus was really trying to say. His primary and immediate concern was the effect of an unforgiving spirit upon the heart and life of the offended party. Ill feelings have a way of festering into hate. Hate is a corrosive force that destroys joy and robs the heart of happiness. Hostile feelings are more injurious to the one who does the hating than they are to the person who is hated. One cannot run the race of the Christian life successfully and carry a grudge on his or her back at the same time.

Joseph freely and fully forgave his brothers of the injury that they had inflicted upon him. He was able to see how God had used even their evil to accomplish a good objective for him (Gen. 45:5; 50:20). Because it is difficult to forgive those who have mistreated us, we need to look constantly unto Jesus, who forgave even those who crucified him, for help in the matter of forgiving.

An ex-convict, who was converted while in prison, told how at the beginning of his prison term the desire for revenge upon some people consumed his thoughts and energies. After he found Christ as his Savior, he was able to forgive and rid his heart of hate. After hate was eliminated, he was able to say, "Now I am a new man."

IV. Lay aside the weight of worry and care.

Undue anxiety and worry are due to a lack of faith. Worry about the future leads to earthly mindedness and a desire to accumulate riches for both the present and the future (1 Tim. 6:9–10).

A. *Worry is useless (Matt. 6:27).*

B. *Worry often comes because we are forgetful of the blessings of the heavenly Father (Matt. 6:28–30).*

C. *Cares and worry are heathenish (Matt. 6:32).*

D. *Cares and worry are injurious (Matt. 6:34).* If we worry about the failures of yesterday and the uncertainties of tomorrow, the load becomes so heavy that we are unable to do the work of today.

If we will accept ourselves as we are (Matt. 6:27) and evaluate ourselves (6:30) and dedicate ourselves (6:33), perhaps we will find it easier to lay aside the weight of worry as we seek to run the race that is set before us.

Conclusion

The Greek athletes who participated in great Olympic games were stripped of every possible hindering weight. There are some things that must be laid aside if you would give yourself to the task of living up to God's will for your life. Do so gladly for the glory of him who gave up heaven and bore a cross on Calvary for you.

WEDNESDAY EVENING, JULY 9

Title: The Sin of Prayerlessness

Text: "God forbid that I should sin against the LORD in ceasing to pray for you: but I will teach you the good and the right way" **(1 Sam. 12:23)**.

Introduction

Samuel, the prophet of God, considered prayerlessness as a sin against the Lord. To live a prayerless life is to be disobedient to the command of God. The spirit and habit of prayer is commanded and encouraged throughout the Bible.

I. Prayerlessness is a sin against God.

To live a life of prayerlessness is to live a life of rebellion against God. Prayer is not just an opportunity; it is a responsibility. Prayer is not just a monologue in which we express our wishes and wants to God; it is a dialogue in which we also listen to God. Through prayer God has designed to give us grace and guidance, correction and instruction as we seek to live according to his will.

To live a prayerless life means we neglect to check into headquarters to find out what "the Boss" wants us to do.

II. Prayerlessness is a sin against self.

We impoverish ourselves when we neglect to pray. Prayer is the divinely ordained channel through which we are to receive those things essential to carrying on the work of God.

Prayerlessness reveals something tragic about our spiritual heart condition. Neglect of the closet of prayer indicates smug spiritual satisfaction, moral laziness, unbelief, and preoccupation with the world.

III. Prayerlessness is a sin against others.

When we spiritually impoverish ourselves by failing to pray, we also rob others of blessings.

Have you ever really wanted a vibrant faith? Do you eagerly covet divine wisdom? Do you hunger for inward strength to understand the sinful pressures about us? These are but just a few of the blessings that come as a result of prayer that affects the lives of those about us.

IV. Developing a prayerful spirit.

A. *Set apart a time in your daily schedule for prayer.*

B. *Pray with faith until you get an answer from God.*

C. *Pray about needs and problems as they arise.*

D. *Follow the Bible examples of prayer.* Study the prayers that Jesus answered positively and those he answered negatively. Adjust your prayers accordingly.

Conclusion

The use of credit cards has greatly increased during recent years. Some companies have issued company credit cards to certain employees. They are authorized to use these credit cards to requisition needed items for the operation of their business, but they may not use them for personal purchases.

Prayer is heaven's company credit card by which we may requisition the things needed for living and working effectively as servants of God.

SUNDAY MORNING, JULY 13

Title: "Praise Ye the LORD"

Text: "In the courts of the LORD's house, in the midst of thee, O Jerusalem. Praise ye the LORD" (**Ps. 116:19**).

Hymns: "All Hail the Power," Perronet

"O for a Thousand Tongues," Wesley

"Praise to God, Immortal Praise," Barbauld

Offertory Prayer: Heavenly Father, today we bring a portion of our income to you. Help us also to bring ourselves and to dedicate all that we are to you as our reasonable worship. Help us to dedicate our bodies as living sacrifices that others may see the beauty of holiness and by so doing come to hunger for a knowledge of Jesus Christ as Savior and Lord. Bless with your Holy Spirit these tithes and offerings so that others will have the joy of knowing Jesus. For Christ's sake. Amen.

Introduction

Psalm 116 begins with a list of the many reasons why the psalmist found it easy to love God. The psalmist closes with the word "Hallelujah," which, when translated, means "Praise ye the Lord."

If we will list the reasons why we love the Lord, an anthem of praise will rise up from our hearts and flow from our lips. The world needs to hear words of praise concerning the God who can produce joy, peace, and harmony in life.

The world goes on in spiritual darkness and disillusionment because we who have experienced God's grace and power have neglected to praise him for his goodness and wonderful works.

I. The psalmist lists some of the reasons why we should praise the Lord.

A. *The psalmist says I love the Lord because:*
  1. He has heard my prayers (v. 1).
  2. He has healed my body (v. 3).
  3. He has delivered me from trouble (v. 3).
  4. He has dealt bountifully with me (v. 7).
  5. He has delivered my soul from death (v. 8).
  6. He has wiped the tears from my eyes (v. 8).
  7. He has delivered my feet from falling (v. 8).
B. *We should praise the Lord because we have experienced his grace.*
C. *Christian privileges demand praise and thanksgiving.*
  1. Prayer.
  2. Christian fellowship.
  3. Service opportunities.
D. *Family mercies call aloud for praise to God.*
E. *National blessings put us under obligation to praise the Lord.* To praise God is our duty to God, to ourselves, and to others (Ps. 146:1–2).

II. The psalmist describes how we can praise God.

A. *"I will walk before the* LORD *in the land of the living" (v. 9).*
B. *"I will take the cup of salvation, and call upon the name of the* LORD*" (v. 13).*
C. *"I will pay my vows unto the* LORD *now in the presence of all his people" (v. 14).*
D. *"I will offer to thee the sacrifice of thanksgiving" (v. 17).*

III. The psalmist tells us when to praise the Lord. "I will pay my vows unto the LORD now" (v. 14).

A. *It is easy to praise God in seasons of prosperity.*
B. *We should also praise him in days of adversity.*
C. *The trusting heart will find many things to praise the Lord for when death knocks at the door.*

IV. The psalmist tells us where to praise the Lord.

A. *In the courts of the Lord's house (v. 19).*
B. *In Jerusalem (v. 19).*
C. *Throughout the whole world.*

V. The effects of praising the Lord.

A. *Praising the Lord promotes the growth of God's kingdom.*

B. *Praising the Lord lessens the suffering of men.*

C. *Praising the Lord will create a deeper love for God and others.*

D. *Praising the Lord will strengthen our faith.*

E. *Praising the Lord pleases God.*

Conclusion

You can be a real blessing to your friends and to your family if you will give expression to the gratitude of your heart for the blessings of God upon you. Christian witnessing is verbalizing the gratitude of your own heart with a view to persuading others to receive Jesus Christ as their personal Savior. May God help you to make your life a continual anthem of praise to God.

SUNDAY EVENING, JULY 13

Title: "The Sin Which Doth So Easily Beset Us"

Text: "Let us lay aside every weight, and the sin which doth so easily beset us" **(Heb. 12:1)**.

Introduction

Most of us have what we call "a besetting sin." By a besetting sin, we refer to some personal weakness or shortcoming. Usually we justify or explain our reason for tolerating this sin to the extent that our conscience does not hurt us too much.

What is your besetting sin? Is it a vile temper? Is it a critical spirit? Is it a sharp tongue? Is it profanity? Could it be spiritual idleness?

Instead of a different sin for each person, the writer of the book of Hebrews is referring to a sin that is common to us all—the sin of unbelief. The sin of unbelief is the sin God's people have been guilty of through the ages. Failure to exercise faith was the undoing sin of the Israelites. Weak faith plagued the early church. Our failure to trust God robs the modern church and the individual Christian of spiritual power and achievement.

The sin of unbelief causes the unbeliever to remain lost and under the wrath of God. It causes the children of God to remain in spiritual infancy.

I. Our unbelief and the Savior.

A. *It is a source of grief to him.*

B. *Lack of confidence disappoints his love.*

C. *Little faith is an insult to his truthfulness.*

D. *Failing to trust him hinders his purposes for us.*

II. The results of this besetting sin.

A. *Imaginary dangers darken the pathway ahead when we do not face the future with a genuine faith in the living Lord (James 4:2).*

B. *Without faith the resources of God that come in response to believing prayer are undiscovered (James 4:2).*

C. *Without faith the fear of failure captures the heart of the one who would be the servant of Christ, and he will attempt only that which is humanly possible (Phil. 4:13).*

D. *Without faith we place limitations on both the power and the activity of God (Ps. 78:41).*

E. *Refusal to trust God dishonors and displeases him (Heb. 11:6).*

III. The cause of little faith.

A. *We have a natural inclination to see obstacles and difficulties and to form opinions on the basis of mere appearances.* We depend too much on human agency alone.

B. *We forget and ignore the presence of God (Zech. 4:6; John 14:12).*

C. *We fail to recognize that faith is both the gift of God and something that we develop as we discover that God is faithful in keeping his promises (Mark 9:23–24).*

IV. The cure for little faith.

How can you put aside that besetting sin of unbelief and grow a great faith?

A. *Put faith in faith.* Instead of trusting alone in human ability and common sense, recognize that the presence and power of God comes into human life through the channel of faith.

B. *Interpret the Bible, not only as a history of what happened in the past, but also as a revelation of what can happen in the present.* Identify with biblical characters and recognize that we can depend on God to respond toward us as he did to them in ages gone by. This is the whole purpose of the challenge in Hebrews 12:1 and the list of witnesses that are marched on to the witness stand of Hebrews 11. Each of these would tell us that God can be depended on and that we can trust him implicitly.

C. *Pray for the gift of an increasing faith (Luke 17:5).*

D. *Place your confidence in the promises of God to the very limit of your ability and capacity (Heb. 11:23).*

Conclusion

We trust God for the salvation of our souls through the death of Jesus Christ on the cross. Let us also trust him with the daily decisions and responsibilities we face.

WEDNESDAY EVENING, JULY 16

Title: The Prayer of a Pastor for His People

Text: "For this cause I bow my knees unto the father of our Lord Jesus Christ" (**Eph. 3:14**).

Introduction

Paul wrote his epistle to the Ephesians while he was in prison. He was separated from them by great distance and by the bonds that imprisoned him.

Paul was a man who believed with all his heart in the power of prayer. He rejoiced in the privilege of prayer. He made much of the opportunity to pray. Again and again we see him on his knees when for all practical purposes his chains fell off and he entered the presence of God on behalf of those for whom he felt a particular responsibility.

The letter to the Ephesians contains two inspired prayers. In the first (1:15–23), he prayed that the Ephesians might have a new insight into the nature of the spiritual realities and a new comprehension of the unique significance of the person of Jesus Christ. The second prayer contains four petitions that his beloved Ephesian friends might be fully equipped to accomplish the purpose of God for their lives.

I. A prayer for inward power (Eph. 3:16).

A. *A power that is divine.*

B. *A power that is communicated by the Holy Spirit.*

C. *A power that is experienced in the inner man, the seat of intellectual and spiritual life.*

For many years Popeye was a famous comic-strip character who found himself in some impossible situations. In times of trouble, he was provided with indescribable energy by eating a can of spinach. For Christians to overcome the evil within and around them and to serve God and fellow humans at the same time, they need energy somewhat comparable to the energy that came from Popeye's can of spinach. This energy is available in and through the Holy Spirit.

II. A prayer that Christ may dwell in your hearts (Eph. 3:17).

A. *The presence of Christ in us is a matter of degrees and advances.*

B. *In some Christ is present, in others he is prominent, and in others he is preeminent.*

C. *Paul was praying that Christ might dwell in their hearts fully so that their total being would be molded and controlled by his dynamic presence.*

III. A prayer for a full comprehension (Eph. 3:18–19).

A. *Paul was praying that his readers might fully understand that which cannot be completely comprehended.*

B. *He was praying that they might know by experience the limitless love of God.*

   1. It is wide without being shallow.

211

2. It is long without being thin.
3. It is deep without being narrow.
4. It is high yet within the reach of all.

IV. A prayer for the fullness of God (Eph. 3:19).

A. *Paul prayed for the Ephesians that they might enter into the fullness of the energies, power, and attributes of God.*

B. *Paul was eager for his people to receive all of the blessings that God is willing and able to bestow.*

Conclusion

Paul's prayers for the Ephesians in a very real sense contained God's promises to us. We can experience this inward power. Christ wants to occupy our lives completely. We can rejoice in and live in this divine love. We also can be filled with the fullness of God. May God grant that it be so.

SUNDAY MORNING, JULY 20

Title: Taking a Good Look at God

Text: "I will lift up mine eyes unto the hills, from whence cometh my help" (**Ps. 121:1**).

Hymns: "O God, Our Help in Ages Past," Watts

" 'Tis So Sweet to Trust in Jesus," Stead

"God Will Take Care of You," Martin

Offertory Prayer: Heavenly Father, because of the multitude of your mercies upon us, we dedicate ourselves to you. Help us to make our time, our talents, and the testimony of our lips at your disposal at all times. We bring our substance in the form of tithes and offerings to meet the expenses of a ministry of rendering mercies in your name. Accept them and bless them in Jesus' name. Amen.

Introduction

The psalmist gives expression to his faith in the Lord who can provide unique help for victorious living in difficult days. Perhaps you have been looking in the wrong direction for help for too long. Everything depends on how and to whom one looks in times of crisis.

Erich Sauer said: "If you wish to be disappointed, look to others. If you wish to be encouraged and experience victory, look upon Jesus Christ" (*In the Arena of Faith* [Grand Rapids: Eerdmans, 1955], 18).

Our age has been described as the age of guided missiles and misguided people. If this is true, it is due to the fact that people have been looking in the wrong direction for guidance and help. Some never lift their eyes to look to God;

they look only to scientists, to military leaders, and to diplomats for national peace and security. Others look to a political party, to labor unions, or to their college degrees to supply them with material prosperity and plenty. The psalmist had discovered that to achieve real victory, one must look to a power higher than one's own personality and to an authority superior to the political party in power.

The psalmist had discovered that only the Lord could provide the help, the happiness, the health, and the hope for which the heart hungers. From the desolate plains of the land of exile, the psalmist declares that he will look to God for help. He speaks of God as his helper, his keeper, and his preserver.

I. Let us look to the Lord for help.

The psalmist anticipates an experience of worship in which he will seek to open up his heart to receive the blessings God has for him. He has discovered that the vital energies of life were restored and strength was renewed through worship (Isa. 40:28–31).

    A. *Help will come for the burdens of life.*
1. Sickness.
2. Sorrow.
3. Disappointments.
4. Limitations.

    B. *Help will come for overcoming the temptations of sin (Ps. 121:7).*
1. Temptations to a life of low morals. Joseph lived a life of purity, and so can we with the help of God. He said to Potiphar's wife, "There is none greater in this house than I; neither hath he kept back any thing from me but thee, because thou art his wife: how then can I do this great wickedness, and sin against God?" (Gen. 39:9).
2. Temptation to live a self-centered life.

    C. *Help will come for the responsibilities of life.*
1. Responsibilities as a citizen.
2. Responsibilities toward the family.

II. Let us look to the Lord for happiness.

    A. *Fullness of joy.* "Thou wilt shew me the path of life: in thy presence is fulness of joy; at thy right hand there are pleasures for evermore" (Ps. 16:11).

    B. *The abundant life.* "The thief cometh not, but for to steal, and to kill, and to destroy: I am come that they might have life, and that they might have it more abundantly" (John 10:10).

    C. *Christianity is no prison house.*

    D. *Some have presented a gloomy caricature of Christianity.* Jesus was no killjoy even though he did seek to lead people to forsake those attitudes and acts that were destructive to human personality and eternal values. Those who heeded his voice gained victory over worry, boredom, and self-centeredness. They developed a great faith in God. They enjoyed a transforming friendship. They were led out of self-centered ways into unselfish service to others, and consequently, they experienced abundant life.

III. Let us look to God for hope.

Our hope in God is based on something more than a wish or a grand "perhaps." Our hope in God is based on his solemn promises.

A. *The hope of forgiveness.* We have not only the hope, but the assurance that our sins have been forgiven (1 John 1:7). This is a part of the gospel to which each of us should respond fully. A burden of unresolved guilt can destroy happiness and peace of mind, and at the same time it disqualifies one from giving a joyful witness concerning the grace and power of God.

Our hope of forgiveness is not based on human effort or moral excellence. The basis of our assurance of full forgiveness is found in the wonderful truth that Jesus Christ died for our sins (1 Peter 1:18–19).

B. *The hope of fellowship.* Children of God can be sustained if they face the future with the hope of a constant fellowship with the living Lord (1 John 1:7).

The psalmist faced the future with a calm confidence because he had the assurance that the Lord would be with him as he walked through the dark, gloomy valleys where danger and possible death lurked. He declared, "I will fear no evil: for thou art with me; thy rod and thy staff they comfort me" (Ps. 23:4).

Conclusion

As the psalmist looked to the Lord for help and happiness and hope, each of us can look to the Lord for a heavenly home at the end of the road. Someone has suggested that to experience abundant happiness in life, one needs to have a happy home, a happy church family, and the assurance of a heavenly home.

All three of these are possible to you and yours through faith in Jesus Christ as Lord and Savior. Take a good look at who he is, what he has done, and what he can do in your life. Receive him today according to your individual needs and according to his purposes of love for you.

SUNDAY EVENING, JULY 20

Title: How Do You Run?

Text: "Wherefore seeing we also are compassed about with so great a cloud of witnesses, let us lay aside every weight, and the sin which doth so easily beset us, and let us run with patience the race that is set before us" **(Heb. 12:1)**.

Introduction

The writers of the New Testament sought by every means at their command to communicate the great truths concerning God and the issues of life. We should not be surprised to discover in the New Testament that there are many references to athletic contests. Particularly in the epistles of Paul do we find figures of speech with an athletic connotation. The people to whom he addressed his epistles were very familiar with the Olympic games.

At least three kinds of athletic games are referred to in the New Testament: racing, boxing, and wrestling. The race is mentioned most frequently. Three different phases of the spiritual life are explained and emphasized by each of these games. The race portrays life as a continuous effort to reach a worthy goal so as to gain a prize (Phil. 3:14). Boxing was used to exemplify our opposition to the evil within us (1 Cor. 9:26–27). Wrestling illustrates the struggle that we must put forth with the powers of darkness around us (Eph. 6:12).

I. The race set before us.

    A. *The new birth is the starting line rather than the finishing line.*
    B. *The "race set before us" is our divinely given task. It is our duty to run.*
    C. *One cannot separate one's personal life of faith from being a runner in the race.* God has appointed that we should be runners.

II. Consider the challenge.

    A. *All can reach the goal.* This includes you.
    B. *All must run and hasten with all available strength.*
    C. *All must concentrate on the goal. It is easy to get sidetracked.*
    D. *All must persevere to the finish line (2 Tim. 4:8).* No one must yield to fatigue on the way.
    E. *All must press forward without pause.*
    F. *All must be careful not to stumble in this obstacle course.*
      1. Intellectual problems.
      2. The failures of others.
    G. *All must be determined to win the noblest and best and in no case be content with reaching only lesser aims.*

III. Consider the prize.

    A. *The praise of the Savior.*
    B. *The highest possible manhood and womanhood.*
    C. *The blessing of helping others.*

Conclusion

The race of the Christian life is hard. Even more chilling is the realization that without Christ's strength dwelling in us, it is impossible to compete. We can be a blessing. We can be joyful. We can have peace. We must ask the Lord for his strength and love to continue and complete the race set before us.

WEDNESDAY EVENING, JULY 23

Title: Prayer in the Time of Danger

Text: "Lord, save us: we perish" (**Matt. 8:25**).

Introduction

Repeatedly in the Scriptures we are exhorted to have the habit of prayer and then not to break that habit. But should we neglect our prayer life, it is still encouraging to notice that our Savior will respond affirmatively for a plea to help in a time of danger.

The event described in the text gives direction for those who sail the sea of life in the present. Let us study it reverently and responsively and allow the Master to speak to our hearts.

I. This incident took place at the end of a busy day.

A. *Christ was a constant worker (John 9:4).*

B. *This passage contains the only reference to Christ sleeping.*

C. *This incident reveals the humanity of Christ.*

D. *It discloses his deity and power.*

II. There arose a great tempest.

A. *The face of the sea looked like a boiling caldron.* The disciples found themselves in great danger through no fault of their own. They were at the mercy of the forces of nature and recognized their helplessness.

B. *The storms of life beat down on us.* There are some who find this difficult to understand. They expect perfect peace and quietness as they make the journey of life.

  1. We face sickness.

  2. Each of us will experience sorrow.

  3. All of us are affected by war with its many troubles and dangers.

  4. Only a very few have financial security.

  5. Uncertainty is an inescapable part of life.

C. *The storm swept down on the disciples even though Christ was present.* Being a Christian does not guarantee that one will face no storms.

D. *The Christian must not expect life to always be smooth.* God has not promised us immunity from danger.

E. *At times it appears that God is asleep and unconcerned.* The psalmist declared, "Behold he that keepeth Israel [thee] shall neither slumber nor sleep" (Ps. 121:4).

III. There was a great cry for help.

A. *Their fear drove them to prayer ("we perish").*

B. *Their faith brought them to the Savior ("save us").*

C. *Christ did not rebuke their fear; he rebuked their lack of faith.* They had little faith in spite of all that they had seen him do.

D. *Christ quieted their fears as the God of grace.* As the God of nature, he commanded the winds to cease their blowing.

E. *Christ still saves those who call on him (Luke 18:13; Acts 2:21; Rom. 10:13).*

IV. There was a great calm.

A. *The storm lost its power.*

B. *Those in the ship at sea rejoiced in peace.*

C. *Christ can give you victory over the storms that beat on your life.*

V. There was a great sense of wonder.

"What manner of man is this, that even the winds and the sea obey him!" (Matt. 8:27).

A. *He is the God-man.*

B. *He is the sinless one who came to save sinners.*

C. *He is the one God appointed to die for our sins.*

D. *He is the one who has conquered death and the grave and lives to be our Leader, Teacher, and Lord.*

Conclusion

While we will continue to pray for help in times of danger and uncertainty, let us also build a great faith by developing the habit of prayer and making sure that we do not break it.

SUNDAY MORNING, JULY 27

Title: The All-Seeing Eye of God

Text: "Whither shall I go from thy Spirit? or whither shall I flee from thy presence?" **(Ps. 139:7).**

Hymns: "Immortal, Invisible," Smith

"There's a Wideness in God's Mercy," Faber

"In Christ There Is No East nor West," Oxenham

Offertory Prayer: Holy Father, we remind ourselves that nothing is hidden from you. You have placed within our care many blessings over which we are to serve as managers for you. Help us to be your servants in every area of our lives. We want to serve you in the world where we earn a living. We come now bringing a portion of the fruit of our labors to present it to you as an act of worship. Accept our offerings and bless them to the increase of your kingdom, to the salvation of the lost, and to ministries of mercy. Through Jesus Christ our Lord. Amen.

Introduction

God is present everywhere. The psalmist had experienced the elation of success, the shame of sin, the burden of sorrow, the joy of forgiveness, and the thrill of service. He had discovered that God was always near to meet the deepest needs of his heart and life.

Have you ever fully grasped the significance of God being everywhere and always present? Does it frighten you or comfort you to know that God's eye has been, is now, and always will be on you? Do you believe that you can hide from him? Are you afraid that he has overlooked you?

God knows our innermost thoughts. He is fully informed concerning our secret ambitions. Nothing is hidden from him.

I. The all-seeing eye of God should help us to abstain from sin.

A. *People choose darkness and secrecy for the perpetration of evil.* People love darkness rather than light because their deeds are evil (John 3:19).

B. *Adam and Eve probably did not even think of God's discovering their sin.*

C. *God saw the evil of the world during the days of Noah.*

D. *The eye of the Lord beheld David commit his double sin (2 Sam. 11:27).*

E. *The eye of the Lord was on Peter as he denied him in Pilate's court (Luke 22:61).* "For God shall bring every work into judgment, with every secret thing, whether it be good, or whether it be evil" (Eccl. 12:14). God "will bring to light the hidden things of darkness" (1 Cor. 4:5).

   1. God sees our selfishness.
   2. God sees our covetousness.
   3. God sees our evil thoughts.
   4. God hears our unkind and untrue statements.

A baffling robbery took place in one of New York's fashionable apartments. No clue as to the identity of the thief was found until a detective noticed an alabaster bust of Hofmann's *Christ* turned to the wall. It yielded the one fingerprint that apprehended the criminal. The robber later explained that he just could not steal with the eyes of Christ looking at him. He had to turn the statue around before he completed the robbery.

II. The all-seeing eye of God should be a great source of comfort and strength.

A. *Abraham was bold and courageous because of his confidence in the abiding presence and constant care of God (Rom. 4:19–21).*

B. *Moses was able to face Pharaoh with courage only because he had confidence in the presence, power, and purpose of his God who was as close to him as his breath.*

C. *The psalmist explains his faith by saying, "Yea, though I walk through the valley of the shadow of death, I will fear no evil: for thou art with me; thy rod and thy staff they comfort me" (Ps. 23:4).*

D. *Jesus promised to his disciples who seek to carry out his commission, "Lo, I am with you alway" (Matt. 28:20).*

   1. He understands perfectly our problems, trials, and troubles.
   2. He understands our weaknesses.
   3. This is what brings the peace that passes all understanding.

Those who have enjoyed the blessing of a sympathetic mother can remember being tucked into bed at night and being assured that all was safe. In our day, as we face risks and possible danger, we need the assurance that God is near to help us.

III. The all-seeing eye of God should challenge us to tremendous effort in unselfish service.

Athletes are inspired to tremendous effort by a crowd of spectators. Most of us are inclined to do a better job if we know that others are going to observe it and approve.

A. *David was able to go down in the valley to face the Philistine giant Goliath because he had faith in the presence and power of God.*

B. *Paul gave himself without reservation to a campaign to evangelize his world that he might have the approval and commendation of his Lord (2 Cor. 5:10).*

C. *Jesus tells us that there will come a day when the good deeds of the righteous will be recognized and rewarded (Matt. 25:31–40).*

Conclusion

The wonder of wonders is that God knows everything that we have done and ever will do yet still loves us. He knows our guilt. He knows our need. He loves us to the extent that he gave his Son to die in our place on the cross.

He wants to save you and use you. He has great plans for your life. Let him have his way in your life.

Seven Blessings from God's Presence

1. Above you—to guard (Deut. 4:39).
2. Underneath—to support (Deut. 33:27).
3. Behind—as a reward (Isa. 52:12).
4. Before—to lead (Isa. 45:2).
5. At your right hand—to protect (Pss. 16:8; 110:5).
6. Round about—to shield (Ps. 125:2).
7. Within—as companion and comforter (Ezek. 36:27; Gal. 2:20).

SUNDAY EVENING, JULY 27

Title: "Looking unto Jesus"

Text: "Looking unto Jesus the author and finisher of our faith; who for the joy that was set before him endured the cross, despising the shame, and is set down at the right hand of the throne of God" **(Heb. 12:2)**.

Introduction

The great heroes and heroines of the faith are assembled in eternity's amphitheater, not as mere spectators who view our struggles in life, but as testators, spiritual cheerleaders, who shout words of challenge and encouragement to us as we seek to run faithfully the race of life. They would declare to us that our God is faithful and can be depended on to keep his promises and to provide us with all that is essential for an effective Christian witness. They would tell us that in him we can be adequate for whatever difficulties or disasters life may bring. They would join in a continuous shout that the prize of divine approval at the end of the way is worth all of the struggle, sacrifice, and suffering involved in the race of life.

Like an enthusiastic and well-trained college cheering squad, they would challenge us to "Hold that line!" when it seems that Satan and all of his cohorts are bound to win a victory and overwhelm us with defeat. They would make the heavens ring with their cry, "We want a touchdown! We want a touchdown!" when we are near the crest of success in either personal spiritual growth or achievement.

Our God is the same God as the God of Enoch. Our God is the God of Abraham, Isaac, and Jacob. These men were made of common clay as you and I are. They achieved success because of the genuineness of their faith in the faithfulness of the God and Father of our Lord Jesus Christ.

The New Testament writer compares the Christian life to a race. When we think of those who participate in a race, we think of speed, strength, skill, strategy, and endurance. There is probably no other form of athletics that demands more of an individual in terms of hard work, training, self-discipline, and endurance.

Not many people are setting spiritual records these days. We have slowed down to a walk. Some of us have sat down to rest; some are asleep. Some are dreadfully sick, and others have actually died—and not from overexertion in running the Christian race.

The inspired writer declares that there is a vital connection between our maintaining a vision of the Christ and winning the race of life.

I. We are to look to Jesus continually.

    A. *Not just a casual glance.*
    B. *Not just a look of understanding.*
    C. *A look that indicates fixation.*

1. Amazement and admiration.
2. Love and loyalty.
3. Gratitude.
4. Worship.

D. *Looking — not just on Sunday.*
E. *Looking to Jesus is not a part-time job, but a full-time vocation.*

II. Looking to Jesus means looking away from everything else.

There are many different places for one to look for success. Many pin their hopes on education, financial resources, friends, and scientific progress; some even depend completely on the government. For success in the Christian life, we must not depend on any of these things. We must take our eyes off things that cannot guarantee success.

A. *There are those who would discourage us.*
B. *There are treasures that would captivate our thoughts and energies.*
C. *There are those who would distract.*
D. *We must beware of even looking to self too much.* Many things only Christ Jesus can do for us.

III. Looking to Jesus is essential if we are to win the prize.

To look to him means to place all of life under his care and guidance.

A. *The prize is not the gift of eternal life.* One must possess life to run in the first place.
B. *The prize can be described in several ways:*
   1. It is the assurance of divine approval and commendation.
   2. It is the satisfaction of a good conscience.
   3. It is the joy of being helpful to others.
   4. It is the inward satisfaction of knowing that you have fulfilled the divine purpose for your life and that you have achieved your appointed destiny.

Paul knew the joy of winning the prize, and as he approached the end of his earthly journey, he was able to declare: "For I am now ready to be offered, and the time of my departure is at hand. I have fought a good fight, I have finished my course, I have kept the faith: Henceforth there is laid up for me a crown of righteousness, which the Lord, the righteous judge, shall give me at that day: and not to me only, but unto all them also that love his appearing" (2 Tim. 4:6–8).

IV. Looking to Jesus brings wonderful surprises.

A. *We look to Jesus for our salvation — forgiveness, new life, eternal life.*
B. *We look to Jesus for instruction.*
   1. The nature and character of God.
   2. The purpose of life.
C. *We look to Jesus for inspiration.*
   1. It is the experience of us all to become discouraged.
   2. All of us need to hear a bugle.

    D. *We look to Jesus for correction and protection.*
      1. We all have a built-in tendency to do wrong, fall short, miss the mark, and go astray.
      2. We stand in daily need of counsel and advice.
    E. *We look to Jesus for direction in times of difficulty.*
    F. *We look to Jesus for comfort in distress.*

Conclusion

God spoke through Isaiah and said, "Look unto me, and be ye saved, all the ends of the earth: for I am God, and there is none else" (Isa. 45:22). Charles Haddon Spurgeon heard a sermon on this text and responded by looking to Jesus for salvation, and Jesus Christ came into his heart. Today there is life for you through Jesus Christ.

> ### *Looking unto Jesus*
>
> *There is life for a look at the Crucified One,*
> *There is life at this moment for thee;*
> *Then look, sinner, look unto Him and be saved,*
> *Unto Him who was nailed to the tree.*
>   *—Harry Dixon Loes*

WEDNESDAY EVENING, JULY 30

Title: The Spirit of the Disciples' Prayer

Text: "But when ye pray, use not vain repetitions, as the heathen do: for they think they shall be heard for their much speaking" (**Matt. 6:7**).

Introduction

An intense study of the Lord's Prayer will reveal that a very definite pattern is proposed for our communion with God and for our bringing petitions to the throne of grace. This prayer, instead of being something to be memorized and repeated, is a perfect pattern, a blueprint or model.

A most important thing to be observed about this prayer is the spirit it encourages.

I. A filial spirit: "Father."

There is a difference between offering prayers to the eternal Creator and presenting personal needs to the heavenly Father. Attention is focused on a parent-child relationship.

II. An unselfish spirit: "Our Father."

The personal pronoun in the perfect pattern for prayer is always in the plural, for we are members of a family. A community of concern is not only encouraged, but is required if we would pray effectively.

III. A reverent and worshipful spirit: "Hallowed be thy name."

Irreverence has been the undoing sin of people through the centuries. Some treat the Holy God as if he were a "chum" or "buddy." We trample into the courts of God with muddy boots on. To pray effectively we must open our eyes to the holiness of God as did Isaiah in the temple (Isa. 6:1–5).

IV. An evangelistic and missionary spirit: "Thy kingdom come."

This petition will be realized ultimately when the Lord returns, but his kingdom comes in the present as individuals make him the Lord of their lives. If we truly offer this petition, we offer ourselves as witnesses for our Lord.

V. An obedient and submissive spirit: "Thy will be done in earth, as it is in heaven."

To experience the grace and power of God and to achieve the purpose of God for our lives, we must cooperate with him even as the angels do who do his bidding in heaven. In offering this petition, we pledge our loving obedience.

VI. A humble and dependent spirit: "Give us this day our daily bread."

In this modern day in which so many are far removed from the process by which we get our bread from God, it is easy to forget how dependent we are on him. By this prayer we are encouraged to ask God's blessings on our daily work that our daily needs might be met.

VII. A confessing and forgiving spirit: "Forgive us our trespasses as we forgive those who trespass against us."

As people stand in daily need of daily food, even so they stand in daily need of cleansing from sin. If we would be happy, we must also forgive those who sin against us. Because unresolved hate festers and produces a poison that corrupts the whole system, we must forgive.

VIII. A cautious and trusting spirit: "Lead us not into temptation but deliver us from evil."

Within one's own strength, no one is adequate to overcome the evil that is within and the evil that is about us. We are in daily need of divine resources if we are to rise above the weakness within and the pressures about us.

IX. A confident and adoring spirit: "For thine is the kingdom and the power and the glory forever. Amen."

All that we are and all that we have comes from the bountiful hand of God. There will be more confidence in our spirit, more gratitude in our hearts, and more prayers on our lips if we will recognize how good our heavenly Father has been to us. He showers many of his blessings on us without our even asking. He is more eager to bless than we are to be blessed.

Conclusion

The spirit of this prayer is more essential than the correct repetition of its words and a proper attention to the sequence of petitions. May the heavenly Father help us to have this proper spirit as we pray.

AUGUST

■ Sunday Mornings and Evenings

On the first Sunday morning of the month, complete the series from the Psalms, and on the first Sunday evening, complete the series from Hebrews 12.

Beginning on the second Sunday, offer a series of morning and evening sermons that complement, supplement, and contrast each other. In addition to providing an opportunity to meet specific needs in the lives of the membership, this series can be used to encourage attendance for the evening services during the summer.

■ Wednesday Evenings

Jesus' parables are featured on Wednesday evenings this month. They serve as vehicles to transport truth today even as they did when they were first spoken.

SUNDAY MORNING, AUGUST 3

Title: Hard-Hearted or Compassionately Concerned?

Text: "I looked on my right hand, and beheld, but there was no man that would know me: refuge failed me; no man cared for my soul" (**Ps. 142:4**).

Hymns: "Blessed Assurance," Crosby

"Day by Day," Berg

"Jesus, I Am Resting," Pigott

Offertory Prayer: Our loving Father, we labor in vain unless we labor for you. We want to work diligently because we love you. We want to strive together in holiness because you command us to be holy as you are holy. And we want to bring to you some of the labor of our hands, from gratitude to you for the strength of your mighty hand that raises us up for every good work. In the name of our Lord Jesus Christ. Amen.

Introduction

Psalm 142 is the heart cry of a physically exhausted, discouraged man. Saul's insane jealousy had forced David to flee as a hare before the hounds. He was a fugitive in hiding from the forces of the king. He was to know no peace until after Saul's death.

During these dangerous years, it was only normal that David should become despondent. At times it seemed that he didn't have a friend in the world. It appeared that the world itself was against him. In a moment of intense loneliness and despair, he found strength in God. We hear him crying out, "I looked on my right hand, and beheld, but there was no man that would know me: refuge failed me; no man cared for my soul" (Ps. 142:4). David voices the despair of his soul in a moment when he felt utterly forsaken. He was sustained only by the inward assurance that God was his refuge.

There may be those in our immediate community who are overwhelmed with a mood of despondency and loneliness. Is it possible that they have the impression that no church is vitally concerned about their spiritual welfare? One does not have to take a scientific survey to know the answer to this question. Not only are there multitudes who have the feeling that no one really cares for them, but there are also multitudes who have no inward assurance that even God cares or is concerned about their welfare. This is due primarily to the failure of Christian witnesses to bear a continuous testimony to God's compassionate concern for all people.

I. The sin of being hard-hearted or unconcerned.

Jesus was both grieved and angered by the hardness of the hearts of the religious leaders of his day (Mark 3:5). They were far more concerned about giving proper consideration to the traditions of their fathers than they were to ministering to the needs of suffering men and women. Before we become too critical of this group who brought grief to the heart of the Savior and provoked his righteous indignation, let us consider our own record.

A. *An unworthy life on our part indicates a lack of concern for the unsaved about us.* We know that only by exemplary living can we create within the hearts of the unsaved a hunger to know our Savior (Matt. 5:16).

B. *The lack of fidelity to the church indicates a lack of concern for the unsaved.* The church is the only institution on earth with a divine commission to make disciples. The Lord is depending on his church to carry out the Great Commission. The unsaved person's only hope is through the ministry and the message of this divinely commissioned church (John 20:23).

C. *To neglect the church's worship services, to support inadequately its programs, and to be so preoccupied as to be unable to be an integral part of its activities indicates a lack of real concern for the unsaved.* Only those who live in an atmosphere of prayer and know some of the basic teachings of the Scriptures can be used most effectively in witnessing to the unsaved.

D. *The new commandment—which requires that we love each other even as Christ loved us—calls for a compassionate heart toward the needs of those who are without God (John 13:34).* For the child of God to demonstrate an attitude of indifference, a condition of being hard-hearted, is inhuman, unnatural, and unchristian.

225

II. Why are we hard-hearted and unconcerned?

 A. *Is it because we are so preoccupied with the cares of the world and with the responsibilities of life?*

 B. *Is it because we have forgotten what it feels like to be without God and without hope and without peace and without the assurance of heaven as our eternal home?*

 C. *Is it because we are ignorant about the actual spiritual condition of those who do not know Jesus Christ and who have not yet put their faith in God?*

 D. *Is our unconcern due to the fact that the Devil has lulled us to sleep and caused us to ignore the fact that all people outside of Jesus Christ are lost?*

 E. *Are we unconcerned because we have failed to tarry in the presence of the cross to discover the measure of God's concern for lost people?*

III. The cause of concern.

The condition of lost people is a condition that should cause genuine concern. The church needs to promote a campaign to increase concern. We need to let the concern of the Savior capture and overflow our hearts. "But when he saw the multitudes, he was moved with compassion on them, because they fainted, and were scattered abroad, as sheep having no shepherd" (Matt. 9:36).

With penetrating insight, Jesus was able to see the heart condition of these people. He suffered for them. He wept over them. They were abusing their privileges and rejecting their responsibilities. Jesus was vividly aware of the waste and wages of sin. He knew that the people were following a pathway that was going to lead to failure and disappointment. He knew the fate that awaited them, and his compassion moved him to do all within his power to save them from the ill-fated destiny of dying under the condemnation and guilt of sin.

The apostle Paul labored under the inward compulsion of a great compassion for the spiritual welfare of people (Rom. 9:13; 10:1).

Perhaps if we were better informed about the spiritual condition of unbelievers, our hearts would be moved with compassion.

 A. *Without Christ people are lost (Luke 19:10).*

  1. They are lost from God and are a loss to God.

  2. They are lost to the church.

  3. They are lost from heaven.

  Have you forgotten what it feels like to be lost?

 B. *Without Christ people have no hope (Eph. 2:12).* Our unsaved friends face a hopeless eternity unless someone can give to them a persuasive witness concerning what Jesus Christ can mean to them. They have no hope of going to heaven without him. Have you known what it is like to be without hope?

 C. *Without Christ man does not enjoy sonship.* While all people are the creatures of God, only those who receive Jesus Christ by faith as Lord and Savior can lift their face in prayer and pray, "Our Father." Until they receive Jesus Christ, they miss this joy and privilege (Gal. 3:26).

 D. *Without Christ people face complete failure.* No one likes to be a loser or a failure. Until people become children of God, they fail to experience life at

226

its fullest. And they face the possibility of being failures throughout all eternity. "What shall it profit a man, if he shall gain the whole world, and lose his own soul?" (Mark 8:36).

E. *Without Christ our unsaved friends will miss heaven.* Heaven is so wonderful that it is beyond the power of human language to describe. The mind cannot even begin to fully comprehend the beauties and the glories of the heavenly home the divine Carpenter is preparing for those who love him. For our unsaved friends to come to the end of life without Christ Jesus as their personal Savior is for them to miss heaven.

F. *Without Christ our unsaved friends face an eternity in hell.* Jesus believed that there was a hell from which to save people. He believed it to the extent that he died a death of unutterable anguish and suffering on the cross to save them from hell. The Scriptures tell us that hell was "prepared for the devil and his angels" (Matt. 25:41). God did not intend for people to go to hell. God has done everything within his divine power to save people from hell.

To save people from hell is one of the primary reasons for the existence of the church in the world today. God is depending on each of his children to share his compassionate concern and to do what we can to persuade people to forsake the way of life that leads to hell. People who follow the life of unbelief and give their allegiance to the Devil are not only permitted, but they are destined, to follow him into hell (Matt. 25:41–46).

IV. The consequences of compassionate concern.

David indicted his contemporaries for being unconcerned about his welfare. Jesus was both grieved and angered by the hard-heartedness of the religious leaders of his day. If we would be better than they then we must let compassionate concern for lost people take command of us. Compassionate concern will express itself in many different ways.

A. *It will take some of our time if we would be useful to God in rescuing the lost from sin.*

B. *The talents with which God has endowed us can be used by the Holy Spirit to persuade others to put their faith in the Christ.*

C. *If we would have treasure in heaven, and if we would make investments that would pay eternal dividends, we must put a minimum of a tithe of our income into the work of God's kingdom.*

D. *Compassionate concern will cause us to bear a winsome testimony concerning what Jesus Christ has done within our own heart in every area of life on a continual basis.* We will want to give a total witness with both our lips and our life.

Conclusion

The United States Navy and other interested parties spent a combined $40 million in the search for Amelia Earhart, the American aviatrix who went down in the Pacific preceding the Second World War. That seems like an awful lot of money for a government to spend searching for one of its citizens, but aren't you glad you live in a country that shows that much concern?

God was so concerned for us that he gave his Son Jesus Christ to die on the cross for us. Because he loves us and cares for us so lavishly, you can trust him implicitly. Decide now to entrust your past, present, and future into his hands.

SUNDAY EVENING, AUGUST 3

Title: Are You Listening?

Text: "See that ye refuse not him that speaketh" (**Heb. 12:25**).

Introduction

When God speaks people must listen. To fail to do so is the height of foolishness. Repeatedly our Lord said, "He that hath ears to hear, let him hear" (Mark 4:9). There are none so deaf as those who will not hear. The psalmist encouraged his listeners to hear with responsive hearts (Ps. 95:7–9). To hear and not to respond is to destroy one's ability to hear the voice of God.

In the epistles to the seven churches of Asia Minor, the living Lord completed each with the exhortation, "He that hath an ear, let him hear what the Spirit saith unto the churches" (Rev. 2:7, 11, 17, 29; 3:6, 13, 22). The repetition of this refrain not only implies but also teaches that people are spiritual receiving stations. The God who spoke in ages past will speak today to those who are willing to hear.

I. The symbolic language of nature (Ps. 19:1–3).

The psalmist was able to see both the power and the grace of God in the beauty of the world and in the immensity of the universe. Are you listening?

II. The historical language of experience.

A. *God would speak to us through history if we had but eyes to see and ears to hear.* The great prophets of the Old Testament had a message from God for their day that is relevant for ours. God has not changed, people have not changed, sin has not changed. The law of cause and effect still works. No new instinct has been added, and no new appetite has been created. The God who rewarded faith and punished wickedness will do the same today.

B. *God speaks to us through the personal experiences of Bible characters.* He directs us to paths of conduct that lead to the right destination.

Concerning a life fully dedicated to the divine will of God, we could listen for a message through the personal satisfaction that comes to the apostle Paul (2 Tim. 4:6–8). Are you listening?

III. The inward language of conscience (Rom. 2:15).

God has placed within the hearts of all humankind a conscience, a sense of moral obligation to do what is right.

The conscience is not always a safe guide, because the content of one's conscience is determined by the teachings that have been received and accepted. If a person has accepted false ideas and a faulty scale of values, he or she could do wrong without any qualms of conscience. Nevertheless, God often chooses to speak to us through our conscience. Are you listening?

IV. The personal language of his witnesses (Heb. 12:1).

That God speaks to people through people is the main point of Hebrews 12. Chapter 11 contains an impressive list of distinguished heroes of the faith. The inspired writer marshals one after another to the witness stand. The purpose of each is to bear a personal testimony concerning the faithfulness of God with a view to encouraging more faith on the part of all who read the record of their experience.

God speaks through his servants today just as he spoke to those whose lives are enshrined in the pages of the Bible. God speaks through pastors, through godly teachers, and through the music of choirs. He may even speak to those who have ears to hear through the words of strangers. Are you listening?

V. The book language of the written Word (2 Tim. 3:16–17).

E. F. Hallock called Bible study "the listening side of prayer." God will speak to each of us daily if we will do as the psalmist did (Ps. 1:1–2). Psalm 119 is a magnificent tribute to how God speaks and blesses the lives of those who will listen to his divine Word.

While the idea appears in many places, the word "success" appears in only one place in the King James Version of the Bible. Success was promised to Joshua if he would let God speak to him and provide guidance through the book of the law (Josh. 1:8). Are you listening?

VI. The direct Word of the living Lord (Heb. 1:1–2).

The living Lord, who has promised to be present in every place and at every time when his disciples come together in his name (Matt. 18:20), will speak to the deepest needs of the human heart. Worship is an experience in which we not only speak to God concerning our needs, but in which we also listen for his word to us. At times we stand in need of rebuke; and at other times we need to be encouraged. On other occasions we need to be commissioned according to his grace; and according to our needs and our opportunities he will speak if we will listen. Are you listening?

Conclusion

Is it possible that God has been seeking to communicate with you and you have been so preoccupied that you have failed to hear his knock at the door? One of the most inspiring pictures of God to be found in all the Scriptures portrays him as taking the initiative and seeking to bring his blessings into each individual's life (Rev. 3:20). If you will hear and open the door, he will come into your life today. If you have the ability to hear, you should respond to him, for even as in your physical life you can lose the ability to hear, you can lose the sensitivity that would make it possible for you to hear the voice of God.

In Washington, D.C., a number of years ago, people were enjoying an afternoon movie. Outside it was snowing hard. Suddenly from within the group there was a shout, "Get out! Get out!" A miner, who had been trained to be cautious in the mines, had heard a sound that revealed that the roof was in the process of caving in. Many heard his shout and escaped while others perished.

WEDNESDAY EVENING, AUGUST 6

Title: The Parable of the Sower

Text: "Behold, there went out a sower to sow . . ." (**Mark 4:3**).

Introduction

Jesus made use of parables to get across some of his greatest lessons. The parable of the sower contains a message for the church and for each individual.

I. The sower.

A. *The Christ.*
B. *All who teach the truth.*
   1. Parents.
   2. Teachers.
   3. Ministers.
   4. Anyone and everyone.
C. *Galatians 6:7–9.*

II. The seed—the Word of God (Mark 4:14).

The children of the kingdom (Matt. 13:38).
A. *The Word of God is living and has tremendous vitality (Heb. 4:12).*
B. *The Word of God is truth.*
C. *The Word of God makes faith possible (Rom. 10:17).*
D. *The Word of God is used by the Holy Spirit in producing the new birth (Rom. 1:16; James 1:18; 1 Peter 1:23).*

III. The soil.

The condition of the soil at planting time largely determines the harvest. This truth can greatly encourage the Christian worker who has become discouraged because of the unresponsiveness of those to whom he seeks to witness. By this parable, our Lord was teaching us that people were not always responsive to him. If we look at this parable mathematically, it is possible that only 25 percent responded genuinely. There are many different responses to the Word of God taught in the classroom, proclaimed from the pulpit, and whispered from one heart to another.

Someone has seen in the four types of soil four conditions of heart: deceived, demonstrative, distracted, and discerning.

A. *Wayside hearers — deceived hearts.* Some hearts are hard and unreceptive and do not have any intention of receiving the Word of God.

    1. Many deceive themselves into believing that they do not need Christ.

    2. Some deceive themselves into thinking that Christian commitment is unimportant.

    3. Other hearts are indifferent. The gospel is not permitted to enter the mind or conscience.

    4. Some neither believe nor disbelieve. They merely ignore it. These people hear the Word of God but let the Devil snatch it away before it has an opportunity to germinate and grow (Mark 4:15; cf. 2 Cor. 4:4).

B. *Stony ground hearts — demonstrative.*

    1. There are many who receive the seed of God's truth in a superficial manner. They make a sentimental emotional response.

    2. The moral nature is not affected.

    3. The intellect and will remain unchanged.

    4. Many are attracted to Christ but never let his teaching get beyond the surface or circumference of their lives. The shallowness of their response becomes painfully evident in a time when moral discrimination or courage is required.

C. *The occupied heart — distracted.* Some of the seed fell on soil that was already occupied by thorny plants. The seed here did not have much of a chance. It is very easy to pack life so full of interests that there is no room for Christ. As life becomes complicated, some have difficulty in establishing priorities.

    1. The cares of this world. Anxiety over the normal routine of life causes some people to become so preoccupied that God is crowded out.

    2. The deceitfulness of riches. The luxuries that are available have a way of becoming considered as necessities. All of us are encouraged by society to desire riches. People judge success in terms of riches. Mammon very definitely is a rival of God for the throne of your heart. Because we call the desire for riches something else, we are in great danger of being deceived.

    3. The lust for other things. Contentment with the necessities of life is a rare virtue. Those who set their minds on material things will find that the acquiring of such, instead of bringing satisfaction, really increases the desire for more things (1 Tim. 6:9–10).

D. *Good ground — discerning hearts.* Some people go to church to take a walk. Some go to laugh and others go to talk. Some go to meet a lover while others go a fault to cover. Some go to meet a friend, while others go because they have time to spend. Those who are wise go to worship God and to hear divine truth.

1. Hear the Word attentively.
2. Hear the Word prayerfully.
3. Hear the Word responsively.
4. Hear the Word obediently.

Conclusion

How do you respond to the Word of God? Do you hear it in a hard-hearted, halfhearted, or wholehearted manner?

SUNDAY MORNING, AUGUST 10

Title: Seven Things That God Hates

Text: "These six things doth the LORD hate; yea, seven are an abomination unto him" **(Prov. 6:16)**.

Hymns: "Crown Him with Many Crowns," Bridges

"Holy Spirit Faithful Guide," Wells

"Jesus Saviour, Pilot Me," Hopper

Offertory Prayer: Heavenly Father, you have blessed us abundantly with all spiritual blessings. You have made available to us not only the necessities but also a surplus. Open our eyes and help us to see the blessings that have come from your gracious hand. Today we give unto you that which is yours, for all that we are and have is yours. Help us to live each day and all of our days for your glory and praise. In Jesus' name we pray. Amen.

Our Lord, because of the perfection of his character, hates only things that are hateful. Some things, because of their very nature, are abominable. If we can discover what is abhorrent to God, we will discover what we also should abhor.

As Christians we should love things that are worthy, and we should hate things that are deadly and destructive.

In the opinion of the wise man, there were at least seven things that provoked the hate of God. They are listed in our text.

I. The Lord hates a proud look.

A. *A proud look proceeds from an egotistical, proud heart.*
B. *The general causes of a proud look are some supposed excellencies, either of birth, fortune, talents, or education; but none of these provides a sufficient excuse for pride.*
C. *Pride puffs people up with self-sufficiency and self-satisfaction so that they despise others and idolize themselves.*
D. *Pride puts self on the throne and God in the gutter.*
E. *The demons fell through pride.* "Pride goeth before destruction, and a haughty spirit before a fall" (Prov. 16:18).

232

II. The Lord hates a lying tongue.

A lie is something spoken with a design to deceive. A person who makes an untruthful statement may, however, just be mistaken rather than purposely lying.

    A. *Truth in our words is of vast importance.*

    B. *There are many sorts of lies and many designs in lying.*

        1. Some lie to make sport.

        2. Others lie to make mischief.

        3. Others lie to promote their reputation.

        4. Others lie to blast the reputation of others.

        5. Others lie to conceal their faults.

    C. *There are many proofs that God hates lying.*

        1. God struck down Ananias and Sapphira (Acts 5:1–11).

        2. The Devil was a liar from the beginning (John 8:44).

III. The Lord hates hands that shed innocent blood.

    A. *Capital punishment is essential in a world that has rejected God.*

    B. *Genesis 9:5–6.*

    C. *Matthew 26:52.*

IV. The Lord hates the heart that devises wicked imaginations.

    A. *The minds of some people are as deep and as dark as hell.*

    B. *Their minds are at work day and night to devise schemes of lust and cruelty.*

V. The Lord hates feet that are swift in running to mischief.

    A. *Wicked imaginations lead to wicked actions.*

    B. *People who feed their minds with filth make haste in doing mischief.* "A good man out of the good treasure of the heart bringeth forth good things: and an evil man out of the evil treasure bringeth forth evil things" (Matt. 12:35).

    C. *These are the very opposite of the actions of our Savior who went about doing good.*

VI. The Lord hates a false witness who speaks lies.

    A. *Perjury is a serious offense before God.*

    B. *"Thou shalt not bear false witness against thy neighbor" (Ex. 20:16).*

    C. *Perjury is not only injurious to the innocent; it also destroys something in the perjurer.*

VII. The Lord hates a person who sows discord among brethren.

    A. *Brethren are sons of one father.*

    B. *"Behold, how good and how pleasant it is for brethren to dwell together in unity!" (Ps. 133:1).*

    C. *"A froward man soweth strife: and a whisperer separateth chief friends" (Prov. 16:28).*

    D. *Some things should not be whispered.* They hurt people and displease God.

1. Is it kind?
2. Is it helpful?
3. Is it true?

Conclusion

The ideal Christian life emphasizes love and a life of devoted service. There are also some great negatives in the life of the true child of God. Diligently he should seek to avoid things that would be displeasing to the heavenly Father. The message of the morning has revealed some of the things that God hates and that we should avoid as if they were deadly diseases. With the help of Jesus Christ as Savior, Teacher, and Guide, we can be found well-pleasing in God's sight.

SUNDAY EVENING, AUGUST 10

Title: Those Whom God Loves

Text: "For God so loved the world, that he gave his only begotten Son, that whosoever believeth in him should not perish, but have everlasting life" **(John 3:16)**.

Introduction

In the morning message we considered seven things that provoke the wrath of God. While God is loving, it must be recognized that one side of love is the hatred of that which threatens the object of love. Tonight we have a more pleasant subject as we consider how we can show love to the God who loves us.

I. Through Moses God declared his love for obedient children.

"Wherefore it shall come to pass, if ye hearken to these judgments, and keep, and do them, that the LORD thy God shall keep unto thee the covenant and the mercy which he sware unto thy fathers: And he will love thee, and bless thee, and multiply thee: he will also bless the fruit of thy womb, and fruit of thy land, thy corn, and thy wine, and thine oil, the increase of thy kine, and flocks of thy sheep, in the land which he sware unto thy fathers to give thee" (Deut. 7:12–13).

   A. *Our obedience is a proof of our love for God.*
   B. *Our obedience is a recognition of his lordship.*
   C. *Obedience on our part is essential for spiritual well-being and success in all kingdom activities.*
   D. *Obedience is an act of the highest wisdom.* Jesus said to his disciples, "If ye love me, keep my commandments" (John 14:15), and "Ye are my friends, if ye do whatsoever I command you" (John 15:14).

II. Through the psalmist the Lord declared his love for the righteous.

"The LORD loveth the righteous" (Ps. 146:8).

A. *We become right with God through faith in and surrender to Jesus Christ our Savior (Rom. 5:1, 18–19).* The only way to be perfectly right with God is to receive the righteousness of Jesus Christ through faith (Rom. 10:4).

B. *We are right with our fellowman as we obey the commandments of our Lord and follow his example of love (Matt. 5:6).*

C. *To enjoy peace with God we must treat our fellow humans right.* We cannot offer acceptable worship and mistreat a brother or sister at the same time (Matt. 5:23–24).

To experience the fullness of God's love, we must deliberately, at all times, seek to do what is right in God's eyes. We must let God's truth regulate our actions at this point, for "All the ways of a man are clean in his own eyes; but the LORD weigheth the spirits" (Prov. 16:2). "There is a way which seemeth right unto a man, but the end thereof are the ways of death" (14:12).

III. Through the apostle Paul we hear that God loves the cheerful giver (2 Cor. 9:7).

A. *Why would God love a hilarious giver?* Surely it is not because he is in need of our gifts. "For every beast of the forest is mine, and the cattle upon a thousand hills" (Ps. 50:10). "If I were hungry, I would not tell thee: for the world is mine, and the fulness thereof" (v. 12).

B. *That is the kind of giver that God is.* God is a liberal, lavish, extravagant Giver. The psalmist praised God for being a spiritual spendthrift (Ps. 103:1–5). John 3:16 describes the boundless love of God. Paul seeks to reveal the riches of God's generosity in the following words: "He that spared not his own Son, but delivered him up for us all, how shall he not with him also freely give us all things?" (Rom. 8:32).

Paul responds to God's generosity by saying, "Thanks be unto God for his unspeakable gift" (2 Cor. 9:15). From these great passages there are certain truths that we should understand and cling to. God is not stingy. God never gives the bare minimum. God never gives grudgingly or reluctantly. God gives royally without measure. For the sheer joy of giving, he overlooks our unworthiness and treats us as we do not deserve to be treated.

C. *Our Lord encourages us to be givers, for abundant life is found in giving.*
1. Jesus teaches us that if we want to find the highest possible happiness in life, we must imitate the generous attitude of God and be a giver.
2. Jesus places before us the example of the poor widow who gave her all (Mark 12:41–44).
3. Study Luke 6:38 and notice that there is one word of command and the rest of the verse is promise.

To become a giver may be as attractive as bitter medicine at first, but those who, by faith, follow the Savior's example, discover that when the deed is done, the taste is like honey.

235

IV. God loves the sinner (Rom. 5:8).

Because of sin and the pointing finger of an accusing conscience, people in their natural state have a tendency to believe that God hates them. Nothing could be further from the truth. From the beginning of time, the Devil has misrepresented the nature and character of God. He seeks to separate people from God. The gospel is the good news of God's love for guilty sinners who need but do not deserve his grace and mercy.

Conclusion

Individually and personally, let's relate ourselves to the God of love. If you need to forsake the life of unbelief and rebellion and come to him who revealed his love on Calvary, then do so right now.

If you want to more fully experience the love of God in your life, then make yourself more lovable through a life of obedient, righteous, and devoted giving of self to God and to others.

WEDNESDAY EVENING, AUGUST 13

Title: The Four Who Were Lost

Text: "I say unto you, that likewise joy shall be in heaven over one sinner that repenteth, more than over ninety and nine just persons, which need no repentance" **(Luke 15:7).**

Introduction

One of the most cherished chapters of the Bible is Luke 15. I like the way it begins: "Then drew near unto him all the publicans and sinners for to hear him."

Much is said about Christ in those words. They mean that those who failed realized that in Christ they would find help instead of condemnation. The publicans and sinners found that he was "a friend of sinners," that he liked to eat with them, and that he gave most of his time to them.

He had hard words for self-righteous people, but he always spoke kindly to those who had missed the way. In fact, the word "sinner" was seldom on his lips. He thought of them as "lost." On one occasion when the people "murmured" because he received sinners, Jesus told them four stories.

In these stories we see four ways of getting lost, four consequences of being lost, and a fourfold quest for the lost.

I. Four ways of getting lost.

A. *Lost through heedlessness—the sheep (v. 4).* The one sheep that was lost was not a bad sheep. He was perhaps no worse than the rest of the flock. His love for the shepherd was just as great as any other member of the fold.

He just kept drifting away from the flock in quest of better grass and greener pastures. Then when darkness fell, he realized he was all alone. Through failing to give heed to the shepherd's call, this sheep got lost.

And this is the way so many get lost. Busy with the pressing affairs of life, they gradually drift from God, his church, and his people. Then in the darkness of some tragic hour, they discover they are all alone — all because of heedlessness!

B. *Lost through idleness — the coin (v. 8).* The coin was the same coin after it was lost that it was before. That which was silver did not now turn to brass. And being lost does not mean a person has no value or character.

The coin was out of circulation and thus "lost." The coin represents service, and when we remove our lives from service to God, we are out of circulation and thus lost.

C. *Lost through willfulness — the prodigal (vv. 12–13).* This younger son was lost because he willed to be lost. He was basically a good son, but he chafed under the rules and expectations of home. So he thought only of the moment, ignored his duty to family and society, and deliberately took off on his own.

In an effort to prove and exercise his "freedom," he became a slave to sin and a slave to a strange man in a distant land. He was lost through his own willfulness.

D. *Lost through haughtiness — the elder brother (vv. 25–26).* This conscientious and honest young man stayed at home and still got lost. He was lost through pride and haughtiness. Being satisfied with himself, he became intolerant toward others and lost to the purpose of his father.

It has been said that if the prodigal had seen his brother before he saw his father, he might have returned to the pigpen! I wonder how your lifestyle and attitude affect others. Do they attract people to Christ or drive them away?

II. The consequences of being lost.

A. *The consequence of helpless distress — the sheep (v. 4).* The sheep was lost not because it had been destroyed, for it was very much alive. It was lost because it had wandered away from the shepherd and the flock and now found itself in a state of helpless distress.

The aimless multitudes with no sense of real purpose in life, no laws to follow, no God to worship, suffer the same consequences of helpless distress.

B. *The consequence of uselessness — the coin (v. 8).* The lost coin still had its value and still had the image of the emperor stamped on it. But being lost, it was useless. Although still the property of its owner, it was of no value.

If you have lost touch with God, you have not lost your value, but you are useless to him and his service.

237

C. *The consequence of degradation — the prodigal (v. 16).* The clean-cut, well-dressed young man was now living in filth and poverty and was clothed in rags. Friends, wealth, self-respect, and virtue were now all gone. But this is the consequence of willfully choosing to leave the Father. Degradation awaits each of us who decides to walk the path away from God.

D. *The consequence of joylessness — the elder brother (vv. 28–30).* Whatever else may be true of this son, it must be said that he was not a happy person. The consequence of his sin of haughtiness was joylessness. When religion is infected by jealousy and pride, there really is little to choose from between being an "elder brother" or a "prodigal."

III. A fourfold quest for the lost.

A. *The quest of Christ (vv. 4–5).* Surely with ninety-nine sheep in the fold, a shepherd would be both content and thankful. But not Christ. As long as one sheep is lost from the fold, he will search "until" he finds it. And when he finds the lost sheep, he will not beat or upbraid it. He will lovingly lift it to his shoulders and gently carry it to the safety of the fold.

B. *The quest of the Holy Spirit (v. 8).* The Holy Spirit sweeps through our lives, removing the dirt of sin until we find ourselves like bright and precious coins restored to useful service.

C. *The quest of the heavenly Father (vv. 20, 28).* The Father always takes the initiative. "We love him because he *first* loved us" (1 John 4:19). And "God so loved the world, that he [taking the initiative] gave his only begotten Son ..." (John 3:16).

D. *The quest of the church (Luke 14:23).* "As my Father hath sent me, *even so* send I you," Christ said (John 20:21). Just as Christ was sent on a quest for souls, so are we sent.

Conclusion

However people may be lost — through heedlessness, idleness, willfulness, or haughtiness — they can be assured there is a Father in heaven who loves them, a Savior who died for them, and a Holy Spirit who seeks to bring them into the fold of safety.

SUNDAY MORNING, AUGUST 17

Title: The Greatest Commandment

Text: "Thou shalt love the Lord thy God with all thy heart, and with all thy soul, and with all thy mind" **(Matt. 22:37)**.

Hymns: "Love Divine, All Loves Excelling," Wesley

"O Love of God Most Full," Clute

"More Love to Thee," Prentiss

Offertory Prayer: Gracious God, help us always to be conscious that we are but stewards of your grace. Help us to be good managers of that which you have entrusted unto our care. Help us this day to bring a tithe and an offering that would indicate the sincerity of our love and deep concern that all of the world might hear the gospel of your redeeming love through the missionary outreach of the church. In the name of our Lord we pray. Amen.

Introduction

People wonder about their primary duty to God. Jesus came that he might teach us an acceptable way to worship and serve. Once we have related our lives to God through faith, our Lord would encourage us to be motivated by his love. The distinguishing characteristic of the Christian religion is that it is built on and expresses itself in terms of love. The very heart of the gospel is that God loves people and has revealed his love in the gift of Jesus Christ.

The writer of the book of Ecclesiastes understood humankind's duty in terms of obedience. "Let us hear the conclusion of the whole matter: Fear God, and keep his commandments: for this is the whole duty of man" (Eccl. 12:13).

Micah, a prophet of the eighth-century BC, defined humankind's duty toward God in a remarkable statement: "He hath showed thee, O man, what is good; and what doth the Lord require of thee, but to do justly, and to love mercy, and to walk humbly with thy God?" (Mic. 6:8).

It remained for Jesus to define the duty of humans toward God in terms of love. "Thou shalt love the Lord thy God with all thy heart, and with all thy soul, and with all thy mind" (Matt. 22:37).

I. There are two main reasons why people do not love God.

A. *People find it difficult to love God because they have not been taught that God is lovable and worthy of their devotion.* They have been told dark and hard things about God that cause them to be frightened. God has been misrepresented. He is blamed for misfortune and tragedy.

From the beginning of human experience, the Evil One has been misrepresenting the character of God. That old Serpent, the Devil, supplied Eve with a subtle suggestion that the Creator God was not a good God, that she and Adam were being deprived of life at its highest and best by

239

the prohibition to eat from the Tree of Knowledge of Good and Evil (Gen. 3:4–5). From that day until this, by every method at his command, Satan has implied that God is not worthy of humankind's faith and trust.

B. *Many do not love God because they do not understand his commandments.* When people do not understand that the nature and purpose of God are motivated by love, they naturally misjudge his commands. They think the divine commands are too restrictive or too demanding. John, the apostle of love, interpreted God's commands in the following manner: "For this is the love of God, that we keep his commandments; and his commandments are not grievous" (1 John 5:3).

II. God is lovable and should be loved (1 John 4:19).

A. *To love genuinely we must recognize the object of love as being worthy of our adoration, devotion, and confidence.* The properties of love are said to be two:
   1. The desire to please.
   2. The desire to enjoy.
B. *God is lovable.*
   1. He is our Creator.
   2. He is our Redeemer.
   3. He is our Guide.
   4. He is our Provider.
   5. He is our Friend.
C. *God's love is immeasurable (John 3:16).*
D. *God's love is unchangeable and unconditional.*
E. *God's love is unfailing.*

III. The demonstration of our love for God.

The psalmist, after citing many reasons for his love for God, asked, "What shall I render unto the LORD for all his benefits toward me?" (Ps. 116:12). There are at least three ways we can demonstrate our love.
A. *Glad obedience.*
B. *Undivided loyalty.*
C. *Unselfish service.*

IV. The quality of our love for God.

A. *Our love should be sincere.*
B. *Our love should be supreme over all other love.*
C. *Our love should be firm and steadfast.*

V. The results of supreme love for God.

A. *It will elevate us to the highest possible manhood and womanhood.*
B. *It will enrich our lives beyond our fondest dreams.*
C. *It will cause others to come to know Jesus Christ as their personal Savior.*

Conclusion

When we understand God's love for us, we will respond in love. We can best discover his love by a visit to Calvary where "God was in Christ, reconciling the world unto himself" (2 Cor. 5:19), for it was there that God "made him to be sin for us, who knew no sin; that he might be made the righteousness of God in him" (v. 21).

> *Were the whole realm of nature mine,*
> *That were a present far too small;*
> *Love so amazing, so divine,*
> *Demands my soul, my life, my all.*
> —*Isaac Watts*

SUNDAY EVENING, AUGUST 17

Title: The Second Greatest Commandment

Text: "And the second is like unto it, Thou shalt love thy neighbour as thyself" (**Matt. 22:39**).

Introduction

As Jesus approached the end of his earthly ministry, he gave his disciples a badge by which they could identify each other. He gave a uniform with which to clothe themselves that would indicate to the world that they were his followers. This badge or uniform is revealed in the following statement: "By this shall all men know that ye are my disciples, if ye have love one to another" (John 13:35).

Christian love has been defined in terms of a persistent, unbreakable spirit of goodwill. Jesus wants us to follow the royal law of love in all of our relationships.

I. The royal law of love (James 2:8).

The royal law of love is the law of the kingdom of heaven. It is the law of the King. It takes precedence over every other law. To obey this law makes life royally happy.
   A. *Love God (Matt. 22:37).*
   B. *Love neighbor (Matt. 22:39).*
   C. *Love wife (Eph. 5:25, 33).*
   D. *Love Christ's disciples (John 13:34).*
   E. *Love enemies (Matt. 5:43–44).* An unloving attitude is a boomerang that comes back on the person who lives by the principle of hate.

II. The law of love described.

   A. *Negatively.*
      1. Not an amiable attitude without backbone.

    2. Not an all-inclusive tolerance that allows the eternal distinctions of right and wrong to be violated.

B. *Positively.*

    1. A spirit that never harbors a grudge.

    2. A spirit that always discovers the best in people because it can see inside.

    3. An attitude that is full of understanding.

    4. An attitude that is wonderfully patient.

    5. A spirit that is utterly pure.

    6. An unselfish spirit of self-giving.

III. The law of love demonstrated (Luke 10:25–31).

A. *Love crosses racial barriers.*

B. *Love crosses religious differences.*

C. *Love moves to action.*

D. *Love suffers inconvenience.*

E. *Love is generous.*

F. *Love is courageous.*

G. *Love is patient.*

IV. The difficulty of love.

A. *People are not easy to love.*

B. *Christian love is something above and beyond natural love.*

C. *In the death of Christ, we see the worth of humankind revealed.*

D. *The love of God is poured out in our hearts by the Holy Spirit (Rom. 5:5).*

Conclusion

To love the world with Christian love, we need to make love personal. We cannot love the whole world all at once, but we can demonstrate Christ's love toward individuals in God's world. As the Holy Spirit leads and as our heart commands, let each of us become the channel through which God's love touches the world.

WEDNESDAY EVENING, AUGUST 20

Title: The Parable of the Tares

Text: "Another parable put he forth unto them, saying, The kingdom of heaven is likened unto a man which sowed good seed in his field: But while men slept, his enemy came and sowed tares among the wheat" **(Matt. 13:24–25).**

Introduction

The parable of the tares among the wheat was taken from nature and was spoken by Jesus in public. It provides us with an explanation for many of the struggles and tragedies of life.

This parable is a picture of life: personal life, family life, community life, national and international life, and church life.

I. We are on a quest for perfection.

    A. *Why can't things be ideal and perfect?*

    B. *Often this quest for perfection produces haughty pride in connection with our achievements.*

    C. *In other instances, this quest for perfection produces an attitude of intolerance.*

    D. *We must all beware of the peril of making a deal with the mediocre.*

II. We are confronted with continuing imperfections.

    A. *There will always be weeds in the field. There are no fields in which only flowers grow.*

    B. *Some search for a perfect church.*

    C. *Thousands are utterly distracted because of the absence of a heavenly marriage devoid of disappointment and discomfort.*

    D. *Somehow we must live with limitations.*

        1. With grace.

        2. Patient persistence.

        3. Humility.

III. The presence of the tares reveals that appearances are deceiving.

    A. *In a hundred different ways, we are offered substitutes.*

        1. For relaxation and the enjoyment of fellowship there are dozens of brands of beer.

        2. Cigarette manufacturers promise such pleasure that millions of Americans are willing to waste their money and take a chance on lung cancer.

    B. *Advertisers proceed on the premise that we are eager to fool ourselves.*

IV. The fruits of a life provide the acid test.

    A. *What comes forth from a tree is the definition of the tree.*

    B. *The sinner does not always reap his wages at high noon.* The impatient, righteous onlookers must wait until day is over.

    C. *Most of us expect the harvest too soon.* "And let us not be weary in well doing: for in due season we shall reap, if we faint not" (Gal. 6:9).

Conclusion

The Last Judgment will be full of surprises. God is more merciful than we are. God is stricter than we are. God is more knowing than we are. We need to rely on his wisdom to keep us in his grace so that we can be part of his bountiful harvest and also bring others in.

SUNDAY MORNING, AUGUST 24

Title: If Every Christian Could Take One Look into Heaven

Text: "In my Father's house are many mansions.... I go to prepare a place for you" **(John 14:2)**.

Hymns: "Majestic Sweetness Sits Enthroned," Stennett

"My Saviour First of All," Crosby

"When We All Get to Heaven," Hewitt

Offertory Prayer: Holy and loving Father, you have given us the rich treasures of your grace. We thank you for every blessing that has come to us in the past. Today we express our gratitude for the blessings you have in store for us in the future. In our tithes and offerings, we bring the fruit of our labors as proof of our gratitude and love. Accept these tithes and offerings as symbols of our desire to give ourselves completely to you. In Jesus' name. Amen.

Introduction

The Bible does not give us all the answers to the questions we may have concerning heaven and hell. Someone has suggested that if we were given a full description of the joys of heaven, it would be impossible for us to be happy here on earth. Although many questions are not answered, we can be grateful for the information we do have concerning the life beyond.

It is impossible to know all until we get to heaven. By means of travel, one is able to learn much about a country and about the people that make up that country. It is impossible to describe fully what we would learn by a trip to heaven. We can only speculate as to the reports that we would be able to give if we could then return to the common walks of man.

In the book of Revelation, a door was opened and John the Revelator heard a voice describing heaven: "And I heard a voice from heaven saying unto me, Write, Blessed are the dead which die in the Lord from henceforth: Yea, saith the Spirit, that they may rest from their labours; and their works do follow them" (Rev. 14:13). The voice came from one who could see the glory and joy of those who had passed on into the home of the heavenly Father. It described those saints as blessed and happy.

If we could take one look into heaven, we would observe a number of things.

I. We would see what God intended for all people.

A. *The Bible begins with man in a garden of delight.*
   1. He was given a pleasant occupation.
   2. He was blessed with beloved companionship.
   3. He enjoyed beautiful surroundings.
B. *Sin thwarted God's plan for all.*
   1. Humans were made to walk and talk with God in a personal relationship and fellowship (Gen. 3:8).

244

2. Unbelief, rebellion, and greed for equality with God broke this fellow-ship, and Adam and Eve were cast out of the garden (Gen. 3:24).

C. *The Bible is a record of God's activities by which he is seeking to help humankind regain the lost paradise.*

1. The Bible opens with man in the garden (Gen. 3) and closes with the redeemed again in a garden (Rev. 22:1–5).

2. The redemptive program of God from the beginning to the present has been designed to help people regain that which was lost because of sin.

II. We would see what God has in store for those who love him (I Cor. 2:9).

A. *Heaven is a prepared place for a prepared people (John 14:3).*

1. Commodious.
2. Beautiful.
3. Comfortable.

B. *Heaven is a place of perfect holiness.* "And there shall in no wise enter into it any thing that defileth, neither whatsoever worketh abomination, or maketh a lie: but they which are written in the Lamb's book of life" (Rev. 21:27).

C. *Heaven is a place of rest (Rev. 14:13).*

D. *Heaven is a place of perfect health (Rev. 21:4).*

E. *Heaven is a place of active service (Rev. 22:3).*

F. *Heaven is a place where rewards for faithful service are bestowed (Rev. 22:12).*

III. We would see what our lost friends are going to miss.

A. *The Scriptures teach that the unsaved will be shut out of heaven and deprived of the blessings that could have been theirs (Matt. 25:41, 46; Rev. 20:11–15).*

B. *The Bible teaches that instead of going to heaven, which God is preparing for those who love him, the unsaved will enter hell as intruders.* They will be unwelcomed guests in a place that was prepared for the Devil and his angels (Matt. 25:41).

C. *Missing heaven will be a tragedy of tragedies.*

IV. We would see why Jesus was willing to die for lost people.

A. *The Savior was willing to die for our sins that we might receive the gift of eternal life and have the privilege of living with God in heaven for eternity.*

B. *He died to save us from hell, but he also died to save us for heaven.*

C. *The privilege of going to heaven is the highest possible destiny and the greatest possible blessing that can be bestowed on a life.*

Conclusion

When we claim the precious promises of God concerning heaven, we will immediately realize how foolish it is to live for this life only. To grasp our Savior's teachings about heaven would do much to destroy our fear of death and would enable us to face the future with more joy and courage. Those who trust in the teachings of our Savior concerning heaven will find much greater joy in living day by day with the issues and values of eternity in mind.

The assurance of going to heaven should challenge every disciple to be a good witness for Jesus Christ so that through his or her telling the story of God's love, many others will come to know Christ as personal Savior.

Unsaved friend, the absolute certainty of death, your need for forgiveness, and the desire for a life and destiny in heaven like that which the Bible describes should challenge you this very day to forsake the life of unbelief and rebellion against God. Jesus Christ can and will forgive your sin and grant you the privilege of entering into the eternal home prepared for those who love God if you will receive him as your Lord and Savior (John 14:6).

SUNDAY EVENING, AUGUST 24

Title: If Every Christian Went to Hell for Five Minutes

Text: "And he cried and said, Father Abraham, have mercy on me ... for I am tormented in this flame" (**Luke 16:24**).

Introduction

The title of this message, "If Every Christian Went to Hell for Five Minutes," supposes an impossibility. It is not the ideal will of God that anyone go to hell. The Scriptures teach that hell was prepared for the Devil and his angels (Matt. 25:41). The whole redemptive program of God is motivated by the dual desire to save people from a destiny in hell and to save them to an eternal fellowship with God in heaven.

Have you ever speculated concerning what you would learn if you could make a five-minute visit into the destiny of the doomed? Have you ever examined your heart and been convicted of the calloused, cold-hearted indifference of your heart toward the spiritual welfare of those for whom our Lord died?

I must say to you that there have been times when I have felt, at least momentarily, that a five-minute trip to hell would be very profitable for my ministry. I must also confess that there have been times when, if I could have sent some of my church members to hell for five minutes and then brought them back, that I would have done so. I say this without malice or hatred or desire for revenge. These thoughts were motivated by a desire to help parents see the awful danger to which they were exposing their children by an attitude of total indifference concerning their spiritual and moral well-being.

I. We would learn that hell is real.

    A. *Hell is not a myth or bad dream or the creation of some fantastic fiction writer.*

    B. *Hell was a reality to our Savior to the extent that he died on a cross to save people from it.*

C. *Hell was a reality to the apostle Paul to the extent that he suffered great privation and hardship and martyrdom that he might communicate the saving gospel to the lost.*

D. *Hell was a reality to the rich man mentioned in the story by Jesus.*
   1. He was in possession of his consciousness.
   2. He described his feelings.
   3. He retained his memory.
   4. He was in a hopeless condition.
   5. He had a concern for his five brothers lest they come into the same torment.

II. Such a trip would cause the church to be aroused from a state of complacency.

A. *The church is not a social club.*

B. *The church is not just a service organization.*

C. *The church is our Lord's rescue squad charged with the responsibility of persuading people to forsake their lives of unbelief and rebellion against God that will eventually put them in hell.*

D. *We greatly admire heroes.* The newspapers contain stories week after week of those who have greatly endangered themselves to save someone from great peril. If the members of the contemporary church really believed that all of those who died outside of Jesus Christ would spend eternity in hell, we would become a community of compassionate concern unlike anything the world has never seen.

III. Such a trip would cause us to recognize the value of being genuinely Christian in all of our conduct.

A. *The most effective sermons ever preached are not those that are uttered over the pulpit.* Unless the gospel is demonstrated in life, the testimony of the lips and the sermon from the pulpit will have no weight or influence.

B. *By referring to his disciples as the salt of the earth and the light of the world, Jesus was emphasizing the value of influence.* People will not believe in our Savior unless we demonstrate that he makes a difference in our lives.

C. *Paul was emphasizing this truth when he said, "Wherefore, if meat make my brother to offend (stumble), I will eat no flesh while the world standeth, lest I make my brother to offend (stumble)" (1 Cor. 8:13).* Our conduct must always be guided by our motive to attract people to our Savior.

IV. Such a trip would vastly influence our personal spiritual growth and discipline.

A. *Prayer would take on a new meaning if we realized that it brought us into vital contact with the eternal God and that through prayer God would be able to work his work within us so as to make us more effective in our witnessing.*

B. *We would become diligent students of the divine Word that we might more effectively meet the personal needs of those to whom we would seek to bear a winning witness.*

C. *We would respond to the church with a much deeper love and with a greater loyalty, because the church is the only institution God is depending on for the evangelization of the world.*

V. Such a trip would enable us to learn why people go to hell.

"They will repent" (Luke 16:30).

A. *People do not go to hell because of the desire or design of God.*

B. *People do not go to hell because they have sinned so greatly that God is unable to save them (Rom. 1:16).*

C. *People go to hell because they refuse to repent (Luke 13:3).*

D. *People go to hell because they live a selfish life of sin (Rom. 6:23).*

E. *People also go to hell because of our neglect to witness and to tell others of God's love (John 20:23).* By obedience to our Lord's command to be witnesses, we become the means whereby people hear the Word and seek forgiveness, and consequently they escape an eternity in hell. For us to neglect to witness is to involve ourselves in guilt for their remaining in their sins. It is almost too terrible to contemplate that people go into eternity unprepared to meet God because of the indifference, unconcern, and failure to bear a witness on the part of those who consider themselves followers of the Lord.

Conclusion

God does not want anyone to go to hell. He has given his Son Jesus Christ to prevent people from going to hell. God has done all within his power to save people. Every Christian should cooperate with him in his work of saving people from a hopeless eternity.

If you have not yet received Christ as your Lord and Savior, do so immediately that you might be prepared for an eternity of fellowship with God.

WEDNESDAY EVENING, AUGUST 27

Title: The Parable of the Pearl of Great Price

Text: "The kingdom of heaven is like unto a merchant man seeking goodly pearls: Who, when he had found one pearl of great price, went and sold all that he had, and bought it" **(Matt. 13:46).**

Introduction

The kingdom of God can be described in two ways. It is the rule of God in the heart. It is moral, not nationalistic. It is spiritual, not material. It is actual, not ideal. But it is also the rule of God in the world. It is social, not individualistic. It is universal, not local. It awaits a final consummation and is not yet complete.

I. The kingdom is spoken of as a hidden treasure, a pearl of great price.

A. *Christian character satisfies deeper needs than anything else can.*

B. *The kingdom answers to humankind's highest aspirations.*

C. *The kingdom is not only a treasure of infinitely finer quality but of longer duration.*

II. Many look for a cheap and easy religion today.

A. *We are bargain seekers.*

B. *We are looking for instant gratification.*

C. *Many want to use Christ as a convenience.*

III. The cost of the best.

A. *The cost is all that a person has.*

B. *The kingdom must be first.*

C. *The kingdom deserves your best.*

    1. Time.

    2. Talents.

    3. Treasure.

    4. Testimony.

Conclusion

The Christian life is often difficult and painful; this cannot be denied. It is valuable, however, in many ways. A key value is the pearl of heaven, for which we can constantly give thanks. This gift or treasure from God, bought with Christ's blood, gives us a more godly attitude toward perseverance in trials.

SUNDAY MORNING, AUGUST 31

Title: What Is God Like?

Text: "The heavens declare the glory of God; and the firmament sheweth his handiwork" (**Ps. 19:1**).

Hymns: "Praise to the Lord, the Almighty," Neander

         "Praise, My Soul, the King of Heaven," Lyte

         "O Worship the King," Grant

Offertory Prayer: Holy Father, you are God, the Maker and Creator of us all. We are your people and the sheep of your pasture. We come before you with thanksgiving and praise. We love you because you have first loved us. We bring our tithes and offerings as indications of the sincerity of our love. Bless these gifts to your glory and to the progress of your kingdom on earth through Jesus Christ our Lord. Amen.

Introduction

Only a fool would say, "There is no God." When David lifted up his eyes and beheld all the glories and beauties of the universe, it is no surprise that he would burst forth in a psalm of praise to God, the author and creator of it all.

249

Today we preach on the assumption that there is a God who has existed from the timeless past and will continue to exist through all eternity. "In the beginning God created the heaven and the earth" (Gen. 1:1). He will continue to exist when heaven and earth are no more.

A human author does not attempt to prove his own existence. He merely prints his name on his book and sends it out into the world. Without any attempt to prove his existence, God places himself in the first verse of the Bible and proceeds to reveal himself, his person, his power, and his purpose in the world.

Through the ages, people have wanted to know what kind of a being God is. With Philip they have said: "Shew us the Father, and it sufficeth us" (John 14:8). They have wanted to know what God looks like and how he feels and acts toward men. They have wondered about his nature, character, and purpose. They have sought to understand his power and his purpose through a study of nature. The text says, "The heavens declare the glory of God; and the firmament sheweth his handiwork."

The Bible is a record of God's self-revelation. Through the ages God has revealed himself to man. The patriarchs, psalmists, and prophets were given insights that were recorded for the benefit of others.

The supreme and final revelation of God comes to humankind through the person and work of Jesus Christ (John 1:18; 14:9; Heb. 1:1–3). He was the eternal God clothed in human flesh, who visited the earth that people might know what God is like (John 1:14).

I. The personality of God.

    A. *God is a person.* God is not an abstract principle or an impersonal power. God is something more than a pantheistic absolute. God is more than the principle behind the universe.

        All of the marks of personality are ascribed to God. He knows. He feels. He loves. He acts. He speaks. He is knowable. The writer of the book of Hebrews speaks of faith in terms of believing that God is, and that he is a rewarder of those who diligently seek him (Heb. 11:6).

        Several ministerial students were engaged in a discussion of various theological questions while making a trip by train. The conversation ceased, and one moved across the aisle to a vacant double seat where he could study. He was no more than seated when a woman who had been listening in on their conversation came and sat down beside him. Apologetically, she asked, "May I ask you a question?" When he assured her that he would be glad to help in any way possible, she asked, "Can you tell me if there is any hope at all of a life beyond?" She then explained that she was en route to the interment service of her grandchild, the ashes of whom she was carrying in her suitcase. Her face showed anxiety and grief.

        Not knowing exactly how to answer, the young pastor asked a question: "What is your concept of God?" After a pause and some serious thought, the grieving grandmother replied, "To me, God is the principle behind the universe." In the discussion that followed, she revealed that she was a member of a church, and for a number of years she had taught a Sunday school class. She also indicated that she had never had a definite answer to prayer. Everyone recognizes that no comfort can come in a time of sorrow from a god who is nothing more than a principle behind the universe. The young pastor sought to comfort her by telling her that God is more than a principle. He is a person who has revealed himself in Jesus Christ.

B. *God is spirit (John 4:24).* God is not limited to space and time as humans are. God is not material and visible as man is. This is difficult to comprehend, and those who have limited themselves to the scientific method find great difficulty in believing at this point.

One of the Ten Commandments forbids the making of graven images. To make any kind of a graven image not only limits the concept of God, but it also misrepresents the nature and character of God.

God is infinite, and humans are finite. God is before, and above, and beyond the power of the human mind to comprehend. He communicates with us on the level of the mind and spirit, and we are able to experience his presence only on that level. We cannot see him with the eye. We cannot grasp him with our hands. But on the level of the mind and spirit, we can have communion with him at any time, any place, and under any circumstances.

That God is spirit should not cause people to stumble into unbelief. There are many things that cannot be fully comprehended with the mind. Electricity is a phenomenon that defies complete comprehension. There are things about telecommunications that seem unbelievable. The immensity of the universe is staggering in its significance. These are things we believe in and relate to even though we do not perfectly understand them.

II. The nature of God's character.

A. *God is eternal (Gen. 1:1; Ps. 90:2).*
  1. The heavens and earth have been here for a long time, but God was here first.
  2. When the heavens are no more, God will still exist.
  3. Humans are but creatures of the day, but God inhabits eternity. God always has been and always will be. He is eternal.

B. *God is holy (Isa. 6:3).*
  1. God is different and distinct from humans.
  2. God is separate and above humans.
  3. God is perfectly good and always right.
  4. God is separate from evil.
  5. God's holiness is the part of his nature that reacts with antagonism toward all sin. Sin is that which destroys people and would destroy God if possible. God's holiness reacts to sin as a consuming fire.

C. *God is omnipotent* (Matt. 19:26).
   1. God's omnipotence is his ability to do everything that can be done.
   2. He is the almighty, all-powerful God.
   3. He always works within the limits of that which is right. He does not act in a contradictory manner.
D. *God is omniscient (Ps. 139:1–6).*
   1. God knows all things.
   2. "He telleth the number of the stars; he calleth them all by their names" (Ps. 147:4).
   3. The hairs of your head are numbered (Matt. 10:30).
   4. He knows the past, present, and future.
E. *God is omnipresent (Ps. 139:7–12).*
   1. This means that God is everywhere present at all times.
   2. We cannot drift beyond the circle of his loving care.
   3. He is with the missionaries who serve on foreign mission fields as well as with the housewife at home caring for her children.
   4. The psalmist declared, "God is our refuge and strength, a very present help in trouble" (Ps. 46:1).
F. *God is great (Ps. 86:10).*
   1. In his creative power.
   2. In his redemptive power.
   3. In his keeping power.
G. *God is love (1 John 4:8).*
   1. Shown in the gift of his Son.
   2. Shown in his daily care.
   3. Shown in his mercy toward sinners.

III. God's present relationship to the world.

A. *He governs it.* It seems at times that the world has gone mad and that nothing can stop it from destroying itself. Some believe that people will turn this world into a cinder heap by means of a nuclear explosion. Those who have been gripped by this fear bear testimony to the absence of a faith in the God who created and who sustains our world. Today the church desperately needs to claim the truth that God is still on his throne and that he is at work in history. This thought can be both comforting and frightening.

B. *God punishes sin and rewards righteousness.* Some would dispute this statement, because at times it seems that the wicked prosper and righteous suffer. A part of God's punishment on sin falls on people in this life. Some of it is reserved for the next life. Some of the reward for righteousness comes in this life, but Scripture teaches that there will also be rewards in eternity.

C. *God offers forgiveness and salvation.* The Bible is a record of God's continuous efforts to rescue people from the consequences of their unbelief and rebellion. Through Jesus Christ, God offers forgiveness and the gift of eternal life to repentant believers.

IV. God's future relationship to humankind and the world.

A. *People will be required to give an account to God (Rom. 14:10–12).*
1. The judgment of God is according to truth (Rom. 2:2).
2. The judgment of God is according to deeds (Rom. 2:6).
3. The judgment of God is without partiality (Rom. 2:11).
4. The judgment of God is with reference to the gospel (Rom. 2:16).

B. *God will reward the faithful and punish the unbeliever (Matt. 25:31–46).*

C. *God will live forever with his children (Rev. 21:1–4).*

Conclusion

A person does not become a child of God by natural birth or by some kind of religious accident. You can become a child of God by a decision to receive Jesus Christ, the Son of God, into your heart. He stands at the front door waiting to enter. He will not intrude where he is not welcome. He has promised to come in if you will invite him (Rev. 3:20). Do so now.

SUNDAY EVENING, AUGUST 31

Title: What Is Man?

Text: "What is man, that thou art mindful of him? and the son of man, that thou visitest him?" **(Ps. 8:4).**

Introduction

Continually people ask: "What am I? Where did I come from? What am I doing?"

There are many conflicting answers to the question "What is man?" Some say that man is but an animal, nothing more than the natural result of evolutionary process, a fortuitous concurrence of atoms, a hunk of protoplasm. Politically, some look upon him as but a servant of the state. Economically, some look upon him as a customer or a potential sucker.

Western civilization is built on the Christian concept that humans are something very special. A study of history reveals that as people respond to the biblical concept of man, that civilization is elevated.

To understand the nature of people, three questions should be answered. "What was man like when he came from the hand of God? What is man like today? What can man become?"

I. What was man like?

A. *Man was the crown and climax of God's creative activity (Gen. 1:27–28).* After everything else had been created and the world was perfectly prepared for the advent of man, he was created by God.

B. *Man was created in the image and likeness of God.* This is a reference to man's spiritual nature rather than a physical likeness. Man was made possessing

253

an intellect, emotions, and a will. He has the power to choose. He has the unique capacity for worship and fellowship with God. He is a worshiping creature. He was commissioned to have dominion over all of God's creation.

C. *Man was made for God.* Only man has the capacity for worship. Of all the creatures, man is the only one who offers prayers and bows down to worship. He alone can give himself freely in service to God.

D. *Man was made innocent and free.* He was not a robot. He was made unstained by sin and was given freedom to believe and surrender in service or to disbelieve and rebel.

II. What is man today?

A. *Man is a being limited by time and space.*

B. *Man is a sinner (Rom. 3:23).*
1. Man has missed the mark of God's calling.
2. Man has fallen short of God's glory.
3. Man's pride finds expression in rebellion and unbelief.
4. Man has become self-centered and self-destructive.

C. *Man is a moral fool.*
1. He is not sensitive to spiritual values.
2. He has a distorted vision of spiritual realities.
3. He can be duped by the Devil. His intellect has been corrupted. His emotions have been warped, and his will has been twisted.

D. *Man is in a hopeless condition (Eph. 2:12).*
1. He is under the sentence of spiritual death (Rom. 6:23).
2. He is under the wrath of God (John 3:36).

E. *Man is the primary object of God's redemptive purpose.*
1. God loves us (John 3:16).
2. Man, in God's sight, was worth dying for. This is the gospel.
3. The Holy Spirit abides in the church and works through individual believers to invite unsaved people to receive Christ.

III. What can man become?

A. *Man can become a son of God (John 1:12; Gal. 3:26).*

B. *Man can become a servant of God (Eph. 2:10).*

C. *Man can become a steward of God.*

Conclusion

If you would find life in its richest quality and if you would live life on its highest level, you would find it only in a relationship to the Creator who has revealed himself as the loving heavenly Father. Man has unique significance only in relationship to God. Man finds meaning and purpose in life only as he lives it by faith in God.

SEPTEMBER

■ Sunday Mornings

The suggested theme for the morning services this month is "Beautiful Pictures of God." The possibilities for such a series are unlimited. Four verbal pictures have been selected for use that can strengthen the faith, deepen the devotion, and challenge the lives of people.

■ Sunday Evenings

To complement or supplement the morning messages, the suggested theme for the evening services is "Beautiful Pictures of God's People." These messages remind us of who we are, what we are to be, and what we are to do if we want to be God's people for this age and time.

■ Wednesday Evenings

The emphasis this month is on how Christians should deal with temptation.

WEDNESDAY EVENING, SEPTEMBER 3

Title: The Worth of Your Soul

Text: "For what shall it profit a man, if he shall gain the whole world, and lose his own soul?" (**Mark 8:36**).

Introduction

Satan appeared to Christ in the wilderness and offered him the greatest prize that was at his disposal to bestow. Satan had all of the kingdoms of the world with all of their glory pass before the Christ. Then he made the offer that these could be his if he would but fall down before his satanic majesty in worship.

Some have failed to recognize the potential appeal of Satan's offer. Christ had come to die on the cross so that the kingdoms of this world might become the kingdom of God. Satan, the father of lies, promised to deliver the entire world if Christ would yield to the suggestion of evil. Satan promised Christ the fulfill-ment of his dreams by means of a detour around the cross. He offered a shortcut to success. He sought to lure Jesus Christ to a path outside the will of God. This was an attempt to buy the soul of Christ and to thwart and to destroy God's great program of redemption. We can be grateful for the fact that the Christ did not sell his soul for this promise of the world.

I. The promise of an impossible gain.

Satan, the prince of this world, continues to promise the world to those who are willing to fall down and worship him. He will promise whatever is necessary to secure and to maintain your allegiance.

    A. *The Devil pays the lowest possible wages (Rom. 6:23).*

    B. *The Devil promises much but gives little. No one has been able to gain the whole world.*

II. The offer of a bad bargain.

All of us are price conscious. We are interested in the cost of everything. This should be true in every area of life including the spiritual. People often fail to count the cost of neglecting their souls. They do not count the cost of buying the world with all of its glitter at the price of losing their souls.

If you could take the coin of your soul and with this currency purchase the world, you would be making a bad deal.

    A. *The world is perishing (1 John 2:17).* Would you purchase valuable perfume if you knew that the flask contained a leak and that the perfume was certain to evaporate?

    B. *The world does not satisfy.* Man was made for God. Deep within the human heart there is a hunger that neither wealth, nor honor, nor pleasure can satisfy. People are spiritual. They need God. Without God, life at its best is but a fraction and will always be incomplete.

    C. *The world is dangerous.* Instead of being your servant, the world would become your master. You would be possessed by the world.

    D. *You cannot take it with you.* It is appointed unto men once to die. Those who have sold their souls in order to win the world will find themselves faced with the sad destiny of having to leave it all.

III. An unanswered question.

The text is an unanswered question in terms of profit and loss. There is no answer concerning what a person can gain, but there is an answer to the question of what he will lose. If you sell your soul and live the life of no faith, for one world only, you lose many wonderful blessings.

    A. *You lose the privilege of having eternal life (John 3:36).*

    B. *You lose the privilege of becoming a child of God (John 8:44).*

    C. *You deprive yourself of peace with God (Isa. 48:22).*

    D. *You miss the life abundant (John 10:10).*

    E. *You miss heaven (Rev. 20:15).*

IV. Count the cost.

    A. *Satan offers you the world with all of its pleasures if you will serve him.* In the end he will pay off with disappointment, death, and destruction.

    B. *Christ offers you life now and life hereafter.* He offers you the freedom to become all that God means for you to be.

Conclusion

You must make the decision regarding the destiny of your soul. You can let Satan have it or you can entrust it into the care of Jesus Christ. If you lose your soul, it is your own responsibility. God has done and is doing all that he can to save you. He will not compel you, but he does invite you to be saved now and forever.

SUNDAY MORNING, SEPTEMBER 7

Title: The God of Hosea

Text: "I will have mercy upon the house of Judah, and will save them by the LORD their God" (**Hos. 1:7**).

Hymns: "O the Deep, Deep Love of Jesus," Francis

"The King of Love My Shepherd Is," Baker

"Love Lifted Me," Rowe

Offertory Prayer: Heavenly Father, we thank you for the gift of life. We praise you for the opportunity to work. We are grateful for the fruit of our labor. We recognize you and praise you as the giver of all good and perfect gifts. With our tithes and offerings we express our gratitude and indicate our desire that others have the privilege of hearing the message of your love. Bless these gifts to that purpose. In Jesus' name. Amen.

Introduction

By the discipline of cruel events, God taught Hosea much concerning the nature and character of Israel's God. Because of Hosea's faith and obedience to God, he was granted insight into the deep spiritual need of his generation and was endowed with a divine message for that hour and for the present.

Hosea was the prophet of the decline, death, and fall of northern Israel. The worship of God had given way to mere ritual. It was a time of moral degeneracy and spiritual adultery. With their lips the people worshiped God, and with their hearts they loved idols. Flagrant immorality, irreverence for the sacred, unfaithfulness, thievery, and drunkenness were the order of the day.

When God wants a specific task performed, he chooses an instrument appropriate to the task. God found in the prophet Hosea a man for the hour. God told him, "Go, take to yourself an adulterous wife and children of unfaithfulness" (1:2 NIV). Hosea was obedient to this command.

The record of the prophet's experience in chapters 1 and 3 has been exposed to a wide variety of interpretations. Some take the passage simply to be a literary device to illustrate a great truth. However, most Old Testament scholars believe that Hosea was directed to marry a woman given to idolatry, an idolatry that was often associated with immorality. At first she was an unchaste woman only in a spiritual sense. She bore to her husband three children, to whom symbolic names were given. Eventually idolatry brought forth its natural fruit, and Hosea's wife

257

became an unchaste woman in a very real sense. Whether she then deserted her husband or was divorced by him is not definitely stated. At any rate, in obedience to the divine command, Hosea recovered his unfaithful wife and restored her to his home.

The first of Hosea's children was named *Jezreel*, symbolizing the overthrow of the dynasty of Israel's ruling king. The second was named *Lo-ruhamah*, announcing that God would have no mercy on Israel. The third was named *Lo-ammi*, symbolizing the utter destruction of Israel. These names have prophetic significance for conditions existing in Israel as Hosea saw them. This period of preparation was not to be completed until the events of chapter 3 had transpired.

As time went by, Hosea began to notice things that caused him to wonder and worry about Gomer. He had known from the very first that she had tendencies toward idolatry. Perhaps he had hoped to win Gomer to Israel's religion. Before too long, Hosea realized his effort was resulting in failure. The names that were given to the second and third children indicated that the prophet recognized he was not their father.

The Bible does not describe the moment of Gomer's departure from the household of Hosea. It is impossible to know whether Hosea cast her out or whether she departed on her own accord. Most scholars believe that Gomer departed of her own free will and became a sacred prostitute in one of the pagan temples of Baal. It is impossible for one to imagine the grief, disappointment, and shame that Hosea must have experienced during these days when the wife of his youth was "beloved of her friends."

It was while Hosea was groping for a solution to his family problems that insight into the episode began to dawn on his consciousness. He was not the only one who had suffered. He began to see that his experience with Gomer was part of a picture of what had been happening to God and Israel for a long time.

God had taken the initiative in establishing a union with Israel. He had delivered them out of Egypt. He had led them into the land that he had designated to be their home. He had shown tender love for Israel and had expected a pure, undivided affection from them. The bond between them was as close and tender as the bond of wedlock.

Israel had been unfaithful to her Maker and spiritual Husband. Israel had sought other lovers and found them in the Canaanite worship of Baal. God had been forsaken by the people on whom he had showered the abundance of his divine love. Consequently, the people were guilty of spiritual adultery. Out of his personal experience, Hosea begins to understand how the unfaithfulness of Israel affected the heart of God.

In spite of Gomer's infidelity and shameful ways of living, Hosea discovered in his heart a continuing love for her and came to interpret this love as the clear command of God to win back his wife to better ways. We read how Hosea went to the slave market, to which Gomer had descended, and purchased her in order that he might redeem her from the depths of infamy into which she had fallen. He dealt with Gomer as he knew God wanted to deal with Israel.

It was a stern and painful education that taught Hosea to understand the relationship between the Lord and Israel. By his personal experience of what infidelity meant, Hosea entered into a new sympathy with the God of Israel who had experienced the same thing at the hands of his people. Dr. H. Wheeler Robinson says that Hosea was thus equipped to preach of the love of God, for his "power was in his wound."

An examination of the book of Hosea reveals at once how deeply the messages it contains are colored by the experience of his marriage. In this experience, Hosea learned certain great truths that we desperately need to heed today.

I. Hosea discovered that God is love.

A. *Hosea has been called the first prophet of grace, Israel's first evangelist.*

B. *God is no impassive observer of the trials and troubles of his people.*

C. *Hosea's message throbbed with an awareness of the loving-kindness of God.*

II. Hosea came to a new understanding of the nature of sin.

A. *Hosea saw sin as spiritual adultery.*

B. *Sin crushes the loving heart of the divine Husband.*

C. *Sin also brings suffering to the guilty.* "For the children of Israel shall abide many days without a king, and without a prince, and without a sacrifice, and without an image, and without an ephod, and without teraphim" (Hos. 3:4).

D. *Israel must go into exile, not because of God's punishment or justice, but because of his redemptive purposes.* God does not merely punish sin, but seeks to bring about the defeat of sin.

III. Hosea came to a new understanding of God's basic requirements.

A. *Hosea's concept of what God required from his people can be summed up in the term* faithfulness.

B. *Hosea's understanding of the love of God caused him to appreciate the demands of love for utter loyalty.*

C. *This can be clearly seen in God's eager desire for the restoration of the marriage relationship.* "I will even betroth thee unto me in faithfulness: and thou shalt know the LORD" (Hos. 2:20).

IV. Hosea understood and explained the necessity of repentance.

A. *Hosea was told to reclaim Gomer, which he did by purchase.* He did not restore her immediately to the position she had occupied formerly as his wife, but rather kept her on probation for an indefinite period of time. Her discipline consisted of certain deprivations (3:3).

B. *Hosea saw that in the presence of defiant wrongdoing, justice and punishment are the highest expressions of love.*

C. *There must be a complete interchange of attitude if Israel is to experience the richest blessings of God's love.*

Conclusion

Hosea speaks to our present generation and tries to convince us that our God is a God of love who suffers because of our unfaithfulness and lack of loyalty. He challenges us to respond to God's love with love that expresses itself in devotion and loyal service.

SUNDAY EVENING, SEPTEMBER 7

Title: "Now Are We the Sons of God"

Text: "Beloved, now are we the sons of God, and it doth not yet appear what we shall be: but we know that, when he shall appear, we shall be like him; for we shall see him as he is" (**1 John 3:2**).

Introduction

All people are the creatures of God. Only those who by faith receive Christ as Savior can truthfully call themselves the children of God. There is no more blessed fact revealed in Scripture or experienced by human souls than that man, created by the merciful hand of God, can become a loving child of God through the miracle of divine regeneration. Sonship is established in the new birth, and it is a nearer and closer relationship to God than that established by God's creative act. This new relationship is tender, affectionate, and glorious, and it is the fundamental basis for all of the sacred, holy, and far-reaching obligations and responsibilities devolved on man.

I. The blessed fact of sonship.

"Now are we the sons of God."

A. *There are many good, but timid, people who have never ventured to say, "I know that I am a child of God."* This hesitation could be due to a number of different factors.

1. Some believe that salvation is a result of God's grace plus human effort.
2. Others would hesitate because of the lack of an outstanding conversion experience.
3. Others would hesitate because they do not understand what the Bible teaches about their relationship to God.

B. *John speaks of sonship with great confidence (1 John 5:13).*

1. God wants his children to have the assurance of their salvation.
2. Those who have been saved can be assured that eternal life is a present possession.

C. *Paul believed that the Holy Spirit provided assurance of sonship (Rom. 8:14–16).*

1. Assurance of sonship should give comfort and security.
2. Assurance of sonship should inspire love and gratitude.
3. Assurance of sonship equips one with a Christian witness.

II. The nature of our sonship.

A. *Our sonship is spiritual.* It is a result of the creative activity of God's Holy Spirit, when we receive Christ into our hearts.

B. *Our sonship is divine.* We become partakers of the divine nature. The nature of God is planted at the life center of the soul (1 John 3:9), and man becomes a new creature in Christ Jesus.

C. *Our sonship is eternal, never ending in its nature.* It is the impartation of eternal life to the soul (John 10:28).

III. The privilege of this sonship.

A. *God becomes our Father.*
1. He is in heaven above and knows the past, present, and future.
2. He knows our needs.
3. He is eager to supply our needs.
4. He loves us.
5. He understands us.
6. He is impartial.

B. *Jesus becomes our Elder Brother.*
1. He is our Savior.
2. He is preparing a place for us.

C. *We become a member of the great family of God.*
1. We are united to those who have gone on.
2. We are united to those who now live.
3. We have a relationship to those who will follow.

IV. The obligations of this sonship.

A. *The first obligation is that of love to God and to our fellow humans.*

B. *Absolute, loving obedience is implied in this relationship. Obedience should rise out of love rather than fear.*

C. *A child of God is to walk worthy of the name he or she bears (1 Thess. 2:11–12).*

Conclusion

The new birth (John 3:3) established the blessed fact of sonship. We become the children of God through faith in Jesus Christ (Gal. 3:26). The faith that saves is much more than mental assent. It accepts Jesus Christ to be all that the Bible claims him to be and trusts him to do all that he has promised to do.

The new birth is mysterious, even as the physical birth is mysterious. While we cannot perfectly and completely understand either, the Scriptures would assure us that "as Moses lifted up the serpent in the wilderness, even so must the Son of man be lifted up. That whosoever believeth in him should not perish, but have everlasting life" (John 3:14–15). Let today be your spiritual birthday.

WEDNESDAY EVENING, SEPTEMBER 10

Title: The Tempter

Text: "Then Jesus was led by the Spirit into the desert to be tempted by the devil" **(Matt. 4:1 NIV).**

Introduction

Our Savior had firsthand experience with the Tempter, that old Serpent, the Devil. Satan sought to lure him away from the place of faithfulness and obedience to the will of God even as he had succeeded in tempting Adam. From both the experience of Jesus and the teachings of the Word of God, we can learn how to be victorious over Satan and his temptations. We need to recognize the reality of the evil forces that are against us. Paul says concerning Satan, "We are not ignorant of his devices" (2 Cor. 2:11). A study of the temptations of our Lord can be very helpful.

I. The temptation of Jesus was real.

A. *It gave proof of his true humanity.*
B. *It was part of his example to us.*
C. *It formed a part of his discipline and prepared him to be a sympathizing intercessor.*
D. *It formed a part of that great conflict in which the "seed of the woman" was to "bruise the head of the serpent."*
E. *To be tempted is not an indication of being exceedingly sinful.*
F. *We become strong and stable by overcoming the temptations toward evil.*

II. The methods of the Tempter.

A. *The Tempter never reveals his strategy.*
B. *The Tempter gently implies that God exists to satisfy our hungers.* "If thou be the son of God, command that these stones be made bread" (Matt. 4:3).
C. *The Tempter encourages us to make a god out of bread.*
  1. You have a natural appetite for bread, so satisfy this appetite.
  2. Since you have a natural desire for pleasure, power, peace, and plenty, abandon yourself to these. Secure these at any cost.
D. *The Tempter comes as a supposed friend and never as a foe (2 Cor. 11:14).*
  1. He dresses neatly, speaks smooth words, and observes perfect manners.
  2. He tempts us with a promise to fulfill a dream long deferred.
E. *The Tempter's voice is indistinguishable from the voice of your own heart.* Until we realize this, we easily can be duped by the devil. John would warn us: "Beloved, believe not every spirit, but try the spirits whether they are of God: because many false prophets are gone out into the world" (1 John 4:1).
F. *The Tempter seeks to separate us from the source of our strength.*

1. Strength comes from surrender to the will of God. Man, even in weakness, depending wholly on God, is stronger than man in strength standing alone.
2. Man, in weakness, is stronger when surrendered to God than his foe, the Tempter.

Conclusion

John, the beloved apostle, would encourage each of us to have faith in the Spirit and power of the Lord who has come to dwell in our hearts. Through him we can be victorious over the Tempter. "Ye are of God, little children, and have overcome them: because greater is he that is in you, than he that is in the world" (1 John 4:4).

SUNDAY MORNING, SEPTEMBER 14

Title: "God Is Our Refuge"

Text: "God is our refuge and strength, a very present help in trouble" **(Ps. 46:1)**.

Hymns: "A Mighty Fortress Is Our God," Luther

"Rock of Ages," Toplady

"Blessed Assurance," Crosby

Offertory Prayer: Heavenly Father, we thank you for the privilege of being coworkers with you in your work of saving the world from the waste and the ruin of sin. Accept our tithes and offerings in order that the gospel might be preached to all nations of the earth. Help us to give our time, our talents, and our treasure, and above all, our testimony unto you. In Jesus' name we pray. Amen.

Introduction

In a day when our nation stands in danger of becoming a cinder heap as a result of an atomic holocaust, this psalm, proclaiming that God is our refuge, has a message that is needed.

Each family can be blessed immeasurably if somehow they can enshrine in their home the picture of God contained in this psalm.

Each person stands in need of a refuge, a place of security, when the storms of life beat down.

I. God is our refuge.

A. *God is our storm cellar when the tornado comes.*

B. *God is our fallout shelter when the events of life explode over our heads.*

C. *God is our high tower when the waves of defeat and disaster beat at our feet.*

God had been all this to Israel when Rabshakeh and the armies of Sennacherib surrounded the city (Isa. 36:13–15; 37:1, 3–7, 33–36).

D. *Every man stands in need of a refuge.*
   1. The pointing finger of an accusing conscience.
   2. The power of sin within ourselves.
   3. The power of the Devil.
   4. The wrath to come.

II. God is our strength.

A. *God provides strength for our infirmities (2 Cor. 12:7–9).*
B. *God provides strength for service (Phil. 4:13).*
C. *God provides strength for our weakness (Isa. 40:29–31).*

III. God is a very present help in trouble.

A. *A help that is not present when needed is of little value.*
B. *God is present when we seek him (Jer. 29:13).*
C. *God is present when we need him (Matt. 28:18–20).*
D. *God is present when we have already enjoyed his presence.*

IV. God is a very present help.

A. *God is more present than the nearest friend can be.*
B. *God is always present.*
C. *God is effectively present.*
D. *God is sympathetically present.*

Conclusion

No one else can trust God for us. No one else can be obedient for us. Our response to him must be immediate and complete.

> *Trust and obey, for there's no other way.*
> *To be happy in Jesus, but to trust and obey.*

Trust God now and obey him day by day, for he is a very present help in trouble.

SUNDAY EVENING, SEPTEMBER 14

Title: "You Are the Salt of the Earth"

Text: "You are the salt of the earth" (**Matt. 5:13 NIV**).

Introduction

In the Beatitudes Jesus sets before us a word picture of the inner spirit of a genuine Christian (Matt. 5:3–9).

The Master Teacher continues the Sermon on the Mount or lecture on Christian discipleship by describing in graphic terms the influence of such Christians.

By using the terms *salt* and *light* to describe the influence of the church, he sets forth a part of its function in the world. The words of the verse in which the text is found imply a conflict, express a compliment, issue a commission, mention a calamity, and deliver a call to consecration.

I. You are the salt of the earth—conflict (Matt. 5:10–12).

It is not right for Christians to follow a policy of peace at any price. They cannot do so and be worthy followers of Jesus Christ. Christianity is revolutionary (Matt. 10:34–38). Some who think of Christianity as something sweet may be shocked at the idea that genuine Christians provoke conflict.

A. *Real Christians are different; they are concerned.*

B. *Real Christians are a constant rebuke to selfishness and sin.*

C. *Christians experience conflict because they interfere with and hinder those who practice injustice and follow a policy of greed.* The presence of a godly person hinders the Devil from having elbow room to do his work. Evil and wicked persons will sometimes be ashamed to show themselves in the presence of purity.

D. *Jesus tells us to rejoice because of this opposition.* Why?

1. We have evidence that we are children of God.

2. This is the pathway to spiritual growth.

3. We follow in the train of the prophets.

II. You are the salt of the earth—compliment.

This is a grave judgment of the world. Apart from God, the earth is seen in Jesus' eyes as getting worse instead of better. He declares that his disciples will save the world from deterioration.

A. *We preserve that which is good.*

B. *We purify that which is worthwhile.*

C. We *season the community, the city, the country, the church, and the home.*

III. You are the salt of the earth—commission.

A. *Salt is a preservative.*

B. *Salt is an antiseptic.*

C. *Salt is a seasoning.*

D. *Salt is positive.*

1. It preserves the standards of a community.

2. It preserves the standards in recreation.

3. It preserves the business structure.

4. It preserves justice and righteousness in politics.

5. It preserves the purity of a city.

E. *Salt is preventative.*

1. It is an enemy of decay.

2. It is a foe of impurity.

3. It is an antagonist of rottenness and decomposition.

IV. If the salt loses its savor—calamity.

If the salt loses its distinctive nature, it also loses the preserving power and becomes dull, sluggish, insipid, flat, and tasteless.

    A. *The individual Christian, through compromise with a contaminating world and through spiritual indifference, can lose his or her saltiness.*

    B. *The church whose membership refuses both the claims and the commission of the Lord can lose its reason for being and consequently become of no value either to God or to people.*

    C. *The sad results:*

        1. No hope for the world.

        2. No joy in the heart of the compromised Christian.

        3. No treasure above.

    D. *Historians tell us that at the beginning of the nineteenth century, England was on the verge of a devastating revolution like the one that almost submerged France.* The revival under the leadership of the Wesleys prevented this tragedy. Today the only thing that can save our world from international cataclysmic destruction is a sufficient number of men and women in positions of authority, possessing the characteristics Jesus describes in the Sermon on the Mount.

V. You are the salt of the earth—consecration.

Every follower of Jesus Christ should seek to be sure that he or she is functioning as the salt of the earth.

    A. *Confession of past failures and present shortcomings is appropriate.*

    B. *An attitude of repentance.* This is a continuing experience as we come to know and accept the mind of Jesus Christ and make him Lord in every area of our affections, attitudes, and ambitions.

    C. *We must be dedicated to the task set before us.*

Conclusion

Salt also creates thirst. While those who are ill disposed toward the gospel resent the presence of those who function as salt to preserve, others are hungry for God, and the genuine Christian is to them like a lump of salt on the tongue. By the beauty of your life and by the happiness of your heart, you can win others to faith in Christ. May God help you to do so.

WEDNESDAY EVENING, SEPTEMBER 17

Title: Have You Tempted God?

Text: "Jesus said unto him, It is written again, Thou shalt not tempt the Lord thy God" (**Matt. 4:7**).

Introduction

In the first temptation the Devil tempted our Savior to satisfy a natural need of his body for food by the selfish use of his divine power. This the Savior refused to do and declared his determination to live by every word that proceeds out of the mouth of God rather than merely living for bread.

Following his defeat in this effort to lead Christ astray, the Devil directed his attack against the source of his strength—his perfect confidence in the Word of God. The ground of Satan's attack was a scriptural promise: "For he shall give his angels charge over thee, to keep thee in all thy ways. They shall bear thee up in their hands, lest thou dash thy foot against stone" (Ps. 91:11–12).

I. Let us examine Satan's approach.

A. *He decided to use the same weapon to achieve victory over Jesus that Jesus had used in winning his victory over the first temptation.*

B. *The Devil said to Jesus, "Since you live by the Word of God, put your trust in God's promises in order to win the people's allegiance."*

C. *The Devil said, "Do something adventurous, something magnificent, something out of the ordinary.* Turn on the glamour and sweep the people off their feet."

D. *In this temptation, the Devil had nothing to say about the will of God for Jesus.*

E. *The Devil emphasized the power of God and urged confidence in that power.*

F. *The Devil, who had risen up against Jesus, was armed to the teeth with Bible passages.* He put on a mask as if he were God and pretended to be a capable counselor for proper conduct. He plucked a passage of Scripture from its context and distorted it with a hellish grimace.

II. Satan's purpose can be discovered.

A. *The Devil wanted to call the signals and thus get the Son of God at his disposal.*

B. *If we will let the Tempter call the signals, he will let us run the plays.*

III. The pathway to victory.

A. *Jesus remembered no commandment of God to the effect that he should leap from a pinnacle of the temple.*

B. *Jesus continued to live by the Word of God—"Again it is written."*

C. *Jesus recognized that presumptuous reliance on God to keep us free from the natural consequences of the laws of nature to which humans are subject proves lack of real faith in God.*

1. We cannot separate cause and effect.

2. We reap what we sow.

D. *Jesus overcame the temptations of the Devil by the purity of his undefiled manhood, by his reliance on the Word of God, and by his obedience to his Father's will.*

Conclusion

Have you put God to an unfair test by trusting him to save you from the consequences of deliberate sin? Are you fooling yourself by believing that you can sow to the flesh and not reap corruption? There are some things that even God cannot do. While he can forgive the guilt of sin, even God cannot save you from the consequences of sin. Do not let the Devil deceive you into believing that he can. Follow the example of the Savior, and do not be guilty of tempting God. Follow the example of the Savior by refusing to trust God to do what even God cannot do.

SUNDAY MORNING, SEPTEMBER 21

Title: "The LORD Is My Shepherd"

Text: "The LORD is my shepherd; I shall not want" **(Ps. 23:1)**.

Hymns: "Guide Me, O Thou Great Jehovah," Williams

"The Lord Is My Shepherd," Montgomery

"He Leadeth Me," Gilmore

Offertory Prayer: Heavenly Father, our blessings have come from your bountiful hand. We thank you for life. We are grateful for forgiveness. We rejoice in the opportunity to serve. You have bestowed on us the privilege of labor, and today, as an act of worship, we bring to you the fruit of our toil. Bless these tithes and offerings for a ministry of mercy to the suffering and ministry of redemption of the lost through Jesus Christ. Amen.

Introduction

Psalm 23 has sometimes been called the Psalm of the Crook. It lies between the Psalm of the Cross and the Psalm of the Crown. If Psalm 22 tells us of the Good Shepherd who died for his sheep, Psalm 23 tells of the Chief Shepherd who is coming again to receive his sheep into his eternal home. Psalm 23 tells us of the Great Shepherd who lives to guide, provide, protect, comfort, and cheer the sheep of his pasture.

Psalm 23 is one of the simplest and loveliest poems ever written. We could do without vast libraries easier than we could do without this little poem, which is as simple as a children's rhyme but as deep as an archangel's anthem.

Psalm 23 records the reflective thinking of an aged man who was a forgiven sinner. The king who had been the shepherd boy and had been taken from the quiet sheepcotes to rule over Israel sings this little psalm of him who is the true Shepherd and King of men. The Twenty-third Psalm reveals that God is tremendously concerned about his creatures and that he will not fail to manifest his personal care in life, in death, and beyond the grave.

In his book *The Shepherd Psalm*, Psalm 23 has been described by F. B. Meyer as a creed.

That is my creed. I need, I desire no other! I learned it from my mother's lips. I have repeated it every morning when I awoke for the last twenty years. Yet I do not half understand it; I am only beginning now to spell out its infinite meaning, and death will come on me with the task unfinished. But, by the grace of Jesus, I will hold on by this Psalm as my creed, and will strive to believe it and to live it; for I know that it will lead me to the Cross, it will guide me to glory.

The first line provides the key to the psalms. Verses 2–6 reveal the rich treasures that belong to those who can truly claim the Lord as their shepherd.

I. The Lord is my Shepherd.

A. *David knew the needs of the sheep.*
   1. Sheep are weak, and they are unable to defend themselves as other animals can.
   2. Sheep are foolish. They will follow a leader into places of great danger.
   3. Sheep are thoughtless. They simply do not have the capacity to evaluate the outcome of their actions.
   4. Sheep are unprotected. They must have a shepherd.
   5. Sheep do not have a built-in sense of direction as other animals do. They go astray very easily.

B. *Sheep need the love and thoughtfulness of a good shepherd who can be a provider, preserver, guide, physician, and friend.* David had found God to meet all of these personal needs of life.

C. *Because the Lord is our Shepherd, we need not suffer the lack of any good thing.* David was speaking with the voice of experience. He was declaring his faith in the fact that he would not suffer the lack of rest, refreshment, nourishment, forgiveness, restoration, fellowship, deliverance from fear, comfort in sorrow, victory over enemies, security in troubled hours, power for service, and a home at the end of the way.

II. Our Shepherd leads us into rest and refreshment.

"He maketh me to lie down in green pastures; he leadeth me beside the still waters" (Ps. 23:2).

As strange as it may seem, the verb translated "he maketh" has within it the idea of force. The psalmist is declaring that the good shepherd forces the sheep to lie down at times so that they might receive rest and refreshment for both mind and soul.

Most of us are activists. We are miserable unless we are going somewhere or doing something. Our lives are barren and frustrated because we have not taken the time to ponder the path of our feet and to meditate on the mercies and purposes of God.

Some of us have burned the candle at both ends to the extent that the body finally demands its sabbath. A poet had this experience and described it as follows:

> *I needed the quiet, so He drew me aside,*
> *Into the shadows where we could confide.*
> *Away from the bustle where all day long*
> *I hurried and worried when active and strong.*
> *I needed the quiet tho' at first I rebelled,*
> *But gently, so gently, my cross He upheld*
> *And whispered so sweetly of spiritual things.*
> *Tho' weakened in body, my spirit took wings*
> *To heights never dreamed of when active and gay.*
> *He loved me so greatly He drew me away.*
> *I needed the quiet. No prison my bed,*
> *But a beautiful valley of blessings instead—*
> *A place to grow richer in Jesus to hide.*
> *I needed the quiet, so He drew me aside.*
>
> —*Alice Hansche Mortenson*

In his book *God's Psychiatry*, Charles L. Allen tells of counseling a nervous, worried, sick man who had achieved material success but somehow had not found inward peace and happiness. He says:

I prescribed the Twenty-third Psalm five times a day for seven days. I insisted that he take it just as I prescribed. He was to read it the first thing when he awakened in the morning. Read it carefully, meditatively, and prayerfully. Immediately after breakfast, he was to do exactly the same thing. Also immediately after lunch, again after dinner, and finally, the last thing before he went to bed. . . . At the end of just one week, I promised things would be different for him (*God's Psychiatry* [Revell], 14).

III. Our Shepherd leads us into paths of righteousness.

A. *Our Shepherd is a competent leader.* The only way he can lead us, because of who he is and what he is, is in the path that leads to the right destination. The divine Shepherd leads his people in the path of righteousness not for his own selfish sake, but because he is a God of integrity who can be trusted.

B. *Our Shepherd is a compassionate leader.* Sometimes the way our Savior leads appears to be difficult and even painful. When such happens we need to remember that our Leader loves us so much that he went to the cross in our stead and that all of his purposes for us in the present are purposes of love.

C. *Our Shepherd is a constant leader.* Like no other earthly friend, the living Lord, that good and great Shepherd of the sheep, can be with us at all times and under all circumstances to provide us with the leadership we desperately need if we are to possess poise and confidence in a chaotic world.

IV. Our Shepherd leads us through the valley of deep gloom and danger.

A. *In talking about the valley of the shadow of death, the psalmist is not talking about death as such.* Instead, he is talking about a deep, dark, gloomy gorge in which danger lurks and in which death could possibly occur. He is talking about an experience of living bountifully when both the present and the future are very uncertain and when fear would capture the soul of the believer.

A mother of three small daughters was facing surgery. She prayed that it would be possible to delay the surgery until her daughters were through school. She was filled with anxiety when her doctor announced that the postponed surgery must not be delayed any longer. With sincere prayers and yet with great fear, she entered the hospital. A short time before the nurse came in to prepare her for surgery, she picked up a magazine and casually opened it. In the center of the page, set off in a block, was a message from God. It leaped into her heart, for she found herself reading, "Yea, though I walk through the valley of the shadow of death, I will fear no evil: for thou art with me; thy rod and thy staff they comfort me" (Ps. 23:4). It was as if God himself had come to speak words of promise to her and to assure her of his loving presence.

B. *Fear often brought sheep closer to the shepherd.* Instead of running in fright, we would be wise if we ran to the Shepherd with our fears and anxieties. Sometimes a green meadow of an abundant life is to be found after walking through one of the dark valleys of life.

V. Our Shepherd leads us into a beautiful home at the end of the journey.

A. *Have you noticed the progression in the psalm?* The shepherd (v. 1) becomes the host (v. 5), and the host becomes the heavenly Father (v. 6). The sheep become the guests (v. 5), and the guests become the children (v. 6). The pasture becomes a tent (v. 5), and the tent becomes the eternal home of the heavenly Father (v. 6).

B. *Jesus promised his disciples that he would prepare a place for them and return again for them (John 14:1–3).* It is because death is the doorway to the home of the heavenly Father that we find that strange but wonderful verse, "Precious in the sight of the LORD is the death of his saints" (Ps. 116:15).

Conclusion

Can you say "The Lord is my Shepherd"? There is much difference between saying, "The Lord is *a* good shepherd," "The Lord is *the* Good Shepherd," and "The Lord is *my* Shepherd." The Good Shepherd knows you, loves you, and pleads with you to hear his invitation to come to him for an abundant, eternal life. He offers to you his guidance and his leadership. Come to him today.

SUNDAY EVENING, SEPTEMBER 21

Title: We Are God's Poems

Text: "For we are his workmanship, created in Christ Jesus unto good works, which God hath before ordained that we should walk in them" **(Eph. 2:10)**.

Introduction

The word "workmanship" in our text is a translation of the Greek word *poiema*, meaning "that which has been made — a work," or "a poetical work," or "a poem." Consequently, even if we feel as if we are very prosaic, the Scriptures declare that we are God's poems. The word implies artisanship, craftsmanship, and skill.

In this remarkable epistle, Paul has been rejoicing in the marvelous grace of God. Grace is God's unmerited favor in spontaneous action toward undeserving sinners. Grace seeks the sinner. Grace satisfies the sinner. God's grace is sufficient for all.

The text refers to four aspects of our great salvation made possible by the grace of God and that make it possible for us to be "God's poems." The text speaks of the divine origin of salvation, the divine method of salvation, the divine purpose for our salvation, and the divine program for the saved.

I. The divine origin of salvation — "We are his workmanship."

A. *Salvation is a divine achievement.* Only God can save a soul.
B. *Salvation is inward and spiritual and has to do with the mind and heart of the one who believes.*
C. *Salvation is dynamic, continuous, and progressive.* Conversion is but the first step in the divine activity (Phil. 1:6). God continues his inward work from the time of conversion until the Christian reaches the end of his or her journey (2:13).
D. *Salvation is incomplete in the present (Rom. 13:11).* Salvation has at least three phases (Phil. 2:12). Salvation should be understood as a past accomplishment, a present process, and a future prospect. The theological terminology is justification, sanctification, and glorification.

II. The divine method of salvation — "created in Christ Jesus."

A. *There is salvation in none other (Acts 4:12).*
B. *Jesus is the only way of salvation (John 14:6).*
C. *Through faith in Jesus we receive the gift of forgiveness (Acts 10:43).*
D. *Through faith in Christ we receive the gift of eternal life (John 3:14; Rom. 6:23).*

III. The divine purpose for our salvation—"unto good works."

A. *Benefits received through salvation (John 3:16).*
1. Should not perish.
2. Have everlasting life.
B. *People are saved for the manifestation of divine grace (Eph. 2:7).* God wants to demonstrate his mercy and grace through the redeemed.
C. *People are saved that good works might result.*
1. Jesus went about doing good.
2. Jesus taught his disciples to pray, "Thy kingdom come. Thy will be done in earth, as it is in heaven" (Matt. 6:10).

IV. The divine program for the saved—"which God hath ordained that we should walk in them."

A. *God does not save a person to continue in sin.* God saves people that in and through them he might carry on his redemptive program in the world.
B. *The privilege of sonship carries with it the privilege of service in the vineyard of the Lord (Matt. 21:28).*
C. *Holy labors await you. Good works are expected of you.*
1. Works of love.
2. Works of obedience.
3. Works of faith.

Conclusion

Have you permitted God's work to begin in your heart? If you have not, why not let him begin his work of love and mercy and grace today. "Behold, now is the accepted time; behold, now is the day of salvation" (2 Cor. 6:2).

Luther Burbank could transform a poisonous plant into something sweet and wholesome. He could take a foul-smelling weed and change it into a beautiful, sweet-smelling flower. Likewise, God can make a beautiful poem out of your life if you will trust him and cooperate with him. He works lovingly, wisely, patiently, and skillfully. Decide today to let him work in your heart and life.

WEDNESDAY EVENING, SEPTEMBER 24

Title: Overcoming Satan

Text: "Resist the devil, and he will flee from you. Draw nigh to God, and he will draw nigh to you" (**James 4:7–8**).

Introduction

Peter speaks of the Devil as a roaring lion. "Be sober, be vigilant; because your adversary the devil, as a roaring lion, walketh about, seeking whom he may devour" (1 Peter 5:8). To fail to recognize the work of the Devil is to be overcome by the Devil.

Alfred J. Hough has written a thought-provoking poem about man's response to the presence and work of the Devil:

The Devil

Men don't believe in a devil now,
As their fathers used to do;
They reject one creed because it's old
For another because it's new.
There's not a print of his cloven foot,
Nor a fiery dart from his bow
To be found in the earth or air today!
At least — they declare it is so!
But who is it mixes the fatal draught,
That palsies heart and brain,
And loads the bier of each passing year,
With its hundred thousand slain?
But who blights the bloom of the land today,
With the fiery breath of hell?
If it isn't the devil that does the work
Who does? Won't somebody tell?
Who dogs the steps of the toiling saint?
Who spreads the net for his feet?
Who sows the tares in the world's broad field?
Where the Saviour sows His wheat?
If the devil is voted not to be,
Is the verdict therefore true?
Someone is surely doing the work
The devil was thought to do.
They may say the devil has never lived,
They may say the devil is gone,
But simple people would like to know
Who carries the business on?

Despite what some people say, the Bible declares the Devil exists. He was created good but fell (Luke 10:17 – 18; 2 Peter 2:4; Jude 6).

The experience of Christ reveals that the Devil exists. Observation tells us that some malignant force is at work in our world. Most of us can testify to personal conflict with the Evil One.

James, who encourages us in the practice of true religion, provides us with suggestions concerning how we can overcome the Evil One. Just remember that the Devil is not omniscient, omnipotent, or omnipresent.

I. "Submit yourselves therefore to God" (4:7).

A. *A positive affirmative suggestion.*

B. *Put yourself under the Holy Spirit's control.*

C. *Make Jesus Christ your Lord.*

D. *God's grace is available to the humble (James 4:6).*

II. "Resist the devil, and he will flee from you" (4:6).

A. *In addition to being in submission to the will of God, we are to resist the Devil.* We are to take our stand against him.

B. *The charge is to resist him — not to attack him.* We must not expose ourselves unnecessarily to danger. We must not be careless about him, but we are to resist him.

1. By stopping our ears and shutting our eyes. The fall of man took place because of Eve's listening and looking. Satan continues to use this approach.

2. By sitting in judgment upon our desires.

3. By lifting our shield of faith. "Above all, taking the shield of faith, wherewith ye shall be able to quench all the fiery darts of the wicked" (Eph. 6:16).

4. By drawing our sword. "The sword of the spirit which is the word of God" (Eph. 6:17). Jesus used the sword of the spirit in overcoming the temptations of Satan (Matt. 4:4, 7, 10).

5. By falling on our knees in prayer (James 4:8). Some may consider this a strange way to fight. Our warfare is different. Prayer brings the power of God into our hearts and lives.

C. *The promise is that if you resist the Devil, he will flee from you (4:7).*

Conclusion

Jesus has overcome Satan. He has bruised his head. If we confront Satan in Christ's name and strength, he will flee. In Christ's presence, Satan is an utter coward.

SUNDAY MORNING, SEPTEMBER 28

Title: "Come; for All Things Are Now Ready"

Text: "A certain man made a great supper, and bade many: and sent his servant at supper time to say to them that were bidden, Come; for all things are now ready" **(Luke 14:16–17)**.

Hymns: "Break Thou the Bread of Life," Lathbury

"The King of Love My Shepherd Is," Baker

"I Hear Thy Welcome Voice," Hartsough

"I Will Arise and Go to Jesus," Hart

Offertory Prayer: Heavenly Father, you are the giver of every good and perfect gift. We thank you for life. We are grateful for health. We rejoice in the privilege of work. We worship by bringing tithes and offerings that represent a portion of our life. Accept and bless these offerings for your kingdom's use. Amen.

Introduction

In the parable of the great supper, our Lord presents a picture of the blessings of Christianity under the figure of a wonderful banquet in which everything has been provided by God who is the generous Host. The world promises much to those who would dive into its pleasures, but those who do so always find more pebbles than pearls. Only God can provide a feast that can satisfy the hunger and thirst of people's souls. The banquet prepared by the God of grace and mercy is for all who will accept the invitation to come. There is food enough for all who will come in all ages.

Throughout the Old Testament the blessings of God's grace are often spoken of as a feast (Jer. 3:15). In this parable our Lord speaks of a great feast, of foolish excuses offered by some, and of the fearful fate of those who reject God's gracious hospitality.

I. We are invited to a feast prepared by the God of grace.

The feast to which God invites us is a banquet that provides adequately for the deepest hungers of the human heart. The blessings freely offered are a richer feast to the soul than the richest dainties are to the body. All the needs of people are supplied at this great supper. All the blessings of the gospel are on display to be enjoyed in a large measure here and perfectly hereafter. Concerning this feast, the psalmist declared, "Thou preparest a table before me in the presence of mine enemies: thou anointest my head with oil; my cup runneth over" (Ps. 23:5). John the revelator looked into heaven and saw the continuation of this feast. "The Lamb which is in the midst of the throne shall feed them, and shall lead them into living fountains of water" (Rev. 7:17).

A. *If your soul is burdened and crushed by a depressing load of grief, be assured that* forgiveness *is on the menu.* God is eager to pardon every sin and forgive

276

every transgression. He can cleanse from all the defilement of sin and deliver you from the power of sin.

B. *The Host at this great feast to which you are invited offers the gift of divine sonship, which carries with it his* Fatherhood. Until people come to Christ, they are creatures with the capacity for fellowship with God, but they become children of God only through the new birth from above.

C. *The* fellowship *at this feast is indescribably wonderful.* God is the high and lofty one who inhabits eternity, but he also grants to each believer access into his divine presence continuously. One of the most beautiful pictures of this truth is contained in Revelation 3:20: "Behold, I stand at the door, and knock: if any man hear my voice, and open the door, I will come in to him and will sup with him, and he with me." Particularly, note the feast and the fellowship with the living Christ serving as the divine Host. No other fellowship is comparable to this.

D. *To sit at the banquet table and enjoy the hospitality of a gracious host implies* friendship. Abraham was called the friend of God. He responded to God's invitation. He trusted God. He obeyed God. He sought to do the things that were pleasing to God. This friendship with God was both enriching and transforming. God is gracious in that he will permit us to be his friends. Jesus said, "Ye are my friends, if you do whatsoever I command you. Henceforth I call you not servants; for the servant knoweth not what his lord doeth: but I have called you friends; for all things that I have heard of my Father I have made known unto you" (John 15:14–15). Jesus is the Friend that every man needs. He is the Friend that sticks closer than a brother.

E. *Among the blessed benefits of this feast is the promise of* fruitfulness. In the same instance in which the Savior spoke of friendship, he also spoke of our bearing much fruit to the glory of God. "Ye have not chosen me, but I have chosen you, and ordained you, that ye should go and bring forth fruit, and that your fruit should remain" (John 15:16). One of our deepest needs is to have the assurance that we are doing something worthwhile. It is encouraging to know that this is a part of the divine provision for us. In fact, this is the primary point of the entire parable. The Jewish leaders of Jesus' day were not bringing forth the fruits of faith or the fruit of the Spirit of God. They were so determined that the Messiah was to fit into their nationalistic and materialistic plans that they were incapable of perceiving the truth of Jesus' claims. Consequently, they were eliminating themselves from the great redemptive feast prepared by a God who wanted to redeem all people from the tyranny of sin and death.

F. *The invitation to this feast carries with it the promise of* future blessedness. "If only for this life we have hope in Christ, we are to be pitied more than all men" (1 Cor. 15:19 NIV). Jesus brings much joy and happiness into our lives during the present. He defined the purpose for his coming in such terms. "I am come that they might have life, and that they might have it more abundantly" (John 10:10). To his disciples on the night before his

277

crucifixion, he said, "These things have I spoken unto you, that my joy might remain in you, and that your joy might be full" (John 15:11).

Christians have happiness, not only now, but also eternally. Do you ever wonder about the state of the saved who have gone on to be with the Lord? John was permitted to hear a voice from heaven that described their condition very briefly, and he was commanded to write, "Blessed are the dead which die in the Lord from henceforth: Yea, saith the Spirit, that they may rest from their labours; and their works do follow them" (Rev. 14:13). The word translated "blessed" has the thought of happiness in it. The voice from heaven was describing the redeemed as happy. This thrilling truth would help us with our grief problems if we would but listen in faith. It would take away much of our fear of death. It would cause us to love our Lord more dearly. It would challenge us to serve him more cheerfully and sacrificially.

II. Foolish excuses were offered.

"And they all with one consent began to make excuse" (Luke 14:18). Excuse making comes naturally to people. At the beginning of time, Adam made an excuse for his sin and actually blamed God for it, for it was God who had provided him with a wife who encouraged him to eat the forbidden fruit. There is a vast difference between an excuse and a reason. The people in the parable did not offer reasons for declining the invitation. They offered excuses, and if one is going to excuse himself from some opportunity or responsibility, one excuse is as good as another. As with most excuses these three had an element of dishonesty.

A. *One man declined the invitation to the feast because of* financial *matters.* "I have bought a piece of ground, and I must needs go and see it: I pray thee have me excused" (Luke 14:18). He permitted his wealth to keep him away from the feast prepared by the God of grace, and thousands of others have been kept back for the same reason. It should be granted that business is important and lawful and must have proper attention, but when material things come between man and God, they become sinful. Money cannot reconcile a man to God. He who has been living for things should reflect on these truths and respond to the invitation to the feast.

B. *A second intended guest offered* feelings of uncertainty *as his excuse for not coming.* He needed to go and prove something. There are many today who decline to come to God for the same reason. They declare that they do not feel certain about the Bible or about this or that doctrine or about which church they should join. They confess their feeling of uncertainty about their ability to live a faithful Christian life. While some of these may indeed be sincere, the majority are evading the call of God's Spirit and are only making foolish excuses.

C. *The third man who was invited used* family affairs *as his excuse.* "I have married a wife, and therefore I cannot come" (Luke 14:20). He was the greatest

sin. People need pardon from past guilt and deliverance from the power and practice of evil.

B. *Jesus is the way out of the failure and the waste of sin.* "What shall it profit a man, if he shall gain the whole world and lose his own soul?" (Mark 8:36). Without salvation a person is a failure throughout all eternity though he or she may have ruled an empire and possessed millions while living on earth. Only Jesus can pay the wages of our sin and deliver us from spiritual death and eternal torment.

C. *Jesus is the way out from the disappointment of sin.* The faithless life always disappoints. No person can play on the Devil's team and be a winner. No one likes to go bankrupt, and yet every person who goes through life without God is following a way that will bring vast disappointment in the end.

II. Jesus Christ is the way through.

A. *Jesus is the way through an uncertain tomorrow.* No one knows what tomorrow has in store. The only thing certain about the future is its uncertainty. Only Jesus, the one who holds the future, can make us adequate for whatever the future holds.

B. *Jesus is the way through the desert of difficulties.* As the children of Israel journeyed through the wilderness for forty years, facing one difficulty after another, as they followed the cloud by day and the light by night, even so we can avoid the steep precipice or the quicksands of moral failure as we follow Jesus closely.

Nowhere are we promised that if we will trust Christ and do right life will be easy and comfortable. God does not always reward us by making life easy. He does promise to be with us, and he assures us that no trial or trouble will be too much for us to bear if we will trust him for help (1 Cor. 10:13).

III. Jesus Christ is the way in.

A. *Jesus is the way into the abundant life.* All people everywhere want an abundant life. Many confused people think that the abundant life of which Jesus spoke is the affluent life. It does not take much study to discover that the affluent life and the abundant life are not to be equated.

Jesus is the way into the forgiveness of sin. His forgiveness is full, free, and forever. An awareness of being clean and pure and right with God is a part of the abundant life.

The assurance of the gift of new life—spiritual life, eternal life, the life of God—is a part of the abundant life Jesus came to make possible (John 3:16). This comes as people receive him and permit him to occupy the thrones of their lives.

B. *Jesus is the way into joy unspeakable.* Jesus was eager that his disciples experience fullness of joy (John 15:11). Joy is a condition of the heart that is much deeper and more permanent than happiness. Happiness is the result of circumstances. Joy is a holy happiness from God that can fill the heart even in the most adverse circumstances.

C. *Jesus is the way into triumphant, true success.* No one likes to be a failure. No one rejoices in losing. Everyone likes to be a winner. By means of faith in and obedience to the Savior, the child of God is able to experience a wonderful success in those matters that really count, both now and throughout eternity.

IV. Jesus Christ is the way up.

A. *Jesus is the way up to our very best.* Man was made to walk and talk with God. He was made to worship and serve God. He was made to live by the law of heaven, which is love rather than to live by the law of the jungle, which is greed and hate.

Jesus makes life complete. Until one comes to know him, life at its best is but a fraction. It has been said that if you want to find the best potatoes, go to Idaho. If you want to find the best cherries, go to Michigan. If you want to find the finest apples, go to Washington. If you want to find the most delicious peaches, go to Georgia. If you want to find the best sailors, go to Annapolis. If you want to find the best soldiers, go to West Point. But if you want to find the finest manhood and womanhood, you must go to Jesus Christ.

B. *Jesus is the way up to God (John 14:6; Acts 4:12).* In Jesus Christ, God comes down to dwell among people. He came to die on the cross for our sins. By his death he removed everything that separates the sinner from God. Through faith in him we are forgiven and received by God as his own dear children.

If we want to know what God is like, we need to look into the face of Jesus Christ and listen to the loving words that fell from his lips.

C. *Jesus is the way up to heaven.* Only Jesus can take a person to heaven when this life is over. This is true because only Jesus was both competent and willing to bear the penalty of our sin on the cross. Because he has paid the penalty for our sins, he is able to offer us the gift of eternal life.

Conclusion

Jesus reveals the only way to God, the truth about God, and the kind of life to be lived with God. Accept him by faith, and you will be on the way and will have the truth. Receive him today, and you can rejoice in being spiritually alive.

SUNDAY MORNING, OCTOBER 5

Title: The Peril of the Soul

Text: "Lift up your eyes, and look on the fields; for they are white already to harvest" (**John 4:35**).

Hymns: "Holy, Holy, Holy," Heber

         "He Lifted Me," Homer

         "Jesus Saves," Owens

Offertory Prayer: Our Father in heaven, we rejoice over the fact that our Savior came into this world to rescue us from the waste and the disappointment of sin. Today we would give of ourselves that others might come to know him as a personal Savior from sin and as a wonderful Friend for the road of life. Accept and bless these tithes and offerings that others might hear the gospel and respond by faith. May your name be honored and glorified. Amen.

Introduction

As the God of heaven looked down on a sinful race, knowing the many perils to which people were exposed, he was moved by his grace and mercy to the extent that he gave his only begotten Son to die on a cross that people might be saved.

As Jesus beheld the needy multitudes, he was moved with compassion on them. He experienced a suffering pain in his heart because he saw them as distressed, despairing, defeated, doomed, and diseased by that fatal malady called sin.

When Jesus looked down on the city of Jerusalem, the Scripture says that as he beheld the city, he wept over it. These were not the tears of a sinner filled with remorse or of a defeated conqueror or of one who felt sorry for himself. Jesus was weeping because of the spiritual condition of people, because of the blessings they were missing in the here and now, and because of the eternal destiny of their souls. He recognized the dangers to which they were exposed, and he wept because of their refusal to be saved.

Jesus sought to impart and to instill within the hearts of his disciples his own compassionate concern and burning enthusiasm for the salvation of unsaved people. He warned them against the universal tendency of people to put off until tomorrow the task of today by saying, "Say not ye, There are yet four months, and then cometh harvest? Behold, I say unto you, Lift up your eyes, and look on the fields; for they are white already to harvest" (John 4:35).

Paul permitted the yearning compassion of the Savior for lost souls to invade every compartment and to fully captivate his heart. Paul considered himself to be under the burden of an oppressive debt to a lost world made up of Greeks and barbarians, wise and unwise, Jews and Gentiles—a debt that could be paid only by the proclamation of the gospel, the power of God unto salvation to everyone who believes. It was he who said, "I have great heaviness and continual sorrow in my heart. For I could wish that myself were accursed from Christ for my brethren, my kinsmen according to the flesh" (Rom. 9:2–3). "Brethren, my heart's desire and prayer to God for Israel is, that they might be saved" (10:1). He also said, "To the weak became I as weak, that I might gain the weak: I am made all things to all men, that I might by all means save some" (1 Cor. 9:22). Because of his compassionate concern for a lost world, Paul could say, "Christ shall be magnified in my body, whether it be by life, or by death" (Phil. 1:20).

Through the centuries when people have permitted the compassion of Christ for unsaved souls to permeate and saturate their hearts, the church has been blessed, souls have been saved, the citadels of evil have been stormed, the moral standards have been raised, and God's work has moved forward in a mighty way. On the other hand, when the disciples of our Lord have ignored the perils to which the souls of people are exposed, their compassion has been chilled and their evangelistic zeal has died, and the church has suffered a stroke, resulting in paralysis.

Indifference on the part of our members, and a cold, compassionless, and complacent ministry in the pulpit are the mud that hinders the wheels of the gospel and the redemptive process. Lack of concern for souls is often the result of a preoccupation with private interests. Many permit themselves to be lulled to sleep by the promises and comforts of materialism. Consequently, in many instances, evangelism has been put on the side track instead of on the main track. The so-called disciples of our Lord have joined the cult of comfort and found themselves a cushion on which to relax instead of bearing a cross for the salvation of a lost world. We have become executive officers on the Lord's sitting squad. We have made of our churches cold storage plants instead of power stations.

Indifference concerning the perils facing our unsaved friends is inhuman, unnatural, and unchristian. Indifference and unconcern often grow out of ignorance or forgetfulness. Again and again we need to remind ourselves of the perils the unsaved face in order that our hearts might be filled with compassionate concern so that we might be compelled to go out and proclaim the gospel of redeeming love.

I. The unsaved face the peril of being forever lost because of the fatal malady of sin.

A. *Jeremiah said, "The heart is deceitful above all things, and desperately wicked" (Jer. 17:9).* Sin has defaced, debased, and degraded the image of God in humans. Human intelligence is darkened, emotion is deadened, and the will is degraded.

Because of this dreadful sickness, his heart is dead in trespasses and sins. At present he is without God, without Christ, without life, and without hope in the world.

B. *Sin always degrades, drags down, debases, defiles, and destroys.* Sin causes suffering, sorrow, and shame. Sin separates people from their better selves, from others, and finally from God. The end result of a life of sin is eternal death, and salvation is to be found only in Jesus Christ. He and he alone as the physician of the soul can cure us and deliver us from this dreadful sickness.

As his messengers, ambassadors, and appointed representatives, we have that which can bring salvation to the heart of sinful humanity.

When Dr. Jonas Salk and his research scientists discovered a vaccine for the prevention of poliomyelitis, the entire world rejoiced. What if Dr. Salk had been secretive and had withheld this vital information that was so welcome to the hearts and minds of fathers and mothers everywhere? His sin would not have been nearly as bad as ours when we withhold from a lost world the news of God's love and redeeming power through Jesus Christ.

II. The unsaved face the peril of complete failures here and hereafter.

A. *Jesus said, "I am come that they might have life, and that they might have it more abundantly" (John 10:10).*

B. *Jesus said, "What shall it profit a man, if he shall gain the whole world, and lose his own soul?" (Mark 8:36).*

C. *Failure here is bad; failure in the hereafter is disastrous beyond our ability to understand.*

III. The unsaved face the peril of experiencing the inflexible justice of a righteous and holy God who will bring every sin into judgment on the Judgment Day.

Jesus spoke of a time when all of the nations of the earth would be gathered before the judgment throne of God; when the righteous would be separated from the wicked as a shepherd would divide his sheep from the goats. Those who were saved would hear the welcome of the Savior while those who had rejected God's love and mercy and salvation would hear the unchangeable decree of eternity ringing in their ears, saying, "Depart from me, ye cursed, into everlasting fire, prepared for the devil and his angels" (Matt. 25:41). The decrees of this judgment are final.

IV. The unsaved face the peril of missing heaven and finding hell as the eternal destiny of their souls.

A. *If we really believed this, we would be out of breath chasing souls.*

    1. John Knox believed it and prayed, "Give me Scotland or I die."

    2. Paul believed it and said, "I am a debtor—I am ready—I am not ashamed of the gospel."

B. *To miss heaven is an irreparable loss, but for people to go to hell is a tragedy that breaks the very heart of God.*

C. *People are not appointed to wrath, but to obtain salvation (1 Thess. 5:9).*

D. *Those who go to hell go as intruders into a place that was not prepared for them (Matt. 25:41).*

V. The unsaved face a great peril of being lost because of our indifference and unconcern (2 Cor. 6:1–2).

    A. *God told Ezekiel that people would perish if he did not warn them (Ezek. 33:7–8).*

    B. *Jesus tells us that by our complacency and indifference and neglect to witness, we are the means of retaining the unsaved in their sins (John 20:23).*

Conclusion

Will the blood of souls be on our hands when we stand before our Maker?

> *Must I go and empty-handed,*
> *Thus my dear Redeemer meet?*
> *Not one day of service give Him,*
> *Lay no trophy at His feet?*
> *Not at death I shrink nor falter,*
> *For my Savior saves me now;*
> *But to meet Him empty-handed,*
> *Thought of that now clouds my brow.*
>   *—Charles C. Luther*

It is inhuman and unchristian for us to neglect to labor in the fields that are ready for harvesting. The unsaved about us are lost but can be saved today. Invite them to come to Christ today. As followers and representatives of Christ, let us labor in the fields that we might lead others to faith in Christ.

If you are among those who have not yet received Christ as Savior, I challenge you to welcome him into your heart now.

SUNDAY EVENING, OCTOBER 5

Title: "Thou Shalt Call His Name Jesus"

Text: "And she shall bring forth a son, and thou shalt call his name Jesus: for he shall save his people from their sins" (**Matt. 1:21**).

Introduction

The angelic announcement to Joseph concerning Jesus followed in the tradition of Isaiah the prophet who had spoken prophetically concerning the person and ministry of the Savior. Before the Christ child was born, the angel announced that he was to be the Savior and that he was to deal with humankind's sin problem.

I. The name Jesus in the Hebrew is Joshua, which means "deliverer" or "savior."

So the name the angel said should be given to Mary's Son was the same as that of two famous characters of the Old Testament. An understanding of their significance for the life of Israel can help us to understand the ministry of the Savior.

A. *Joshua, the leader and deliverer.* Following the death of Moses on Mount Nebo, the leadership of the Israelites was commended to a man named Joshua (Josh. 1:1–2). Joshua was to finish the task of leading the children of Israel across the Jordan River and into the Promised Land. He was to lead them in the conquest of Canaan. Through their united efforts, they were to possess their inheritance. Joshua was one of the real heroes of Israel and was known as a deliverer of the people.

B. *Joshua, the high priest.* A second Old Testament hero who wore the name Joshua was the high priest who worked with Zerubbabel in rebuilding the temple and restoring pure worship (Hag. 1:1; 14:2–5).

Joseph would have recognized the unique significance of this divinely given name, which was prophetic of the fact that the Savior would deliver his people from the slavery of sin and enable them to enter the divine inheritance. Jesus the Savior would enable people to worship God in spirit and in truth.

II. Consider Jesus the Savior.

A. *Jesus saves from the penalty of sin.*
1. From the beginning of time the penalty of sin has been spiritual death (Gen. 3:3; Ezek. 18:4; Rom. 6:23).
2. The good news of the gospel is that Christ paid the penalty for our sins (1 Cor. 15:3; 1 Peter 2:22–24; 3:18).

B. *Jesus saves from the power of sin.*
1. Sin is a universal fact. All of us are sinners (Rom. 3:23).
2. Humans are slaves of sin (Rom. 6:16).
3. Paul declares that only through Jesus Christ can a person be delivered from the power and practice of sin (Rom. 7:24–25).
4. A life of victory over the power of sin is possible through Jesus Christ (Phil. 2:13; 4:13).

C. *Jesus will save us from the presence of sin.* The writer of the Epistle to the Hebrews speaks of a time when we shall be saved from the very presence of sin (Heb. 9:28). We shall be like him, for we shall see him as he is (1 John 3:2). Our sinful nature will be no more, and we shall be like the Savior (Phil. 3:20–21). Paul rejoiced in the assurance of a resurrection, at which time our salvation would be complete (1 Cor. 15:51–57).

Conclusion

The Christ who was born in Bethlehem came to save us from the penalty of sin, from the power and practice of sin, and ultimately from the presence of sin. The believer can speak of salvation in three tenses: "I was saved from the penalty of sin when I first trusted Jesus Christ as my Savior. I am in a process of being saved from the practice of sin. Someday I will be saved from the very presence of sin."

Jesus came to be your Savior. He offers you a great salvation. You cannot buy it with money or earn it with good works. You can only receive it as a free gift through the faith that accepts him to be all that he claims to be and then trusts him to do all that he has promised to do.

WEDNESDAY EVENING, OCTOBER 8

Title: God Gives the Increase

Text: "I have planted, Apollos watered; but God gave the increase" (**1 Cor. 3:6**).

Introduction

Those who regularly attend the prayer services of their churches have no doubt that our Lord clearly commanded his disciples to be witnesses to his redemptive achievements with a view to persuading unbelievers to place their faith in him as Savior and Lord. Every Christian is to be a witness now. Every Christian is to be a witness always. World evangelism involves individual believers going about from place to place bearing personal testimony to the meaning Christ Jesus has brought into their lives. The entire world could be evangelized in ten years if all Christians would take seriously the command of our Savior (Matt. 28:18–20; Luke 24:45–48; Acts 1:8).

Why have we been disobedient? There are many possible answers to that question. It is difficult to give one full and complete explanation for our failure to be joyful witnesses.

Our text infers two possible answers to the question of why we fail to be winning witnesses. The first is that many of us labor under the impression that everything depends on us. This frightens us into silence as we face the possibility of telling another person how to be converted and become a child of God. We unintentionally usurp the place and work of God if we think in these terms. The farmer realizes that the harvest of an abundant crop depends on something other than the effort of his hands, as necessary as that is. We need to learn this in the spiritual realm if we are to please our Lord and bless the unsaved people about us.

The second possible explanation for our failure to be good witnesses for our Lord is our failure to give proper regard to the power of the gospel itself.

The life principle in the seed causes it to germinate and grow, not the anxiety or effort of the farmer who planted it. Do we really believe that a personal testimony by a believer is the gospel that is the power of God unto salvation unto everyone that believeth (Rom. 1:16)? The writer of Hebrews says, "For the word of God is alive and active. It cuts more keenly than any two-edged sword, piercing as far as the place where life and spirit, joints and marrow, divide. It sifts the purposes and thoughts of the heart" (Heb. 4:12 NEB). God spoke through Isaiah concerning the divine power of the inspired word. "It shall not return unto me void, but it shall accomplish that which I please, and it shall prosper in the thing whereto I sent it" (Isa. 55:11).

What do the text and these other passages say to believers who are convicted of their personal failure to be good witnesses for the Lord Jesus?

I. Our work is not the same for everyone.

"I planted and Apollos watered." By his reference to "planting," the apostle speaks of his original mission in which he established the church in Corinth (Acts

18:1 – 4). By "watered" he refers to Apollos's work later on, which was comparable to one who would irrigate a farm after the seed had been planted. He uses the aorist tense, which refers to a single action completed in the past time. God does not expect the same ministry or testimony from all of us. There is no fixed form into which each of us must fit as the servants of the Lord.

Paul, because of the particular time, and because of his unique personal experiences with God, had his own spiritual contribution to make to the church at Corinth. The ministry and message of Apollos would be different by the very nature of the case. Are you waiting until you can render a service exactly like some Paul that you have known? Or perhaps you see yourself as a waterer like Apollos. The important thing is that each of us be about the task in our own unique manner, which is the result of our experiences and circumstances.

II. Planting and watering are necessary for a harvest.

Planting and watering must be done by the farmer or he will starve. Others will go hungry if he fails to plant. In the spiritual realm, many think only of the glamour and glory of the harvest. Whoever heard of a farmer who could go and prepare the soil, plant the seed, cultivate and irrigate the fields, and reap a harvest all in the same day? That would be some operation. There are those who become discouraged as they labor in the fields that are white unto harvest because they are not able to see such a miracle. A new term is being seen in the literature relating to evangelism — "cultivation evangelism." This is what Paul is talking about. One plants, another waters, someone else harvests, but it is God who gives the increase.

In courts of law, seldom is a decision reached on the basis of the testimony of a single witness unless there is ample evidence that substantiates that testimony. It is also true that seldom is a soul converted because of the testimony of a single Christian witness in complete isolation from all other Christians. Usually it is the testimony of many witnesses that causes an unbeliever to put confidence in Jesus Christ as his or her personal Savior. "Paul planted, Apollos watered." Have you been planting the divine seed in the hearts of others? Have you been irrigating the crops planted by the efforts of those who have gone on before you? It is of eternal importance that all of us do our job faithfully and cheerfully.

III. God is always the one who gives the increase.

If the farmer did not have faith in the life principle within the seed, he would not put forth the effort to prepare the soil and plant the seed. It would be foolish to plant seed if it were not for the warming and drawing power of the sun. The farmer has to put confidence in a power outside and beyond himself; he has no other alternative.

The same is true in the spiritual realm. God and God alone can bring about conviction of sin and the awareness of a need for forgiveness in the cold, dead hearts of the unsaved. He does this by means of the warmth and power of the gospel message as it comes through the lives and lips of his children. Only God

291

can impart the gift of new life, heavenly life, spiritual life, eternal life to human souls.

Conclusion

When we accept the truth deep within our hearts that only God can impart the gift of new life and make that truth a vital part of our faith, our personal witnessing will be revolutionized. Fear will depart and faith will fill our hearts. We will be able to joyfully bear a winning witness when we come to realize that our task is simply to plant and water and let God do the rest.

SUNDAY MORNING, OCTOBER 12

Title: Do the Right Thing with Jesus

Text: "What shall I do then with Jesus which is called Christ?" **(Matt. 27:22)**.

Hymns: "Joyful, Joyful, We Adore Thee," Van Dyke

"Blessed Redeemer," Christiansen

"The Old Rugged Cross," Bennard

Offertory Prayer: Heavenly Father, you gave your Son to die on the cross for us. You have given to us the Holy Spirit to dwell within our hearts. You have given us eternal life, which causes us to hunger after you and to love you. Today we give ourselves completely to you. Accept our tithes and offerings as tokens of our desire to belong completely to you. Through Jesus Christ our Lord. Amen.

Introduction

The Roman governor Pilate asked the question in our text and gave the wrong answer. In so doing, he lost all that was worthwhile in both time and eternity.

Today will you ask the question that he asked? May God help you to answer it in a manner that will bring the blessings of God upon you. You will note that it is a personal question, a pressing question, and a present question.

I. Who is this Jesus?

A. *He is the fulfillment of Old Testament prophecy (Acts 10:43).*

B. *He is the Son of God (Matt. 3:17).*

C. *He is a divine and authoritative teacher (Matt. 7:29).*

D. *He is your sin bearer (John 1:29).*

E. *He is the conqueror of death and the bestower of immortality (2 Tim. 1:10).*

F. *He is the only Savior (Acts 4:12).*

G. *He is the one whom God has anointed to be your King (Phil. 2:9–11).*

II. Wrong reactions.

You may react in a variety of ways to Christ.

A. *You may act as if you are unaware of his presence.*

B. *You may assume an attitude of complete indifference.*
C. *You may forget that he exists.*
D. *You may evade him.*
E. *You may be actively hostile and resentful.*
F. *You may keep him on the circumference of your life.*

III. Proper responses.

A. *Receive him as an honored guest into your life (Rev. 3:20).*
B. *Trust him as your dearest Friend (John 15:14).*
C. *Listen to and heed his teachings as heaven's infallible Teacher (Matt. 7:29).*
D. *Follow him as a loving leader (Matt. 4:19, 22).*

Conclusion

Pilate sought to evade a decision concerning Jesus Christ. He sought to use Herod and Barabbas as scapegoats for his own conscience. He did the wrong thing with Jesus. You may reject him rather than accept him. You may deny him instead of confessing him. You may shut him out instead of letting him come in.

Do the right thing with Jesus, because more than anything else, you need Jesus Christ as your Savior. Do the right thing with Jesus, because Jesus needs you so that he can bless your family and your neighborhood with the richest blessings of God. The choice is yours. It is never right to do the wrong thing with Jesus Christ. It is always right and wise to do the right thing with Jesus. Do the right thing with him now.

SUNDAY EVENING, OCTOBER 12

Title: "Consider Your Ways"

Text: "This what the LORD Almighty says: 'Give careful thought to your ways' " **(Hag. 1:7 NIV).**

Introduction

People desperately seek to read the signs of the times. This is true in every area of life. People in every walk of life put forth an earnest effort to interpret the factors that contribute to either success or failure. They are eager to succeed in their personal affairs.

We live in a day in which politicians of both major parties mount their soapboxes and place all of the nation's trouble on their political opponents. Diplomats and statesmen work double time to formulate a foreign policy that will correct as many of the mistakes of their predecessors as possible and at the same time outthink and outmaneuver the diplomats of potential enemies. Military leaders make recommendations that they hope will guarantee survival in this fearful age of splitting atoms, whirling satellites, and destructive missiles.

The truth is that we, the people of these United States, find ourselves in a condition similar to one that existed during the latter days of the kingdom of Judah, when Jeremiah, God's sensitive-hearted prophet, said, "I hearkened and heard, but they spake not aright: no man repented him of his wickedness, saying, What have I done? Every one turned to his course, as the horse rusheth into the battle" (Jer. 8:6).

Instead of always seeking to blame someone else for the trouble in which we find ourselves, we need to be honest and make a sincere appraisal of our own ways of thinking and behaving. We need to come face-to-face with the question, "What have I done?" During the days of Jeremiah, people refused to face this question because they were too busy thinking about and discussing the failures of others.

At a later time, God's spokesman Haggai stepped onto the stage of Israel's history with the sobering challenge: Consider your ways. Are they wise? Are they truly profitable? Will your ways end well?

Calamity had befallen the nation, and God sent Haggai as a spokesman to interpret the calamities to the people. Briefly stated, Haggai declared to the people that at the root of their trouble was the fact that they had left out God. They had postponed doing his will and had given him a secondary place in life.

I. Haggai analyzed the resulting conditions of excluding God.

  A. *Haggai discovered that theirs was a life of fruitless toil.* "Ye have sown much, and bring in little" (Hag. 1:6).

  B. *Haggai observed that theirs was a life of unsatisfied hunger and thirst.* "Ye eat, but ye are not filled with drink" (Hag. 1:6).

   1. Their appetites were focused on things that could not possibly satisfy.
   2. To feed their bodies people often starve their souls.
   3. Only God can satisfy the soul.

  C. *Haggai said that their godless lives were dependent on futile defenses.* "Ye clothe you, but there is none warm" (Hag. 1:6).

   1. The storms of life will blow on us all. The winters of life will come for all of us. They are unbearable if God is not close by to help.
   2. How can people face the awful possibility of this uncertain age without God and not go mad?

  D. *Haggai declared that the godless life is one of fleeting riches.* "He that earneth wages earneth wages to put it into a bag with holes" (Hag. 1:6).

   1. Jesus said, "For what shall it profit a man, if he gain the whole world, and lose his own soul?" (Mark 8:36).
   2. "A man's life consisteth not in the abundance of the things which he possesseth.... But God said unto him, Thou fool, this night thy soul shall be required of thee: then whose shall those things be, which thou hast provided? So is he that layeth up treasure for himself, and is not rich toward God" (Luke 12:15, 20–21).

      Consider your ways. Are they wise? Are they truly profitable? Will they end well?

II. The pathway to spiritual and moral calamity is revealed.

A. *The people walked in the path of postponement.*
   1. Men do not say, "never"; rather, they say, "not yet."
   2. Conscience will not permit us to say, "never." Our conscience does permit us to procrastinate.
   3. The present is the golden hour of opportunity. God always calls "now."

B. *The people followed the path of selfishness, which is idolatry.* They placed self on the throne of their soul instead of permitting God to occupy the place that rightfully belongs to him (Hag. 1:2–4).
   1. Self-love will hinder all effort to repair and build the temple of God.
   2. They were more concerned about their own comfort and luxury than about the things of God.
   3. Theirs was the selfish indifference of an ungrateful and an unfaithful people.
   4. The pursuit of material things caused them to neglect spiritual realities.
   5. They judged success in terms of things. They had a false scale of values.
   6. Selfishness and self-love prevent us from making sacrifices of tithes, time, and talents to the cause of Christ.

      Are you earning wages and putting them in a bag that has a hole in the bottom?

III. The call for obedience (Hag. 1:12).

A. *The time is now—for us to take seriously our relationship to Christ. He is our Lord.*

B. *The time is now—for us to give ourselves to the deepening and enriching of our own spiritual lives.*

C. *The time is now—for us to dedicate our all to Christ.*

D. *The time is now—for us to bear a continual and winning witness for our Lord.*

Consider your ways. Are they wise? Are they truly profitable? Will they end well?

Conclusion

You need forgiveness, and forgiveness is available through Jesus Christ. You need friends, and Jesus is a Friend who sticks closer than a brother. You have delayed entirely too long. Decide to let Christ come into your heart. He would speak to you now and invite you to become a member of the family of God. Hear him and heed him now.

WEDNESDAY EVENING, OCTOBER 15

Title: Personal Witnessing

Text: "He that goeth forth and weepeth, bearing precious seed, shall doubtless come again with rejoicing, bringing his sheaves with him" **(Ps. 126:6)**.

Introduction

This text implies a command to be a witness, a seed sower of the divine truth. It mentions the privilege of being a seed sower of God, sowing the divine truth in the hearts and lives of others. It makes a promise that the sower will reap a harvest.

Perhaps the fear of failure is one of the reasons why so many people hesitate to be a personal witness. The fear of failure can paralyze one into inactivity. In the matter of personal witnessing, the fear of failure is one of our greatest hindrances.

We are afraid of failing our Lord. We are afraid of failing those to whom we bear a witness. We are afraid of failing and thus wounding our foolish pride. We are afraid of the depression that accompanies failure.

If we are to witness, we must overcome the paralyzing effects of fear. Perhaps several truths can help us overcome this fear. The text implies a command, mentions a privilege, and makes a promise.

I. Personal witnessing is the will of God for you.

A. *To Abraham, God said, "Be thou a blessing" (Gen. 12:2).*

B. *To his apostles our Lord said, "Ye shall be my witnesses" (Acts 1:8).*

C. *The Holy Spirit came that every believer might be a spokesperson for God (Acts 2:17).*

II. The living Christ has promised to be with you (Matt. 28:20).

A. *Some of us hesitate to witness because we are afraid those to whom we witness might ask some questions we could not answer.* Jesus has promised to be with us to help us with all of these.

B. *In the parable of the soil, there are four kinds of soil.* The condition of the soil determines to a large degree the success of a crop. The condition of an individual's heart will determine to a large degree your success. Jesus did not win everyone to faith. We are not called to or required to achieve success. Our primary call is to be a witness, and our living Lord has promised to be with us.

III. The Holy Spirit is present to bless your word of testimony and the Word of God.

A. *Hebrews 2:7–8.* Even as the unsaved person must hear and respond to the Holy Spirit, the disciple must hear and heed the commandment of the Holy Spirit to witness. When the Holy Spirit places a burden of concern

296

on our heart for a particular person, the Holy Spirit is also working in the heart of the person who needs the witness.

B. *Hebrews 4:12.* The Word of God is different from any other word. The Word of God is dynamic and creative. It penetrates the heart and is used by the Holy Spirit to effect the spiritual birth in the heart of the sinner who believes (John 16:8–11).

IV. Your personal experience with Christ is the most essential element for this task.

A. *Not education.* Educational achievements do not necessarily equip a person for personal witnessing.

B. *Not even years of experience in the ministry are the best equipment.*

C. *A fresh, vital, up-to-date experience with Christ is the primary factor.*

Often young Christians are much more successful in witnessing than Christians of many years because they are eager to tell what Jesus has done for them. A young preacher who blunders in every possible way sometimes achieves more success than a pastor who is mature and experienced. While this may be the case, it should not be so. If the inexperienced preacher achieves success, it is usually due to the freshness of his or her personal experience with Jesus Christ. How fresh is your experience? Are you talking about a Jesus of ancient history, or is he your contemporary?

V. Witnessing individually is the most effective form of Christian service.

A. *Witnessing individually is the most effective and at the same time the most neglected form of Christian service.*

B. *Individual needs can be met better.*

C. *Personal witnessing allows dialogue between the witness and the unsaved person.*

D. *Personal witnessing is the most natural method.*

E. *Personal witnessing is the method recorded most in the New Testament.*

F. *Personal witnessing is the only method that will reach the overwhelming majority of those about us.* They do not come to services conducted inside the church.

Conclusion

Those who serve God as personal witnesses will come with rejoicing, bringing their sheaves with them. The law of the harvest declares that if a man continues to sow, in due season he shall reap a harvest. If no seeds are sown, there can be no harvest (1 Cor. 3:6–7).

SUNDAY MORNING, OCTOBER 19

Title: The High Cost of Rejecting Jesus

Text: "He came unto his own, and his own received him not. But as many as received him, to them gave he power to become the sons of God, even to them that believe on his name" **(John 1:11–12)**.

Hymns: "Praise to God, Immortal Praise," Barbauld

"Christ Receiveth Sinful Men," Neumeister

"He Included Me," Oatman

Offertory Prayer: Heavenly Father, you have given your very best to us and for us. We praise you for the privilege of receiving the gifts of forgiveness and eternal life. Today we bring tithes and offerings that represent a portion of our lives. We offer them to you, praying that you would help us to give ourselves completely to you. Through Jesus Christ our Lord. Amen.

Introduction

All of us are price conscious. We continually look for bargains. We refuse to purchase some things because of their high cost. Someone has condensed his financial philosophy into the following statement: "When a man's outgo exceeds his income, his upkeep has become his downfall."

We live in a day of high-pressure advertisement in which the "soft sell" is used most effectively. Many people live on a financial precipice because they have failed to put a brake on their appetites. Easy credit and balloon payments have just about destroyed them.

Has it ever occurred to you that the cost of rejecting Jesus Christ as your Lord is much higher than the cost of accepting him as the Lord of your life? Instead of thinking in terms of what it is going to cost you to become a Christian, consider what it is going to cost you to refuse Christ and shut him out of your heart and life.

The text paints for us a picture of the Christ as he confronts the human heart. He is eager to bring to one's life the blessings of God. He offers to you these blessings. For you to refuse him automatically means that you deprive yourself of the blessings that only he can make available to you.

Shutting Christ out of your life is very costly. Consider some of the privileges and blessings of which you deprive yourself when you refuse to hear and heed his voice.

I. The privilege of divine sonship.

While humans were made in the image and likeness of God, that image has been marred by sin. People have the capacity for worship, and it is possible for them to be more than a creature of God. They can become children of God through a spiritual birth as they put their faith in Jesus Christ as the Lord of their lives (John 1:12; Gal. 3:26).

II. The joy of forgiveness.

All people are sinners. The wages of sin is death. There is not one among us who is not a sinner. All of us stand guilty before God. There is no way by which we can atone for our own sin.

God in his grace and mercy offers us the gift of forgiveness through faith in a perfect Savior who died a substitutionary death for our sins. In offering the gift of forgiveness, Jesus declared, "If ye believe not that I am he, ye shall die in your sins" (John 8:24). Only through Jesus Christ can our sins be forgiven and the penalty removed (Acts 10:43).

A pastor tells the story of how he carried money and food to the house of a poor widow. He knocked on the door repeatedly but there was no reply. Later he learned that she was inside and thought it was her landlord knocking because he wanted his rent. We can understand why she hesitated to open the door, but by neglecting to do so, she deprived herself of that which she desperately needed. Some think that the Christ comes as a robber or a thief to impoverish them, and they refuse to heed his knocking at the door. He would bestow on them the joy of forgiveness.

III. The peace of God.

Some people know the peace that comes as a result of enjoying financial security. A much larger group know the peace that the assurance of good health provides. Peace is a blessing for which the hearts of all people hunger. There are many different kinds of peace. The Scriptures tell us though, "There is no peace, saith the LORD, unto the wicked" (Isa. 48:22). Fear takes possession of the soul of the person who has no faith in God as he or she contemplates the state of the present world and the issues of eternity.

There is no peace comparable to the peace that is possible for the soul of a person through faith in Jesus Christ. To entrust one's past, present, and future into his hands makes possible a peace of heart and mind that is impossible to define.

To be prepared for death financially can give a person wonderful peace. Some have sought to gain this peace by the purchase of stocks, bonds, property, and insurance.

To be prepared for death legally can provide a person with wonderful peace. While the average person will never have a large estate to pass on, it would be exceedingly wise for each couple to at least organize debts so that an administrator would know how to take care of them in case they were killed accidentally. Every person needs a will.

The greatest peace we can have comes through knowing that we have trusted Jesus Christ as Savior and are prepared to meet all of the eventualities of eternity. It has been truthfully said that we are not really prepared to live until we are also prepared to die. The peace of assurance that everything is right between the soul and God comes through faith in Christ (Rom. 5:1).

IV. A continuing companionship.

To reject Jesus Christ as Savior costs one the privilege of his companionship along the road of life. Being a genuine Christian is something infinitely more than straining all of one's spiritual muscles to achieve some coveted excellence. Genuine Christianity is something more than living up to a code of conduct. Vital Christianity is a continuing relationship to the living Christ.

The Christ who loved us to the extent that he was willing to die on the cross in our place was divine to the extent that he conquered death and the grave. The apostles lived and labored in the consciousness of his abiding presence. The living Lord has walked down through the corridors of time to the present. He is our eternal contemporary.

He is present to commend, to counsel, to command, to share, and to call us forth to an ever-increasing life of faith and faithfulness that becomes more satisfying with the passing of every year.

To turn a deaf ear and to refuse to hear and to heed his request for entrance into your heart and life will cost you the privilege of his companionship.

V. The home at the end of the road.

Deep within the hearts of people there is a hunger for a home. Rare indeed is the person who wants to be a rolling stone throughout all of his or her life. The messianic age is pictured as a time when every man shall sit under his own vine and fig tree. This speaks to a deep heart need of every person.

While Jesus did not answer all of the questions that we might like to ask, he did talk about the home of the heavenly Father that is at the end of the pathway of this life (Matt. 25:34; Luke 16:22; John 14:1–3; Rev. 21:1–4).

This home of the soul is a prepared place for a prepared people where purity will be the rule and blessings will be perpetual. Heaven is a place where rewards will be bestowed upon the children of God for the deeds they have done to bring honor and glory to God (Rev. 22:12). Heaven will be a place of perfect holiness where sin will not enter in to defile (Rev. 21:27). Heaven is a place where sorrow, sickness, pain, and death are banished. Only those who have received Jesus Christ into their hearts and lives will be received into the home of the heavenly Father (John 14:6). For you to reject him automatically means that you deprive yourself of this home at the end of the way.

Conclusion

Jesus Christ comes to your heart's door and knocks for entrance. He does this by means of the ministry of the church. He will seek his way into your heart through hymns. He will use the Scriptures to reveal God's love for you and your need for that which only God can do for you. By means of the hunger of your heart for the Bread of Life and by the emptiness of your life without God, he requests the privilege of coming into your heart as Savior.

Christ is no intruder. He will not come in unless he is welcome. The choice is yours. The cost of rejecting him is exceedingly high. The benefits of receiving him cannot be fully described. Make your decision for him today.

There's a Stranger at the Door

There's a stranger at the door; let Him in;
He has been there oft before, let Him in.
Let Him in, ere He is gone, let Him in, the Holy One,
Jesus Christ, the Father's Son, let Him in.
Open now to Him your heart, let Him in;
If you wait He will depart, let Him in;
Let Him in, He is your Friend,
He your soul will sure defend,
He will keep you to the end,
Let Him in.

—Jonathan Bush Atchinson

SUNDAY EVENING, OCTOBER 19

Title: The Marks of the New Birth

Text: "We know that we have passed from death unto life, because we love the brethren" **(1 John 3:14).**

Introduction

The new birth, a birth from above, a birth of the Spirit, is absolutely essential to be a part of the kingdom of God and to enter heaven at the end of life. The new birth signifies an entrance to a new life. It is described as a resurrection experience in which new life is given to that which was dead (Eph. 2:1). Paul described it as a creative act on the part of God (2 Cor. 5:17).

The new birth is definite. It is complete. It is permanent. It is wrought in the heart by the Holy Spirit as an individual responds to God in repentance, placing faith in the Lord Jesus Christ (Acts 20:21). The new birth is miraculous and mysterious, but very real.

Tonight we want to look at five distinctive marks, five hereditary characteristics or proofs and evidences of the new birth. Not all five of these characteristics are as evident in each child of God as they should be or as they can be.

A child will resemble his or her ancestors. The child of God will favor his or her heavenly Father in character and disposition. Often when a new baby is born, those who come to visit the mother and see the baby will immediately make some comment about who the baby favors. It is pretty difficult to be accurate in stating

301

dogmatically who the baby favors, but distinctive resemblances will be in evidence as time goes by.

One of the great tragedies as far as the kingdom of God is concerned is that too many of God's children remain infants and never fully develop their divine potential.

At this point the importance of both heredity and environment cannot be overemphasized. In the new birth we receive the nature and character of God in embryonic form. Environment and the manner in which we respond to opportunities and responsibilities will determine the degree to which we demonstrate the distinctive characteristics of our heavenly Father.

The five distinctive characteristics that are considered can disturb or they can comfort and challenge. If you lack these characteristics, then you should be disturbed about your own spiritual relationship to God. If you possess these characteristics, you can be assured that yours is a saving faith that has made you a child of God.

I. The twice-born possess a new appetite for righteousness.

It is a law of nature and also a law of the kingdom of God that every living creature, shortly after birth, has an appetite for food. This law holds true for those who have been born into the family of God.

A. We should hunger and thirst after righteousness (Matt. 5:6).

B. We should thirst for God (Ps. 42:1–2).

C. What is your spiritual diet?
1. Devotional study of the Bible?
2. Guided Bible study in the Sunday school?
3. Open-mindedness to truth?
4. Regular worship habits?

Absence of appetite indicates either disease or death. If you have no hunger for the things of God, you are either dreadfully sick or you are spiritually dead.

II. The twice-born have a new adoration for God.

A. *Some people ignore God, forget God, fear God, hide from God, run from God, defy God, distrust God, or hate God.*

B. *The twice-born love God (1 John 4:19).*

C. *The twice-born love God's children as well as the lost world (1 John 4:7–8).*

III. The twice-born have a new attitude toward sin.

A. *The new birth introduces a new nature that has an aversion for and abhorrence of sin (Gal. 5:17).*

B. *The presence of the Holy Spirit within the hearts of new converts creates an intense desire for holiness of life (1 John 3:8–10).*

C. *God works on the inside of new converts and helps them to see that sin is destructive by its very nature and causes them to want to avoid sin rather than to cling to sin (Phil. 1:6; 2:13).*

IV. The twice-born have a new affection for the people of God (I John 3:14).

The basis for the assurance that a person has experienced a divine birth is found in love for the church, the family of God. In our normal family relationships, we are always interested when a child is born, a marriage is performed, or a death occurs. We are sad when a member of the family experiences a misfortune. We rejoice when success is achieved. Within the church family there will be a deep concern in the hearts of the membership one for another. If you are among those who say that it is easy to love God but you have no love for the people of God, it is time for you to be disturbed about yourself.

V. The twice-born possess a new ambition—to do the will of God in their lives (I John 2:17).

The will of God is not something a cold, cruel fate would impose on us. Rather, it is something for us to rise up to instead of something from which we should run. Paul's question on the road to Damascus should describe our continuing attitude toward the will of God: "Lord, what wilt thou have me to do?" (Acts 9:6).

Conclusion

As you examine your life in the light of these five characteristics or marks of the twice-born, what is your verdict? Congratulations if you see in your own heart these traits that have come to you through the spiritual birth. If they are absent, then may God help you to hear the good news of how Jesus Christ was lifted up on the cross so that whosoever believeth in him should not perish but have everlasting life. You can experience now this spiritual birth from above by yielding your heart and life to Jesus Christ in obedient faith.

WEDNESDAY EVENING, OCTOBER 22

Title: The Effective Evangelistic Church

Text: "And daily in the temple, and in every house, they ceased not to teach and preach Jesus Christ" **(Acts 5:42)**.

Introduction

It is difficult for us to recapture the character and spirit of the early church. We often equate a church with a building. The early church had no buildings of its own. In many respects it is impossible for the contemporary church to be exactly like the early church.

Each local congregation must reexamine itself against the example of the early church as it functioned as the body of Christ.

I. Let us evaluate our church.

   A. *Are we a missionary church?*

   B. *Are we a musical church?*

C. *Are we a friendly church?*

D. *Are we a worshiping church?*

E. *Are we a ministering church?*

F. *Are we a redeeming church?*

G. *Are we an evangelistic church?* This is perhaps the area in which we drop beneath the New Testament ideal most dramatically.

II. Evaluate the early church.

A. *They were overwhelmed by the greatness of God's immeasurable love for lost people.*

B. *They were captivated by a deep conviction of the desperation of lost people.*

C. *They were thrilled by the tremendous power of the gospel.*

D. *They were encouraged by the consciousness of the personal presence of the living Christ.*

E. *They were energized by the power of the Holy Spirit.*

All these attitudes should characterize the membership of a church in our day.

III. A practical program of evangelism.

A. *Daily.*
1. Not annually.
2. Not semiannually.
3. Not weekly.
4. But "daily."

B. *In the temple.* The temple was the normal place of worship. God's people did not consider it a place to go only on the Sabbath. It is tragic that many of our church facilities are used for only a few hours one day each week.

C. *In every house.*
1. The unsaved do not come to our churches.
2. The unsaved are not going to come to the church unless they are sought and drawn by a spiritual hunger created by a Christian's personal testimony (Rom. 3:11).
3. We are commanded to go to them.

D. *They ceased not to teach and preach.*
1. They were persistent.
2. They were persuasive.

E. *They presented Jesus Christ.* Our message has always been the good news of God's love as revealed in Jesus Christ. The gospel is good *news* rather than good *advice.*

Conclusion

The early church was responsive to the commission of the Lord. Gratitude motivated them. The need of the unsaved pulled at their heart strings. The joy of being a bearer of good news excited them. The delightful pleasure of experiencing a degree of spiritual success kept them at the job. May God help us to follow in their steps.

appointments are inevitable, inescapable, and unavoidable. Each of us, without exception, will keep these appointments with God on time. We will be unable to postpone or to secure a reappointment. These two appointments are mentioned in the text. "It is appointed unto men once to die, but after this the judgment."

I. Our appointment with God in death.

A. *Most of us are allergic to the thought of death.* We do everything in our power to avoid thinking about the subject. We maintain the best health possible in order to postpone the possibility of death as long as possible.

B. *Great wealth will not enable you to avoid keeping this appointment.* Whether your name be Ford, Rockefeller, or J. Paul Getty, it will still be necessary for you to meet your appointment with God in death.

C. *Great piety will not enable you to escape death.* Abraham, Isaiah, John, Paul, Augustine, Martin Luther, Charles Haddon Spurgeon, Pope John Paul II—all have died.

D. *Great political power will not enable you to avoid an appointment with death.* George Washington, Abraham Lincoln, Franklin D. Roosevelt, Winston Churchill, John F. Kennedy, and Ronald Reagan have all gone out into eternity through the doorway that we call death. It may be in the cleanliness of a hospital room or in the familiar surroundings of your home, or it may be in a car crash or the blast of a bomb that death will come. The time is uncertain, but all of us will meet God at the time of death.

II. Our appointment with God in judgment.

"It is appointed unto men once to die, but after this the judgment." Man does not march off into oblivion through the doorway of death. He goes out to meet God in judgment where he will give an account of the life he has lived. This is the testimony of the Scripture from the book of Genesis to the end of the book of Revelation.

A. *Romans 2 tells us that the judgment of God will be according to truth.* It is the truth, the whole truth, and nothing but the truth that people will give an account of when they stand before God. This is what most people dread (v. 2).

B. *The judgment of God will be "to every man according to his deeds" (Rom. 2:6).* Both the good and the evil are recorded in the divine computer, and in the day of judgment a man will face his total record.

C. *God will show no partiality to a favored group (Rom. 2:11).* In some places a man's political affiliation affects the justice that he receives. In many places the color of a man's skin determines how he will be treated in a court of law. A man's financial resources can be used to enable him to evade many of the demands of justice. Such will not be the case when people face an impartial God on the day of judgment.

D. *The gospel and the divine truth of the Word of God will be the standard by which people are judged (Rom. 2:16).* On the Judgment Day people will not be judged by public opinion. No effort will be put forth to secure a self-evaluation. People will be judged by the truth of God.

E. *The date has been set and the Judge has been appointed (Acts 17:31).* The judgment will be universal in scope, the verdict final.

III. Our appointment with God at Calvary.

The most important appointment that God has made with man is at Calvary where "God so loved the world that he gave his only begotten Son, that whosoever believeth in him should not perish, but have everlasting life" (John 3:16). Here is the place where God has appointed that we meet with him in order that we might be prepared to meet him in death and on the Judgment Day without fear of being lost and rejected.

A. *At Calvary the awful, vile, evil nature of our sin is most dramatically disclosed.* When we behold Calvary and recognize that Jesus died a substitutionary death under the penalty of sin, we will cease to ignore, to hide, to explain away, and to treat lightly the fact of sin. God has appointed that we meet him at Calvary where Jesus Christ was bruised for our iniquities and where the chastisement of our peace was placed on him. God would have us meet him at Calvary where he "hath made [Christ] to be sin for us, who knew no sin; that we might be made the righteousness of God in him" (2 Cor. 5:21).

B. *When we come to Calvary to meet God, we see the awful penalty of sin.* It is the law of God and a fact of history that "the soul that sinneth, it shall die" (Ezek. 18:20). On the cross Christ was meeting the penalty of our sin. Either sinners must let the death of Christ meet the requirements of God's holy law for them, or they must meet and pay that penalty for themselves.

C. *God has appointed that we meet him at Calvary that we might learn the divine estimate of the worth of a soul.* We live in a world in which human life is cheap. In a world with an exploding population, there are many who do not consider themselves to be of much worth. People can see their worth at Calvary as at no other place. Here God demonstrates the extent to which he will go to save the soul of a person. Here the sinless Savior died as a sinner for us that we might be able to live in the presence of God as if we had never sinned.

D. *God would have us meet him at Calvary where he revealed the height and depth and the length and breadth of his love for lost men and women.* While it is impossible for us to understand why he should love us, we can rejoice and respond to that love by faith.

Conclusion

If you will come by faith to the foot of the cross and accept and receive Jesus Christ as your Lord and Savior, you will receive as the gift of God the forgiveness of your sin and the new life Jesus offers. By so doing, you will be prepared, not only for these two inevitable, inescapable appointments with God in death and on the Judgment Day, but also you will be prepared to live the abundant life in the here and now. If you have not already done so, may God help you to do so now.

WEDNESDAY EVENING, OCTOBER 29

Title: Witnessing with Urgency

Text: "Behold, now is the accepted time; behold, now is the day of salvation" **(2 Cor. 6:2).**

Introduction

The words of our text have been quoted by Christian witnesses to unbelievers to encourage them to make an immediate decision to trust Jesus Christ as a personal Savior. Very definitely they teach that God wants to save the sinner right now.

Actually these words were not directed by the inspired writer to the ears of unbelievers. They were addressed to those who were already disciples to encourage them to witness with urgency.

Many of us have misunderstood the purpose of God's grace and have interpreted God's purposes toward us selfishly. To live as if we were the only objects of God's concern is to waste the grace of God (2 Cor. 6:1). From a human perspective, it is difficult for us to see how God's grace is wasted when it results in our salvation. When we look at the bestowal of God's grace from a divine perspective, we immediately see that his grace has been wasted on us if we are nothing more than a reservoir. God wants us to be conduits or channels through which his redemptive purpose can reach others.

Paul was both challenging and rebuking our Lord's disciples at Corinth. He was rebuking them because they were not bearing a continual witness, and he was challenging them to get on with their task because God wanted to save the unsaved immediately.

Procrastination is not only the thief of time, but it also deprives the unsaved of the good news of God's grace when we do not witness with a note of urgency. So let us focus our attention on the world now. Now is the acceptable time as far as God is concerned. God is in the business of forgiving and redeeming sinners now.

I. The urgency of the present.

A. *Our Lord recognized the urgency of doing today's work today (John 9:4).* Our day of opportunity to witness will soon turn into the darkness of night. The unsaved person's day of opportunity to hear the gospel will soon turn into night.

B. *All of us are guilty of procrastination (John 5:35).* When wheat is ripe, it is a golden yellow. If the harvest is delayed, the wheat will turn white. If it is harvested at this stage, it will deteriorate and be of no value at all. Our Lord saw the lost world as a field that was white already unto harvest. He was encouraging urgency.

II. Men are lost now.

Some labor under the impression that people are not lost until the end of life. They are mistaken. While there is still hope that those people will be converted, they are lost now if they have not trusted Christ as their Savior. Only the slender thread that we call life is keeping them out of hell right now. If those of us who claim to be the followers of Jesus Christ would face up to this truth, perhaps it would thaw the ice in our hearts and melt the lead in our feet.

A. *"The son of man is come to seek and to save that which was lost"* (Luke 19:10).

B. *"He that believeth on him is not condemned: but he that believeth not is condemned already, because he hath not believed in the name of the only begotten Son of God"* (John 3:18).

C. *"He that believeth on the Son hath everlasting life: and he that believeth not the Son shall not see life; but the wrath of God abideth on him"* (John 3:36).

III. Now is the time for serious thought (Isa. 1:18).

If the saved and the unsaved alike would think seriously about the issues and values of eternity, changes would take place. The saved would urgently seek to persuade nonbelievers to put their faith in Jesus Christ, and the unsaved would be more receptive and responsive to the counsel.

A. *"Boast not thyself of tomorrow; for thou knowest not what a day may bring forth"* (Prov. 27:1).

B. *"So teach us to number our days, that we may apply our hearts unto wisdom"* (Ps. 90:12).

IV. Now is the time for repentance.

"God ... now commandeth all men every where to repent" (Acts 17:30). God commands the unsaved to repent now. They cannot repent yesterday; they are not invited to repent tomorrow. He invites people to forsake a life of no faith and to confess their sin today.

Conclusion

We sin against God, we sin against unsaved people, and we sin against ourselves when we fail to recognize the urgency of our being a witness today. Tomorrow may be too late for us individually, and tomorrow may be too late for the person to whom we would communicate the good news of God's love.

A savings and loan company had a large clock on the front of their building. Three words in bold letters were printed across the face of the clock: "TIME TO SAVE." It is also time for us to be good witnesses for the Lord Jesus today and every day until our Lord returns or until he calls us home.

NOVEMBER

The theme for the month is stewardship. Behind every message should be a desire to lead people into a deeper experience of faith and commitment to God.

■ Sunday Mornings

The Sunday morning theme is "Stewardship: God's Way of Saving Us from Selfishness." Most of us fail to realize that human selfishness is the main source of many of the frustrations that upset and disturb happiness. The primary purpose of these messages is to lead people to see how God would deliver us from the tyranny of the material.

■ Sunday Evenings

The theme for Sunday evenings is "Living the Abundant Life." The purpose of these messages is to show how the abundant life is to be discovered, not by the way of affluence, but by the deliberate and devoted giving of self and substance in service to God and to others.

■ Wednesday Evenings

The Wednesday evening messages are designed to strengthen the faith and commitment of church leaders as they communicate the stewardship teachings of the Bible to the rest of the church.

SUNDAY MORNING, NOVEMBER 2

Title: Trumpeting the Gospel

Text: "For from you sounded out the word of the Lord" (**1 Thess. 1:8**).

Hymns: "A Mighty Fortress Is Our God," Luther

"Revive Us Again," Mackay

"Faith Is the Victory," Yates

Offertory Prayer: Eternal God and Father of our Lord Jesus Christ, today we come directly into your presence in the name of our Savior who died for us and offered his blood as an atonement for our sin. We come bringing our tithes and offerings. We come to do more than meet the expenses of this particular church. We come to express our love and gratitude to you, our God and our Savior. In Jesus' name we pray. Amen.

Introduction

On Paul's second missionary journey, he preached in Thessalonica on three Sabbath days. Many people were converted and formed the nucleus of what was to become a vigorous, thriving church.

Those who were converted lived such consistent Christian lives that they were conspicuous in the midst of a corrupt heathen community. Their lives were loud proclaimers, effective witnesses, to the transforming difference that Christ makes in life when he is trusted and is served as Lord. The difference they demonstrated was so obvious that they became a subject of conversation for all who had contact with them.

In describing the winsome testimony of this congregation of believers for Christ, Paul used a word that was ordinarily used in describing the blast of a trumpet. They were "trumpeting the gospel." Their lives were so close to the living Lord that their influence was felt and their message was heard as positively as the clear, ringing, loud, penetrating, melodious, rousing notes of a trumpet.

For Christ's sake, from each of us and from all of us collectively, there should go forth a Christian testimony as clear, as melodious, as harmonious, and as beautiful as the piercing notes of a trumpet. Only as we accept and respond to the privileges and responsibilities of the priesthood of all believers is there any hope for winning the world to faith in Christ.

In speaking on this text Alexander Maclaren says that "the church is God's trumpet." Through the church God would speak of his love, his mercy, his power, and his purpose of grace to those who are lost and in sin. The trumpet needs to sound forth. The world needs to hear the sound of God's trumpet. To properly appreciate Paul's commendation, it should be recognized that the trumpet is a musical instrument that has been used through the centuries by the military. It has been used for a number of different purposes.

I. The trumpet was used to issue a challenge.

There is an old Jewish legend to the effect that each morning in heaven the trumpets ring out so that all can hear. After Lucifer, son of the morning, had been cast out of heaven, he was asked what he missed most. He replied, "I miss most of all the trumpets that were sounded forth in the morning." The world misses the sound of God's trumpet. The trumpet that would challenge saint or sinner to a life of faith and obedience must understand and appreciate its message and mission.

A. *If we are to be God's trumpet in the world to challenge the hearts of people, we need to go again to Gethsemane's gloom and come to a new understanding of the awful weight of sin borne by our Savior.*

B. *We need to visit Golgotha's bloody brow and see both the awful penalty of sin and the indescribable love of God for sinners.*

C. *We need to visit the empty tomb and discover that ours is a living Savior who has conquered death and the grave.*

314

D. *We should go with the apostles to the Upper Room and tarry until we have been clothed with the power of God, and in that power we should face the world and let the trumpet sound forth.*

We should listen to the note of victory and confidence and courage.

> *He has sounded forth the trumpet*
>   *That shall never sound retreat;*
> *He is sifting out the hearts of men*
>   *Before His judgment seat.*
> *O be swift, my soul, to answer Him!*
>   *Be jubilant, my feet!*
> *Our God is marching on.*
>
> *—Julia Ward Howe*

The story is told that on one occasion the troops of Napoleon were despondent and in great danger of experiencing a defeat when someone inquired as to whether it would be advisable to have the trumpets sound a retreat. Napoleon, the great military leader that he was, issued an order for the opposite and commanded that the trumpeter play a march. The troops responded and victory was achieved. The church and the world need to hear the sound of the trumpet.

II. The trumpet was used to announce good news.

In ages gone by, the messenger of the king would pass through the land and at certain places along the road a trumpeter would sound the trumpet. The people would assemble, and there an official from the king's court would read the message of the king. Sometimes the message was good. Sometimes it was bad.

The heavenly Father used an angel to announce the birth of the royal child, and instead of a single trumpet, an angelic choir sang a glorious anthem to herald the good news of the birth of a Savior. Today God would use you personally and the church collectively to announce to a needy world that salvation is available through Christ.

A. *Christ came to reveal that God is love.*

B. *God's love is a sacrificial self-giving love.*

C. *The supreme revelation of his love is giving his Son on the cross.*

D. *God's love offers salvation to all through Jesus Christ.* This salvation includes the forgiveness of sin, the promise of power to live a victorious life over evil in the present, and a life of endless fellowship with God for eternity. This is the message we are to announce to the world as clearly and as forcefully as the notes of a trumpet.

III. The trumpet was used to warn of dangers.

For thousands of years, cities were warned of possible danger by a trumpeter who was charged with the responsibility of being a watchman. God spoke to Ezekiel concerning his responsibility as the watchman who was to use a trumpet to warn the people of approaching danger. "But if the watchman see the sword

315

come, and blow not the trumpet, and the people be not warned; if the sword come, and take any person from among them, he is taken away in his iniquity; but his blood will I require at the watchman's hand" (Ezek. 33:6).

God spoke to Isaiah and instructed him to warn the nation as a trumpeter of the evil consequences of sin in the following way: "Cry aloud, spare not, lift up thy voice like a trumpet, and shew my people their transgression, and the house of Jacob their sins" (Isa. 58:1).

A. *America's greatest danger is not terrorists.*

B *America's greatest danger as a nation is to be found in the peril of forgetting the God who has made us great.* It is so easy for a great nation to become proud and haughty and self-sufficient and selfish. The moral confusion that threatens our nation can be traced to either our forgetting or ignoring the will of the God who has made us great. Both individuals and the community need to hear the warnings of God and the lessons of history. The church needs to be God's trumpet today to warn our nation concerning the certain results of forgetting or ignoring God.

IV. The trumpet was used to announce victory.

When the battle was over and the victorious armies returned home, the arrival of the commanding officer was announced by a fanfare of trumpets in loud, exultant, melodious, and penetrating notes. When our Lord returns to earth for his own, his arrival will be announced not by the sad, sobbing wailing of a flute, but with the piercing, shattering notes of a trumpet.

A. *"Behold, I shew you a mystery; we shall not all sleep, but we shall all be changed, in a moment, in the twinkling of an eye, at the last trumpet: for the trumpet shall sound, and the dead shall be raised incorruptible, and we shall be changed" (1 Cor. 15:51–52).*

B. *"The Lord himself shall descend from heaven with a shout, with the voice of the archangel, and with the trump of God: and the dead in Christ shall rise first" (1 Thess. 4:16).*

> When He shall come with trumpet sound,
> Oh, may I then in Him be found;
> Dressed in His righteousness alone,
> Faultless to stand before the throne.
> On Christ, the solid Rock, I stand,
> All other ground is sinking sand,
> All other ground is sinking sand.
> —Edward Mote

Conclusion

We as individual members can help our church be God's trumpet in our community and even around the world. We have God's good news to announce concerning a great God who loves sinners. We have the responsibility of warning the lost of the dangers to which they expose themselves. We have the privilege of waiting and listening for the sound of the trumpet that will announce the final and ultimate victory of our Lord and his coming.

Individuals served as God's trumpet during the apostolic days, and the world heard the gospel. As individuals responded by faith and faithfulness to the newly rediscovered truth of the priesthood of every believer, thousands followed the leaders of the Reformation and shook the world. May God help each of us to be one of his trumpeters today.

SUNDAY EVENING, NOVEMBER 2

Title: Communicating the Gospel with Confidence

Text: "So, as much as in me is, I am ready to preach the gospel to you that are at Rome also" **(Rom. 1:15).**

Introduction

The apostle Paul stood with his face toward the city of Rome, the queen city of the empire, the place of poets and legislators, the scene of imperial grandeur where the magnificence of wealth and power was on constant display. With great confidence in his gospel to meet the deepest need in the hearts of the people in this mighty metropolis, Paul was eager to preach the gospel to them. Paul was convinced that the gospel of Jesus Christ was the only solution to the problem of the world's sin.

Paul's gracious enthusiasm grew out of his confidence in the power of divine love, the power of eternal truth, the power of moral judgment, and the power of the living Spirit of God, which had been demonstrated time and time again when the gospel was communicated.

Paul used a negative approach to express a positive truth. He was declaring that the gospel had never caused his face to blush. It had never let him down.

We need to be infected with Paul's enthusiasm. We need to be possessed by a passion for souls. We need to be convinced that the gospel is the solution to our problems: individual problems, national problems, and international problems.

I. Paul was confident of the source of his gospel.

The gospel was born in the heart of God. It was disclosed in Bethlehem. It was demonstrated on Calvary.

II. Paul was confident of the substance of the gospel.

A. *Many have thought of Christianity as primarily in terms of good advice.*
B. *The gospel is good news about God as he has revealed himself in the person, life, death, and resurrection of Jesus Christ.*
C. *Many sermons fail to be gospel sermons because they do not contain good news about God.*

317

D. *Your personal witness to an unsaved friend should center in the good news of God's love demonstrated in the gift of Jesus Christ for us.*

III. Paul was confident of the scope of the gospel.

A. *The angelic announcement to the shepherds declared, "Fear not: For behold I bring you good tidings of great joy, which shall be to all people" (Luke 2:10).*

B. *The gospel invitation includes all people irrespective of color, class, condition, or station in life.*

C. *The blessings of the gospel are needed by all.*

D. *The blessings of the gospel are easily within the reach of all.*

IV. Paul was confident of the success of the gospel.

"It is the power of God unto salvation" (Rom. 1:16).

A. *Even a little child can trust.*

B. *Salvation comes to us through the channel of faith, that it might be by grace (Rom. 4:16).* By faith a sinner could receive Jesus Christ from a grounded submarine on the bottom of the ocean. By faith an astronaut speeding through space or living at the space station could accept the gospel invitation and entrust his or her soul into the care and custody of the Savior.

Conclusion

As followers of Jesus Christ, we, like Paul, can communicate the gospel with great confidence. Our Savior came to save. Our Savior died to save. Our Savior lives again to save. Our Savior will use our mouths to communicate the message of God's great salvation if we will make ourselves available to him and cooperate with him in his continuing quest to save.

WEDNESDAY EVENING, NOVEMBER 5

Title: "What Is That in Thine Hand?"

Text: "And the LORD said unto him, What is that in thine hand?" **(Ex. 4:2).**

Introduction

Moses was given three signs by which he was to verify his divine appointment as God's leader of Israel.

1. The sign of the rod.
2. The sign of the leprous hand that was cleansed.
3. The sign of the water that became blood.

I. What is that in thine hand?

A. *Just a simple shepherd's rod.* It became the visible symbol of the invisible God (Ex. 4:2).

B. *David had a simple slingshot and five smooth stones (1 Sam. 17:40).*

C. *The lad had a boy's lunch (John 6:9).*

D. *The maid in Naaman's house had a simple story of one who could heal (2 Kings 5:13).*

II. What you have is enough.

A. *God does not expect us to do that which is beyond our ability or capacity.*

B. *God does not require more than we are able to do.*

III. What has God placed in your hand?

A. *The gift of speech?*

B. *The gift of song?*

C. *The gift of intelligence?*

D. *The gift of leadership?*

E. *The gift of teaching?*

F. *The gift of serving?*

G. *The gift of working?*

IV. Use God's gift or lose it.

A. *Train yourself to use it.*

B. *Learn from failure.*

C. *Seek continually to improve.*

D. *Dare to begin.*

E. *Dare to fail.*

F. *Dare to try again.*

Conclusion

Many of us are in situations where it seems impossible for God to meet our needs, let alone help us to react to those circumstances with faith and integrity. Yet this is exactly what he promises. Let us ask God for his presence to be real in our lives, his strength to conquer our sins.

SUNDAY MORNING, NOVEMBER 9

Title: The Rich Fool's Twin Brother

Text: "So is he that layeth up treasure for himself, and is not rich toward God" (**Luke 12:21**).

Hymns: "Guide Me, O Thou Great Jehovah," Williams

"I Love Thy Kingdom, Lord," Dwight

"Take My Life, and Let It Be," Havergal

Offertory Prayer: Heavenly Father, we rejoice in this day that you have made. We worship you and praise you with all of our hearts, for out of the abundance of your unwasted fullness, you have blessed us. We bring our tithes and offerings that others might hear the story of your love, grace, and mercy. Accept these tithes and offerings and bless them for your purposes, in Christ's name. Amen.

Introduction

Several years ago the picture of a young man appeared on the front page of the *Courier Journal*, the morning newspaper of Louisville, Kentucky, with the question, "Have you seen this young man?" The young man had suddenly and mysteriously disappeared. His parents were hoping that he had decided to leave home and that he would soon be back. The police officials were afraid that he had been kidnapped. In an effort to inform the public that he was missing, they wanted a picture. To get a picture in the earliest edition of the paper, a photographer took a picture of the identical twin brother of the missing man, and it was his picture that appeared in the *Courier Journal*.

Every now and then we see people on the street whom we mistakenly identify as a friend or acquaintance because of some striking resemblances. Probably many of us have been spoken to by a stranger because he or she identified us with someone else.

Did you ever study the Bible from the standpoint of discovering a brother or a cousin? Occasionally we can find an identical twin brother in one of the biblical characters. Some find a twin brother in Jonah because they are running from God's good will for their lives. Others find a twin brother in Peter because he was impulsive and talkative. Many find a twin brother in John Mark who started well but who dropped out at the halfway point (Acts 13:13). They are quitters as he was. It should be said of John Mark that he redeemed himself by renewing his loyalty, and eventually he became the author of the second gospel. Some can find a twin brother in David. He was a great sinner. Let it be said on his behalf that he was also a great confessor, and he acknowledged his sin and experienced forgiveness and cleansing.

If we would study the Bible profitably, we need to identify with the characters to discover how God would meet our spiritual and moral needs. Paul said to the Roman Christians, "For whatsoever things were written aforetime were written for our learning, that we through patience and comfort of the scriptures might have hope" (Rom. 15:4). We can learn much by identifying and participating vicariously with biblical characters as we study God's Word.

In the scriptural text for this message, Jesus warns us against the danger of being a twin brother of the rich fool. Why would God call this man a fool? Are there valid reasons for this verdict of divine wisdom? If we can discover the reasons for this divine verdict, perhaps we can avoid the same destiny.

I. Negative considerations.

A. *Nothing is said about the man being dishonest, vulgar, or untruthful.*
B. *It is not said that he was prejudiced, cynical, or jealous.*

320

C. *He did not consider himself a fool.* He appeared to be a rather capable and confident individual.

D. *He was an owner of property.*

E. *He was a hard worker.*

F. *Most likely he was a wise and shrewd planner.*

G. *No doubt he used the best agricultural methods known in his day.*

H. *This man was successful.*

I. *It can be assumed that this man was greatly admired by some.*

Many of us would have been happy to have been like him; thus, we are his twin brother.

II. Valid reasons for the divine verdict.

Both Moses and Jesus warn us, "It is written, Man shall not live by bread alone, but by every word that proceedeth out of the mouth of God" (Matt. 4:4).

A. *He moved forward on the false premise that one could satisfy his soul with things.* "Soul, thou has much goods laid up for many years; take thine ease, eat, drink, and be merry" (Luke 12:19).

Are you living under the impression that wealth, pleasure, education, fun, trinkets, gadgets, fame, power, or position can meet the deepest needs of your heart and life? Things, by themselves, cannot satisfy the deepest longings of the soul.

A hungry man does not rush to a pile of sawdust to satisfy his hunger pangs. A thirsty man does not rush down to the seaside to quench his thirst with salt water. A laboring man does not go to the county fair to buy cotton candy to replenish his bodily strength. To do so would be foolish. Yet he who did this would be no more foolish than the man who tries to satisfy the deepest hunger of his heart with material things.

B. *With the accumulation of things, the rich fool's selfishness increased.* There are sixty-four words in his dialogue with himself. Eleven of these are personal pronouns. He thought not of God nor of his fellowman who needed help, but only of himself. A man wrapped up in himself alone always makes a very small package. I hope that you are not his twin brother.

C. *The rich fool forgot his two partners: God and society.* God is the giver of all good gifts, and everything is to be used under his judgment and guidance. Every blessing that we receive is bestowed upon us in order that we might be a blessing to others. We have not even begun to live the abundant life until we recognize this truth. I hope you are not the rich fool's twin brother.

D. *The rich fool lived for the present time alone and forgot eternity.* He lived for one world only. He forgot that he was a creature of eternity and that one day he would give an account to his Lord. How sad it is for the man who is looking for oil when he puts his total resources into the drilling of one hole and it turns out to be a duster. Disappointed, indeed, will be the woman who puts all of her eggs in one basket and then drops them. I hope you are not the twin brother of the rich fool.

E. *The rich fool saw living in terms of getting instead of giving.* It is easy for us to think of the happy life as being inseparably associated with an abundance of materialistic things. We live in a materialistic society that judges success in terms of physical properties, bank accounts, and stocks and bonds. The whole point of this parable is to warn others against this false way of defining the primary purpose in life. Jesus would warn us and observation would shout at us that happiness is not always determined by the possession of things. I hope that you are not the twin brother of the rich fool.

F. *The rich fool worshiped a false god, and a false god always disappoints.* Money and position can do many things for us, but there comes a time when money and position cannot meet the deepest needs of life. Only as we have our faith in the eternal God of grace and mercy and build our life around his teachings can we be sure that we will be adequate for all of the eventualities of human existence.

III. The fearful sentence and the disturbing question.

A. *"Thou fool, this night thy soul shall be required of thee" (Luke 12:20).* Life at its longest is brief. Only as we are prepared for death are we really prepared for living. The rich fool based all of the emphasis on living and forgot that one day he was going to die.

B. *"Then whose shall those things be, which thou hast provided?" (Luke 12:20).* One thing is certain. There will be no pockets in a shroud. Five seconds after death, the hand of the multimillionaire is not able to write a check for five dollars.

The only way by which it is possible for us to transfer the valuables of this life into spiritual treasures for the next life is by means of spiritual investments in the hearts and lives of others. Only the soul can go through the strainer that we call death. Only as we have communicated the message of God's grace into the hearts and lives of others so as to persuade them to become believers will we be able to take our treasures with us.

IV. God's will for you is that you be wise.

A. *The wisest act of wisdom would be for you to receive Jesus Christ into your heart and life as Lord and Savior.* You need to build your life on the foundation of the divine truths he spoke.

B. *Let him be the authoritative teacher for your life (Matt. 7:26–29).* Let his mind become your mind. Let his thoughts be your thoughts. Let his will be your will.

C. *Participate with him in redemptive activity.* You can do this by working to help bring the unbelieving world to faith in the good God.

D. *Invest your time, talents, testimony, and your all in that which is valuable both in time and eternity.*

322

Conclusion

You have one advantage over the rich fool. If you have been following his example, it is not too late for you to change your course and recognize the place that belongs to God in your heart and life. Define your efforts in relation to him and lay up treasures in heaven rather than putting them all in a barn here on earth.

SUNDAY EVENING, NOVEMBER 9

Title: Investing in Gilt-Edged Securities

Text: "Lay not up for yourselves treasures upon earth, where moth and rust doth corrupt, and where thieves break through and steal: But lay up for yourselves treasures in heaven, where neither moth nor rust doth corrupt, and where thieves do not break through nor steal: For where your treasure is, there will your heart be also" (**Matt. 6:19–21**).

Introduction

Many think of Jesus only in terms of his being concerned about spiritual matters. Some have limited him to the life after death. They do not feel that he has a relevant message for life in this modern age. To think in these terms is to miss completely the impact of his wonderful life. He is more than a Savior of the soul. He wants to guide us into abundant life (John 10:10).

In the words of our text, Jesus gave utterance to a principle that should touch every area of your life. As heaven's wonderful Teacher, he has a word for us concerning some safe investments. All of us are interested in making wise and profitable investments.

People's acquisitive instincts are inborn and have not changed through the centuries. Because they want to walk by sight rather than by faith, they are constantly tempted to confuse the means of living with the end of living.

The pressures of making a living often crowd out the desire to live a great and significant life. Jesus had much to say about our relationship to the material world and our concern for the necessities of life. He warns us against the peril of letting material things separate us from God.

In the words of our text, the Savior assumes the role of our investment Counselor. He would advise us as to how we can invest our time, talents, and treasure so as to prosper permanently.

I. Jesus points out the insecurity of earthly treasure.

A. *Earthly treasure is subject to destruction from* within — *by the moth.* The moth was symbolic of all that can destroy on the inside. Wealthy people in the Middle East would often have large investments in clothes, carpets, and other perishable materials. These could be ruined by moths.

B. *Earthly treasure is subject to destruction from* without — *by rust.* Much of that which we purchase will deteriorate with the passing of time. The sale value of a new car experiences a sudden drop the moment it is driven out of the showroom. Fire, storms, and floods can render our investments valueless. Most of the things for which people struggle are perishable.

C. *Earthly treasures are subject to destruction from* beneath — *"thieves break through and steal."* There are many factors over which the individual has no control that can rob us of our valuables.

1. War or natural catastrophe can destroy our investments.
2. Inflation causes savings to shrink.
3. Depression causes investments to decrease in value. Earthly treasure alone is a bad investment. It isn't permanent. One has to go off and leave it to someone else (Eccl. 2:17–19).

D. *Jesus is not prohibiting the saving or accumulating of money.* The seventh commandment implies the right to accumulate property.

1. It is God who gives us the power to get wealth (Deut. 8:18).
2. God wants to bless people with prosperity.

E. *Jesus warns us against letting earthly treasure become the chief object in life.*

1. Earthly treasure does not satisfy.
2. Earthly treasure is perishable (1 John 2:17).
3. Earthly treasure will have to be left behind.
4. Concentration on earthly treasure prevents one from laying up treasure in heaven.

II. Jesus pointed out the security of heavenly treasure (Matt. 6:20).

A. *The bank of heaven will never go broke.*
B. *Moths and rust will not corrupt.*
C. *Thieves will not break in and steal.*
D. *Invest your time in the service of God.*
E. *Invest your talents and energy in the service of God.*
F. *Invest your tithe as a minimum in the work of God.*

1. Because of what it will do to and for you.
2. Because of what it will do for your church.
3. Because a lost and needy world waits.
4. Because God says that we are to do so.

III. Proper investments are highly important.

A. *Our heart follows our treasure.* Our heart is always located where our treasure is located. "Where your treasure is there will your heart be also" (Matt. 6:20). This is the whole point of this investment counsel of Jesus. He is encouraging us to invest in the kingdom of God rather than putting our heart into that which is purely material and temporary.

B. *Christ wants us to make a wise investment.* We could waste our substance by an unwise investment. He who lives for this world only is making a very foolish investment of his life and resources. The rich fool is a case in point. He was rich in the eyes of the world but a pauper in the sight of God (Luke 12:21).

Conclusion

"What shall it profit a man if he shall gain the whole world and lose his own soul?" (Mark 8:36). Jesus encourages us to invest all that we are in eternal things—things that will pass through the strainer of death. By so doing we live the full life here, and heaven will be richer and more wonderful hereafter.

WEDNESDAY EVENING, NOVEMBER 12

Title: Economic Consecration

Text: "The earth is the LORD's and the fullness thereof; the world, and they that dwell therein" (**Ps. 24:1**).

Introduction

In the world of our day, two great economic systems are engaged in a struggle that could win our present civilization. Only time will reveal which, if either, survives.

Socialism is built on the premise that a person owns property that is to be controlled by society, as far as possible, instead of by the individual. Capitalism is built on the premise that a person owns property that is to be controlled by the individual, as far as possible, instead of by society.

Christianity would speak to both socialism and capitalism and say, "You are built upon a falsehood. God is the owner of the earth and all that dwell therein." If we all could accept the truth that God is owner and we are stewards, we would see a vast transformation in our human relationships.

I. Pagan ideas of ownership have made a battlefield out of our world.

    A. *We are theological believers and economic infidels.*

    B. *People have shut God up inside the church building.*

    C. *Someone has said, "Godless economics is worse than atheistic evolutionism."*

        1. Atheistic evolution shuts God out of the distant past.

        2. Godless economics shuts God out of the present.

II. It is time for Christianity in general and the Christian in particular to face up to the neglected truth of God's ownership and our stewardship.

    A. *Stewardship of property is God's cure for the cancer of covetousness.*

        1. The sin of covetousness is deceptive.

        2. We permit ourselves to judge success in terms of the material.

        3. We let gadgets become our god.

        4. We put the material before spiritual.

325

B. *Stewardship of property is the material side of personal consecration.*
 1. In consecration Christians give what they are to God.
 2. In stewardship Christians give what they have to God.

III. We need to rediscover the truth that God is owner and we are managers.

A. This discovers and revitalizes the church.
B. This discovers and helps to recover the lost passion for the souls of people.

Conclusion

The worship of mammon is a great foe to kingdom advance. If a person is captivated by the ambition to be an owner, he or she faces the strong possibility of becoming less and less concerned about the eternal things of the spirit. Our American form of Christianity faces the peril of decaying in the midst of modern luxury if the economic significance of original Christianity is not rediscovered.

SUNDAY MORNING, NOVEMBER 16

Title: Modern Motives for Tithing

Text: "And this stone, which I have set for a pillar, shall be God's house: and of all that thou shalt give me I will surely give the tenth unto thee" (**Gen. 28:22**).

Hymns: "Glory to His Name," Hoffman

"A Child of the King," Buell

"Our Best," Kirk

Offertory Prayer: Heavenly Father, we acknowledge you as the giver of every good and perfect gift. We praise you for your generosity and kindness toward us. We rejoice over your grace as the basis of your dealings with us. Help us to recognize how blessed we are so that we might be moved by love in serving you. Through Jesus Christ our Lord. Amen.

Introduction

Scarcely anything is more important than the Christian's motive. A motive is that which moves. What the mainspring is to a watch or the motor is to an automobile, the Christian's motive is to his work and worship. A proper motive is vital in the matter of our giving. The motive behind the gift determines the real worth of the gift. It would be wonderful if the motive behind all that we do in the work of God was a pure love for Christ. Such is not the case and never has been. A study of the Bible reveals that God has appealed to many motives in order to stimulate his children to be and to do that which was right. If we will examine our hearts closely we will discover that mingled motives are behind most of our actions.

In nearly every church there is a group of members who have committed themselves to the practice of tithing year in and year out. They contribute one-tenth of their income to the Lord through their church. A consideration of the motives that lead them to do this can be both informative and challenging.

I. Many Christians are faithful tithers because of a desire to acknowledge God's ownership of all things (Ps. 24:1).

Many sincerely believe that the tithe is the rent they pay to the divine Land-owner for the use of that which belongs to him (Lev. 27:30).

II. Many Christians tithe because they desire the blessings promised to the tither (Mal. 3:10).

It should be recognized that this is a selfish motive. If this is the only motive, it is very possible that the tither will not continue his or her habit for a great length of time.

Thousands will bear a sincere testimony to the effect that God blesses the tither materially. They have found it much easier to meet their financial obligations with nine-tenths of their possessions plus his leadership and guidance. The Bible clearly teaches that we rob ourselves when we are guilty of robbing God of our tithes and offerings (Mal. 3:9). The practice of tithing does not impoverish. Tithing leaves enough for the individual or family to meet their financial needs. It costs more not to tithe than it does to tithe. One's capacity to receive God's blessings is determined in a large degree by his or her willingness to be a giver.

III. Some Christians tithe for the personal satisfaction of having an investment in the most important enterprise on earth (Matt. 28:18–20).

Jesus Christ was God's great messenger to the world to communicate his love. Christ committed to his church the task of carrying the message of salvation to every part of the world. While individual Christians are to bear their own personal testimonies with their lives and their lips, the practice of tithing is considered to be the divinely appointed financial plan by which they help meet the material needs of advancing the kingdom of God on earth.

Tithing links us with God in his great worldwide program of redemption. Through our tithes and offerings, we have a part in the saving of the lost world beyond the circle of our own personal witnessing. Tithing puts each of us in touch with the whole world.

IV. Tithing makes the growth of personal faith possible.

An increase of faith in all of the promises of God is one of the rich fruits of the practice of tithing. All of us agree that a greater faith in God is indeed a rich blessing. Many have discovered that when they begin to trust God with their money, they find it easier to trust God in other areas of life. The practice of tithing permits God to prove his divine trustworthiness. God honors his promises. The

Bible is a book of promises, and the Christian's faith will be greater when these promises are discovered and claimed by faith.

V. A fresh sense of reality and vitality in worship has been discovered by those who tithe.

Genuine worship is an experience in which we give all that we have to God and at the same time we receive what God has for us. One cannot be a mere spectator and genuinely worship. If we would receive all that God is and has for us, we must give of ourselves and of our substance to him. When Jesus warned against the perils of laying up treasures on earth and encouraged his disciples rather to lay up treasures in heaven, his primary purpose was to assist them in worshiping only him who is worthy of worship. He concluded by saying, "For where your treasure is there will your heart be also." Our interest follows our money. We tie our hearts to our investments. Worship is vital and real only when we are investing in the kingdom of God.

VI. Many Christians tithe in order to permit God to partner with them in their economic lives.

By recognizing the ownership of God and the stewardship of man, people have found a partial cure for the cancer of covetousness. We live in a materialistic world that measures success by a materialistic standard.

The Christian is under constant pressure to live only for materialistic things. To believe that real life is to be found in material things is to be guilty of covetousness and idolatry. To be genuinely Christian, we must let God into our economic lives and give us guidance as we make, spend, save, and give away money. Our God is just as concerned about how we make our living as he is in what we do during worship on Sunday evening.

VII. Many Christians are tithing because tithing is a tangible way in which they can prove their love for the Lord.

God loved us and gave his Son for us. Genuine love always seeks to find a way by which it can properly express itself. Words that express affection are shallow and cheap if appropriate deeds do not verify their truthfulness. We need to sing of our love for the Lord, but we also need to prove our love in a significant way.

Conclusion

What is your motive for giving? Most likely you are controlled by mingled motives. Jesus believed that there was more happiness, more joy, more adventure, more excitement, more satisfaction to be found in a life of giving than could possibly be found in a life dedicated to receiving and having.

Jesus believed this to the extent that he gave himself utterly and completely for us. We will discover the way of gladness and joy when we follow his example and live in order to be givers rather than receivers. To begin the practice of tithing is to take a major step in that direction.

SUNDAY EVENING, NOVEMBER 16

Title: Around the World on a Magic Carpet

Text: "Go ye therefore, and teach all nations, baptizing them in the name of the Father, and of the Son, and of the Holy Ghost" (**Matt. 28:19**).

Introduction

From the literature of the ancient East, we read of a legendary magic carpet that could transport one who stood on it to any place desired. In a moment's time, one could be carried incredible distances. Tonight, by the aid of the Holy Spirit, I would seek to place each of you on a magic carpet of inspired imagination and transport you around the world, so that you might discover the desperate needs of the world in which we live. I would then by means of this magic carpet take you back to those events of unique spiritual significance that provide us with both a message that our world needs and the motivation that we must have if we would carry that message to our world.

I. A visit to Mount Olivet.

Before we begin our journey around our modern world, let us make a visit to Mount Olivet and listen closely to one who conquered death, hell, and the grave. As we listen, he reveals his purpose of worldwide redemption: We are to make disciples. He promises his personal presence: "I am with you always." His inexhaustible power is available to us.

We need to hear afresh the Master's magnificent claim. We need to stand at attention as we hear the Master's trumpet-toned command. We should rejoice with joy beyond measure because of the Master's promise of a marvelous companionship.

After twenty centuries of Christian history, the church finds itself in the embarrassing position of having been disobedient to the Master's mandate to the extent that the majority of the inhabitants of this earth are still not Christians.

The world is becoming more pagan with the passing of every year. Christianity becomes more of a minority movement every day.

II. Visit our modern world.

By means of our magic carpet, let us travel around the world and seek to discover the world's need for Christ.

    A. *From the angel's perspective, our world is filled with fear.*
        1. Countries are involved in wars and internal conflicts in many parts of the world.
        2. Terrorists strike in a variety of places and manners all over the world.
    B. *Our world is filled with hate.*
        1. One nation hates another.
        2. One race hates another.
    C. *From our position in outer space, we see a world filled with selfishness.*

1. On an individual level.
2. On national and international levels.

D. *From our magic carpet, we behold a foolish world.* People have become captivated and fascinated by the technical marvels of our age. They worship at the shrine of science. They are interested in breaking all kinds of speed records. They construct more and more complex computer technology. They invest the bulk of their resources on temporal things. They give their deepest devotion and their greatest energy to athletic achievements and scientific research and leave spiritual matters and matters of social justice untouched.

E. *From our magic carpet, we see a world groping in spiritual darkness.*
1. Some have shut God out.
2. Many have shut God in. They have refused to turn him loose in their lives.

F. *From our magic carpet, we can see thousands of our churches that are seemingly unconcerned about the spiritual destitution of those about them.*

III. Reaction and response.

A. *Alarm.* As those who claim to have the truth about God, we should be greatly alarmed by our coldhearted complacency toward the desperate spiritual needs of our world. The impact we as Christians are making is very difficult to discern. It is embarrassing to have to confess that we are not seriously engaged in a crusade to win this generation to faith in our Lord.

B. *Compassion.* The alarm and concern for the world in which we live should provoke compassion in the hearts of Christians. When Christ beheld the multitudes, his heart was filled with a trembling agony of concern that led him to go to the cross that people might be saved.

NASA has giant electronic ears listening for sounds from outer space. May God grant to us ears that can hear the cries of distress from hearts that are in spiritual darkness in our world. The space agency has also placed satellites in orbit around the earth to photograph cloud formations so as to predict the weather. May God give us eyes that will see the desperate needs of those about us.

C. *Frustration or defeatism.* One possible reaction to our magic carpet journey around the world is to be overcome with the immensity of the tasks before us. An attitude of defeatism could easily become the prevailing spirit. To adopt this attitude is to forget both the presence of the living Lord and the power of the gospel to save.

D. *A crusade of compassion.*
1. Jesus believed that there was hope for the world (Matt. 28:18–20).
2. Paul believed that there was hope for his world (Rom. 1:14–16).

3. If we will but revisit Calvary, the empty tomb, and the upper room, and respond to the compassionate command of our living Lord, there is hope for our world.

IV. Motivation for the task.

If we would be adequately motivated for the overwhelming task that confronts us, we must get on our magic carpet and make a trip.

A. *Visit Calvary.* Calvary is where God so loved the world that he gave his only begotten Son (John 3:16). Calvary is where we see the Lamb of God taking away the sin of the world (John 1:29). Calvary is where Christ himself bore our sins in his own body on the tree (1 Peter 2:28).

Calvary is where Christ was wounded for our transgressions and bruised for our iniquities, where the chastisement of our peace was upon him, and where, by his stripes, we are healed (Isa. 53:6).

Calvary is where God commended his love toward us, in that while we were yet sinners, Christ died for the ungodly (Rom. 5:8). Calvary is where the cry echoes, "Believe on the Lord Jesus Christ and thou shalt be saved" (Acts 16:31).

B. *Visit the empty tomb.* By means of an inspired imagination, let us visit the empty tomb. Visit the empty tomb where tragedy was transformed into triumph. Visit the empty tomb where Christ was declared to be the Son of God with power (Rom. 1:4).

Visit the empty tomb where Jesus was declared to be a divine and infallible Teacher. Visit the empty tomb where we learn that death has been conquered and the grave wins no lasting victory (1 Cor. 15:57). Visit the empty tomb where Christ is declared to be the adequate and all-sufficient Savior (Heb. 7:25).

Visit the empty tomb where immortality was demonstrated beyond any shadow of a doubt (Rev. 1:18). Visit the empty tomb where we discover that our Lord is our contemporary in this day in which we live (Matt. 28:20).

Visit the empty tomb where we see demonstrated the exceeding greatness of the power of God that is available to us who believe (Eph. 1:19).

Conclusion

By prayer we can ride a magic carpet through every portion of the world and bring the blessings of God upon the work of his witnesses. A convert on a mission field expressed a desire to study geography so as to pray for other Christians more individually. God can hear your prayer and answer on the other side of the world.

The offering plate can become a magic carpet by which the effort of our hands and the energy of our lives can be used in publishing the good tidings of redemption to a lost and needy world.

The real imperative in the Great Commission is to be found in the word that is translated "make disciples." The word translated "go" is really a participle with the force of an imperative. It literally means, "in your going about from place to place, make disciples." Each of us needs to get on with the wonderful opportunity of telling others about our Savior.

WEDNESDAY EVENING, NOVEMBER 19

Title: Self-Robbery

Text: "Your iniquities have turned away these things, and your sins have withholden good things from you" **(Jer. 5:25)**.

Introduction

On a Monday morning, a pastor entered the church. His office had been vandalized and his study had been ransacked. The drawers had been pulled out, and the contents emptied on the floor. The file cabinet had been pried open, and each file folder had been systematically opened and the contents permitted to drop. The thief was rewarded by finding an envelope that contained five dollars that had been sent to the church in the mail.

Someone commented, "If I were going to steal something, the last thing I would break into would be a church. I just can't think of anything much worse than robbing a church." Most of us would register a similar attitude. The church is sacred. It belongs to God and to his people. Its purpose is to serve and to help, and the great majority of us would not think of deliberately robbing or stealing from the church.

"Will a man rob God?" (Mal. 3:8). This question from the past should penetrate our hearts. And if we think about it for long, we will arrive at the conclusion that people have been guilty—persistently—of robbing God. From the time when Adam lived in the Garden of Eden, Adam robbed God of that place in his own heart that belonged to God. As Adam robbed God, he was also guilty of self-robbery. He robbed himself of innocence, peace of mind (security), fellowship with God, and the highest possible manhood. He brought upon himself a sinful nature.

I. We rob ourselves when we rob God of our time.

A. *Thomas Edison said, "Time is the most important thing in the world."*

B. *Providence plays no favorites in its distribution of time, for all of us share it in equal quantities.* God has given us twenty-four hours in every day and 8,760 hours in every year. If we live to the age of seventy, it means that God has trusted us with 613,200 hours.

C. *Life at its longest is brief and uncertain.*

   1. The psalmist said, "Teach us to number our days, that we may apply our hearts unto wisdom" (Ps. 90:12).

2. Jesus said, "I must work the works of him that sent me, while it is day: the night cometh, when no man can work" (John 9:4).

D. *It is a tragedy to waste time; once it is gone it can never be recaptured.*
1. Idleness.
2. Reading frivolous literature.
3. Peddling gossip.
4. Lying in bed longer than necessary.

E. *Stewardship of time.*
1. Begin the day with prayer and worship.
2. Plan wisely.
3. Work diligently.

F. *The Lord's Day.* A good steward will never get so busy that he does not have time to worship.
1. Worship.
2. Service.
3. Rest.

II. We rob ourselves when we rob God of our talents.

A. *God has a purpose for every life.*
1. We have native endowments. Each talent is a holy responsibility—a God-given opportunity.
2. We have opportunities to acquire necessary skills.
3. We must not bury our talents.

B. *We must render an account of our stewardship and talents.*
1. Talents increase with use.
2. Talents should be used every day.

C. *The road of faithfulness in little things leads to the city of larger opportunities.*

III. We rob ourselves when we rob God of our treasure and particularly when we rob him of our time.

The people of Malachi's day had lost consciousness of the abiding presence of God. They were troubled, perplexed, and insecure. We can be guilty of the same sin and expect the same consequences.

A. *We rob ourselves of a good conscience.*
B. *We rob ourselves of the joys of a great partnership.*
C. *We rob ourselves of rewards in heaven.*
D. *We rob ourselves of blessedness and happiness in this life.*
E. *We rob ourselves of the approval of God.*

Conclusion

It is time for us to wise up to the foolishness of self-robbery. God has far more to give us than we can possibly acquire by our efforts alone. God is eager to bestow these gifts upon you now. He waits upon your faith and your surrender to his will. The time for us to give ourselves unreservedly into the service of our God is now.

The Bible does not encourage us to make a decision tomorrow. It speaks to us in the present.

SUNDAY MORNING, NOVEMBER 23

Title: "What Shall I Render unto the LORD?"

Text: "What shall I render unto the LORD for all his benefits toward me?" **(Ps. 116:12)**.

Hymns: "We Gather Together," Baker

"Count Your Blessings," Oatman

"Make Me a Channel of Blessing," Smyth

Offertory Prayer: Heavenly Father, we thank you for your bountiful blessing upon our land and its people. We offer you the gratitude of our hearts and the praise of our lips. We bring to you our offerings, which represent the bounty of the land and the fruits of our efforts. Accept them and bless them in advancing your kingdom. Help us to give ourselves to you. In Jesus' name. Amen.

Introduction

How long has it been since you took time out to count your blessings? It would be a profitable experience for you to sit down with pencil and paper and list the ten blessings for which you are most grateful. Which blessing would you place at the top of the list?

If we would think more about what God means to us, there would be more of an attitude of gratitude within our hearts. The psalmist went to the trouble of enumerating the blessings of God. His list is found in Psalm 116:1–8. After listing the blessings of God, he discovered some of the reasons why he should have a great love for God.

I. The sincere question of a grateful heart.

After contemplating the many wonderful blessings of God, the psalmist gave voice to a question, "What shall I render unto the LORD for all his benefits toward me?" (Ps. 116:12).

    A. *This was a personal question.*

    B. *This was a proper question.*

        1. Gratitude required this question.

        2. Logic raised the question.

        3. Honor sought for an answer.

II. The response of a grateful heart.

    A. *"I will take the cup of salvation" (Ps. 116:13).* Evidently, the psalmist is here expressing the desire to fully experience and to fully become all that God

334

would have him to be. He determined to drink fully the cup of salvation and to let God's will be done perfectly in his life. God has purposes for us that are beyond our fondest dreams.

B. *"I will walk before the* LORD *in the land of the living" (Ps. 116:9).* The psalmist was aware of the abiding presence of God. He was aware that everything was open to God. This awareness was to strengthen him in the struggle against sin, and it was to inspire him in his struggle to do his best.

C. *"I will pay my vows unto the* LORD *now in the presence of all his people" (Ps. 116:14).* A vow was a promise made, as it were, in the presence of God.

   Many people hesitate to obligate themselves with a vow or a promise. Those who have accepted definite obligations in the kingdom of God are those who in some moment of holy awe and dedication made decisions or vows that lifted them above the level of the average and the mediocre into the realm of the extraordinary. The psalmist not only proved his love for God by his vows, but he lifted himself to higher achievement in doing so.

D. *"I will offer to thee the sacrifice of thanksgiving" (Ps. 116:17).* Because of his recognition of and response to the goodness of God, the psalmist was eager to live a life that would be an anthem of praise to God. His continuing attitude of gratitude was a sacrifice acceptable to God.

III. Love responds to love.

John the beloved apostle said, "We love him, because he first loved us" (1 John 4:19).

A. *The decisions of the psalmist were not made as a result of fear of divine wrath or punishment.*

B. *The psalmist was not motivated by a cold sense of responsibility and duty.*

C. *We see no evidence of an attempt to bargain with God or to purchase God's favor.*

D. *In these words of lavish praise there is no evidence at all that the psalmist was a braggart who was merely boasting of how good God had been to him.*

E. *Pure gratitude and thanksgiving welled up within his heart and overflowed.* Human love responded to divine love, and gratitude became one of the major motives that controlled his life.

Conclusion

May God give us eyes that can see how good God has been to us. May God grant to us hearts that can recognize the divine blessings that have come to us through human channels. May God help each of us to so live that we can be a blessing and a channel through which the blessings of God can reach others.

SUNDAY EVENING, NOVEMBER 23

Title: The Law of Self-Realization

Text: "For whosoever will save his life shall lose it; but whosoever shall lose his life for my sake and the gospel's, the same shall save it" **(Mark 8:35)**.

Introduction

There are certain great principles or natural laws by which we live and by which the universe functions. Biological laws must be observed. Mathematical laws affect us all. Natural laws are silently and constantly at work, with the law of gravity being a case in point. Governmental laws regulate our business and professional relationships.

Likewise, certain great spiritual principles or laws govern life and happiness.

A. *The law of retribution.* "Be not deceived; God is not mocked: for whatsoever a man soweth, that shall he also reap. For he that soweth to his flesh shall of the flesh reap corruption; but he that soweth to the Spirit shall of the Spirit reap life everlasting" (Gal. 6:7–8).

B. *The law of sin and death.* "For the wages of sin is death; but the gift of God is eternal life through Jesus Christ our Lord" (Rom. 6:23). This verse states three truths that affect us all:
1. The wages of sin is death.
2. Salvation is through Jesus Christ.
3. Salvation is the free gift of God.

C. *The law of self-preservation.* "For whosoever will save his life shall lose it; but whosoever shall lose his life for my sake and the gospel's, the same shall save it" (Mark 8:35).

In words that should shock us as if they were written in letters of fire, the Teacher from heaven tells us that the only way to find real life, rich life, full life is through self-sacrifice and self-renunciation to do the will of God and to improve the welfare of others.

The great majority of us think of real life in terms of ease, comfort, luxury, and security. We need to face the fact that one can have all of these in abundance and still not really be happy. Gadgets do not have the capacity to satisfy the human soul. There is a vast contrast between the popular ideas of today and the philosophy Jesus taught.

The law of the principle of self-realization through sacrificial giving is listed six times in the Gospels: twice in Matthew (10:39; 16:26), twice in Luke (9:24; 17:33), once in Mark (8:38), and once in John (12:25).

I. Jesus, our Lord and Savior, lived by this principle.

A. *Jesus asked his disciples to give up their occupation.* He had done so.

B. *Jesus asked his disciples to make family relations secondary to the work of the kingdom.* He had done so (Matt. 8:19–22; 10:35–39).

336

C. *Jesus asked his disciples to forsake safety for danger.* He had done so (Matt. 10:16–24). Jesus never tried to bribe people by the offer of an easy way. He did not offer them peace; he offered them glory. Jesus offered his disciples poverty, misunderstanding, criticism, and a cross. He came not to make life easy, but to make people great.

D. *Jesus became obedient unto death, even the death of the cross, that he might be our Savior (Phil. 2:7–8).* By so doing, he glorified the Father, provided salvation for people, and experienced the highest possible destiny for his life.

This principle of self-realization through sacrifice is not limited to religion. In the days of World War II when Sir Winston Churchill took over the leadership of the British Empire, all that he offered the people of England was "blood, sweat and tears." All of us will agree that as the people responded, this was England's finest hour.

In the field of athletics, the man whose primary purpose is to protect himself and to escape injury never becomes a star player, an outstanding quarterback, or the strong man on the line. Only the man who gives his very best achieves significant success.

II. History is full of noble examples of those who have lived by this principle.

A. *John Bunyan spent twelve years in a British prison rather than cease preaching the gospel as he understood it from his study of the Bible.* From his prison cell came a book we know as *The Pilgrim's Progress,* a story of such universal appeal that it has been translated into more than one hundred languages and still delights both old and young alike in all parts of the world, even though it was written more than three centuries ago.

B. *All of us are familiar with the inspiring life of Albert Schweitzer.* No doubt many considered him to be a fool when he went back to medical school for six years to prepare himself for a ministry in the jungles of Africa. Albert Schweitzer never regretted his decision.

C. *John the Baptist lived by this principle.* "He must increase, but I must decrease" (John 3:30).

D. *The priest and Levite did not believe in this law (Luke 10:30–36).*

E. *The rich young ruler did not accept this philosophy of life (Matt. 19:16–22).*

III. If we would live a rich, full, satisfying Christian life, we cannot ignore the principle that self-realization comes through self-sacrifice.

A. *If we would be true followers of Christ we must say no to self and yes to Christ.*

B. *We must say no to our natural love of ease and comfort.*

C. *We must say no to every course of action based on self-seeking and self-will.*

D. *We must say no to the instincts and the desires that prompt us to touch and taste and handle forbidden things.*

E. *We must spend ourselves lavishly in the service of our King and in the interest of those for whom our Savior died.*

F. *We must say yes to the will of God and to the call for self-giving love.*

Conclusion

The great historian Edward Gibbon tells the story of a monk named Telemachus. He first went into the desert to live alone in prayer, fasting, and meditation so as to save his soul. This did not satisfy. He realized that he must serve others if he would serve God.

After many months of travel, he finally came to Rome, which was officially Christian. He arrived while the city was celebrating the triumph of a great general over the Goths. The soldiers went to the churches and then to the arena for the gladiatorial games. Christians were no longer thrown to the lions, but those captured in war had to fight to the death to entertain the populace. Eighty thousand people were present. The gladiators addressed the emperor before the contest: "Hail, Caesar! We who are about to die salute you."

Telemachus was horrified. Men for whom Christ died were killing each other to amuse an audience that considered itself Christian. He leaped into the arena and stood between them. They stopped. "Let the games go on!" roared the crowd. They pushed the hermit aside. Again he came between them. An order was given. A sword rose and flashed, and Telemachus lay dead. A stunned silence filled the arena. A holy man had been killed. The games ended and never began again. The death of Telemachus was more useful to humankind than his life. Through the hermit's sacrifice of himself, he rendered a far greater service than was possible by living. In death he found the realization of a purpose that has greatly blessed the world.

WEDNESDAY EVENING, NOVEMBER 26

Title: Robbing God

Text: "Will a man rob God? Yet ye have robbed me. But ye say, Wherein have we robbed thee? In tithes and offerings" (**Mal. 3:8**).

Introduction

Some have been surprised that Jesus would be interested in what people contributed to the kingdom of God. Some have considered him to be too spiritual to be concerned about such material things. On at least one occasion while in the temple, Jesus sat near the treasury and was watching as the people made their contributions. He was intensely interested in what was taking place.

The writer of Hebrews declares that Jesus Christ is the same yesterday, today, and forever (Heb. 13:8). He is the Christ who was interested in the offerings of both the rich man and the poor widow, and he continues to be profoundly interested in our gifts. It has been said that money talks. Nowhere does it speak more loudly than when one is faced with an opportunity to make an investment in the kingdom of God.

1. Our gifts indicate our love for God.
2. Our gifts indicate our interest in the extension of God's kingdom.

3. Our gifts indicate where our treasure is.
4. Our gifts indicate whether God or mammon is first in life.
5. Our gifts indicate whether we are being obedient to God.
6. Our gifts indicate whether we are trying to be faithful stewards.
7. Our gifts indicate whether our heart is in the work of the Lord.

Evidently God watched the treasury during the days of Malachi, for through this prophet the people were indicted with robbing God, which is a rather serious charge. We must grant the possibility that such could be true today. If people robbed God then, it is possible they do so now.

I. The cause for this sin.

A. *Many are uninstructed.* Some could honestly plead innocence because they have not been taught the Bible plan of Christian stewardship.
B. *Many have been misinstructed.* Some have taught that God requires less of us under grace than he did of the Israelites, who sought to obey the law of Moses. The emphasis in the New Testament is on total dedication rather than giving a tithe as a symbol of one's acknowledgment of God's ownership. This would require more of us than did the Mosaic law.
C. *Many are guilty of robbing God because of little faith.* They have not been encouraged by someone's personal testimony to exercise faith in God's promises to the tither (Mal. 3:10). God is able and does give to the individual far more than we are able to give to his kingdom's work.
D. *Many are guilty of robbing God out of covetousness.* Webster defines covetousness: "to covet, to desire, to long for, especially something belonging to another."

    Jesus defines covetousness in terms of believing that real living is to be found in the possession of an abundance of things (Luke 12:15). To judge success in terms of material things, to live for the wealth of this world, is to be guilty of covetousness according to Jesus. Covetousness causes us to rob God.
E. *People's natural tendency to procrastinate has caused many to delay plans to become a tither.* All of us hesitate to do that which requires discipline and sacrifice.

II. The curse that accompanies this sin.

A. *The smile of God's approval is removed (Mal. 3:9).*
B. *It would be a low motive for a person to tithe solely with an expectation of financial blessings.* However, it is the testimony of many tithers that God has blessed them in their economic life because of their acknowledgment of God's ownership and their stewardship in tithing.

    The blessings of God are withheld from the nontither (Mal. 3:9). Someone has said that you can always buy more with nine dollars when God's blessings are upon those nine dollars than you can with ten dollars when God's blessings are withheld.

I have yet to see a faithful tither get into financial difficulty because of the practice. But I have seen many people in financial difficulty because of their neglect to let God come into their economic life.

C. *One misses the joy of partnership with God in his worldwide program of redemption that is made possible by the tithes and offerings of his people.*

III. The cure for this sin.

A. *Recognize and acknowledge God's ownership of everything (Ps. 24:1).*
B. *Recognize that stewardship is God's program for strengthening our faith.*
C. *Permit God to share with us the burden of his concern for a lost and needy world.*
D. *Recognize that all things material are temporary and that only that which is invested in the souls of people can go with us into eternity.*
E. *Tarry at the foot of the cross until devotion to Christ wells up within and overflows your heart.*
F. *Dedicate your all to the glory of God.*

Conclusion

If you are a consistent tither and God has blessed your heart in so doing, when the opportunity presents itself, bear your testimony for the glory of God and for the strengthening of the faith of someone who needs encouragement to trust God more fully in his or her economic life.

If you have not yet discovered the joy of being a tither, I challenge you to become a tither. If you do not have faith to make the full decision, then take a step in the right direction, and begin by increasing your regular contribution today.

SUNDAY MORNING, NOVEMBER 30

Title: Truth That Is Stranger Than Fiction

Text: "Heal the sick, cleanse the lepers, raise the dead, cast out devils: freely ye have received, freely give" (**Matt. 10:8**).

Hymns: "Love Divine, All Loves Excelling," Wesley

"Something for Thee," Phelps

"All Things Are Thine," Wittier

Offertory Prayer: Our Father, help us to see how richly and abundantly you have bestowed your blessings upon us. Help us to recognize the presence of your loving purpose in all of the events and gifts that you bring into our lives. Today we bring the fruit of our labors and place them on the altar as an act of worship and adoration. We express the gratitude of our hearts and at the same time share the good news of your love with a lost and needy world. Accept our tithes and offerings and bless them to the salvation of the unsaved in this community and to the uttermost parts of the earth. In Jesus' name. Amen.

Introduction

Truth is often much stranger than fiction. This is particularly true with reference to the love of God for sinners. The blessings God freely offers to us seem too good to be true. People find it difficult to believe that God loves them and that he has rich and wonderful gifts to bestow upon them freely. In fact, people often stumble over this truth to the extent that they deny God the privilege of truly demonstrating his love and bestowing the gifts of his divine heart upon them.

We live in a grasping, greedy, materialistic, self-centered society that believes that the highest possible human happiness is to be found in the acquiring and accumulating of those things that can be assigned a monetary value. Once this way of life has been accepted as normal, it is most difficult to believe that God is any different from man. Because people are selfish and greedy and stingy, it is easy to assume that God must have the same nature. It becomes almost impossible to think of God in terms of pure love whose greatest delight is found in the lavish giving of that which is truly beneficial to those who trust him. Most people think of God in terms of his wanting something from them or in terms of his wanting to prevent them from achieving or experiencing something upon which they have set their heart.

Even those who profess to be followers of Jesus Christ find it difficult to believe that God is really a God of grace who freely bestows the gift of salvation upon those who come to him by faith, receiving Jesus Christ as the Lord of life (Eph. 2:8–9). This is truth that is stranger than fiction. It seems just too good to be true.

I. God is a giver.

God never deals with people on the basis of their financial worth or merit. Salvation is not dependent on what a person does or how good he or she is. God's salvation and mercy come to us because of his love and grace. Because he loves us, he gives.

The great God of heaven revealed and demonstrated the greatness of his love for us in the gift of his Son, Jesus Christ, on the cross of Calvary. "He that spared not his own Son, but delivered him up for us all, how shall he not with him also freely give us all things?" (Rom. 8:32).

II. Freely ye have received.

Just what have we received so freely from God? In the market of the world, a price must be paid for everything of value. It is surprising to discover that God does not sit behind a counter offering various blessings for sale. He is the God of grace and mercy. He bestows the blessings and joys of heaven freely.

Our Savior charged nothing for what he did. He came from heaven freely. He went about doing good freely. He healed the sick. He gave sight to the blind. He made the deaf hear. He made the lame whole. He brought hope and cheer to the distressed. All of these things he did without a price tag attached.

341

Christ Jesus, the Lamb of God, went to the cross and suffered agony of soul and body that he might put away our sin and bring us to God freely. He tasted the awfulness of a death for sin for us. On the first Easter morn, he came forth triumphant over death and the grave to demonstrate the reality of the eternal life God has promised to those who trust him. He did this freely.

By the grace of God, the forgiveness of sin is free. Forgiveness cannot be purchased. The removal of guilt cannot be merited. Forgiveness is free, full, and forever to those who come to Jesus Christ in genuine repentance and sincere faith.

Eternal life, a present possession that will continue for ages without end, is a free gift of God (Rom. 6:23). It cannot be bought. It cannot be stolen. It cannot be merited. The only way to receive it is as a gift of God.

The peace of God is a gift from God to those who receive Christ as the Lord of life.

The gift of the power of the Holy Spirit is one of the good gifts of the heavenly Father to those who live a life of obedience (Acts 5:32).

The heavenly home at the end of the road of this life is the free gift of the Carpenter of Galilee who has gone to prepare a place for those who love and trust him. There will be no real estate sales in heaven. The mansions of the Father are free to his children.

III. Freely give.

The only proper response to the gracious and giving activity of God is for his children to follow the divine example. At no place are our selfishness and lack of faith revealed so clearly as at the time when we have an opportunity to be a giver. The overwhelming majority of us do not subscribe to the basic philosophy of Jesus who said, "It is more blessed to give than to receive" (Acts 20:35).

We normally treat this verse as if it were a gimmick to get at our pocketbook. Our pocketbook protection instinct causes us to miss the point completely. The Savior was not talking about an offering plate. He was talking about a total way of life. He was saying that while the receiver may experience a joy, a satisfaction, and a thrill in receiving, the person who lives to be a giver will have even more adventure, more joy, and more satisfaction. This principle works in the secular realm as well as in the spiritual. Our Savior was not using double-talk to deceive people. He was speaking from personal experience. He came from heaven to be a giver. He lived and labored to be a giver. He died on the cross and arose from the dead, all for the purpose of giving because of the love in the heart of God.

The happiest people on earth are not necessarily those who possess the most. The people who are truly happy are those who interpret success not in terms of what they can get but in terms of service and help they are able to give. You can never find happiness by searching for it. It will always elude the seeker. Happiness comes to those who give themselves lavishly to a cause bigger than themselves.

Conclusion

Freely ye have received, freely give. Give God your heart, your mind, your time, and your energy. Give yourself in helpful service to others. It is only through giving that you will enjoy real living. Is this a truth that is stranger than fiction? Try it and see.

> *Give as you would if an angel*
> *Awaited your gift at the door.*
> *Give as you would if tomorrow*
> *Found you where giving was o'er.*
> *Give as you would to the Master*
> *If you met His loving look.*
> *Give as you would of your substance*
> *If His hand the offering took.*
> *—Author unknown*

SUNDAY EVENING, NOVEMBER 30

Title: "In Every Thing Give Thanks"

Text: "In every thing give thanks: for this is the will of God in Christ Jesus concerning you" (**1 Thess. 5:18**).

Introduction

Many people find it difficult to be grateful to God for his many blessings in this time of insecurity. We need to realize that every age has been an age of insecurity. The only thing different about this age is that people have the power to leave civilization in ruins more speedily and totally than ever could be dreamed of before. Men and women have always been vulnerable beings exposed to all kinds of dangers and preserved only by the providence and mercies of God.

If we take counsel of our fears in this time of insecurity, we shall be overcome with fright. Instead, we should fix our minds on the blessings and gifts of the great and good God who still sits on the throne of the universe.

The apostle Paul urged Christians to maintain an attitude of gratitude. He exhorts us, "In every thing give thanks: for this is the will of God in Christ Jesus concerning you" (1 Thess. 5:18).

He instructs us to be grateful as we pray. "Let your moderation be known unto all men. The Lord is at hand. Be careful for nothing; but in every thing by prayer and supplication with thanksgiving let your requests be made known unto God. And the peace of God, which passeth all understanding, shall keep your hearts and minds through Jesus Christ" (Phil. 4:5–7).

I. "Thanks be unto God for his unspeakable gift" (2 Cor. 9:15).

The greatness of God's gift of salvation through Jesus Christ was indescribably wonderful.

 A. *Indescribably wonderful is the love that thought it.* Our salvation was born in the heart of a loving God.

 B. *Indescribably wonderful is the love that brought it.* The baby born in Bethlehem's stable came to be our Savior.

 C. *Indescribably wonderful is the love that wrought it upon the cross.* "Christ died for our sins" (1 Cor. 15:3).

II. "Now thanks be unto God, which always causes us to triumph in Christ" (2 Cor. 2:14).

Through Jesus Christ, God is at work in all things to bring out every possible good for those who love him, and look to him for guidance and help (Rom. 8:28).

 A. *He causes us to triumph in our days of decision.*

 B. *He causes us to triumph in hours of difficulty.*

 C. *He causes us to triumph even in the defeats of life.*

III. "But thanks be to God, which put the same earnest care into the heart of Titus for you" (2 Cor. 8:16).

Paul was always grateful for his fellow laborers and helpers in kingdom service. He was especially grateful for Titus who assumed a responsibility of spiritual guardianship for many new converts.

 A. *We should be grateful to God for parents who have served as spiritual guardians and guides.*

 B. *We should be grateful to God for teachers who have stimulated us both by their example and by their efforts to lead us to a greater grasp of the truth.*

 C. *We should be grateful to God for Christian friends who have led us closer to God.*

IV. "But thanks be to God, which giveth us the victory through our Lord Jesus Christ" (1 Cor. 15:57).

This is one of Paul's climactic statements as he concludes this treatise on the resurrection of Christ and the final resurrection of the saints. Through Jesus Christ we can be confident of ultimate victory.

 A. *Victory in sickness and in suffering.*

 B. *Victory over sin.*

 C. *Victory over death.*

 D. *Victory over the grave.*

 E. *Victory throughout eternity in the heavenly home of God.*

Conclusion

There is a very close kinship between the word *think* and the word *thank*. If we would consistently spend some time meditating on the blessings of God to us through Jesus Christ, we would make it possible for the beautiful flower of gratitude to grow in the garden of our hearts. We would then have both the faith and the grace that would make it possible to thank God in everything.

DECEMBER

■ Sunday Morning and Evening Services

A consideration of the messianic titles ascribed by Isaiah to the coming Savior can be both informative and inspirational. Such a series can do much to create an attitude of reverent awe and worship during this season.

■ Wednesday Evenings

The Wednesday evening services also are centered in the coming of the Christ and the manner in which different individuals and groups responded to him.

WEDNESDAY EVENING, DECEMBER 3

Title: The Reception of Christ

Text: "He came unto his own, and his own received him not" (**John 1:11**).

Introduction

Jesus has been treated many different ways by people. The variety of ways in which different people have received and treated Jesus Christ is noteworthy.

I. The wise men received him as "the King of the Jews."

A. *They sought him.*
B. *They worshiped him.*
C. *They presented gifts to him.*

II. Herod treated him as a usurper, a rival, a disturber.

"Then Herod, when he saw that he was mocked of the wise men, was exceeding wroth, and sent forth, and slew all the children that were in Bethlehem, and in all the coasts thereof, from two years old and under, according to the time which he had diligently inquired of the wise men. Then was fulfilled that which was spoken by Jeremiah the prophet, saying, In Rama was there a voice heard, lamentation, and weeping, and great mourning, Rachel weeping for her children, and would not be comforted, because they are not" (Matt. 2:16–18).

A. *The wicked have always resented the Savior's presence.*
B. *He is still one who would usurp the power of sin and enthrone himself upon the throne of our heart.*

III. Nicodemus received him as a teacher sent from God (John 3:2).

A. *It is still the verdict of the century, "Never man spake like this man" (John 7:46).*

B. *Christ claimed to be heaven's anointed Teacher and promised both safety and stability to the lives of those who put into practice his teachings (Matt. 7:24–29).*

IV. Some received him as a prophet (Matt. 16:14).

A. *Some thought he was John the Baptist.*

B. *Some thought he was Elijah.*

C. *Others thought he was Jeremiah.*

V. Some received him as "The Lamb of God, which taketh away the sin of the world" (John 1:29).

Following the resurrection, Thomas was to recognize him as "my Lord and my God" (John 20:28).

Conclusion

"He came unto his own, and his own received him not" (John 1:11). Is this description of the Jewish people a description of your response to Jesus Christ? During this Christmas season, let each of us receive him gladly and fully as the Lord of life and as the infallible guide to the abundant life.

SUNDAY MORNING, DECEMBER 7

Title: God's Greatest Gift

Text: "For unto us a child is born, unto us a son is given" **(Isa. 9:6)**.

Hymns: "Jesus Shall Reign Where'er the Sun," Watts

"Angels from the Realms of Glory," Montgomery

"Glory to His Name," Hoffman

Offertory Prayer: Our Father and our God, you who are the author and giver of every good and precious gift, to you we would give thanks for your unspeakable gift to us, even Jesus Christ, your Son and our Savior. Today we give ourselves and our substance in grateful worship to you. Bless these gifts to the honor and glory of your name. Amen.

Introduction

God's greatest gift to people is often overlooked at Christmastime. We concentrate our attention on the gifts the good and gracious heavenly Father sends our way. The prophet foretold the giving of God's greatest gift—his only begotten Son (Isa. 9:6).

It is a tragedy of tragedies that so few have properly related themselves to the Christ who was born in Bethlehem and laid in a manger. The wise men came requesting: "Where is he that is born king of the Jews?" (Matt. 2:2). We should be asking: "Who is he? What do you think of Christ?"

Is Jesus Christ merely a mythical or legendary figure? Is Christ simply the most notable figure on the pages of history? His birthday gave the world a new era dividing the past from the future at a focal point. His spirit has given the world its most immortal paintings. His love has inspired the world's masterpieces of art, sculpture, and music. His influence has inspired earth's greatest philanthropies. More books have been written about him than have been written about all of the kings who have ruled from earthly thrones.

Who is this Son whom God has given?

I. God has given unto us a supernatural Son.

A. *Jesus was supernaturally conceived and born of the Virgin Mary.*

B. *Christianity is built and based on a supernatural Christ.* You can have Buddhism without Buddha and Confucianism without Confucius, but you can't have Christianity without Christ. Christianity is more than a creed or code. It is a fellowship with a risen and living Christ.

Those who would reject the virgin birth, explain away Christ's miracles, and deny his resurrection have only a pale, powerless, poor anemic human Christ who has no power with which to save a sinful race.

II. God has given unto us a sinless Son. Christ was "in all points tempted like as we are, yet without sin" (Heb. 4:15).

A. *Christ refrained from all willful transgression.*

B. *He was the very essence of personal purity.*

C. *The verdict of the Roman governor Pilate was "I, having examined him before you, have found no fault in this man touching those things whereof ye accuse him" (Luke 23:14).*

At the time of Jesus' baptism, a voice came from heaven expressing the complete, divine approval of Christ (Matt. 3:17). There was a second expression of divine approval at the time of the transfiguration (Matt. 17:5). The resurrection of Christ was a public demonstration of the divine acceptance of his substitutionary death on the cross.

III. God has given us a Son who suffered as our substitute.

A. *The prophet Isaiah foretold the substitutionary death of the suffering servant of God (Isa. 53:5–6).*

B. *The angel told Joseph that the unborn child of Mary was divine and that he would be the Savior of his people (Matt. 1:21).*

C. *When John the Baptist introduced Jesus to his disciples, he called him the one who would bear the sin of the world (John 1:29).*

D. *Jesus defined his objective for coming into the world in terms of giving his life as a ransom for many (Mark 10:45).*

E. *Jesus described himself as the Good Shepherd who lays down his life voluntarily for his sheep (John 10:11).*
F. *Paul declared that while we were still rebel sinners against God, God loved us and Christ died for us (Rom. 5:6).*
G. *The sinless one, by a divine decree, was made to be sin for us that he might suffer in our place and we might be saved from the penalty of sin (2 Cor. 5:21).*
H. *He who was rich beyond imagination became a pauper that we, through his poverty, might be made indescribably rich (2 Cor. 8:9).*
I. *God's greatest gift, his sinless Son, suffered for us sinners that he might return us to God (1 Peter 3:18).*

IV. God has given us a Son who is an all-sufficient Savior.

A. *He takes care of the past by the pardon of every sin and the forgiveness of every transgression.*
B. *He takes care of the present by his abiding presence.*
  1. He is the mind of God speaking out to man.
  2. He is the voice of God calling out to man.
  3. He is the heart of God throbbing out to man.
  4. He is the hand of God reaching out to man.
  5. He is the Savior who can meet the deepest needs of the human soul.
C. *He takes care of the future by providing a home at the end of the road.*

Conclusion

Have you received the royal Guest into your heart? It is time to let him in. Do not ignore him or shut him out. Accept God's greatest gift by receiving his Son as the Lord of your heart and life.

SUNDAY EVENING, DECEMBER 7

Title: "His Name Shall Be Called Wonderful"
Text: "And his name shall be called Wonderful" **(Isa. 9:6)**.

Introduction

A study of the messianic titles bestowed on the wonderful Savior by the prophet Isaiah can help us enter the Christmas season with reverence and awe for Christ. Christmas should cause us to focus our attention on Christ and on God's great redemption of us through him. The names that were given to him can help us to understand God's gracious and loving purposes for us.

Names mean little to us. We use them merely as labels to identify one person in contrast to another. In the land and time of our Savior, this was not the case. Names were significant. The name given to a child might be an expression of gratitude, the declaration of a hope or dream, or even a prayer on behalf of the parents. Occasionally parents would give to their children a name of prophetic significance. Some names were deeply religious in nature. The name of a city, a mountain, a village, or a home was often an indication of some spiritual experience that the individual or the people had had with God.

The names and titles given to God contain a revelation of his person, his character, and his purposes toward humankind. The names by which God chose to make himself known to his people are part of the self-revelation by which, "at sundry times and in divers manners," he led his people into the knowledge of himself. The divine names reflect rays of heavenly truth that should be set in our spiritual firmament to burn forever and forever.

I. Wonder of Wonders.

A Celtic proverb describes our Savior as a "Wonder of Wonders and every wonder is true." God has done many wonderful things for us in and through Jesus Christ. We need to have our eyes opened to recognize all that God has done and proposes to do for us through our wonderful Savior.

   A. *He is wonderful in his grace as well as in his greatness.* He came on a mission of grace to meet the deepest needs in the hearts and lives of men and women. With great grace he continues to work wonders in the lives of those who trust him.

   B. *He is wonderful in his mercy as well as in his majesty.* He who was sinless came to bring mercy and forgiveness into the hearts and lives of people who were alienated from God. With great majesty he marched toward the cross and the tomb, and with divine power he conquered death and the grave to be our Savior.

   C. *He is wonderful in his patience as well as in his power.* With infinite patience he works in the hearts and lives of those who trust him to produce miracles of grace. The creative, redeeming power of God was upon him and continues to flow from him into the hearts of those who respond to his love. A poet came face-to-face with this wonderful Christ and responded in the following manner:

   > *I stand amazed in the presence*
   > *Of Jesus the Nazarene.*
   > *And wonder how He could love me,*
   > *A sinner, condemned, unclean.*
   > *How marvelous! how wonderful!*
   > *And my song shall ever be:*
   > *How marvelous! How wonderful!*
   > *Is my Saviour's love for me!*
   > —*Charles H. Gabriel*

II. A wonderful Savior.

   A. *He is wonderful because of who he is.* Who is this Jesus Christ whose birth we celebrate in December? Is he to be thought of only as the best man who

350

ever lived on earth? He was. Are we to think of him only as a remarkable teacher who taught with authority as no one had ever taught before? He did. The Scriptures teach us that Jesus Christ was uniquely different from all other people.

1. Jesus Christ was the God-man. He was the eternal God clothed in human flesh (John 1:1; 14:9). He came to reveal the nature and character of God to man.

2. Jesus Christ was the eternal God who came to be our Savior (Phil. 2:5–11). He did not begin to be when he was born and laid in Bethlehem's manger. This was but the beginning of the visible manifestation of the eternal God who clothed himself in human flesh for the suffering death on the cross. Paul speaks of this "self-emptying" of the Savior who laid aside his divine glory in order that he might become incarnate.

    Because of his sacrificial, substitutionary death on the cross, Christ has been exalted to the right hand of God and should be the object of our worship and adoration (Phil. 2:9–11).

B. *He is wonderful because of what he said.* Through the centuries some people have gained immortality through the words that fell from their lips. Patrick Henry will always be known for saying, "Give me liberty or give me death." John F. Kennedy's words "Ask not what your country can do for you; ask what you can do for your country" will be quoted as long as free people live. And Martin Luther King will be known for "I have a dream."

    Because the words that fell from Christ's lips contained divine truth concerning eternity, they continue to live to bless the lives of people. His message is as relevant now as it was when first spoken.

C. *He is wonderful because of what he did.* The Scriptures tell us that he went about doing good. The unique ministry he performed was that relating to his substitutionary death on the cross. The prophets had foretold how he would deal with human sin (Isa. 53:5–6). After his resurrection the fact that "Christ died for our sins" was at the very heart of the gospel of the early church.

> *He took my sins and my sorrows,*
> *He made them His very own;*
> *He bore the burden to Calv'ry*
> *And suffered and died alone.*
>
> *—Charles H. Gabriel*

D. *He is wonderful because of what he can do for you.* All of us are indebted to others who have and who will continue to render valuable service to us. Most of us owe a debt of gratitude to former teachers, our family physician, our banker, or others who might have assisted us in a time of need. To Jesus Christ we owe our greatest debt of gratitude.

1. He can forgive your every sin and cleanse you from all unrighteousness.

2. He can bestow upon you the wonderful gift of eternal life.

3. He can provide you with guidance and help as you face the future.

III. Is he wonderful to you?

A. *This wonderful Savior who is completely God and perfectly man wants to bring the very life of God into your life if you will let him (John 10:10; cf. 1:11–12).*

B. *This wonderful Christ would continue his ministry of mercy in you and through you if you are willing.* Annie B. Russell sought to describe the wonderful Jesus.

> *There is never a day so dreary,*
> *There is never a night so long,*
> *But the soul that is trusting Jesus*
> *Will somewhere find a song.*
> *There is never a cross so heavy,*
> *There is never a weight of woe,*
> *But that Jesus will help to carry*
> *Because He loveth so.*
> *There is never a care or burden,*
> *There is never a grief or loss,*
> *But that Jesus in love will lighten*
> *When carried to the cross.*
> *There is never a guilty sinner,*
> *There is never a wandering one,*
> *But that God can in mercy pardon*
> *Through Jesus Christ, His Son.*

Conclusion

Because Jesus is a wonderful Savior—wonderful in his person, in his purpose, in his presence, and in his power—you would be wise to trust him and yield your heart and life to him.

WEDNESDAY EVENING, DECEMBER 10

Title: Gifts for the King

Text: "And when they were come into the house, they saw the young child with Mary his mother, and fell down, and worshipped him: and when they had opened their treasures, they presented unto him gifts: gold, and frankincense, and myrrh" (**Matt. 2:11**).

Introduction

Many think of Christmas in terms of what they are going to receive. Children are taught from infancy to look forward to Christmas, for at that time many presents will be coming their way. Many adults are inclined also to think in these terms, or they may dread having to purchase gifts.

Only a very few really have and enjoy the true spirit of Christmas in the spirit of unselfish, devoted giving. Perhaps more than at any other time of the year, people permit a spirit of sympathy to overflow their hearts, which leads to unselfish giving.

People all over the world will receive gifts sent to them by loved ones, and they can enjoy these tokens of love insofar as they themselves have been faithful in giving. Billions of dollars are spent for presents every year.

Did you ever wonder where and when the giving of Christmas gifts originated? Let's go back to the first Christmas and there observe how it was celebrated.

I. God gave his Son.

    A. *Matthew 1:21: "And thou shalt call his name JESUS, for he shall save his people from their sins."*

    B. *Luke 2:10–11: "And the angel said unto them, Fear not: for, behold, I bring you good tidings of great joy, which shall be to all people. For unto you is born this day in the city of David a Saviour, which is Christ the Lord."*

    C. *John 3:16: "For God so loved the world, that he gave his only begotten Son, that whosoever believeth in him should not perish, but have everlasting life."*

    D. *2 Corinthians 9:6: "Thanks be unto God for his unspeakable gift."*

    E. *Romans 6:23: "The gift of God is eternal life."*

II. The angels gave a song.

"And suddenly there was with the angel a multitude of the heavenly host praising God, and saying, Glory to God in the highest, and on earth peace, good will toward men" (Luke 1:13–14).

    A. *They could not give a Savior.*

    B. *They could not give silver or gold.*

    C. *They could not tell of his saving power from personal experience.*

    D. *They could sing a song.*

        1. They sang to the glory of God and of goodwill among those upon whom God's favor rests.

        2. We are never too poor to sing.

Charles Wesley prayed:

> *O for a thousand tongues to sing*
> *My great Redeemer's praise,*
> *The glories of my God and King,*
> *The triumphs of His Grace!*

Francis H. Rowley vowed:

> *I will sing the wondrous story*
> *Of the Christ who died for me.*
> *How He left His home in glory,*
> *For the cross of Calvary.*

Yes, I'll sing the wondrous story
Of the Christ who died for me,
Sing it with the saints in glory,
Gather'd by the crystal sea.

III. The shepherds gave a story.

"And when they had seen it, they made known abroad the saying which was told them concerning this child" (Luke 2:17).

A. *They received the witness.*
B. *They believed the testimony.*
C. *They proclaimed the good news abroad.*
D. *We can testify by our lives and with our lips of the "wondrous works of God."*

IV. The wise men gave of their substance.

"And when they had opened their treasures, they presented unto him gifts: gold, and frankincense, and myrrh" (Matt. 2:11).

A. *They sought the Savior.*
B. *They worshiped the Savior.*
C. *They indicated their devotion and reverence in the giving of costly gifts — the best that could be obtained.* Howard B. Grose wrote lyrics urging us to do the same.

Give of your best to the master,
Give Him first place in your heart;
Give Him first place in your service,
Consecrate, ev'ry part.
Give, and to you shall be given,
God His beloved Son gave;
Gratefully seeking to serve Him,
Give Him the best that you have.

V. Mary gave submission.

"And Mary said, Behold the handmaid of the Lord; be it unto me according to thy word" (Luke 1:38).

A. *This was a giving of more than a song, a story, or of substance.*
B. *Mary gave her life, her soul, her complete self.*
C. *She faced misunderstanding, criticism, and possible death.* She put her faith in God.

VI. The Bethlehemites gave a stable.

"And she brought forth her firstborn son, and wrapped him in swaddling clothes, and laid him in a manger; because there was no room for them in the inn" (Luke 2:7).

A. *Mary gave her all; the Bethlehemites gave a stall.* What a contrast!

B. *There was no room for the Christ child.*

Conclusion

What are you going to give Christ today? A song? You can. A testimony? You may. A gift? You should. A life? You ought. Charles C. Luther asks a probing question:

> *Must I go, and empty-handed,*
> *Thus my dear Redeemer meet?*
> *Not one day of service give Him,*
> *Lay no trophy at His feet?*
> *Not at death I shrink nor falter,*
> *For my Saviour saves me now;*
> *But to meet Him empty-handed,*
> *Thought of that now clouds my brow.*

SUNDAY MORNING, DECEMBER 14

Title: "His Name Shall Be Called Counselor"

Text: "His name shall be called ... Counselor" **(Isa. 9:6)**.

Hymns: "Angels We Have Heard on High," Old French Carol

"The First Noel," Old English Carol

"O Come, All Ye Faithful," Wade

Offertory Prayer: Holy Father, with reverent awe we approach your throne of grace to offer our gifts as a token of our love and gratitude for your grace and mercy. Multiply these tithes and offerings as Christ multiplied the loaves and fishes to the end that suffering might be relieved and that the unsaved might come to know the Christ as Lord and Master. Help each of us to dedicate our all to you through Jesus Christ our Lord. Amen.

Introduction

Throughout history the achievements and outstanding traits of character of great people have been inscribed on statues and memorial monuments in order that others may know what they have accomplished. By so doing we preserve the memory of the race.

The unique thing about the messianic titles of the Savior in the book of Isaiah is that these character traits and achievements were inscribed on the prophetic parchment seven hundred years before his birth.

North of Beirut, Lebanon, there is a site called Dog River. Looking down on the modern highway and railroad that skirt its base stands an ancient stone mountain whose face is adorned with figures of old world rulers whose military achievements are set forth in a series of panel inscriptions hewn some five or six inches in depth and averaging about seven feet in height and three feet in breadth. In this international hall of fame, great conquerors of the ancient world meet to tell of exploits that resulted in the enslavement of millions and to boast of conquests that included practically all of the biblical world. Among the earliest of these inscriptions is that of the great Egyptian Pharaoh Rameses II who is represented as offering a sacrifice to the god Amon-Ra in commemoration of Syrian conquests in 1240 BC.

Six hundred years later (670 BC) Esarhaddon, returning from an invasion of Egypt, recorded on a panel next to that of Rameses II, his victory over Tirhakah, Ethiopian ruler of Egypt. There are also inscriptions made by Sennacherib, Tiglath-pileser III, and Shalmanaser III. In later days Greeks, Romans, Arabs, and Crusaders made theirs.

The words of the text containing the prophetic inscription set forth the titles and ministry of the Christ seven hundred years before his birth. He was the fulfillment of the prophecy. This inscription describes him as a wonderful counselor or "a wonder of a counselor."

Our world is groping for counsel. On an international level, the finest brains of the world are brought together in the United Nations to attempt to work out the problems that face the nations of the world.

On the national level, the president of our country seeks the counsel of the most capable advisers.

On a personal level, we seek financial counsel from our banker, investment broker, or some trusted business friend. If we are in need of legal counsel, we seek out a good lawyer. Often marriage counsel is sought from a pastor. Conscientious parents seek educational counsel from their children's teachers.

We all have times when we stand in need of a trusted counselor who can listen to our problems and sympathize with our pain and serve as a sounding board for our ideas.

Seven hundred years before Christ's miraculous birth, the prophet declared that a Savior would come to serve as a counselor.

I. Christ is competent to be your Counselor.

He is competent because of who he is, what he has done, and what resources of wisdom and knowledge are in him.

A. *He is a compassionate counselor.*

B. *He is a consistent counselor.*

C. *He is a confidential counselor.* To him we can confess our sins in the confidence that he will forgive us and that our confidence in him will never be betrayed.

II. Christ is constantly present to be your Counselor.

He has promised, "Lo, I am with you alway" (Matt. 28:20). He has also promised, "Where two or three are gathered together in my name, there am I in the midst of them" (Matt. 18:20). Ours is a living Savior who comes to dwell in the heart of the believer in the person of the Holy Spirit (John 14:16–18).

   A. *He will counsel you by means of the Scriptures you memorize and hide away in your heart.*
   B. *He will counsel you by means of his church, which is his body in the world.*
   C. *He will provide you with counsel through sermons you hear.*
   D. *He will counsel you by means of spiritual songs you listen to.*
   E. *He offers you counsel in the quietness of the closet of prayer if you will listen.*
   F. *He will counsel you through great books if you will read.*
   G. *He will counsel you through words spoken by good and great Christians if you will develop their friendship.*
   H. *He will counsel you through open and closed doors of opportunity.*

III. The character of his wonderful counsel.

   A. *He will search for and find that which is commendable in your life.* He did this as he wrote to the seven churches of Asia Minor.
   B. *He will discover and denounce that which is destructive in your life.* When we go to a physician for a physical examination, we expect him to discover anything that is contrary or harmful to our physical well-being. Unless he does, it would be difficult to take steps to prevent the spread of infection. The spiritual physician will at times rebuke and warn us of that which is dangerous in our moral and spiritual makeup.
   C. *He will envision that which is possible and challenge us to a greater faith and to a higher achievement.* Jesus always sees the best in others.

IV. The consequences of his counsel.

   A. *His counsel will provide us with invaluable assistance in our quest for consistent Christian conduct.*
   B. *By means of his counsel, our chances of a complete conformity to the mind and spirit of Christ will be much more likely.*
   C. *Constant preparedness for all eventualities in life can be our experience as day by day we follow the counsel of our living Savior.*

Conclusion

The wonderful Counselor counsels the weary and worn, "Come unto me, all ye that labour and are heavy laden, and I will give you rest. Take my yoke upon you, and learn of me; for I am meek and lowly of heart: and ye shall find rest unto your souls. For my yoke is easy and my burden is light" (Matt. 11:28–30).

SUNDAY EVENING, DECEMBER 14

Title: "His Name Shall Be Called the Mighty God"

Text: "His name shall be called ... The mighty God" **(Isa. 9:6)**.

Introduction

With prophetic insight the prophet looked forward seven hundred years to the birth, life, death, and resurrection of the Savior and wrote a tribute of praise to him. It is remarkable, indeed, to see how Christ fulfilled that which the prophet had foretold by divine inspiration.

It was a miracle of miracles and a wonder of wonders that God chose to become a baby. The "Ancient of Days" became the "Infant of Days." The eternal one entered time. God gave his only beloved, sinless Son to suffer for us (John 3:16).

The names ascribed to the Messiah represent spiritual significance and application. The Messiah was and is wonderful because of who he is, because of what he said, because of what he did, and because of what he can do. He is a wonder of a Counselor because he is divinely competent, constantly present, compassionate, and consistent.

In every age people have stood in awe of those who possess great power or authority. This has been true in every area of life. We speak of people as being powerful in finance or politics or science. We may have failed to recognize the stature and authority of our Savior whom the prophet described as "The mighty God."

I. The mighty God is the need of the hour.

A. *We need to have faith in a great Savior who has the ability to accomplish for us a complete redemption.*

B. *We need a Savior who can command the full allegiance of both intellect and emotions, and before whose authority we can gladly bow.*

C. *The modern Christian could be blessed by an experience similar to that of Isaiah, revealing to the eye of his soul the sovereign holiness and majestic authority of the God of Israel.* We must study Revelation where the twenty-four elders fall down before the one who sits on the throne and say in unison, "Thou art worthy, O Lord, to receive glory and honour, and power: for thou hast created all things, and for thy pleasure they are and were created" (Rev. 4:11).

II. Our Savior is the mighty God.

A. *He overcame Satan in the wilderness temptation experience.* He stood invulnerable against all of the shafts of Satan.

B. *He overcame the world by a sinless life.*

C. *He overcame the flesh in the Garden of Gethsemane.*

D. *He overcame sin on the cross.*

E. *He overcame death and the grave in the resurrection.*

358

III. His name: The mighty God.

    A. *His is an exalted name (Phil. 2:9– 10)*. Charles Lamb said, "If Shakespeare were to come into this room, we would rise to do him honor. If Christ were to enter this room, we would bow before him in worship."

    B. *His is a saving name (Acts 4:12)*.

        1. "She shall bring forth a son, and thou shalt call his name Jesus: for he shall save his people from their sins" (Matt. 1:21).

        2. "He came unto his own, and his own received him not. But as many as received him, to them gave he power to become the sons of God, even to them that believe on his name" (John 1:11– 12).

        3. "These are written, that ye might believe that Jesus is the Christ, the Son of God; and that believing ye might have life through his name" (John 20:31).

His name stands for his person, his power, and his redeeming activity. He bore our sins and our sorrows on the cross. He provides for us a perfect righteousness. He can convert the hardest heart. He can provide grace for the weakest sinner.

He will one day raise the dead, judge the world, and destroy sin. He will give his saints the privilege of entering the eternal home of God.

Conclusion

Come and put your trust in Jesus Christ, the mighty God, the wonderful Savior, the competent Counselor. Let him help you with all of your troubles and needs. Take to him your griefs, your failures, and your troubles, and he will give you comfort and strength. He is able and eager to save all who are willing to come to God by him.

WEDNESDAY EVENING, DECEMBER 17

Title: The Song of the Angels

Text: "Glory to God in the highest, and on earth peace, good will toward men" **(Luke 2:14)**.

Introduction

Songs fill the air at Christmastime. Christmas carols are heard everywhere. Perhaps the pattern for this was set by the angelic hosts who announced the birth of the Christ child. [Select a corresponding hymn or chorus to sing with each part of the outline.]

I. An angel announced to Joseph the forthcoming birth of the Savior (Matt. 1:18–21).

II. An angel announced the Savior's arrival to the shepherds (Luke 2:8–12).

III. An angelic choir sang an anthem of praise at the time of Christ's birth (Luke 2:14–15).

IV. The angels ministered to Christ immediately following his victory over temptation in the wilderness (Matt. 4:11).

V. Angels announced to Mary that the Christ had conquered death and the grave (John 20:12–13).

VI. Angels explained Christ's ascension and prophesied his personal return to earth for his own (Acts 1:10–11).

Conclusion

We perform the function of angels when we sing of the Savior. It is proper to join our hearts and lips together in singing about our wonderful Savior. Christianity is the only religion that has put a song into the hearts of humankind.

SUNDAY MORNING, DECEMBER 21

Title: "His Name Shall Be Called the Everlasting Father"

Text: "His name shall be called ... the everlasting Father" (**Isa. 9:6**).

Hymns: "Majestic Sweetness Sits Enthroned," Stennett

"The Head That Once Was Crowned," Kelly

"Great Redeemer, We Adore Thee," Harris

Offertory Prayer: Eternal Father, giver of eternal life and bestower of all blessings, to you we come to offer the love of our hearts, the praise of our lips, and the fruit of our labor. As the wise men of old brought precious gifts of their substance, even so today we bring our tithes and offerings in sincere worship to him whom you have appointed to be our King. Accept these gifts and bless them to the increase of your kingdom. Amen.

Introduction

The title Everlasting Father has caused some difficulty to believers through the ages. They have wondered why that name was prophetically ascribed to him who in human nature was a "Child born" and a "Son given" for the salvation of people. The name "Father" has normally been associated with the first person of the Godhead.

To properly understand this title, we must note that the name given is not "Father" but "The everlasting Father." In the East men were often given a name or a title that signified some quality or characteristic for which they were famous. One could be a father of wisdom or a father of folly or a son of wisdom or a son of folly. James and John were called the "Sons of Thunder."

This particular messianic title speaks of the coming Savior as "the Father of perpetuity, the Father of eternity, the Father of the forever." To be the everlasting Father is to be characterized by eternity. It refers to Christ's lordship of eternity.

I. This title is an emphatic assertion of the Messiah's deity.

It distinctly sets him apart from sinful man, whose life has been compared to a vapor that appears for a while and then fades away.

A. *To the Savior is ascribed ageless, timeless being and character.* In this respect he is uniquely different from others.

B. *Our Savior is the Eternal One (John 1:1, 14).*

   1. The Messiah came and lived on this earth, died for our sins, and lives again as the Lord of life and death (Rev. 1:18).

   2. In the midst of a changing world, we worship and serve the unchanging Christ (Heb. 13:8).

C. *Our Savior, the Father of eternity, is immune to the limitations of time.* He is as young as the morning; he is as youthful as the daybreak. Time cannot tarnish the glory of his person. Age after age reveals his ability to achieve miraculous results in the lives of those who trust him.

II. The Messiah is "The everlasting Father" because he is the giver of eternal life.

A. *Everlasting life can be a present possession (John 3:36).*

B. *Eternal life is the gift of the Good Shepherd (John 10:27–29).*

C. *Eternal life is through Jesus Christ alone (Rom. 6:23).*

III. The promised Messiah, the Child born, the Son given, is "The everlasting Father" in the sense that he provides for his own.

A. *He provides tender, loving care for the children of God.*

B. *Faithfully he abides with those who trust him and work to carry out his wishes (Matt. 28:20).*

C. *With infinite wisdom he seeks to train us to bear much fruit (John 15:2).*

D. *The Messiah provides safety for those who trust him with a faith that causes them to follow (John 10:28–29).*

IV. The title "The everlasting Father" declares that the Messiah will never vacate his office (Rev. 1:18).

The Savior whom we worship at Christmastime did not come into existence at the time of his birth in Bethlehem. He always was. In this event the eternal God clothed himself in the garments of human flesh that people might better understand the nature and character of the true God. What the Savior was, he is and shall be forever.

A. *He ever lives to provide companionship and counsel.*

B. *He ever lives to love and to lift us toward our divine destiny.*

C. *He seeks continually to save people from both the penalty and power of sin.*

D. *He constantly exercises the concern of a father's loving heart.*

Conclusion

The Savior continues to be "The everlasting Father" in his ability and availability to meet the deepest needs of the human heart. He can introduce you to the true God who has revealed himself in terms of love and mercy and grace as well as in terms of holiness and justice.

As the Father of eternity, he is eager to bestow on you the gift of eternal life. This life is more than endless duration. It is a new quality of life — the very life of God. Recognize him, respond to him positively, and this will be the most wonderful Christmas of all.

SUNDAY EVENING, DECEMBER 21

Title: "His Name Shall Be Called the Prince of Peace"

Text: "His name shall be called ... The Prince of Peace" **(Isa. 9:6)**.

Introduction

We have been looking at the prophetic messianic titles of the Christ child who was born and placed in a manger. Each title was prophetic of the ministry he was to render. His glory and greatness are proclaimed. His names are glorious in their wondrous claims. His titles are famous throughout God's vast domain.

Each of Christ's names contains a divine promise. In the title Prince of Peace, we see the highest title of all. He is to be the answer to the heart's deepest need. The foregoing titles culminate in this title.

The magnitude of his task is revealed in this title. He is to make it possible for humans to be at peace with God and to live at peace with one another. Sin has created a woeful need for a divine prince who can restore the primitive peace.

I. The heart of man hungers for peace.

A. *The desire for peace is universal.*

1. America wants peace.
2. The war-torn nations of the Middle East want peace.
3. People involved in conflicts all over the world want peace.

B. *Why have we failed to achieve peace?*

1. We have achieved the highest standard of living the world has ever known.
2. Due to medical research, our longevity continues to increase.
3. Prosperity prevails, but there is an absence of peace.
4. Substitutes for the Prince of Peace have been accepted. Nations are not encouraged to depend on God for peace. We place our faith in the armed forces and in a variety of weapons. Individuals have accepted

substitutes for the Prince of Peace. They look to education, wealth, friends, and health for peace. All of these disappear, and turmoil prevails in the heart.

II. Peace is the gift of God.

A. *The priests of the Old Testament were instructed to bless the people with a benediction of peace.* "The LORD bless thee, and keep thee: The LORD make his face shine upon thee, and be gracious unto thee: The LORD lift up his countenance upon thee, and give thee peace" (Num. 6:24–26).

B. *The psalmist recognized peace as one of the blessings of God.* "The LORD will give strength unto his people: The LORD will bless his people with peace" (Ps. 29:11).

C. *The prophet Isaiah perceived that true peace comes from a right adjustment of life to the will of God.* "Thou wilt keep him in perfect peace, whose mind is stayed on thee: because he trusteth in thee. Trust ye in the LORD for ever: for in the LORD JEHOVAH is everlasting strength" (Isa. 26:3–4).

D. *The apostle Paul believed that the heavenly Father is the giver of peace.*
   1. "Be careful for nothing; but in everything by prayer and supplication with thanksgiving let your requests be made known unto God. And the peace of God, which passeth all understanding, shall keep your hearts and minds through Christ Jesus" (Phil. 4:6–7).
   2. For the Thessalonians he prayed, "Now the Lord of peace himself give you peace always by all means" (2 Thess. 3:16).
   3. "God is not the author of confusion, but of peace" (1 Cor. 14:33).

E. *Apart from God there is no peace.*
   1. "There is no peace, saith the LORD, unto the wicked" (Isa. 48:22).
   2. When Israel rebelled during the days of Jeremiah and the peace of God departed, one of the Israelites said, "We looked for peace, and there is no good; and for the time of healing, and behold trouble!" (Jer. 14:19).

   Without God people are out of step with eternity. They do not come to grips with the ultimate values of life.

III. Jesus Christ is the only source of real peace.

A. *The Prince of Peace is peaceful in his disposition.*
   1. He bears long with his enemies.
   2. He endures much at the hands of his friends.
   3. He is always accessible and available.
   4. He is always ready to forgive.

B. *Peace is the disposition for which the Savior was renowned.*

C. *Peace is the blessing he died to purchase (Rom. 5:1).*

D. *Peace is the blessing he lives to bestow (John 20:21).*
   1. In Christ we cease to war among ourselves.

363

2. Christ delivers sinners from their follies, passions, and the evil that destroys.

E. *Christ is peace.* He bestows peace, exercises peace, and delights in peace.

IV. The peace that Christ offers.

Most people are eager to have the peace that can be understood. This kind of peace is based on money in the pocketbook, in a secure position in the family, in business, and in a healthy body.

The peace Jesus gives cannot be won on a battlefield or purchased with money or secured through medicine. His peace is not that of the conquering sword but of a prevailing spirit.

A. *His peace is not the peace of stagnation or inactivity.* He does not provide us with a spiritual narcotic to keep us from facing reality. Neither is his peace the peace of freedom from inward temptation or outward suffering.

B. *The Prince of Peace brings peace from God and gives us peace with God.*
1. His peace is the peace of surrender to the rule of love.
2. His peace is the peace of fellowship with God the heavenly Father.
3. His peace is the peace of self-control through spiritual power and divine energy.
4. His peace is the peace of assurance that our sins have been forgiven.
5. With his presence it is possible for one to walk with poise in the midst of storms and calamity.

Conclusion

If Jesus is to bring to us the peace of God, we must crown him King of our empire and make him Lord of our lives. If we let his will become our will, we will discover ourselves in harmony with God and the laws of the universe. Life will be lived without the evil effects of destructive tension. The prophet said, "Thou wilt keep him in perfect peace, whose mind is stayed on thee: because he trusteth in thee" (Isa. 26:3).

WEDNESDAY EVENING, DECEMBER 24

Title: Christ the Lord

Text: "For unto you is born this day in the city of David a Savior, which is Christ the Lord" (**Luke 2:11**).

Introduction

During the Christmas season, emphasis is placed on the birth of the Christ child in Bethlehem. We sing about the Virgin Mary, the angels, the mysterious star, and the wise men. We stand in awe of the angelic proclamation, "For unto you is born this day in the city of David a Savior, which is Christ the Lord."

With the end of the Christmas celebration comes also the end of the calendar year. This is a fitting time, in reflecting on the meaning of Christ's coming into the world, to consider also his claim on our lives as people who belong to him. What does it mean that "Christ is Lord"?

I. A Savior: They needed one.

A. *The nation was enduring a destructive political tyranny.*

B. *The nation was suffering economic insecurity.*

C. *The nation was burdened with religious traditionalism and a cold formalism.*

D. *Spiritual bankruptcy was the order of the day.* The whole world, then as well as now, stands in need of salvation from sin and selfishness.

II. Who is this Child born, this Son given?

A. *The Christ child is the one anointed by God to be our Savior.*

B. *The Christ child was the fulfillment of the prophetic dreams and announcements.*

C. *The Christ child was the Son of God in human flesh.* He was the God-man. He was the eternal God clothed in the flesh of a baby.

III. The nature of Christ's lordship.

A. *The absolute lordship of God is emphasized throughout the Old Testament.* First priority belongs to God. When people gave God first place, life was meaningful.

B. *The lordship of the Christ was declared by the mysterious star that announced his birth.*

C. *Christ's lordship over the angels is revealed by the anthem of annunciation (Luke 2:13–14).*

D. *Christ is Lord over nature.* The winds and the sea obey his commands.

E. *Christ is Lord over disease and death.* Death and disease flee from him like frightened dogs.

F. *Christ is Lord over sin, Satan, death, and the grave.* He lived a life of perfect purity on earth. He overcame every temptation of Satan and conquered death and the grave.

IV. The Lord is love.

A. *Because Christ left heaven and came to earth as a human to give his life as a sacrifice for our sin, God appointed him to be Lord over everything and everyone (Phil. 2:5–11).*

B. *Because of what Christ did and because of what he can do in your life, you should make him the Lord of your life.*

1. Trust him as Lord for salvation (Rom. 2:10).
2. Confess him as Lord for the assurance of salvation (Rom. 10:10–13).

Conclusion

The basic sin of us all is the rejection of the lordship of God. People foolishly believe that they can find their highest happiness in ways other than the ways of

God. Only if we are willing to make Jesus the Lord of our lives will we find him to be the Prince of Peace who brings the joy of salvation into our hearts.

For Christ to be the Prince of Peace, a coronation service must take place; you must make him King of your heart. Do it now.

SUNDAY MORNING, DECEMBER 28

Title: Joy to the World

Text: "And the angel said unto them, Fear not: for, behold, I bring you good tidings of great joy, which shall be to all people" **(Luke 2:10)**.

Hymns: "Angels We Have Heard on High," Traditional

"Hark! The Herald Angels Sing," Wesley

"Joy to the World," Watts

Offertory Prayer: Father, we thank you that you have given us joy through the sufferings of Jesus for us. We ask you to strengthen us and to perfect us in Christ so that we may joyfully give of ourselves. Bless these tithes and offerings as part of ourselves. In Jesus' name. Amen.

Introduction

The angel's announcement to the frightened shepherds was intended to produce great joy. The message was one of good tidings, which were to bring joy to the hearts of all people everywhere.

I. The need for joy.

The world needs a religion of joy. Many factors contribute to an unhappy frame of mind.

A. *The present world crisis.*

B. *Personal past failures.*

C. *The competitive and materialistic spirit of our age.*

D. *Disappointment by others.*

These factors contribute to a spirit of pessimism. In the midst of these distressing circumstances, it is somewhat difficult to be joyous. We need to remind ourselves that a sour-faced Christian is a very poor advertisement of what Christ can do for a person.

A student of anatomy has said that it takes thirteen muscles to smile and sixty-five muscles to frown. If this is so, some of us are overworking ourselves by wearing a frown instead of a smile. A sincere smile on the face is the outward expression of joy in the heart.

Jesus came into the world that people might be filled with joy. Most of the painters and poets have given the world a false concept of the character and nature of Jesus Christ. They have painted him as a sad, melancholy, morbid, unhappy individual. Because of this impression, many have the opinion that a

Christian must never smile. Some judge the quality of one's piety in terms of the length of one's face. The great majority of those who are not yet disciples of our Lord believe that all enjoyment of life is over when one becomes a Christian.

II. Jesus was joyous.

Have you ever asked, "What kind of a man was Jesus Christ?" Was he a joyful individual or did he forever wear a frown?

Jesus had a magnetic personality. His disciples detected in him something for which their hearts hungered. They perceived that he had come into the world to make available abundant, lasting, and true joy to the hearts of people.

A. *The Pharisees were scandalized because Jesus did not fast and pretend to be pious.*
B. *Jesus described himself as a bridegroom.*
C. *Something about Jesus caused mothers to want to bring their children to him.*

III. Jesus desired joy for others.

A. *Jesus desired that his followers be filled with joy.* "These things have I spoken unto you, that my joy might remain in you, and that your joy might be full" (John 15:11).
B. *Concerning the privilege of prayer, Jesus said, "Ask, and ye shall receive, that your joy may be full" (John 16:24).*

IV. The Babe in Bethlehem's manger was born to be a Savior from sin.

A. *The absence of joy in the hearts of people can be traced to sin and all that this little three-letter word stands for.* Christ was born to deal with humankind's sin problem.
   1. The Savior came to bear the penalty of our sin.
   2. The Savior who died but lives again can deliver us from the power of sin.
   3. Ultimately, this Savior, whose birth brought joy to the angels, will one day bring to each of us who trusts him the joy of being saved from the very presence of sin.
B. *This Savior seeks to produce joy in our lives by displacing fear with faith.* People have always been afraid of the possibility of not having adequate resources for the future. In his Sermon on the Mount, Jesus taught his disciples to trust in the greatness of God and to work without worrying (Matt. 6:25–34).

   As his disciples faced the future, they feared personal failure, and he sought to encourage them with a promise of his continuing presence (Matt. 28:19–20).

   People have feared to face the curtain that we call death, and Jesus sought to bring joy by assuring his disciples of a prepared place for a prepared people.

Conclusion

Jesus thought of bringing joy into the hearts and lives of people as one of the primary motives for his coming into the world, for he said, "I am come that they might have life, and that they might have it more abundantly" (John 10:10). You must let Jesus Christ be born in your heart and live as a guest in the house of your life if you want to know the fullness of joy about which the angels sang.

SUNDAY EVENING, DECEMBER 28

Title: Wise Men from Everywhere

Text: "Now when Jesus was born in Bethlehem of Judaea in the days of Herod the king, behold, there came wise men from the east to Jerusalem" (**Matt. 2:1**).

Introduction

Wise men from the East, students of the stars, came to worship the Christ child. How far had they traveled? To the east of Jerusalem were the deserts of Arabia, the valleys and plains of Mesopotamia, the vast empire of India, the mysterious land of China. How had these men seen the star in the East? How did they know it was the Messiah's star? It is impossible to answer these questions.

From the mysterious East came the wise men, seeking to worship a child with gifts of mystic meaning. Gold was a tribute to a king, frankincense a gift for deity, and myrrh symbolic of the suffering to come.

Perhaps it is a good thing that we do not know too much about these wise men, for we can see them as representative of all who have the true wisdom of the Spirit that causes them to follow by faith the heavenly light that ever guides them in their quest for the real meaning of life. The wise men represent all in every age who have been people of faith and action. Their message for all who would be wise in this century is that we should seek wisdom.

Poet Jean Carter Cochran questions these wise men in imagination.

> Wise man, tell me, what did you see
>   That made you travel so far?
> Stranger, I followed the radiant light
>   Of a splendid, flaming star.
> Wise man, tell me, what did you hear
>   In that land where you did stray?
> Stranger, I heard an angel's song
>   That rings in my heart alway.
> Wise man, tell me, what did you find
>   That makes your countenance so bright?
> Stranger, I found a heavenly King
>   Born on that Holy Night.

I. The wise men of old would tell wise men from everywhere to follow the light that God gives.

A. *The birth of Jesus was signaled by a supernatural phenomena—a star.* If at his death the earth trembled, the veil of the temple was torn, and the sun refused to shine, we should not think it strange that at his birth a star stood over his cradle while a great multitude of the heavenly host sang, "Glory to God in the highest."

B. *We cannot tell what star the wise men saw.* It was their profession to watch the heavens. Some heavenly brilliance indicated to them the entry of a king into the world.

C. *There are many events and inward hungers, desires, and conflicts, which, if we were to recognize and interpret them properly, would lead us to seek the Savior who can bring meaning, beauty, purpose, and power to our lives.*

II. The wise men of old, like wise men from everywhere, rejoiced when they found the Savior.

A. *Christ produces joy in the hearts of those who seek and find him as Lord and Savior.*

B. *Many desire the fruit of faith in Christ before they receive him as Lord and Savior.*

C. *You must let Christ come into your heart if you want to experience joy and peace.*

> *If Christ a thousand times in Bethlehem be born,*
> *Until He is born in me, my soul is all forlorn.*

III. The wise men of old, like wise men from everywhere, worshiped the Savior.

A. *They fell down before him and paid homage to him as the King of the Jews.*

B. *No person should worship that which is less than the highest. No person should worship anything or anyone less than God.*

C. *Worship is the highest and most noble activity of the soul.*

D. *Genuine worship is the climax of wisdom.* Only through worship do we accept the essential dignity of humankind.

E. *The wise men of old found in the Child a revelation of God, and they worshiped him.*

IV. The wise men of old would encourage wise people from everywhere to open their treasures and present gifts to the Christ.

A. *According to the Bible, the wise men did this spontaneously.*

B. *Each man gave his best gift to the Christ child — his utmost to the Highest.*

C. *The wise men perceived that the Christ child was not just a baby, but the King, to whom the tribute of God was rightfully due.*

D. *Is it not astonishing that the gift of frankincense should symbolize that worship to be offered only to deity?*

E. *How utterly beyond explanation is the last gift of myrrh, foreshadowing a life of sacrifice and suffering, prefiguring Gethsemane and Calvary.*

F. *The nature of the gifts is most significant.*

    1. Gold, the king of metals, is a gift suitable for a king. Jesus was born to be a King. He was to reign, not by force, but by love; and he was to rule over people's hearts, not from a throne, but from a cross. We do well to

remember that Jesus is King and therefore we must always meet him in total submission.

2. Frankincense is the gift for a priest. It was a sweet perfume used in the temple sacrifices. The function of a priest is to open the way to God for people. That is what Jesus did. Through him we can enter into the very presence of God.

3. Myrrh is the gift for one who is to die. Myrrh was used to embalm the bodies of the dead. Jesus came into the world to die.

These three gifts given at the cradle of Christ foretold that he was to be the true King, the perfect High Priest, and the supreme Savior of people.

V. The wise men returned by a different road.

The wise men were warned not to go back home by the way which they had come—that is, by way of Herod's palace.

A. *After discovering Christ, people walk a different road.*

B. *Wise people walk a spiritual "King's highway."*

C. *Wise people walk the way of holiness.*

D. *Wise people walk in the pathway of peace.*

Conclusion

The wise men of the past sought the Savior. They worshiped him as deity and gave him the very best they had. If you and I would be wise, we likewise would seek the Savior. He alone is worthy of worship. He alone deserves the very best of our time and talents and treasure. Let us make the decisions that we need to make this day that we might follow in the trend of these wise men.

WEDNESDAY EVENING, DECEMBER 31

Title: A Call to Christian Consecration for the New Year

Text: "Ye are washed, but ye are sanctified, but ye are justified in the name of the Lord Jesus, and by the Spirit of our God" (**1 Cor. 6:11**).

Scripture Reading: 1 Corinthians 6:11 – 18

Introduction

Suppose you were to go to the ticket window of your local airport and say, "I want a ticket." The clerk would ask, "To where?" And you would say, "Well, anywhere; for what places do you have tickets?" The ticket salesperson would say immediately, "How stupid! You'll never get anywhere, for you don't know where you want to go." Too often we approach the new year in just that fashion—without goals and without sound resolutions. Before us spread in panoramic view, yet with a deep veil separating us, is a whole new year of adventuresome living. Spiritually, we should and can see a great breakthrough into many hearts that are steeped in the blackness of sin as they come to know Christ a Savior and Lord and thus come into the sunshine of his saving grace.

For us as individuals, it can be the greatest year yet if we do the following:

I. Resolve to make this the most wonderful year yet.

It should be a wonderful year because:

A. *There is a wonderful relationship between you and the Lord of all life, Jesus Christ.*
1. We must know him as Savior by a personal encounter without which there is no knowledge of him. "Except a man be born again, he cannot see the kingdom of God" (John 3:3).
2. We must know him intimately through day-to-day fellowship with him. A dear saint once said to her pastor, "Pastor, I could not get through a day without an active fellowship with my Master. I am constantly in an attitude of prayer."
3. We must know him as Lord of our daily lives. We should make no decisions without first consulting our Master; we should wait for his instructions and leadership each day of our lives.

B. *There is a thrilling anticipation of what lies ahead.* We ought to be spiritually excited about the new year and what can be accomplished for the Lord.

C. *Because we have systematized our enthusiasm for the coming year.* Following are three methods by which you can systematize your enthusiasm and cause it to produce for you during the coming year:
1. Write down the things that you want to accomplish during the coming year, numbering them 1, 2, 3, etc., thus, having down in black and white something definite toward which to work.
2. Study your job, its requirements, its possibilities, and its potentialities for at least one hour each day for five days a week. If you will do this honestly, you probably will be looked on as an expert in your field within five or six years.
3. Spend at least thirty minutes per day in deep meditation concerning ideas for the improvement of your job, jotting down at least a half dozen or so of these ideas. Perhaps at the end of the week you will discover that out of the many ideas jotted down, there will be at least one great idea that will carry you forward in your work.

   Most of these ideas just enumerated have concerned themselves with secular life. As Christians we could well afford to carry out these ideas for self-improvement. The Christian faith is in a time of great competition with ideologies that grab the imagination of the youth of our land. We need to know our weaknesses, our strengths, and the best methods of communicating our faith.

II. Resolve that we will live positively this year.

A. *Endeavor to control life and not to let it control you.* In the face of calamities, endeavor to turn catastrophes into blessings.

371

B. *Do not wait for your wishes and dreams to come true.* Go out and face life head-on and help those dreams and visions to come true. Young William Carey, a shoe cobbler in England, wanted to do more for missions in India. He heard a harsh rebuke: "Sit down young man; when the Lord gets ready to save the heathen, he will do it without your help." William Carey thought otherwise and packed up and went to India to tell the unreached about Jesus Christ's saving power.

C. *Venture out, dare, live thrillingly as Christians.* Desiring to see the lost people of our community come to know Christ personally, let us dare to believe that they can be won if we are willing to be Christ's missionaries carrying the good news of his love for the lost.

We would like to see our church be able to meet all of its obligations in the support of the great mission undertaking and in its local areas of need. Let us determine to bring into the Lord's storehouse a tithe of our income.

III. Resolve that we are going to be better people than we were last year.

A. *As a nation we seem to be facing anarchy.* There is on every hand violence, immorality, psychological confusion, and spiritual ignorance and indifference. We need new life in our nation. The only way to obtain this is for individuals in our nation to find new life in Christ Jesus.

B. *As individuals we can expect to have a better year only by being better people.* We can be better people only if we will surrender to the saving power of Christ Jesus. If we are already truly Christians, we can be better people only if we let Christ truly be the Lord of our lives.

Conclusion

At the end of the old year and at the beginning of the new year, let us make spiritual resolutions that will be meaningful to our lives and to the lives of those around us. Let us look toward the upcoming year with a high degree of spiritual expectancy, seeing the next twelve months as a challenge. We will have opportunities to witness for Christ such as we have never had before. Let our motto during the coming year be, "For me to live is Christ" (Phil. 1:21).

Miscellaneous Helps

MESSAGES ON THE LORD'S SUPPER

Title: Precious Memories of Jesus

Text: "And when he had given thanks, he brake it, and said, Take, eat: this is my body, which is broken for you: this do in remembrance of me" (**1 Cor. 11:24**).

Introduction

Do you have a favorite photograph of your parents? Is this photograph a snapshot that was taken without your loved ones being aware that they were being photographed, or is it a portrait made by a professional photographer? Is your favorite photograph also one that your parents would prefer that you have? Photographs help us to preserve our memory of loved ones. They recall pleasant memories and bring delight to the heart.

What is your favorite photograph of yourself? Is it a serious pose, or is it some sort of action picture? The New Testament can be studied as a picture album. It contains many verbal pictures of God as he has revealed himself in the person of Jesus Christ.

I. Christ on the mount.

One of the most beautiful pictures of Christ to be found in the Scriptures is that of him seated near the crest of the mountain with his disciples about him. Here he taught them the principles and characteristics of being ideal citizens of his kingdom in this life. This picture of Christ should be preserved in our memory in order that we might recognize the importance of following his teachings.

II. Christ on the ship.

Another beautiful picture of Christ that we should hang on the walls of our memory is that of him in the boat with his disciples when the storms beat down on them. Christ stood and, with sovereign power, rebuked the winds and commanded the waves of the sea to be quiet. This memory of the Christ can give us peace and poise as we face the storms that will sweep into our lives from time to time.

III. Christ in Bethany.

Jesus loved to go to the home of Mary, Martha, and Lazarus. They treated him as an honored guest. They were a blessing to him, and he was a blessing to them. We find him coming to them in an hour of sorrow when death had invaded the family circle. With a sovereign power that was frightening, he commanded the dead to rise, and Lazarus came forth from the tomb. We need to treasure this memory of the Savior if we want assurance that death is a defeated foe and that the grave will have no final victory over us.

IV. Christ on the cross.

Of all the pictures that the New Testament contains concerning the Christ, this is the picture that he would have us turn to more than any other. We know this because he instituted the Lord's Supper and commanded, "As often as ye do this, do it in remembrance of me." Because his heart was filled with infinite and indescribable love for us, we can be assured that his motive was not selfish for wanting to recall this memory to our mind's eye, but rather he was trying to meet the deepest need in our life.

    A. *Christ would remind us that sin is our deadly enemy and that God, at any price, would deliver us from anything that would ruin our lives.*

    B. *Christ would remind us of the self-giving love of God for people which is beyond our human ability to comprehend.*

    C. *Our suffering Savior was thus seeking to convince us once and for all, and yet repeatedly, that all of the purposes of God toward us are motivated by love and grace.*

Conclusion

By inspired imagination, hang this picture of our suffering Savior on the wall of your memory. Meditate on God's love for you, and respond with love and faith and obedience to him.

Title: Proclaiming the Lord's Death

Text: "For as often as ye eat this bread, and drink this cup, ye do shew the Lord's death till he come" (**1 Cor. 11:26**).

Introduction

A reverent, worshipful observance of the Lord's Supper is a dramatic proclamation of the redemptive act in which Jesus Christ, the sinless, stainless, spotless Son of God, died for the sins of a lost world. This is a message that believers and unbelievers alike need to have repeated regularly.

I. The death of Christ reveals the divine hatred of sin.

    A. *Sin is a dark and dismal reality.*

    B. *Sin is a transgression of God's holy law.* This law is designed to regulate the lives of the creatures made in the image of God so as to produce maximum well-being if followed.

    C. *Sin is an attitude of selfishness that leads to acts of rebellion against God.*

    D. *Sin is a destructive and degrading attitude that causes life to drift downward.*

    E. *Sin is a wicked, malignant force that does not work for righteousness.*

    F. *Sin is a deadly disease in the soul that has darkened the intellect, deadened the emotions, and degraded the human will.*

G. *Sin has produced a spiritual death in human souls by separating them from their Creator.*

II. The death of Christ revealed the holiness and justice of God.

Some have a sentimental concept of God. They picture him as a doting grandfather who is very indulgent and tolerant.

A. *The death of Christ on the cross reveals that God does not pass lightly over sin nor treat it with an indulgent attitude.*

B. *God does not ignore sin.*

C. *Sin, because of its very nature, must be punished and obliterated.*

D. *Mysteriously and miraculously, God himself, in the person of Jesus Christ, suffered for our sins.* "For he hath made him to be sin for us, who knew no sin; that we might be made the righteousness of God in him" (2 Cor. 5:21). "For Christ also hath once suffered for sins, the just for the unjust, that he might bring us to God, being put to death in the flesh, but quickened by the Spirit" (1 Peter 3:18).

III. The death of Christ reveals the immeasurable love of God.

A. *Following the resurrection and the coming of the Holy Spirit on the day of Pentecost, the early Christians were overwhelmed with the grace of God's redeeming love when they thought of the death of Christ.* "Forasmuch as ye know that ye were not redeemed with corruptible things, as silver and gold, from your vain conversation received by tradition from your fathers; but with the precious blood of Christ, as the lamb without blemish and without spot: who verily was foreordained before the foundation of the world, was manifest in these last times for you" (1 Peter 1:18–20).

B. *The sacrificial love of God was infinitely costly.* God gave his only begotten Son to die on the cross as the only adequate way of dealing with our sin.

C. *God loved the sinner long before Christ died on the cross.* Someone has said, "There was a cross in the heart of God long before there was ever a cross on Calvary's hill."

IV. The death of Christ makes forgiveness and remission of sins possible.

"To him give all the prophets witness, that through his name whosoever believeth in him shall receive remission of sins" (Acts 10:43). The desire to forgive, to cleanse, to deliver, to set free from sin originates with God. "But God commendeth his love toward us, in that, while we were yet sinners, Christ died for us" (Rom. 5:8).

A. *Forgiveness is full.* The psalmist speaks of God, "Who forgiveth all thine iniquities" (Ps. 103:3).

B. *Forgiveness is free.* "But the gift of God is eternal life through Jesus Christ our Lord" (Rom. 6:23). Forgiveness cannot be purchased or earned. It can be received only as a free gift of God.

C. *Forgiveness is forever.* "I, even I, am he that blotteth out thy transgressions for mine own sake, and will not remember thy sins" (Isa. 43:25).

Conclusion

As we partake of the elements of the Lord's Supper, let us be reminded of the awful nature of our sins that made it necessary for Jesus to die as a substitute in our place. Let us be overwhelmed with the gracious wonder of God's love for us. As willingly and as completely as Jesus Christ gave himself, let us give ourselves in service to him for others. Because he died for us, let us live for him.

Title: A Visit to Calvary

Text: "Surely he hath borne our griefs, and carried our sorrows.... But he was wounded for our transgressions" (**Isa. 53:4–5**).

Introduction

As Jesus instituted the Lord's Supper, he instructed his disciples, "As oft as ye do this, ye do it in remembrance of me." By this he was suggesting the possibility of his disciples making a visit to Calvary by inspired imagination.

We learn much through travel and observation. One can travel by train, by bus, by automobile, or by plane. One can also travel by means of reading a good book, attending a travelogue, or watching a television program.

Many Christians would like to visit the Holy Land and actually walk where our Lord walked. Some will have this joy, but the majority will never be able to visit Jerusalem except by inspired imagination.

In observing the Lord's Supper, let us make a trip by inspired imagination to Calvary and with eyes of the soul behold our Savior on the cross.

I. We need to visit Calvary to discover our sinfulness.

People have a natural tendency to ignore, conceal, excuse, or explain away their sin. Once we make a visit to Calvary and see Jesus bearing the guilt, the shame, and the penalty of our sin, we will find it almost impossible not to confess and forsake our sin.

II. We need to visit Calvary to discover the nature of our God.

A. *Many of the greater religions of the world have pictured God as possessing all of the vices of humans.*

B. *Calvary reveals the greatness of our God's grace and mercy toward sinners.* It was on Calvary that Christ Jesus obtained our redemption from the penalty of sin.

   1. This was redemption by love.
   2. This was redemption by substitution.
   3. This was redemption by sacrifice and suffering.

376

III. We need to visit Calvary to discover the world's only hope of salvation.

    A. *There are many false messiahs.*

        1. Some trust wealth.

        2. Some put their faith in education.

        3. Some have made a god out of science.

    B. *Only Jesus Christ can give a new heart and a new life.*

IV. We need to visit Calvary for inspiration of service.

    A. *In the elements of the Lord's Supper, we are dramatically reminded of how completely and how freely Jesus Christ gave himself for us.*

    B. *By his faith and dedication to the will of God, Jesus Christ inspires us to follow his example.*

    C. *God will bring to fruition every act of self-denial and self-surrender for the sake of the gospel.* He raised Christ from the dead, and he will bless your every sacrifice and effort.

Conclusion

By inspired imagination, Isaac Watts visited Calvary and penned beautiful words that continue to challenge the hearts and lives of those who love the Lord.

> *When I survey the wondrous cross*
> *On which the Prince of Glory died,*
> *My richest gain I count but loss,*
> *And pour contempt on all my pride.*
>
> *Forbid it, Lord, that I should boast,*
> *Save in the death of Christ, my God!*
> *All the vain things that charm me most,*
> *I sacrifice them to His blood.*
>
> *See, from His head, His hands, His feet,*
> *Sorrow and love flow mingled down;*
> *Did e'er such love and sorrow meet,*
> *Or thorns compose so rich a crown?*
>
> *Were the whole realm of nature mine,*
> *That were a present far too small;*
> *Love so amazing, so divine,*
> *Demands my soul, my life, my all.*

Title: What Is the Lord's Supper?

Text: "This cup is the new testament in my blood: this do ye, as oft as ye drink it, in remembrance of me" (**1 Cor. 11:25**).

I. The Lord's Supper is a memorial service.

"Take, eat: this is my body, which is broken for you: this do in remembrance of me" (1 Cor. 11:24).

A. *Memorials are erected to honor great lives.*
B. *Memorials commemorate great deeds.*
C. *Memorials keep memory alive.*
D. *Memorials serve to instruct.*

II. The Lord's Supper is a time of communion.

"The cup of blessing which we bless, is it not the communion of the blood of Christ? The bread which we break, is it not the communion of the body of Christ?" (1 Cor. 10:16).

As an act of worship, we enter the experience of forgiveness through the blood of Christ, and we feed our souls on the spiritual relationship of him who is the Bread of Life.

III. The Lord's Supper is proclamation.

As you partake of the elements of the Supper of our Lord, you proclaim to your own heart and to others your faith in the fact that Christ Jesus gave himself on the cross for our sins. He demonstrated the divine opposition to sin and a divine determination to redeem us. He demonstrated the love of God.

IV. The Lord's Supper is a time of self-examination.

"But let a man examine himself, and so let him eat of that bread, and drink of that cup" (1 Cor. 11:28). We are not to examine ourselves to see whether or not we are worthy so as to deserve to partake, but we are to examine the manner and motive in which we participate. This should be a most soul-searching experience as we reverently contemplate that Jesus died for our sins.

V. The Lord's Supper is a time for expression of gratitude.

"And when he had given thanks, he brake it, and said, Take, eat: this is my body, which is broken for you: this do in remembrance of me" (1 Cor. 11:24).

It is interesting to attempt to contemplate that for which our Savior offered thanks as he instituted the Lord's Supper. We can offer thanks for the love of God and for the sacrifice of Jesus Christ. We can offer thanks for the full forgiveness of our sin and for the new life that has come to us through him.

VI. The Lord's Supper is a silent but loud prophecy.

"For as often as ye eat this bread, and drink this cup, ye do shew the Lord's death till he come" (1 Cor. 11:26).

Conclusion

Until the heavens roll back as a scroll and the Lord himself descends from heaven with a shout, his disciples will come together from time to time to partake of these elements that proclaim the assurance of the forgiveness of sin and to reveal that a divine Savior has died that we might have life and have it more abundantly.

MESSAGES FOR CHILDREN AND YOUNG PEOPLE

Title: Choosing a Foundation for Life

Text: "Therefore whosoever heareth these sayings of mine, and doeth them, I will liken him unto a wise man, which built his house upon a rock" (**Matt. 7:24**).

Introduction

The Empire State Building stands 103 stories tall. It reaches 1,253 feet, or almost one-fourth of a mile in height. If all the materials that went into the construction of this building had been loaded onto one train, it would have been 57 miles long. The building contains 10 million bricks, over 6,000 windows, 75 miles of water pipes, and 5,000 feet of electric wiring. This gigantic building houses 25,000 people and could house as many as 80,000 per day. This gigantic structure, weighing in excess of 303,000 tons, needed a tremendous foundation, so the engineers excavated until they reached solid granite, the basic rock of our earth. On this rock they laid the foundation for the Empire State Building.

Even a child can understand that a great building must have a solid foundation if it is to withstand the winds and storms of time. As a building must have a firm foundation, so must our lives be built on a solid foundation if they are to withstand the pressures and strains of life.

Before Jesus began his teaching ministry he was a carpenter. It is possible that he had assisted in the building of homes. In the Sermon on the Mount, he gives us instructions and specifications for building a Christian life. Spiritually speaking, each of us has a house to build and a rock on which to build it, and we need to build it so that the storms will not destroy it.

I. Jesus spoke of two foundations on which one can build his life—the sure foundation and the faulty foundation.

The foundation for the Empire State Building was not more important to its owners than the foundation of your life is to you.

    A. *Faulty foundations.* You can build your life on something shoddy and shabby that will prove to be unsafe when the storms of life beat down on you.

        1. Some build their lives on a materialistic foundation.

        2. Some build their lives around pleasure. They are eager to enjoy the excitement of anything that will intoxicate for the moment.

        3. Some build their lives on the foundation of common sense. They put their faith in education and science and fail to realize that while both of these are good, they are not a safe foundation on which to build a life.

    B. *The sure foundation.* Faith in Jesus is the sure foundation. We must build on that foundation a life of obedience to God. Life will cave in on the person who shuts God out of his or her life.

II. The storms of life are certain to come.

In the conclusion of the Sermon on the Mount, Jesus speaks of rains descending and winds blowing and waves beating against the house of a person's life. There is no immunity or escape from the realities of life.

A. *You may experience a storm of sickness or the death of a loved one.*
B. *Disappointment and disillusionment may come.*
C. *You may experience a storm of temptation and evil influences.*
D. *A storm of financial loss and the pinch of poverty may hurt you.*
E. *Life will not always be easy; consequently, the foundation on which you build your life is of tremendous importance.* Christ would encourage you to build your life and faithfulness on the will of God.

III. The two endings: One life stood and one life collapsed.

A. *The life of faith and obedience is stable and secure.*
B. *The life that is not founded on Christ perishes.*

Title: The Peril of Flunking

Text: "But I keep under my body, and bring it into subjection: lest that by any means, when I have preached to others, I myself should be a castaway" (**1 Cor. 9:27**).

Introduction

Would you be surprised to learn that the apostle Paul lived constantly aware of the possibility of flunking? He looked upon his missionary ministry somewhat as a course of study to be followed for the glory of God. He knew that if he did not apply himself, he would fail to be the good minister of Jesus Christ that he was capable of being.

In the text he speaks of how rigidly he disciplines himself lest after having preached to others he might become a spiritual castaway. The word translated "castaway" was a technical word used by those engaged in the business of making pottery. It was a term that applied to a cracked pot, a vessel that would not pass inspection, that could not be used as the potter intended it to be used. Paul was constantly seeking to conduct himself in a manner that would merit the praise of the Savior.

Have you ever been afraid of flunking out in school? Possibly all of us at some time or another have neglected to make proper preparation and have found ourselves in real difficulty as we faced an examination. To find oneself in this condition is indeed painful. Has it ever occurred to you that there are other areas than the academic in which it is possible to flunk?

I. You can flunk in the matter of finances.

A. *If you are dishonest in the matter of paying your debts and meeting your obligations, you are certain to flunk out as far as finances are concerned.*
B. *If you dedicate your life solely to the making of money, you may become a millionaire.* However, to live only for money and for material things is actually to experience failure as far as the highest possible happiness in life is concerned.

II. You can flunk out in your family.

A. *The Bible is very clear at the point of insisting that one both respect and obey one's parents in the Lord (Eph. 6:1–3).* To be disobedient to those who are in a

380

position of responsibility for you and over you is to do irreparable harm to your sense of values. It is the will of God that you be respectful and obedient to your parents.

B. *It is your privilege and responsibility to live a life of moral purity so as to be worthy of the best possible marriage.* It is possible for you to ignore the moral teachings of God while you are young, to the extent that you deprive yourself of the chance for a happy and wholesome family life as an adult.

III. You can flunk out with your friends.

A. *He who would have friends must show himself friendly.* If you want friends, you must be worthy of the friendship of others.

B. *Our friends will either lift us up or drag us down.* If you choose the wrong kind of persons with whom to build your closest friendships, you will be responsible for degrading yourself.

IV. You can flunk out in the enjoyment of fun.

A. *Everyone enjoys having fun.* Nearly all are seeking a life of fun.

B. *Many things that promise fun and pleasure actually produce the opposite.* We live in a day and time in which immorality is common. Drinking beer and using narcotics are glamorized. Temptation to evil almost always comes in some form of a promise of pleasure.

Sin is destructive. By its very nature, sin drags down and destroys, wrecks and ruins. We should beware of the so-called fun that produces failure instead of success.

V. You can flunk out in the matter of faith.

Some put their faith in themselves. Self-confidence is a valuable asset, but one needs a greater god than self.

Conclusion

The apostle Paul encourages us to put our faith in the Lord Jesus Christ. Let him become your Coach as you play the game of life. Let him be your Teacher who will show you how to live the abundant life. Let the Christ become your Friend who will always be with you as you trust him and follow him. By so doing you can be assured of avoiding the peril of flunking and can make a good grade in the school of life.

Title: Youth Makes the Choice

Text: "Choose you this day whom ye will serve" (**Josh. 24:15**).

Introduction

God did not make us to be robots without the power of self-determination. God made us free to choose our own way and our own destiny. All of us rejoice in

381

the privilege of choosing for ourselves. We should be wise enough to recognize that when we choose a certain road, we automatically choose the destination to which that road leads.

Wise young people recognize their need for guidance in making the best possible choices for their lives. The need for such guidance and leadership is one of the most important reasons why all young people should become Christians. They can then let Jesus guide them as they make the choices that will determine their destinies.

I. Youth is a time of decision.

Life consists of decisions. We cannot avoid the responsibility for making decisions. When we awake in the morning, we are confronted with the decision to get up immediately or to remain in bed for a while. Throughout all of the day we continually make decisions. This is a picture of life.

A. *You face the decision concerning the object of your worship in life.* Some decide early to worship the true God who has revealed himself in the person of Jesus Christ. With heart, mind, soul, and body they dedicate themselves to him. Others choose to worship things, and so they place material things on the throne of their lives. They organize their lives around securing properties and material things, and they bow before a false god of material things. Some decide to worship self. They organize their lives around themselves. But to worship any god other than the true God will prove disappointing.

B. *During your youth you will face the opportunity and responsibility of choosing a mate for life.* No other earthly decision will affect your human happiness more than your choice of the person who is to be your companion in marriage. You not only need the guidance of your heart and your mind, but you also need the guidance of the Lord Jesus Christ in making this choice.

C. *Another decision you will face in youth is the decision concerning your life's vocation.* How will you earn a living? What will be your profession? To what will you dedicate your energy? With the uppermost part of your intellect, may you choose a profession with the guidance and leadership of the Lord Jesus Christ.

II. Youth is a time of dedication.

A. *Many young people are dedicated devotedly to athletics.* Life seems to revolve around athletic events at school. They participate with tremendous enthusiasm.

B. *Others dedicate their lives to having fun.* They seek excitement and adventure. They are on a quest for one thrill after another. While no one wants life to be dull, it should be recognized that some forms of fun can be very destructive and can bring great harm into one's life as well as into the lives of others.

C. *Even while you are young, you would be exceedingly wise to dedicate yourself with enthusiasm to the worship and work of God.* This does not necessarily mean that you must enter some type of church-related vocation. It does mean that you should trust Jesus Christ as your Savior and let him guide you in your home, your school, your social life, and as you look forward to a professional life.

III. Youth can be a time of desecration.

It is a tragedy that some desecrate their lives to the extent that they almost completely destroy the possibilities for living a full and happy life later on.

A. *One can waste educational opportunities.* By choosing to ignore one's opportunities and responsibilities while still a youth in school, one can rob oneself of the opportunity for a rich and full life and of one's earning potential later on. Consequently, he or she deprives a future family of that which he or she could have achieved. May God help you to see the tremendous opportunity that is yours of developing your intellect and the skills that you will need after you become a man or a woman.

B. *It is possible to live a life of dissipation even in the early days of youth that can seriously imperil the possibility of a happy marriage and a good reputation in later life.* Some live under the false impression that every boy must go through a period of foolishness in which he sows his wild oats. You should be wise enough to recognize that "whatsoever a man soweth, that shall he also reap" (Gal. 6:7). What you do today will determine what you are tomorrow. It is impossible to sow a crop of wild oats, even in the foolish days of youth, and escape a certain harvest somewhere down the line. May God help you to decide to live a life of purity in the present.

IV. Youth is a time of destiny.

Someone has said that decisions determine destiny. When you get to the end of the way, you will have discovered that your destiny was determined by the decisions you made along the way. Your tomorrow is wrapped up in the decisions that you make now.

A. *Moses achieved his great destiny because he made a decision in his youth to worship and to serve God with all of his heart and life (Heb. 11:24–25).*

B. *From early youth Joseph gave himself in worship and service to God.* He decided to live a life of personal purity in a time when he was sorely tempted to compromise his faith and his morals. Because of this decision and other decisions, he was able to achieve his destiny, and he became the prime minister of Egypt.

C. *We read in the Old Testament about a boy named Daniel who made a decision to live a life of faithfulness to God.* "But Daniel purposed in his heart that he would not defile himself with the portion of the king's meat, nor with the wine which he drank: therefore he requested of the prince of the eunuchs that he might not defile himself" (Dan. 1:8). Because of this decision that Daniel made in his youth to be loyal and faithful to God, he was strengthened and equipped by God to become the great man that he became later on.

Conclusion

We are where we are today because of the fork in the road we chose yesterday. Young people, you are at a fork in the road. You have an opportunity to choose the high road that leads to success or the low road that leads to disappointment, failure, and desecration.

Youth is a wonderful time in life. God promises to help you to use it wisely—if you want his help—as you face the decisions that will determine your destiny.

Title: Limiting God

Text: "Yea, they turned back and tempted God, and limited the Holy One of Israel" **(Ps. 78:41)**.

Introduction

The inspired writer spoke of the fact that ancient Israel did something which at first glance would appear to be impossible. He declared that the followers of Moses put limitations on God.

The Bible teaches us that God is the Creator of the universe, that he made man from the dust of the earth and breathed into his nostrils the breath of life. The Bible speaks of him as being all-powerful, all-knowing, and present in all places at all times. How would it be possible for anyone to limit a God like this? Moses was declaring that the people of Israel were individually limiting God as to what he could do in and through their lives. They hindered his gracious work in their lives. They prevented God from having the place that belonged to him. They restricted his activity. They thwarted his purposes. They shut him out of their thoughts, their ambitions, and their actions. For all practical purposes, they tied the hands of the loving God so their lives would not be used of him.

Israel was journeying toward the Promised Land. God was leading and seeking to bless them, yet they limited him.

I. The way God was limited.

A. *They forgot his wonderful works in the past (Ps. 78:11).* Consequently, they were afraid of the future.
B. *They questioned the goodness of God in spite of the fact that he had been lavish in the gifts he bestowed (Ps. 78:19).*
C. *They did not place confidence in God to be trustworthy and dependable (Ps. 78:22).*
D. *They were insincere and untruthful to God (Ps. 78:36).*

II. The results of limiting God.

A. *The heart of God is grieved.* Like a loving parent, God is eager to bestow on his children the gifts they need for facing the crises and responsibilities of life.

384

As parents grieve when their children refuse to cooperate and respond to their opportunities, even so God grieves when we limit him.

B. *They experienced spiritual poverty and deprivation (Ps. 78:60).* Because of their lack of faith and the spirit of rebellion that filled their hearts, God withdrew and left them to their own resources. When people rebel against God, they impoverish their lives.

C. *Others are robbed of potential blessings when they limit the work of God in and through their lives.*

III. Limiting God in the present.

Did you know that it is possible for us to limit God in the present in the same manner Israel limited God in the past?

A. *You can limit God by refusal to trust him.* Jesus was unable to do mighty works in Nazareth because of their unbelief (Mark 6:5–6).

B. *By neglecting the means of spiritual growth, you can deprive yourself of the spiritual muscle that you would need to carry heavy responsibilities in the future.* Even as it is necessary that you attend school to develop intellect, so you need to give yourself to Bible study and witnessing that you might be prepared for greater opportunity for service in the future.

Conclusion

Years ago there was a Western song titled "Don't Fence Me In." The cowboy wants to be free to ride the range without restrictions and hindrances. God would like to have complete freedom to work his good work in your heart and life. Don't fence God out.

Title: Youth's Time Is God's Time

Text: "Remember your Creator in the days of your youth" **(Eccl. 12:1 NIV)**.

Introduction

You are fortunate to be young. You are the envy of all who are aged. Youth is a priceless possession. It is sought after by those who have lost it. You have read of the early explorer Ponce de León who sailed from Europe to the New World in search of a legendary fountain of youth. As a young person you enjoy the blessings for which he was searching.

Youth is the springtime of life. It is the time of sowing and planting. Youth is the time of developing habits that can give great promise for the future.

There are many reasons why you should trust Jesus Christ as your Savior while you are young and determine to serve him as Lord throughout all of your life. The writer of the book of Ecclesiastes would encourage you to "Remember your Creator in the days of your youth" (Eccl. 12:1 NIV).

I. It is much easier to trust and follow Christ early in life.

This is so because the habits of sin have not yet enslaved you and patterns of evil conduct have not yet been developed.

A. *Many people expect to become a Christian some day.* The tragedy is that many delay the decision to let Jesus Christ become their Savior until it is too late.

B. *The wisest decision you could make would be to trust Jesus Christ as your Savior in the present, and then you can have him as your Friend throughout all of your life.* He wants to guide, teacher, and help you all the way along the road of life.

II. You have a whole life to give to God now.

A. *It is tragic to waste life, for life is the gift of God.* Because life is so precious, it should be used wisely. Once time is gone, it cannot be recalled.

B. *Dedicate yourself to Christ now.* By so doing you will have time to prepare for a life of service both to God and to others. Your greatest study opportunities are immediately before you. God has blessed you with talents. If you will develop what he has given you and study hard, you will have much more to place at the disposal of God when you reach maturity.

C. *In the morning of life give the whole day to the Lord who gave his life completely for you on the cross.*

III. Christ can keep sin out of your life.

A. *What many people do in the first years of their lives makes their last years miserable.* The things that you choose to do now make an impact on your life that will affect the balance of your life. It is exceedingly important that you have Jesus Christ as your Savior in order that he might not only forgive your sin, but also assist you in avoiding that which could destroy you.

B. *He who has fallen into great sin has nothing to boast about.* Sin by its very nature is destructive. It corrupts, defiles, and ruins. It separates a person from his or her better self. Sin grieves the heart of God and prevents us from achieving our highest and best in life. Jesus Christ would guide you so as to avoid that which would destroy you.

C. *On one occasion the psalmist said, "Thou hast delivered my feet from falling" (Ps. 56:13).* The Savior wants to prevent you from getting into something of which you would be ashamed and that would destroy your reputation. He wants to lead you in paths that lead to the right destination both in this life and in the next.

IV. The possibility of becoming hardened to the gospel is avoided.

A. *In the Scriptures we are warned, "Today if ye will hear his voice, harden not your hearts" (Heb. 3:7–8).* To hear the gospel and the call of Christ and not heed it is to do something to your spiritual eardrum that will make it more difficult for you to hear his call the second time. It is a dangerous thing to hear the call of God and not respond. While your heart is tender and your life is young, you would be exceedingly wise to respond to the good news of God's love for you.

B. *It is dangerous to walk away from God into the dark.* Every time you hear the call of Jesus Christ and turn a deaf ear, you are actually turning away from God and walking into spiritual darkness. This is always dangerous, because the farther you walk, the deeper the darkness and the greater the danger becomes.

V. You have no guarantee of tomorrow.

The average life expectancy is now in the eighties and many people live well into their nineties, but many of us will not live to that age. In a day of deadly diseases and dangerous highways, hardly a year goes by that some friend, even among the young, is ushered into eternity. This is another reason why you should determine to let Jesus Christ be your Lord and Savior while you are still young.

In the Bible everyone is encouraged to respond to God's love and grace and mercy now. Nowhere in all of the Word of God are you encouraged to wait until you are twelve or twenty or fifty. You are invited to come to Jesus Christ now. Yesterday has flown into the tomb of time. Tomorrow is still just a dream, and it is in the womb of time. We have today, and today is the time when you should respond by faith to Jesus Christ. Trust him as your Lord and Savior now.

Title: Follow the Leader

Text: "Follow me, and I will make you fishers of men" **(Matt. 4:19)**.

Introduction

When I was a boy I used to play Follow the Leader with my friends. The leader would seek to outdo the other boys in the stunts that he was able to perform. The leader might climb a tree and act like a monkey, swinging from one limb to another. If we were swimming, the leader might dive into deep water or swim across deep water or dive from a high diving board. Those who were playing the game with him would follow until they "chickened out." It was an exciting and dangerous game. Sometimes the leader would act in a very foolish manner, and others, recognizing his foolishness, would refuse to follow. Some have found themselves in great difficulty in a game like this by following the wrong kind of leader.

Have you ever thought of a Christian as one who was following the leader? Jesus Christ, at the beginning of his ministry, told his disciples, "Follow me." On another occasion, when Jesus was passing by the place where the publicans were collecting taxes for the Roman government, he came face-to-face with a young man named Matthew and said to him, "Follow me. And he arose and followed him" (Matt. 9:9). At the conclusion of his ministry, Jesus said to Simon Peter, "You must follow me" (John 21:22 NIV). One of the best ways to think of the Christian life is to think of it in terms of following the Leader—Jesus Christ. Someone is bound to ask, "Where will Jesus Christ lead us?"

387

I. Jesus will lead you to dedicate yourself to the will of God.

In the Gospel of Luke, we read how that at the age of twelve Jesus visited the temple in Jerusalem. He was concerned about doing the will of God even at this age. Later he said to Mary and Joseph, "Wist ye not that I must be about my Father's business?" (Luke 2:49). One does not have to wait until one is full-grown before becoming involved in the work of God. In early childhood you can decide to let Jesus Christ be your leader and your Lord, and you can be about your Father's business.

II. Jesus will lead you into a right relationship with your parents.

We read in the Scriptures how that after Jesus had made this trip to Jerusalem, he returned to Nazareth and was subject to his parents. Luke's gospel tells us that Jesus "increased in wisdom and stature, and in favour with God and man" (Luke 2:52). God holds parents responsible for the manner in which they conduct themselves toward their children and for providing guidance for their children. God wants parents to be his helpers in teaching children the way of life. God holds you responsible for your reactions and response to your parents. If you will follow the leadership of Jesus Christ, he will lead you into right attitudes and into a right relationship with your parents.

III. Jesus will lead you in regular habits of worship.

Soon after Christ began his public ministry, he made a return visit to Nazareth. Luke's gospel tells us, "And he came to Nazareth, where he had been brought up: and, as his custom was, he went into the synagogue on the sabbath day, and stood up for to read" (Luke 4:16). As you need food to supply energy for your body, so you need worship for the growth of your spiritual life. Christ will lead you in both public worship and private worship. He will lead you to the house of prayer and worship every Lord's Day and to special activities during the week. Christ will also lead you in private worship as you study your Bible day by day and as you talk with God in prayer concerning the needs and problems of your life.

IV. Jesus will lead you to give yourself for others (Acts 10:38).

Jesus "went about doing good." He believed that the highest possible happiness was to be found in the giving of self in service to others. Consequently, he gave himself fully and freely in order to be helpful to others.

Jesus gave encouragement to those who were distressed. He gave hope to those who were depressed. He gave food to the hungry. He gave guidance to the uncertain. He gave comfort to the grieving. Finally, he gave his life fully on the cross for us. Jesus believed with all his heart that his highest destiny was to be found in the giving of himself completely to God for others.

Christ will lead you to define your purpose for living in terms of the service that you could render to other people, rather than in terms of how much you could get out of other people. May God help you to decide to follow him in a life of giving.

V. Christ will lead you into the heavenly home.

At the end of a life of worship and work, Jesus Christ will lead you into the heavenly home at the end of the way that he has been preparing for those who love him. Jesus said, "I go to prepare a place for you. And if I go and prepare a place for you, I will come again, and receive you unto myself; that where I am, there ye may be also" (John 14:2–3). To neglect to follow Jesus is to miss the highest possible success in life and to deprive oneself of following him into the heavenly home at the end of the way.

Conclusion

The happiest people on earth are not necessarily the most popular or the wealthiest. The happiest people that you know are those who have given their hearts and lives to Jesus Christ and are sincerely and honestly seeking to follow him day by day and week by week. You would be exceedingly wise to let Jesus Christ lead you throughout all the days of your life.

FUNERAL MEDITATIONS

Title: "Comfort One Another with These Words"

Text: "Wherefore, comfort one another with these words" **(1 Thess. 4:18).**

Introduction

By his victorious resurrection from the dead, Jesus assured his disciples of the reality of eternal life. He assured them that because of his grace and power, they likewise would experience eternal life (John 14:19).

The disciples lived in the constant hope that our Lord would fulfill his promise to return and that he would fully establish his kingdom on the earth during their lifetime. The years became decades, and as some of the Jesus' followers entered eternity through the doorway that we know as death, it was only normal that those who remained should be concerned about the fate and welfare of those who died. By divine inspiration, Paul wrote to give them both information and comfort.

I. "I would not have you to be ignorant, brethren" (I Thess. 4:13).

The New Testament has much to say about the eternal home of the redeemed. While all of the minute questions that we might ask are not answered in the Scriptures, we are provided with enough information to comfort the hearts of those who know Jesus Christ as Savior.

II. Our sorrow is not the sorrow of those who have no hope.

It is only normal that we experience sorrow and grief when death removes a loved one from our midst. We grieve because of our loss. Death has deprived us of the joys and privileges of that one's presence. In this sense our grief is for us.

Our Christian faith tells us that death has separated us from our loved one for a time and not forever. One day we shall go to be with our loved one, and the pain of separation will be a thing of the past.

III. Those who have died in the Lord are with the Lord (I Thess. 4:14).

Paul declares that when the Lord returns to the earth, he will have with him those who died before his personal return. Departed believers are with the Lord (2 Cor. 5:8).

Heaven is the dwelling place of God. Wherever God is, there is heaven. The writer of the book of Revelation records, "And I heard a voice from heaven saying unto me, Write, Blessed are the dead which die in the Lord from henceforth: Yea, saith the Spirit, that they may rest from their labours; and their works do follow them" (Rev. 14:13).

IV. At our Lord's return the resurrection will occur (I Thess. 4:16–17).

Ultimate and final victory over death and the grave will be experienced by the redeemed when our Lord returns triumphantly to the earth. Death shall be no more. Separation from Christian loved ones will be a thing of the past. The eternal home of God will become the dwelling place of all of the redeemed. The inspired writer speaks of that time. "And I heard a great voice out of heaven saying, Behold, the tabernacle of God is with men, and he will dwell with them, and they shall be his people, and God himself shall be with them, and be their God. And God shall wipe away all tears from their eyes; and there shall be no more death, neither sorrow, nor crying, neither shall there be any more pain: for the former things are passed away" (Rev. 21:3–4).

Conclusion

Those who know Jesus Christ as Lord and Savior can be greatly comforted by these precious promises when death comes to claim a member of the family. We can be comforted by pleasant memories of the departed. We can be comforted by the presence of friends. Our greatest source of comfort is to be found in the genuineness of our own faith in the Christ who said, "I am he that liveth, and was dead; and, behold, I am alive for evermore" (Rev. 1:18).

May God grant to each of us the faith in this living Lord that will make him real to us in the time of grief.

Title: "Death, Be Not Proud"

Text: "I am he that liveth, and was dead; and, behold, I am alive for evermore" (**Rev. 1:18**).

Introduction

John Donne, a famous English preacher known as the poet's poet, was born in 1573 and went to be with the Lord in 1661. In one sonnet he personifies death and speaks to death as only a Christian can.

Death, be not proud, though some have called thee
Mighty and dreadful, for thou art not so;
For those whom thou think'st thou dost overthrow
Die not, poor Death, nor yet canst thou kill me.
From rest and sleep, which but thy pictures be
Much pleasure, then from thee much more must flow;
And soonest our best men with thee do go—
Rest of their bones and souls' delivery!
Thou'rt slave to fate, chance, kings and desperate men,
And dost with poison, war, and sickness dwell;
And poppy or charms can make us sleep as well,
And better than thy stroke, Why swell'st thou then?
One short sleep past, we wake eternally,
And Death shall be no more: Death, thou shalt die.

This is the mature Christian's concept of death. John Donne recognized that through Jesus Christ the believer would ultimately have victory over death. This faith is needed by each Christian, and it means more and more as time goes by.

I. From the beginning of recorded history, people have feared death.

A. *People have feared the grip of death since Cain murdered Abel.*
B. *Death invades the family circle, and those left behind are deprived of their dearest and most precious relationships.*
C. *Death is a constant reminder to people of their fallen condition.* People were and are sinners. Sin and death entered the world at the same time.

II. Death has been a conqueror.

A. *Death has been a robber.*
B. *Death has been an enemy.*
C. *Death has been a despoiler of human hope and love.*
D. *Death has been a grim reaper.*
E. *Death conquered the strong: Samson, Goliath, and Gideon.*
F. *Death conquered the wise: Solomon, Paul, Augustine, Origen, Gladstone, and Webster.*
G. *Death has conquered the wealthy: Croesus, Rockefeller, Morgan, and Astor.*
H. *Death has conquered the holy and the good: patriarchs, prophets, apostles, and martyrs.*

III. Death is a defeated foe.

A. *Jesus came to earth "for the suffering of death" (Heb. 2:9).*
B. *Christ entered the country of death to destroy the power of the Devil and death (Heb. 2:14–15).*
C. *"Whom God hath raised up, having loosed the pains of death: because it was not possible that he should be holden of it" (Acts 2:24).*

D. *"But now is Christ risen from the dead, and become the firstfruits of them that slept"* *(1 Cor. 15:20).* The devout Israelite would bring the firstfruits of the harvest and dedicate them to God as an expression of gratitude for the full harvest that was to follow. By the term "firstfruits," the inspired writer is declaring that those who trust Christ will also experience victory over death and the tomb.

E. *The resurrection was more than just a demonstration of divine power.* It presented an exhibition of the reality of life and immortality beyond death for those who know Jesus Christ as Savior and Lord (2 Tim. 1:9–10).

F. *Christ said, "Because I live, ye shall live also" (John 14:19).* Faith in Christ enabled the revelator to see a vision of the new heaven and the new earth and to hear a voice out of heaven saying: "Behold, the tabernacle of God is with men, and he will dwell with them, and they shall be his people, and God himself shall be with them, and be their God. And God shall wipe away all tears from their eyes; and *there shall be no more death,* neither sorrow, nor crying, neither shall there be any more pain: for the former things are passed away" (Rev. 21:3–4, emphasis added).

G. *The inspired writer was permitted to hear a voice from heaven describing the condition of the righteous dead, and he was commanded by the voice from heaven to write, "Blessed are the dead which die in the Lord" (Rev. 14:13).* The word "blessed" carries with it the idea of happiness; the inspired writer is actually saying, "Happy are the dead who die in the Lord."

IV. Consider death.

A. *The fact of death is certain.*

B. *The time of death is uncertain.*

C. *Death is life's last frontier.* Each man must discover it for himself. No one escapes it.

D. *Leon Marsh said, "Death may come in infancy, youth, the prime of life, or old age.* There is never a time when it should surprise us, and yet never a 'right' time for dying."

V. Death gives us many warnings.

A. *Empty chairs at home.*

B. *Death abroad in the land.*

C. *The decline of health.*

D. *The advance of age.*

Conclusion

Because Jesus Christ is "able also to save them to the uttermost that come unto God by him, seeing he ever liveth to make intercession for them" (Heb. 7:25), we should trust him implicitly when sorrow comes or when we face our own departure from this life. It is both the divine will and within divine power to replace death with life. God would replace our fear with faith. He would dispel our grief with joy. With John Donne, let us speak to death and say:

> *Death, be not proud . . .*
> *One short sleep past, we wake eternally,*
> *And Death shall be no more:*
> *Death, thou shalt die.*

Title: "The God of All Comfort"

Text: "Blessed be God . . . the God of all comfort" **(1 Cor. 1:3).**

Introduction

[Read Psalm 23 and John 14:1–6.] In the words of our text, the inspired writer speaks of our God as being the Father of mercies and the God of all comfort. Here God is described as one who deals with us in mercy and who is eager to provide us with all comfort. The word translated "comfort" literally means to "call to one's side." It is the same word Jesus used to describe the Holy Spirit (John 14:16; 16:7). The English word "comfort" is from a Latin word that means "to be brave together."

I. God is aware of our need for comfort.

A. *As we meet the disappointments and face the duties of life, we desperately need the companionship of the loving God.*

B. *Crises will occur along the road of life in which every person stands in need of the comforting presence of the redeeming Savior (Ps. 23:4).*

C. *The experience of death is before us all.* A calm faith in a home at the end of the road can provide comfort and assurance to every believer (John 14:1–6).

II. God has provided a way of comfort for us.

A. *"The wages of sin is death; but the gift of God is eternal life" through faith in his Son, Jesus Christ (Rom. 6:23).* This eternal life is a present possession of those who trust him as Lord.

B. *Christ Jesus, the sinless, stainless, spotless Son of God, died on the cross for our sins to remove everything that would separate us from God.* Having redeemed us by his own precious blood, he is able to bring each believer unto God because he has conquered death and the grave and is our living Savior (1 Peter 3:18).

C. *He entered death and destroyed the power of the Devil in order that he might deliver us from the fear of death (Heb. 2:14–15).*

III. The assurance of life beyond.

Job asked, "If a man die, shall he live again?" (Job 14:14). The centuries rolled by without an authentic answer to that question. It remained for Jesus Christ to

393

declare, "I am the resurrection, and the life: he that believeth in me, though he were dead, yet shall he live" (John 11:25). He also said, "Because I live, ye shall live also" (14:19).

One of the primary purposes of the book of Revelation is to reveal the ultimate triumph and victory of Jesus Christ over all forces and powers that are in opposition to God. One of these is death. The risen Christ appeared to John in transfigured glory and declared, "I am he that liveth, and was dead; and, behold, I am alive for evermore, Amen; and have the keys of hell and of death" (Rev. 1:18). Here he declares his sovereignty over life, death, and the abode of the dead. By means of the keys, he declares his control over life and death. It is his will that his followers have life and have it more abundantly. In this faith let us face the future without fear. With courage and cheer let us live each day with the issues and values of eternity ever in mind.

Title: Heaven

Text: "I go to prepare a place for you" (**John 14:2**).

Introduction

When a family learns of the possibility of a move from one state to another, immediately they become intensely interested in their prospective new community. Since all of us hope to go to heaven some day, we should be vitally interested in knowing as much about our future home as possible. The Bible is the only source of authentic information concerning the eternal home of those who trust Jesus Christ as Savior. We should study the Bible diligently to learn as much about heaven as possible.

I. Heaven is a place of perfect holiness.

"And there shall in no wise enter into it any thing that defileth, neither whatsoever worketh abomination, or maketh a lie; but they which are written in the Lamb's book of life" (Rev. 21:27). It is a prepared place for a prepared people.

Only those who have been redeemed by the blood of the Lamb and have experienced a spiritual birth that imparts to them a nature like unto the nature of God could possibly enjoy heaven. Heaven is not just a place of continued existence. The life that we receive through Christ Jesus is qualitative as well as quantitative.

II. Consider the health of heaven.

On earth there is no perfect health. In youth we enjoy next-to-perfect health, but as time goes by, health slowly departs and life comes to an end usually because of sickness. The inspired writer says that in the new heaven "there shall be no more death, neither sorrow, nor crying, neither shall there be any pain: for the former things are passed away" (Rev. 21:4). There will be no more colds, no more fever, no more exhausting pains, and no more hospitals. There will be no more headaches, stomachaches, backaches, or heartaches. No one will be bowed down with the infirmities of old age. Each will walk with the step of an athlete, forever young and vigorous.

III. Consider the music of heaven.

John speaks of the sound of the harps and the songs of the redeemed (Rev. 14:2–3). There is nothing more inspiring than beautiful music. There will be choirs of white-robed children singing with the voices of cherubs. There will be choirs of patriarchs and prophets and choirs of apostles. Anthem will follow anthem and chorus will follow chorus. David will be there with his harp. Gabriel will be there with his trumpet. Congregation will join congregation, and the scepter of eternity will beat time to the music. Hearts will be lifted and souls will be continually transformed by the glory of the music of heaven.

IV. Consider the reunions in heaven.

A. Good-bye *is a sad word in every language.* No one likes to be parted from a loved one. Separation from a loved one is what causes us to be sad when death removes that loved one from us.

B. *In heaven there shall be no more death to separate us from those we love.* When we get to heaven, we will be reunited with those who have gone before. We will be welcomed at the pearly gates. We will be welcomed as we walk down the golden streets. We will be welcomed by the river of life. We will be welcomed at the heavenly Father's house.

Conclusion

Jesus Christ and Jesus Christ alone is the way to heaven. "Jesus saith unto him, I am the way, the truth, and the life: no man cometh unto the Father, but by me" (John 14:6). Jesus Christ, the divine Carpenter, has gone to prepare a place for those who trust him and love him and follow him.

With faith let us trust him now, and in faithfulness let us follow him. To know him now and to walk with him through life is to experience a foretaste of heaven here and now.

Title: "The Death of His Saints"

Text: "Precious in the sight of the LORD is the death of his saints" (**Ps. 116:15**).

Introduction

Death is always a solemn and serious experience. It is not, of necessity, a gloomy, melancholy subject. For the Christian it can be one of God's most wonderful blessings.

The death of an unbelieving sinner is indeed a sad and tragic experience. It would mean the end of a wasted life and the beginning of a hopeless eternity. For the children of God, such is not the case.

I. His saints.

God's children are called saints.

A. *God's children are called saints not because we are without sin or because we have achieved a degree of piety that puts us beyond the temptation to sin.*

B. *We are called saints because we have been saved from the penalty of sin.* We are in a process of being saved from the power and practice of sin as God works his good work within our hearts and lives. The New Testament speaks of all believers as saints. They are the dedicated ones who belong to God by a decision of commitment to Jesus.

II. The death of the saints.

God looks at the death of his saints from an entirely different perspective than the way we view death. From our perspective, death takes our loved ones from us. We experience a sense of loss. We are robbed of their presence, of their affections, and of their activities. From God's perspective, it is through the doorway of death that his saints, his children, come into the eternal home where perfect holiness and perfect happiness are the unending experience of all of the redeemed.

All of us have experienced the sadness of having someone depart for a brief journey. A father or mother may go away on a business trip. Children may go away to college or to join the military. The time of departure is always sad, but the return of loved ones is always an occasion of joy. By the vehicle of death, God's saints journey to him.

III. The blessing of a Christian death.

A. *God wants to bless his saints with rest from their labors.*

B. *God wants to bless his saints with relief from suffering.*

C. *God wants to reward his saints for their faithfulness.*

D. *God wants his saints to come home.*

WEDDINGS

Title: Prewedding Conference

A pastor assumes that when a couple comes for a wedding ceremony, they look upon the wedding ceremony as having religious significance. Christian marriage is more than just a legal contract; it is the beginning of a divine institution. As such the pastor should plan the service as a religious ceremony. In an effort to assist the couple to find the highest possible happiness and the greatest possible success, I have a policy of having a prewedding conference with every couple whose ceremony I perform. In this conference one of my major purposes is to get acquainted with the couple and to establish a relationship that would make it possible for them to return for counsel and help at a later time if they face unusual difficulties adjusting to each other.

I never perform two ceremonies alike. Each wedding should be tailored to fit the specific occasion.

In this conference, we discuss the fact that success in marriage is determined like success in any other enterprise. Success is almost always the result of plain hard work combined with a determination to succeed.

I discuss with the couple the nature of love and warn them that if romantic love is the only factor bringing them together, they are in great danger of experiencing failure in marriage. I discuss with them the nature of love using three Greek words, *eros, philia,* and *agape.* In this discussion I point out that usually romantic love comes first, but that if the marriage is to succeed, there must also be filial love based on a recognition of the character and worth of the other as an individual. They need to be the kind of individuals that their companion would genuinely appreciate even if they were not married. Agape love is sacrificial, self-giving love—the Calvary kind of love. I point out that in the happy Christian marriage, there needs to be a combination of love on these three different levels—sexual, social, and sacrificial. I then fill out the Premarital Conference Information Sheet.

Premarital Conference Information Sheet

Date of conference _____ Date of wedding _____

Groom _____ Birth date _____ Age _____

    Residence _____ Phone _____

    Occupation _____ Phone _____

    Religious affiliation _____

Bride _____ Birth date _____ Age _____

    Residence _____ Phone _____

    Occupation _____ Phone _____

    Religious affiliation _____

Details of Wedding

    Place of wedding _____ Date _____ Hour _____

    Place of rehearsal _____ Date _____ Hour _____

    Witnesses _____ Relationship _____

    _____ Relationship _____

    Number of ushers _____ Number of bride's attendants _____

    Others in wedding party _____

    Assisting minister, if any _____ Organist _____

    Double or single ring ceremony _____ Vocalists _____

    What men are wearing _____

    What minister should wear _____

    What rooms of church are needed _____

    Any extra janitorial service required _____

    Florist _____ Caterer _____

    Request of changes in wording or ceremony _____

Couple will reside at _____

    Is above temporary or permanent address? _____

    Who will usually know permanent address? (relationship) _____

    Name _____ Address _____

Known _____ Dated _____ Engaged _____

I. People involved in your marriage.

   A. *Your parents.*
   B. *Your community.*
   C. *Your church.*
   D. *The state.*
   E. *The schools.*
   F. *God.*
   G. *Unborn children.*
   H. *You.*

II. The continuation of courtship.

   A. *Watch personal attractiveness.*
   B. *Give attention to the little courtesies of life.*
   C. *Cultivate mutual interests.*
   D. *Avoid criticizing your companion in public.*
   E. *Resolve that all conflicts will be settled before the day ends.*

III. The new relationship.

   A. *The problem of in-laws.*
   B. *Plans for the operation of a home.*
   C. *A cooperative spirit is important.*

IV. Practical matters.

   A. *Health.*
   B. *Keeping out of debt.*
   C. *Living within your income.*
   D. *Planning for children.*
   E. *Keeping your love in spiritual repair.*
   F. *Recognizing the presence of God by sharing your income with him.*
   G. *Maintaining a family altar.*

V. Personal growth and development.

   A. *Give attention to what you read.*
   B. *Engage in play.*
   C. *Restful recreation.*
   D. *The danger of alcoholic beverages.*

VI. The problem of physical adjustment.

Some books you may find helpful are Ed Wheat, *Love-Life for Every Married Couple* (Zondervan, 1980); Herbert J. Miles, *Sexual Happiness in Marriage* (Zondervan, 1982); Lewis B. Smedes, *Sex for Christians* (Eerdmans, 1994); Les Parrott III and Leslie Parrott, *Questions Couples Ask* (Zondervan, 1996), *Love List* (Zondervan, 2002), and *I Love You More* (Zondervan, 2005).

VII. Spiritual matters.

Title: Marriage Ceremony

Holy and happy is the sacred hour when two devoted hearts are bound by the enchanting ties of matrimony. Marriage is an institution of divine appointment and is commended as honorable among all men. Marriage is God's first institution for the welfare of the race. In the quiet bowers of Eden, before the forbidden tree had yielded its fateful fruit or the Tempter had touched the world, God saw that it was not good for the man to be alone. He made a helpmate suitable for him and established the rite of marriage while heavenly hosts witnessed the wonderful scene in reverence.

The contract of marriage was sanctioned and honored by the presence of the power of Jesus at the marriage in Cana of Galilee and marked the beginning of his wondrous works. It is declared by the apostle Paul to be honorable among all men. So it is ordained that a man shall leave his father and mother and cleave unto his wife, and they twain shall be one flesh, united in hopes and aims and sentiments until death alone shall part them.

If you, then, _____ (groom) and _____ (bride), after careful consideration and in the fear of God, have deliberately chosen each other as partners in the holy estate, and know of no just cause why you should not be so united, in token thereof you will please join your right hands.

Groom's Vow

_____ , will you have this woman to be your wedded wife, to live together after God's ordinance in the holy estate of matrimony? Will you love her, comfort her, honor her, and keep her in sickness and in health, and forsaking all others keep yourself only unto her as long as you both shall live?

Answer: I will.

Bride's Vow

_____ , will you have this man to be your wedded husband, to live together after God's ordinance in the holy estate of matrimony? Will you love him, honor him, and keep him in sickness and in health, and forsaking all others keep yourself only unto him so long as you both shall live?

Answer: I will.

Vows to Each Other

I, _____ (groom), take you, _____ (bride), to be my wedded wife, to have and to hold from this day forward, in prosperity or adversity, in sickness or in health, in advances or reverses, to love and to cherish till death do us part, according to God's holy ordinance, and thereto pledge you my trust.

I, _____ (bride), take you, _____ (groom), to be my wedded husband, to have and to hold from this day forward, in prosperity or adversity, in sickness or in health, in advances or reverses, to love and to cherish till death do us part, according to God's holy ordinance, and thereto I pledge you my trust.

Then are you each given to the other for richer or poorer, for better or worse, in sickness and in health, till death alone shall part you.

Throughout history the ring has been used to seal important covenants. The golden circlet, most prized of jewels, has come to its loftiest prestige in the symbolic significance which it vouches at the marriage altar. Its untarnishable material is the purest gold. Even so may your love for each other be pure and may it grow brighter and brighter as time goes by. The ring is a circle, thus having no end. Even so may there be no end to the happiness and success that come to you as you unite your lives together.

Do you, _____ (groom), give this ring to your wedded wife as a token of your love for her?

Will you, _____ (bride), receive this ring as a token of your wedded husband's love for you, and will you wear it as a token of your love for him?

Do you, _____ (bride), give this ring to your wedded husband as a token of your love for him?

Will you, _____ (groom), receive this ring as a token of your wedded wife's love for you, and will you wear it as a token of your love for her?

Having pledged your faith in and love to each other in the sight of God and these assembled witnesses, and having sealed your solemn marital vows by giving and receiving the rings, acting in the authority vested in me as a minister of the gospel by this state, and looking to heaven for divine sanction, I pronounce you husband and wife.

Therefore, what God has joined together, let no man put asunder. [Prayer.]

Title: Mutual Subjection to the Will of God

On this high and holy occasion when two devoted hearts are bound together by the enchanting ties of Christian matrimony, we should rejoice in the glad consciousness that this is a part of God's good plan for humankind. Marriage is more than just a human arrangement. Christian marriage should be something infinitely more than a legal contract between two individuals, for marriage is a divine institution that was born in the heart of God and designed to produce the highest possible human happiness.

Since marriage is a divine institution, we should look to the Scriptures for guidance and help if we would achieve the highest possible success in this most important of human relationships. One of the most beautiful passages dealing with the mutual responsibilities of the husbands and wives is found in Paul's epistle to the Ephesians.

[Read Ephesians 5:21–33.]

I would call your attention to the fact that in the first verse of this passage both the husband and the wife are encouraged to recognize the absolute lordship of Christ in the marriage relationship. Marriage should not be entered into lightly or without inward assurance that the union of your two lives into one is according to the will of the Savior. This verse implies that God is to have first place and that we are responsible unto him for the manner in which we relate ourselves to our companion in marriage.

This passage of Scripture compares the relationship of the husband and the wife to the mystical relationship that exists between Christ and his church. The passage emphasizes the mutual responsibilities within the marriage relationship rather than the rights and privileges of the relationship.

The passage contains a commandment to the husband to love his wife in a twofold manner. First of all, the husband is commanded to love his wife "even as Christ also loved the church, and gave himself for it" (Eph. 5:25). This is sacrificial love that places the welfare of the wife before the husband's own private welfare. The second command to the husband is that he is to love his wife even as he loves his own body (v. 28). By a combination of sacrificial love and self-love, the husband is to devote himself to the welfare and best interest of his wife.

The Scripture contains two commandments also to the wife. Verse 22 encourages the wife to recognize her husband as the head of the household, and verse 33 exhorts the wife to "see that she reverence her husband." Nothing is said about the wife loving her husband, though it is implied. Genuine and abiding love is based on respect. We can safely assume that it is the purpose of God that the wife should so conduct herself that the husband will find it easy to love her even as Christ loved the church.

The Vows

[Use the vows of your choice.]

The Rings

Throughout history the ring has been used on important occasions. In ages gone by, the official seal of the empire was often worn as a signet on the hand of the reigning monarch and was used to authenticate documents of the state. But the golden circlet, the most prized of jewels, has reached its loftiest prestige in the symbolic significance that it vouches at the marriage altar.

[Hold the ring(s) up before the bride and groom.]

The wedding ring is an object of great beauty. This is true because it is made of a precious metal that will not tarnish with the passing of time. I would remind you as we look at this ring that at one time it was but crude ore in the depths of the earth. Someone discovered it, mined it, and refined it, master craftsmanship was brought to bear upon it, and the result is this beautiful ring.

Today you bring to your marriage the raw materials of character, unselfishness, love, truthfulness, honesty, kindness, and courtesy. Combine these materials together with master craftsmanship and continued effort, and you will discover that even as there is no end to the ring, there will be no end to the happiness and joy you can experience together as husband and wife. Give to your companion a place second only to your Lord. Place your own private, personal welfare at a lower rung of the ladder, and you will discover that as the ring does not tarnish, so your relationship as husband and wife will be more beautiful and more precious with the passing of every year.

As a permanent reminder of the vows you have made and entered into on this holy occasion, you will now give and receive this (these) ring(s) as a solemn seal to be known by all.

[Present the ring(s) and suggest that it (they) be put on the finger.]

In a moment of high and holy dedication, you have solemnized your marriage vows. Acting in the authority vested in me as a minister of the gospel by this state, I take great joy in pronouncing you husband and wife. What God therefore has joined together, do not let anything put asunder.

[Prayer of benediction.]

[Address the groom.] You may now claim your bride with a kiss.

Title: Permanent Love

On this happy occasion when relatives and friends come together to witness the solemnization of marriage vows, let us all unite our hearts in prayer for this couple that they might demonstrate a love for each other that will grow and increase and become more beautiful with the passing of each year.

[Prayer of invocation.]

The Bible teaches us that God is a God of love. We are not to interpret this as being romantic love, but it should be recognized that romantic love is a part of God's good purpose for humankind. The divine Creator created us in a manner that makes it possible for humans to find completion and fulfillment and companionship in this most sacred of human relationships that we call marriage. It is a part of God's will that a man should fall in love with a woman and that a woman should fall in love with a man and that they should desire to enter into a lifelong relationship as husband and wife.

The Bible would teach us and experience would verify that romantic love needs to combine with unselfish, self-giving Christian love if you are to find the highest possible happiness as husband and wife.

In Paul's great chapter on love, he describes the properties and characteristics of the love that is permanent and that brings beauty and happiness into the lives of those who live in an attitude of Christian love. These properties are described most beautifully in 1 Corinthians 13:4–8. [The minister may then read these verses.]

These verses describe both the negative and positive characteristics of the love that can grow more beautiful with the passing of each year. If it is your desire to enter into the rights and responsibilities of a Christian marriage, you will indicate such by the joining of your right hands.

Groom's Vow

_____ , will you have this woman to be your wedded wife, to live together after God's ordinance in the holy estate of matrimony? Will you love her, comfort her, honor and keep her in sickness and in health, and forsaking all others keep yourself only unto her so long as you both shall live?

Answer: I will.

Bride's Vow

_____ , will you have this man to be your wedded husband, to live together after God's ordinance in the holy estate of matrimony? Will you love him, honor him, and keep him in sickness and in health, and forsaking all others keep yourself only unto him so long as you both shall live?

Answer: I will.

Vows to Each Other

I, _____ (groom), take you, _____ (bride), to be my wedded wife, to have and to hold from this day forward, in prosperity or adversity, in sickness or in health, in advances or reverses, to love and to cherish till death do us part, according to God's holy ordinance, and thereto I pledge you my trust.

I, _____ (bride), take you, _____ (groom), to be my wedded husband, to have and to hold from this day forward, in prosperity or adversity, in sickness or in health, in advances or reverses, to love and to cherish till death do us part, according to God's holy ordinance, and thereto I pledge you my trust.

Then are you each given to the other for richer or poorer, for better or worse, in sickness and in health, till death alone shall part you.

The ring is a perfect circle, having no end. It is the prayer of your pastor, your relatives, and your friends that there will be no end to the happiness and success that you experience in marriage. You will now exchange your wedding rings as a symbol of your promises to love each other without fail to the end of your earthly lives.

[The bride and groom will then place the wedding bands on each other's hand.]

In the presence of your relatives and friends, and in the very presence of God, you have made vows to each other, binding upon you by the laws of this state, by the laws of God, and by the love you have in your hearts for each other. You have sealed these vows by the receiving and giving of your wedding rings. Acting in the authority vested in me as a minister of the gospel, by this state, I take great joy in pronouncing you husband and wife. What therefore God has joined together, let nothing put asunder.

[Suggest now that the groom claim his bride with a kiss, and the recessional will follow.]

Title: A Home Wedding

It is most appropriate that we should gather together here in the home to solemnize the sacred rites by which a new home and a new family come into existence. As we begin, let us approach the throne of grace for divine approval and assistance for this couple.

[Prayer of invocation.]

On this happy occasion, let us be reminded that the home is God's first institution for the welfare of the race. In the quiet bower of Eden, before sin had touched the world, God saw that it was not good for the man to be alone. "And the Lord God said, It is not good that man should be alone; I will make him an help meet for him" (Gen. 2:18).

In commenting on these verses, someone has said that it is significant to note that Eve was made from a rib from the side of man rather than from the foot or the head. It was not intended that the woman should be trodden upon by man, and neither was she to rule over him. The rib was taken from the side, indicating that she would be very dear to his heart, that she should enjoy his protection and walk by his side as both a supplement and a complement, and that the two of them together should ever attempt to form a perfect union.

The relationship of husband and wife is to have top priority over all other human relationships. From the beginning it was said, "Therefore shall a man leave his father and his mother, and shall cleave unto his wife: and they shall be one flesh" (Gen. 2:24). After marriage the husband is to have first place in the love and loyalty of his wife, and the wife is to have first place in the love and loyalty of her husband.

The contract of marriage was honored and approved by our Savior by his presence at a marriage in Cana of Galilee. It was at this wedding feast that our Savior performed his first miracle that manifested his glory (John 2:1–11).

The writer of the book of Hebrews declares that marriage is accepted as an honorable relationship among all people (Heb. 13:4).

[If the bride wishes to be "given" in marriage, the minister should now ask, "Who gives this woman to this man in marriage?"]

If you, then, _____ (groom) and _____ (bride), after careful consideration and in the fear of God, have deliberately chosen each other as partners in the holy estate of matrimony, and know of no just cause why you should not be so united in token thereof, you will please join your right hands.

Groom's Vow

_____ , in taking this woman to be your lawful and wedded wife, do you promise before God and these assembled witnesses to love her and to honor her and to cherish her in sickness and in health, and forsaking all others be to her in all things a true and faithful husband until death alone shall part you?

Answer: I will.

Bride's Vow

_____ , in taking this man to be your lawful and wedded husband, do you promise before God and these assembled witnesses to love him and to honor him and to cherish him in sickness and in health, and forsaking all others be to him in all things a true and faithful wife until death alone shall part you?

Answer: I will.

Then are you each given to the other for richer or poorer, in sickness and in health, in advances or reverses until death alone shall part you.

[The minister shall receive the ring(s).]

The wedding ring is a perfect circle, thus having no end. As such it symbolizes our hopes and prayers that there shall be no end to the happiness and joy that you experience as husband and wife.

Do you, _____ (groom), give this ring to your wedded wife as a token of your love for her?

Answer: I do.

Will you, _____ (bride), receive this ring from your wedded husband as a token of his love for you, and will you wear it as a token of your love for him?

Answer: I will.

(Groom) _____ , you will now place the ring upon your bride's finger.

Do you, _____ (bride), give this ring to your wedded husband as a token of your love for him?

Answer: I do.

Will you, _____ (groom), receive this ring as a token of your wedded wife's love for you, and will you wear it as a token of your love for her?

Answer: I will.

(Bride) _____ , you will now place the ring on the groom's finger.

Here in the presence of your relatives and friends, and in the eyes of God, you have made vows to each other binding upon you by the laws of this state and by the laws of God. You have sealed these solemn and sacred vows by the giving and receiving of these rings. Acting in the authority vested in me as a minister of the gospel, by this state, I take great joy in pronouncing you husband and wife.

[Lead in a prayer of benediction. Then say to the groom, "You may now claim your bride with a kiss."]

SENTENCE SERMONETTES

The most used word in hell is *I*.

Every self-centered person is a disintegrating person.

God obeys every law he demands of us.

You are not made to be the center of the universe.

A grain of wheat remains a solitary grain unless it falls into the ground and dies.
    If it dies, it bears a rich harvest.

We learn as we obey and in no other way.

Sin is, has been, and ever shall be the parent of misery.

Everybody surrenders — to something.

The function of every Christian is to be a part of the body of Christ.

Prayer is a dialogue rather than a monologue.

Through the church Christ acts, and without the church he cannot act.

All useful work is work for God.

Faith is the settled conviction that certain things are true.

Missions is not a sideline. It is the lifeline of the church.

Some have turned the Great Commission into a great omission.

Religion is man-made. The gospel is God-given.

Religion is good views. The gospel is good news.

The test of the vitality of religion is to be seen in its effect upon society.

If you would avoid criticism: say nothing, do nothing, and be nothing.

We are a product of our thoughts.

The chief end of prayer is the friendship of God himself.

Life is fragile: Handle with prayer.

The smallest deed is better than the grandest intention.

When it comes to giving, some people stop at nothing.

Time and eternity are never far apart.

The best things in life are caught, not taught.

"Trouble" is only "opportunity" in work clothes.

Happiness is not a destination, but a daily way to travel.

Christ is the "centerpiece" of the human race.

God does not have to run his train on our track.

Every sin has three parts: temptation, hesitation, and participation.

"One look-see is worth a thousand say-so's" — *Chinese proverb.*

Worry is interest paid on trouble before it is due.

Untold millions are perishing — *untold!*

A man may give without loving, but he cannot love without giving.

Do you really pray or just worry on your knees?

You cannot kill time without injuring eternity.

Self-indulgence is the law of death; self-denial is the law of life.

SUBJECT INDEX

INDEX OF SCRIPTURE TEXTS

Glocalization

How Followers of Jesus Engage a Flat World

Bob Roberts Jr., Author of Transformation

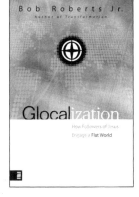

If you want to know where and how the church is going to grow, think local and global. Think glocal.

Glocal is Bob Roberts's term for the seamless connectedness between the local and global. That connection is affecting the church in ways that never could have been imagined in the first-century church, or even the twentieth-century church. And it's creating unprecedented opportunities for individuals and churches—for you and your church—to live out their faith in real time across the world.

Glocalization offers a vision of the unprecedented changes of our times and how they are impacting the church. Discover how these changes will transform the way churches define their mission and how Christians relate to one another and to the world. This provocative book turns the traditional mission-agency model upside down and shows how transformed people and churches can make a glocal (global and local) impact.

Glocalization offers an exciting vision for churches and individuals who want to reach this changing world for Christ.

Hardcover, Jacketed: 0-310-26718-8

Pick up a copy today at your favorite bookstore!

ZONDERVAN®
.com

They Like Jesus but Not the Church

Insights from Emerging Generations

Dan Kimball

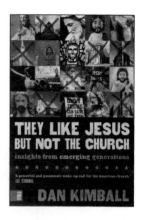

Many people today, especially among emerging generations, don't resonate with the church and organized Christianity. Some are leaving the church, and others were never part of the church in the first place. Sometimes it's because of misperceptions about the church. Yet often they are still spiritually open and fascinated with Jesus.

This is a ministry resource book exploring six of the most common objections and misunderstandings emerging generations have about the church and Christianity. The objections come from conversations and interviews the author has had with unchurched twenty- and thirty-somethings at coffee houses. Each chapter raises the objection using a conversational approach, provides the biblical answers to that objection, gives examples of how churches are addressing it, and concludes with follow-through projection suggestions, discussion questions, and resource listings.

Softcover: 0-310-24590-7

Pick up a copy today at your favorite bookstore!

A Little Guide to Christian Spirituality

The Journey of a Life Lived with God

Glen G. Scorgie

Navigating the contemporary spiritual maze is a challenge. This book will help readers:

- Think clearly about Christian spirituality
- Understand its basic dynamics, and
- Utilize classic and contemporary resources with discernment

Join Glen on his sabbatical pilgrimages to Iona Abbey in Scotland, spiritually significant sites in Italy and Turkey, and renewal centers in North America. Listen as he provides brief profiles of memorable people and places from the rich history of Christian spirituality. Consider his rediscovery that Christian spirituality is about living all of life before God in the transforming and empowering presence of his Spirit. This biblically informed book traces the contours of such an encompassing spirituality. It offers a simple yet comprehensive model with three dimensions:

- A relational dimension (Christ with us)
- A transformational dimension (Christ in us), and
- A vocational dimension (Christ through us)

It is not meant to replace any of the devotional classics or any of the many helpful contemporary treatments of Christian spirituality. It is a companion volume to the rest — a modest-sized, reliable guide to the whole field.

Softcover: 0-310-27459-1

Pick up a copy today at your favorite bookstore!

ZONDERVAN®
.com

Everything You Want to Know about Jesus

Well ... Maybe Not Everything but Enough to Get You Started

Peter Downey and Ben Shaw

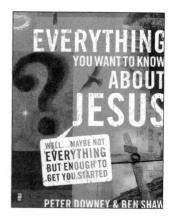

Jesus is the most influential person who ever lived, but for many of us, he has ceased to be a real person. We have sanitized him with pious jargon, framed him in stained glass, and reduced him to a religious puppet who floats through biblical landscapes dispensing Christian cliches and nice advice. It's time for a fresh look at the man this book describes as "a square peg in a society of round holes."

Whether you are new to Jesus or just want to rediscover him with fresh eyes, this is the book for you. No dry theological treatise, it is written in an engaging, sometimes even humorous, style. In short, readable chapters, you will get a tour of important background info and fascinating history that will bring to life the era in which Jesus lived. Then you will read about his birth, his adult ministry and teaching, and the crucial last week of his life on earth. You will catch a glimpse of the impact and excitement as news of Jesus spread around the world. And finally, you will be inspired to think about what Jesus means for us today.

Softcover: 0-310-27337-4

In the Steps of Jesus

An Illustrated Guide to the Places of the Holy Land

Peter Walker

In the Steps of Jesus presents a visually stimulating tour of the places Jesus visited and ministered in during his time on earth as recorded in the Gospels. Each location is addressed separately and includes such cities as Capernaum, Nazareth, and Jerusalem. Full-color photos bring to life the ancient world of the Bible few will ever be able to visit in person. With every page, the reader will gain greater insight into the history, geography, and unique features of these historic places.

A must-have reference book for those interested in the study of the New Testament and the life of Christ.

Hardcover, Printed: 0-310-27647-0

Pick up a copy today at your favorite bookstore!

Life Sentences

Discover the Key Themes
of 63 Bible Characters

Warren W. Wiersbe

"Scripture frequently sums up a man's life in a single sentence."

This observation by the great preacher Charles Spurgeon launched Warren Wiersbe on a study of the lives of prominent Bible characters. Interested in more than biographical facts, Wiersbe sought out the themes of each person's life as reflected in the pages of Scripture. How does the Bible summarize this person's life? What is the key to understanding his or her character? How do I see my own life reflected in the life of this person?

Here is the fruit of this study. A popular reference book with a pastoral and devotional flavor, *Life Sentences* takes you into the lives of sixty-three men and women who encountered an extraordinary God. For each, Wiersbe identifies a verse that sums up that individual's life and then reflects on the lessons to be learned, both positive and negative. Not only will you be challenged by these examples, but also you will be stimulated to consider what your "life sentence" will be.

Life Sentences is an ideal reference tool for teachers, Bible study leaders, and preachers seeking to bring Bible characters to life. But it is written from a pastor's heart, so it also makes ideal devotional reading for anyone who wants to more clearly understand the Bible and apply it to life.

Softcover: 0-310-27282-3

Pick up a copy today at your favorite bookstore!

Halley's Bible Handbook with the New International Version—Deluxe Edition

Henry H. Halley

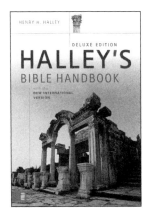

Clear. Simple. Easy to read. Now in full color for its twenty-fifth edition, this world-renowned Bible handbook is treasured by generations of Bible readers for its clarity, insight, and usefulness. *Halley's Bible Handbook* makes the Bible's wisdom and message accessible. You will develop an appreciation for the cultural, religious, and geographic settings in which the story of the Bible unfolds. You will see how its different themes fit together in a remarkable way. And you will see the heart of God and the person of Jesus Christ revealed from Genesis to Revelation.

Written for both mind and heart, this expanded edition of *Halley's Bible Handbook* retains Dr. Halley's highly personal style. It features brilliant maps, photographs, and illustrations; contemporary four-color design; Bible references in the easy-to-read, bestselling New International Version; practical Bible reading programs; helpful tips for Bible study; fascinating archaeological information; easy-to-understand sections on how we got the Bible and on church history; and helpful indexes.

Hardcover, Printed: 0-310-25994-0

Pick up a copy today at your favorite bookstore!

Moving On—Moving Forward

A Guide for Pastors in Transition

Michael J. Anthony and Mick Boersma

For most pastors and church staff members, gone are the days of serving at the same church for twenty or thirty years. What's more, the landscape of pastoral hiring has changed, with the advent of more sophisticated search committees, the Internet, and professional search firms. But the fine art of changing churches or moving to a new career isn't something most of us learned in seminary.

Whether you are searching for your first position or are a seasoned veteran wrestling with if, when, and how to move on, *Moving On — Moving Forward* will help you navigate the ins and outs of the ministry employment maze. Based on research with nearly 200 pastors who themselves have gone through transitions, this book uniquely addresses the needs of people in ministry. It deals with the crucial and sometimes painful emotional and familial issues involved in ministry transition. And it is immensely practical and informed by many real-life examples.

Topics covered include dealing with search committees, writing a letter of resignation, preparing a resume, negotiating compensation, and more. The book includes charts and worksheets.

Softcover: 0-310-26776-5

Pick up a copy today at your favorite bookstore!

We want to hear from you. Please send your comments about this
book to us in care of zreview@zondervan.com. Thank you.

ZONDERVAN.com/
AUTHORTRACKER
follow your favorite authors